Shakespeare in Our Time

Shakespeare in Our Time

A Shakespeare Association of America Collection

Edited by
Dympna Callaghan and
Suzanne Gossett

Bloomsbury Arden Shakespeare
An imprint of Bloomsbury Publishing Plc

B L O O M S B U R Y
LONDON · OXFORD · NEW YORK · NEW DELHI · SYDNEY

Bloomsbury Arden Shakespeare

An imprint of Bloomsbury Publishing Plc

Imprint previously known as Arden Shakespeare

50 Bedford Square	1385 Broadway
London	New York
WC1B 3DP	NY 10018
UK	USA

www.bloomsbury.com

BLOOMSBURY, THE ARDEN SHAKESPEARE and the Diana logo are trademarks of Bloomsbury Publishing Plc

First published 2016

© The Editors and Contributors 2016

British Library Cataloguing-in-Publication Data
A catalogue record for this book is available from the British Library.

ISBN: HB: 978-1-4725-2042-5
PB: 978-1-4725-2041-8
ePDF: 978-1-4725-2044-9
ePub: 978-1-4725-2043-2

Library of Congress Cataloging-in-Publication Data
A catalog record for this book is available from the Library of Congress

Typeset by Fakenham Prepress Solutions, Fakenham, Norfolk NR21 8NN
Printed and bound in United States of America

In tribute to J. Leeds Barroll, founder of the Shakespeare Association of America.

CONTENTS

PREFACE

At some undocumented moment in April 1616, the life of William Shakespeare ended and his astonishing afterlife commenced. This volume marks two milestones: the 400th anniversary of Shakespeare's death and the 44th anniversary of the founding of the Shakespeare Association of America (SAA). Our dedication honors the distinguished scholar who conceived of the organization in 1972 and who served as executive officer for its inaugural conference in 1973.

An interim landmark was the first "modern" edition of Shakespeare's plays in 1709. Adding a biographical account, editor Nicholas Rowe observed that "the knowledge of an author may sometimes conduce to the better understanding of his book." Knowledge and understanding, research and interpretation—these continue to occupy us centuries later. But the nascent SAA was also perfectly poised to register the revolution in Shakespeare studies that occurred within a decade of its formation. Many groundbreaking acts of political, theoretical, and performative analysis are associated with contributors to this volume, some with the author of our Afterword.

For much of this work, the SAA was an incubator. Our second executive officer, Ann Jennalie Cook, pioneered a program of conference seminars to complement formal panel sessions. In the seminars, senior scholars have sat with their juniors, women with men, faculty from small colleges with those from research universities, all at the same table and on equal footing. The seminars have produced an untold number of discoveries and debates, mentorships and partnerships.

How can one volume capture the SAA experience? *Shakespeare in Our Time* represents half the SAA's institutional history, featuring member-elected presidents over the course of the past twenty-two years. The chronology of officers has determined the content order of the collection. Thus, we begin with Phyllis Rackin, president in 1993–4; follow with Bruce R. Smith, president in 1994–5; and proceed accordingly to Rebecca Bushnell, president at press time. There are just two exceptions to this principle of organization: presidents Meredith Skura (2000–1) and Anthony B. Dawson (2001–2) were unable to take part, and Robert Miola and Gary Taylor write in their steads. Two presidents, Suzanne Gossett (2011–12) and Dympna Callaghan (2012–13), do not offer essays, having served as editors of the volume. The project was first conceived and approved by their boards of trustees (who have recused themselves as contributors).

The authors of our keynote essays consulted with the trustees about commissioning the shorter, satellite essays in each chapter. The intent is further to sample the richness of Shakespeare studies and the diversity in our membership. Soon after its establishment, the SAA welcomed a strong contingent of scholars from Canada. During the term of our third executive officer, Nancy Elizabeth Hodge, the membership grew even more international. Here, we include essays by Shakespeareans from England, India, New Zealand, and Switzerland, as well as Canada. Four hundred years on, "Shakespeare" can be a universal language, a way of communicating across cultural difference about human relations and humanist values.

As the successor to Dr. Hodge, I am grateful to the many officers and members who have shown such care for and commitment to this organization. They take the SAA forward in the high-minded, even-handed, and open-hearted spirit of its founder, Leeds Barroll.

Lena Cowen Orlin

LIST OF CONTRIBUTORS

Pascale Aebischer, University of Exeter, Exeter, UK

Sarah Beckwith, Duke University, Durham, USA

David Bevington, University of Chicago, Chicago, USA

Gina Bloom, University of California Davis, Davis, USA

Lara Bovilsky, University of Oregon, Eugene, USA

James C. Bulman, Allegheny College, Meadville, USA

Rebecca Bushnell, University of Pennsylvania, Philadelphia, USA

Patricia Cahill, Emory University, Atlanta, USA

Dympna Callaghan, Syracuse University, Syracuse, USA

William C. Carroll, Boston University, Boston, USA

Bradin Cormack, Princeton University, Princeton, USA

Lena Cowen Orlin, Georgetown University, Washington D.C., USA

Margreta de Grazia, University of Pennsylvania, Philadelphia, USA

Christy Desmet, University of Georgia, Athens, USA

Mario DiGangi, City University of New York, New York, USA

Frances E. Dolan, University of California Davis, Davis, USA

Lynn Enterline, Vanderbilt University, Nashville, USA

Lukas Erne, Université de Genève, Geneva, Switzerland

Mary Floyd-Wilson, University of North Carolina at Chapel Hill, Chapel Hill, USA

Alan Galey, University of Toronto, Toronto, Canada

Marjorie Garber, Harvard University, Cambridge, USA

Suzanne Gossett, Loyola University Chicago, Chicago, USA

Stephen Greenblatt, Harvard University, Cambridge, USA

Stephen Guy-Bray, University of British Columbia, Vancouver, Canada

Andrew Hartley, University of North Carolina at Charlotte, Charlotte, USA

Diana E. Henderson, Massachusetts Institute of Technology, Cambridge, USA

Peter Holland, University of Notre Dame, Notre Dame, USA

Adam G. Hooks, University of Iowa, Iowa City, USA

Jean E. Howard, Columbia University, New York, USA

Heather James, University of Southern California, Los Angeles, USA

Coppélia Kahn, Brown University, Providence, USA

David Kathman, Independent Scholar, Chicago, USA

Gail Kern Paster, Folger Shakespeare Library, Washington D.C., USA

Alysia Kolentsis, University of Waterloo, Waterloo, Canada

Ania Loomba, University of Pennsylvania, Philadelphia, USA

Julia Reinhard Lupton, University of California Irvine, Irvine, USA

Laurie Maguire, University of Oxford, Oxford, UK

Sonia Massai, King's College London, London, UK

Russ McDonald, Goldsmiths, University of London, London, UK

Madhavi Menon, Ashoka University, Delhi, India

Steve Mentz, St. John's University, Queens, USA

Robert S. Miola, Loyola University Maryland, Baltimore, USA

Barbara A. Mowat, Folger Shakespeare Library, Washington D.C., USA

Michael Neill, University of Kent, Canterbury, UK

Scott L. Newstok, Rhodes College, Memphis, USA

Lois Potter, University of Delaware, Newark, USA

Karen Raber, University of Mississippi, Oxford, USA

Phyllis Rackin, University of Pennsylvania, Philadelphia, USA

Mary Beth Rose, University of Illinois at Chicago, Chicago, USA

Kathryn Schwarz, Vanderbilt University, Nashville, USA

Jyotsna G. Singh, Michigan State University, East Lansing, USA

Bruce R. Smith, University of Southern California, Los Angeles, USA

Ian Smith, Lafayette College, Easton, USA

Tiffany Stern, University of Oxford, Oxford, UK

Gary Taylor, Florida State University, Tallahassee, USA

Henry S. Turner, Rutgers, The State University of New Jersey, New Brunswick, USA

Daniel Vitkus, University of California San Diego, La Jolla, USA

Wendy Wall, Northwestern University, Evanston, USA

William N. West, Northwestern University, Evanston, USA

Susanne L. Wofford, New York University, New York, USA

David Houston Wood, Northern Michigan University, Marquette, USA

W. B. Worthen, Barnard College, Columbia University, New York, USA

Paul Yachnin, McGill University, Montreal, Canada

Georgianna Ziegler, Folger Shakespeare Library, Washington D.C., USA

Introduction

Dympna Callaghan and Suzanne Gossett
Presidents, Shakespeare Association of America
2012–13 and 2011–12

"[I]t is impossible to limit the purposes for which the language of Shakespeare may be studied" wrote Helen Kate Furness in her Preface to *A Concordance to Shakespeare's Poems* (1874). She presciently anticipated the myriad possibilities opened up by Shakespeare's writing which, over a hundred years later, remains at the forefront and the core of contemporary literary study. Focusing her speculations, Furness imagined ever more microscopically honed close readings in imitation of the scholarly attention bestowed upon classical literature. She envisaged a time to come, "if it has not already," when Shakespeare's "use of every part of speech, down to the humblest conjunction, will be criticized with as much nicety as has been bestowed upon Greek and Latin authors." Ready evidence that her projections on this score were correct can be found, for example, in the much-discussed pronominal problem of the *Sonnets* and in the work of queer philology. Writing forty-six years before American women got the vote, and nearly a century before the Civil Rights movement and Stonewall, she could not, however, have imagined that such careful close reading might be combined with matters—had names for them even existed—that would no doubt have seemed at a very great distance from Shakespeare's plays: ecological criticism, queer studies, disability studies, psychoanalytic criticism, race and gender studies, to name a few. Other areas such as performance studies, textual criticism, contextual criticism, book and theatre history are rather more easily translated back into the critical idiom of Furness's era, but even these aspects of the field have undergone such revolutionary changes since the dawn of the twentieth century that it is unlikely she would recognize them. In part, by sheer dint of archival labor, we now know vastly more about Shakespeare and about his plays and poems, as well as about almost every dimension of early modern life. Scholars have uncovered hitherto unknown or unexamined documents on matters ranging from agriculture to the zodiac. Indeed, the topics and themes of the field have expanded exponentially not only since Furness's time but even within the presidential chronology of twenty years covered by this book.

Arguably, however, even more significant than the new topics which have populated the field are the modes of inquiry that have arisen as new foci have revolutionized scholarly approaches to Shakespeare by means of theoretical and methodological innovation. To take one of the most far-reaching and transformative critical discourses as an example of the kind of shift to which we refer, namely feminist criticism, it is now commonly understood that sex and gender cannot be addressed alone but must be read in conjunction with race, class, identity, and the body. Similarly, Shakespeare's cross-dressed heroines, once understood as somewhat titillating renditions of heterosexual femininity, may now be read in terms of current debates about transsexuality and addressed in relation to early modern discourses about tribadism. While these developments are not the products of a natural evolution or progression, but of the deliberate and spirited interventions of fiercely committed scholarship, the transformations they have effected can be traced back through the history of Shakespeare criticism. Thus, current work on these issues has its roots in the explicitly political agenda of feminist scholarship in the 1970s, which tended to advocate for female characters as oppressed and misunderstood victims of patriarchy. It can be traced back further still through the nineteenth century to the genteel explorations of Anna Jameson into the girlhoods of Shakespeare's heroines, which were in turn preceded by the long-standing discussion about women characters in Shakespeare.

Shakespeare is simultaneously entirely a product of his time and invariably ahead of it, and indeed ahead of our time, so that some new dimensions of Shakespeare studies may strike us as having always been present in Shakespeare's language, embedded in the fabric of his composition and lying dormant to await the momentous occasion of "discovery." In other instances, however, new avenues and objects of inquiry may appear to function as creative and often extraordinarily productive anachronisms that, variously, are and are not authorized by the text. For example, although ecological criticism is far from indifferent to Shakespeare's representations of nature, it is also engaged with a broad field of inquiry, intimately bound up with the political struggle over natural resources, the climate crisis, the depletion of fossil fuels, and the ways in which boundaries are being redrawn, literally and conceptually, between the human and the nonhuman—both animate and inanimate. *Shakespeare In Our Time* is therefore the outcome of the complex synergy between the text itself and what the great variety of readers have brought to it, up to and including the present.

Attention to Shakespeare's language thus has the capacity to enter into ever-new forms of engagement with the present, as well us to lead us back again to the words on the page. Shakespeare also provides a focal point for those of us interested in sixteenth- and seventeenth-century literature and enables us to function as custodians of knowledge who nurture not just awareness of the past but also vigorous engagement with it. Furthermore, Shakespeare can be and has been used strategically, by, among others, the contributors to this volume, to make expansive arguments about the advent of modernity and the role of literary and theatrical culture in shaping and responding to its developments, especially in relation to economic transformation, religious schism, and the dawn of colonialism. Indeed, the topic of every section in this book from historicism to source studies has seen major transformations, fueled by the vigorous intellectual engagement of generations of Shakespeare Association of America (SAA) members not only with the historical past but also with the imperatives of their own historical moments.

The central and vital question implicitly addressed by this volume is, why do we continue to pursue intellectual projects in relation to Shakespeare? The answer is that Shakespeare remains a vital link to the past and a powerful testament to the relevance of history and historicity for the twenty-first century. Shakespeareans are uniquely positioned in relation to the cultural imperative both to redeem the literary and to explain that the past is the most radical place that exists in our society. Most of all, studying Shakespeare, as Furness suggested, permits us to access the immense potentialities of language, by reading closely, questioning assumptions, destabilizing terms, and finding the stories behind the words we use in order to allow us to become more fully conscious of how the past inhabits the present. "Shakespeare" thus functions as a synecdoche for the nexus between the literary and cultural inheritance of the past and that of the present, and Shakespeare studies has become a field where it is possible to discuss what culture means—both high culture and culture in the most catholic sense of the word—and a space where we can examine the function and consequences of the human impulse towards image making and mimesis.

While *Shakespeare in Our Time* aims to offer a scholarly snapshot of work within the broader field of Shakespeare studies, this book is not intended as a museum piece. We hope that the essays included here will provoke further discussion, in and out of the classroom, and that the book will be useful to all readers in offering a sense of the directions of current research, areas of scholarly contention, emergent areas of inquiry, and potential divergences within a given approach. The debates and discussions here—each section consisting of a longer essay, when possible by a former SAA president, and two shorter contributions by members of the organization—can be entered at any point in the volume, since read with and against one another the essays generate debate and demonstrate the dynamism and diversity of our field.

Sometimes tightly woven, sometimes in tension and at odds with one another, the topics and subfields included here represent the mesh of intellectual engagement, the friction as well as the rapprochement, that constitutes Shakespeare studies in this anniversary year. Such tensions are evident in the critical differences among contributors here, and for this reason, the editors have not tried to erase disagreements, to give but one example, by imposing uniformity on the dating of Shakespeare's plays. Consisting of parallel lines as much as converging avenues of inquiry, all of the dimensions of this arena of intellectual energies are part of the ongoing cultural conversation about Shakespeare. Every contributor in this volume is part of the network of scholarship that connects students, teachers, and seminar participants, and in this sense each of them is much indebted to the wider constituency of the SAA. If the essays that follow demonstrate anything, it is that Shakespeare studies is a living, breathing, growing arena of scholarly concentration and a powerful argument in favor of the necessity and the rewards of intellectual labor. What the scholars included here have in common, along with all SAA members, is a collaborative commitment to Shakespeare and an awareness of the aesthetic achievement his work embodies. The current volume is written both in celebration and commemoration of that fact and as an invitation to deepen the networks that continue to inform Shakespeare studies.

1

Feminism

Why Feminism Still Matters

Phyllis Rackin
President, SAA 1993–94

"Feminism" is the only area of Shakespeare scholarship represented in this volume designated by a name that originated in, and is most frequently associated with, a political movement rather than a subject of academic study. Its inclusion here is gratifying but not surprising because by now feminist work has become a familiar presence in the repertory of Shakespeare scholarship—so familiar, in fact, that it sometimes seems a bit outworn. But many of us can still remember the days when feminist approaches to Shakespeare were so unfamiliar that they were often dismissed as too "trendy" and tendentious to be truly scholarly. These charges are seldom heard nowadays, at least in scholarly circles, where it is now widely recognized that all scholarship, even the most apparently "objective," cannot help but be inflected by its writer's interests, desires, and social location and that the dialogue between our present historical situation and the past historical material we study constitutes the matrix where all our scholarly projects take their shape and acquire their reasons for being.

In light of this recognition, both the earlier charge that feminist scholarship was too "trendy" to be taken seriously and the current suspicion that it is now somewhat passé, can themselves be seen as trendy. In fact, it is difficult to imagine any scholarly pursuit that is not trendy. The recurrent dream of a scholarship that will ascend (or escape) to the empyrean realm of timeless, transcendent truths itself becomes most attractive at particular historical moments. During the McCarthyite 1950s, for instance, aesthetic questions dominated the study of literature. This was a time when applicants for positions at New York's publicly supported institutions of higher education were required to sign loyalty oaths before they could be hired, and tenured professors were brought up before the House Un-American Activities Committee and asked whether they had ever been members of, or had ties to, the Communist Party (and some of them lost their jobs for refusing to answer). Current emphases in Shakespeare studies are equally suggestive. Ecocriticism and queer theory are obvious examples; but we might also want to consider the implications of the fact that although the ahistorical formalism of the 1950s is still discredited, aesthetic questions are again popular, along with bibliography and antiquarianism, newly configured as "history of the book" and "the study of material culture." And more and more scholars are finding that classical texts and the intricacies of religious doctrine had a profound influence on the playscripts that William Shakespeare produced for the popular commercial stage. We are all learning from this scholarship, and feminists have made good use of these approaches in their own scholarly work. But although all these approaches can tell us a lot about the interests and motivations that shaped the writing of Shakespeare's plays, our current fascination with them can tell us just as much about the interests and motivations that shape our own scholarly choices.

In the case of feminism, those interests and motivations are easy to trace. The emergence of feminist approaches to literature in the last quarter of the twentieth century was energized by an active feminist political movement and by feminist scholars' desire for an improvement in women's status in the here-and-now of their own lives—at home, in the academy, and in the larger world in which they lived. In the academy, as Elaine Showalter famously observed, although many women studied literature, what the English major gave them was an education in negative capability. The authors we studied were almost always men, as were the professors who taught us and the critics and scholars whose work we read. And what all these men taught us, although this was never explicit or even recognized, was how to read like a man. This unexamined bias shaped all our study, but nowhere more so than in the case of Shakespeare, the male writer who stood at the center of the masculine canon we studied. The great contribution of feminist scholarship was to encourage women to approach Shakespeare's plays, not as honorary men, but from our own points of view as women. This is not to say that the work we produced was monolithic. From the beginning, feminist Shakespeare scholarship has been multivocal and multifocused, as various as the intellectual interests and the personal experience and commitments of the scholars—too numerous to name in this short essay—who produced it. Feminist scholarship became a battleground in the subversion/containment debate of the period. Some of us invoked Shakespeare's authority in support of our own aspirations, finding in his plays endorsement for a feminist vision *avant la lettre*. Others, turning to his plays for early traces of our own marginal status, found evidence of entrenched patriarchy and of women's subordination and disempowerment. But despite the disagreements among us, there is a very important sense in which the project of feminist scholarship, like the project of feminism itself, was a collective effort, and the political implications of what we wrote, although not always explicit, were inevitably there. They are still there now, when feminist approaches have gained recognition as an accepted mode of scholarly work even among writers whose personal political commitments remain unexamined.

The vehemence of the initial opposition to feminist Shakespeare criticism, the ridicule and denunciations that were circulated in the popular press as well as academic conferences and publications, should not have surprised us. Shakespeare's writings still have an authority unequalled by any other secular texts: because of the cultural capital that has accrued to the name of Shakespeare, feminist revisions of his work, if accepted, could have real cultural—and therefore political—consequences. But once that work gained a toehold in academic journals and booklists, it was confronted by other attempts to discredit it, this time from within the academy itself. The first charge, easiest to answer, was that our work was unhistorical. This claim was relatively easy to refute because it was based on a view of history that was just as much biased by a masculinist perspective as the literary criticism that invoked it. Since feminism was also changing the ways

historians thought about the past, historically-minded feminist
critics could turn to history to refute those charges. Feminist historians recorded the achievements of exceptional women both in
life and in literature and the other arts; they edited and published
forgotten texts written by women, and they incorporated them
into the courses they taught. They combed the archives for previously unexamined evidence of the active lives that ordinary women
lived. The repressive prescriptions so often quoted to demonstrate
the ubiquitous power of patriarchy in Shakespeare's England were
called into question by the retrieval and analysis of documents that
recorded married women's ownership, management, and contes-
tation of their husbands' claims to various kinds of property and
demonstrated that women's control over household property—both
de facto and *de jure*—was far more extensive than a too-simple
understanding of the doctrine of coverture had seemed to suggest.
Feminist historians also challenged the anachronistic assumption
that the division between the public arena of male economic
activity and the private domestic space of women's enclosure was,
as previous scholars had often assumed, already firmly entrenched
in precapitalist England. All this evidence of the life experiences of
women in Shakespeare's England complicated and broadened our
conception of the horizon of awareness that would have shaped
their, and their male compatriots', responses to his plays.

In demonstrating that Shakespeare's countrywomen were not
always as marginalized and repressed as we had been taught to
believe, feminist historicist scholars gave women—students as
well as critics and teachers—the material to contest our own
marginalization as readers of Shakespeare's plays. It goes without
saying, but it probably bears repeating, that the entire enterprise of
Shakespeare scholarship rests on the worth of the plays themselves—
not only as cultural capital and as commercial theatrical products,
but also as the objects of delight and appreciation by generations
of playgoers and readers. Feminist Shakespeare criticism has, and
has had, real political implications but, in the first instance, what
matters is our—and our students' own—experience of the plays.
One of the most significant achievements of feminist/historicist
scholars was to challenge the long-standing belief that Shakespeare
and his fellow dramatists wrote for an "all-male" theatre. Women,
they showed, were deeply involved in the business of professional
theatrical production; and they were also influential consumers

of plays, not only as patrons of theatrical companies but also as paying customers in the playhouses and as owners and readers of printed playtexts. If the plays were to be commercially successful, as they were designed to be, they had to please the women who were Shakespeare's paying customers as well as the men.

Once we take seriously the fact that Shakespeare's plays were designed to appeal to an audience that was not exclusively male, many assumptions that limited previous interpretations are called into question. Good examples are the assumptions that Shakespeare's representations of female power and his depiction of male fears of cuckoldry would always have resonated with anxieties that playgoers brought to the theatre. Once we turn our attention to the life experiences and possible responses of female playgoers, our view of powerful heroines, such as Cleopatra, and jealous husbands, such as Othello, will surely change. We will pay more and closer attention to Cleopatra's triumphant suicide and Emilia's denunciation of Othello's jealousy, and we may also remember how popular Queen Elizabeth was among her subjects, that Shakespeare's jealous husbands are always mistaken, and that their jealousy always leads to trouble, both for themselves and for the innocent women they suspect.

At this point, as the inclusion of "Feminism" in this volume attests, feminist perspectives have been well integrated into the methodology of Shakespeare criticism and scholarship, for and by men as well as women. Feminist perspectives can foreground material that would otherwise remain unexamined or even overlooked, and even when feminist scholars analyze familiar material, they are likely to ask different questions and reach different conclusions. Feminist perspectives have also transformed the ways we teach Shakespeare's plays. Reminding students that the plays were designed for an audience that was not exclusively male encourages them to take serious account of facts that, although they were always apparent, most of us had previously discounted or ignored. In the case of *The Merchant of Venice,* for instance, previous readings tended to focus on Shylock; but we might want to pay more attention to Portia: a quick glance at the statistics in any concordance shows that Portia has more lines in the script than he does and a quick glance at a plot summary shows that she is the only character who plays a central role in all three of the plots that constitute the play—not only the story of the three caskets but also the bond plot that culminates in the Venetian courtroom and the ring plot that forms the basis for the main action in Act 5. In the case of the English history plays, critics and teachers have long been accustomed to tracing the development of Prince Hal into King Henry V in the three plays that they often called "The Henriad," but they have paid very little attention to the fact that the only character who plays a role in four of Shakespeare's English history plays is Margaret of Anjou, and to Margaret's own development during the course of those plays.

A feminist perspective can also interrogate the process of canon formation. The plays that modern scholars have chosen to emphasize probably tell us more about our own assumptions than about the beliefs that informed the responses of Shakespeare's first audiences. In the case of Shakespeare's English history plays, it pays to notice which plays have the most (*Richard III*) and the least (*Henry IV, Part 1*) space for female characters, not only to interrogate the reasons we've favored the plays in which female characters are marginalized but also to see what this recognition does for our readings of the plays themselves. Our paradigmatic Shakespearean tragedy is *Hamlet*; how would our conception of Shakespeare's tragedies be altered if it were *Antony and Cleopatra*? And how would our interpretation of that play be altered if we remembered that Antony dies in Act 4, which means that all of Act 5 is firmly centered on Cleopatra. In the case of the late romances, the patriarchal fantasy played out in *The Tempest* has given that play pride of place, but it is worth noting that the only female character who appears in that play is Prospero's young daughter, Miranda. We might want to pay more attention to the other plays in that group, all of which feature far more—and more powerful—roles for female characters.

Comedy is generally conceded to be the genre that gives the greatest scope for female characters, and critics have often turned to Shakespeare's comedies for evidence of his and his audiences' assumptions and expectations about women's roles in the world they inhabited. But here too the canon of plays we have chosen to emphasize may have distorted our conclusions. A play often cited as evidence of women's subordination is *The Taming of the Shrew*, but that play seems not to have been well received in Shakespeare's time. There are only three recorded references to it before 1649; and it is the only one of Shakespeare's plays that provoked a theatrical "reply" during his own lifetime. That sequel was John Fletcher's *The Woman's Prize or The Tamer Tamed*, in which the tables are turned on Petruccio. It is interesting to speculate how different our conception of Shakespeare's view of women's place in marriage might have been if we had focused on *The Merry Wives of Windsor*, a play that was much better received in the seventeenth century than it is today, and one in which powerful women dominate the action. Examples like these suggest a historical basis for taking a more generous view of women's place than recent scholars have found in their own version of the Shakespearean canon.

The appeal to history, while initially called into service as a platform for the discrediting of feminist readings, thus provided the materials for supporting them. But the second major academic attack on feminist criticism, which came from a less predictable source, was more difficult to refute, because it rested on a more solid foundation, both political and intellectual. Because feminist work was motivated by a desire for political change, its politics were necessarily progressive, and this necessity opened it to a set of criticisms from other progressive movements. In the case of feminist Shakespeare criticism, scholars argued that feminist analysis, like the feminist political agenda, focused too narrowly on issues that affected heterosexual, white, middle-class women. In response to these charges, the feminist agenda has broadened to incorporate issues affecting people disempowered by their racial, sexual, and economic status; and feminist literary criticism has had to broaden its agenda to take these factors into account. Othello is not simply a jealous husband, he is also a Moor, and Iago's motivations include both racist contempt and class resentment. Cleopatra is not simply a woman; she is also a queen, and she is not simply a queen: she is the tawny-skinned Queen of Egypt.

However, it is equally important that critics who argue from those perspectives remain mindful of women's issues. The best of recent Shakespeare criticism has done exactly that, and one of the great achievements of feminist criticism is its success in enriching other critical perspectives, which, while not specifically feminist, have been broadened by including considerations of sex and gender in their analyses. Ecocriticism is a notable example, but there is not a single category of Shakespeare studies named in the table of contents to this volume that has not been and cannot be further enriched by feminist scholarship, and not a single one of them that cannot broaden and enrich feminist analysis. Women are as multifarious as humanity itself, and our situations, desires, needs, abilities, disabilities, races, nationalities, and allegiances are not exhausted by a monolithic classification based on our status as female. Nonetheless, the work of a specifically feminist mode of criticism is far from finished. With the widespread acceptance of gender as a conceptual tool, there is a danger that criticism designated as "feminist" will lose its political compass and will be valued only for its contributions to other modes of inquiry. At this point, it is important to remember that the *raison d'être* of feminist scholarship and the criteria by which we should evaluate it are more than academic, because teaching and scholarship do not exist in a vacuum. In the case of contemporary American life, for instance, there is ample evidence that women are still disadvantaged in every area we examine. Women's wages are still lower than men's, women are still underrepresented on the editorial boards of newspapers, the entertainment industry, the leadership of corporations, and the seats of political power, and reproductive rights are still under siege: the list is far from complete. We still have a long way to go, and the ways we interpret Shakespeare's plays have real consequences as well as real causes in the present.

Just Imagine

Kathryn Schwarz

In 1930, *Just Imagine* earned eccentric distinction as the first science fiction musical of the sound era. Set in 1980, the film portrays a society in which, as an ominous voiceover informs us, "everyone has a number instead of a name, and the government tells you whom you should marry." A conventional romantic comedy plays out in a fabulous future tinged with dystopian nostalgia. One small, almost incidental scene captures the tension: a young heterosexual married couple holds a brief conversation about children, then the man pushes a vending machine button. A baby boy pops out. In the background, a character transported from 1930 says, "Give me the good old days."

In 1968, Ti-Grace Atkinson wrote "The Institution of Sexual Intercourse," which appeared in *The New York Free Press* and *Notes from the Second Year* before being anthologized in Atkinson's own collection *Amazon Odyssey* (1974). Beginning with the premise, "the concept of sexual intercourse is a political construct, reified into an institution," Atkinson imagines the consequences if intercourse were detached from reproduction. "This change is beginning to be within our grasp with the work now being done on extrauterine conception and incubation," she notes. Atkinson speculates that, if somatic intimacy were no longer a requisite, it might become a choice: "perhaps we could discover what the nature of the human sensual characteristics are from the point of view of the good of each individual instead of what we have now which is a sort of psychological draft system of our sexualities." But she argues that cooperative sensuality would require a language, "transcribed into gestures appropriate to a particular experience," which we do not yet know. We would need an ethical vocabulary of touch, with protocols for structure, use, and style: "for example, at what point do you have a dialect? and, what would count as a metaphor?"

These improbably congruent fantasies raise questions about ideological as well as bodily lines of descent. In both the film and the essay, a dominant ideology (sexual reproduction, or "the good old days," or the bad old days of here and now) shades toward the residual. But can we term its successor an emergent ideology? Is either the vending machine or the extrauterine incubator an inevitable product of historical progress? Hardly. These are counter-factuals, which irrupt into social logic and, with the promiscuous flick of a sideways glance, reveal alternatives to social time. What vocabularies do we have for counterfactual temporalities, those histories and futurities to which standard rules do not apply? From the *OED*, we have the tantalizing phrase "fugitive propositions." We also have fiction.

I begin with counterfactual generation to foreground the thought experiment as a vital force in feminist thought. As activists, as theorists, and indeed as Shakespearean critics, we sustain that sideways glance, applying rigorous analysis to potentialities which may or may not be extant in practice or subject to proof. Such speculative porosity leads us to mine new archives for material that does not support dominant narratives. It motivates us to scrutinize dominant narratives in search of the other stories they tell. It causes us to devise or engage theoretical paradigms that alter our angles of incidence. And—perhaps not quite often enough—it persuades us to trust fiction as fiction, shaped by, but not bound to, historical conditions of production. When fiction is unfaithful to quotidian circumstance, when it flirts with imaginative possibilities and trifles with notional causalities, it animates our own infidelity to the systems, precepts, and facts we can know all too well. Atkinson concludes her speculations with a grim assessment: "It is as if our understanding of the sense of sight were modeled on the experience of being punched in the eye instead of on experiences such as seeing a Tunisian watercolor by Paul Klee. One might infer the possibility of assault from the art but not the possibility of art from the assault. We are unfortunately in the latter position." I suggest, with precarious optimism, that the "we" who congregate here might access a different position, from which our engagement with art has enabled us to infer something other than the cognitive violence of the norm.

Within the frame of my opening examples, a thought experiment might yield a proposition such as this: there is curiously little evidence that Shakespearean texts endorse sexual reproduction as a guarantor of patrilineal inheritance. While this is not a novel insight, it compresses familiar phenomena into the shape of something strange. We have history plays, such as *Richard II*, in which legitimacy offers no defense against pragmatic usurpation. We have short-lived sons whose mothers authenticate but cannot save their lineal entitlements: Coriolanus, Mamillius, Edward in *Henry VI, Part 3*, Arthur in *King John*. We have repudiated and repatriated daughters (Cordelia, Perdita) who stand or fall as the sole frail hope of continuity. We have Lucius, the son of Titus, whose paternity is less relevant than his army of Goths. We also have what I would term generative mysteries: What is the status of pregnancy in *All's Well*, or of betrothal in *Measure*? Does even a wise father know his own child? Can a patriline revivify if a disavowal is withdrawn? How many children had Lady Macbeth? My question is whether we must distinguish between knowledge and ignorance, between skepticism and faith, or whether we might allow these variations on reproductive futurity to cumulate toward a language of alterity.

Of course we might; our discipline does not proscribe avenues of inquiry, however firmly we may foreclose them for ourselves. Here it seems worth lingering for a moment on the changeling in

A Midsummer Night's Dream. What can he be if not a child detached from the institution of sexual intercourse? In Titania's account, he is born to a votaress who conceives by power of suggestion (maybe). In Oberon's account, he is the son of an Indian king (unspecified). These stories can be reconciled with one another if we assign the votaress a royal sexual partner, although—to paraphrase Hippolyta—it must be our imagination then, and not theirs. But the stories cannot be reconciled with a social imperative that verifies paternity through married chastity. The sexual intercourse that facilitates Oberon's possessive claim is Titania's bestial, enchanted, adulterous liaison with a translated mechanical. If these transactions fulfill a social covenant, it must be the one proposed by Roland du Jardin in *A Discourse of the Married and Single Life* (1621): "If thou desirest to have children of thine owne, I wil tell thee what thou shalt doe: Cause the mother that beares them, to bestowe them as a gift upon thee, wherupon thou maist then, without lying, say they are thine owne." As an extorted gift of provisional tenure, the changeling is a sign of sexual energies that exceed orthodox vocabularies. Is this what would count as a metaphor?

This is not to say that Shakespeare eschews or escapes the doctrine that privileges patrilines at the expense of women. Such an argument simply speaks a "no" made intelligible by the default position to which it responds. I argue instead—as many others have argued—for the value of unintelligibility, of doubt, of ground that shifts beneath our feet. In her 1985 essay "Anti-Historians," Phyllis Rackin describes the effect of women on the masculinist project of history plays: "historiography itself becomes problematic, no longer speaking with the clear, univocal voice of unquestioned tradition but re-presented as a dubious construct, always provisional, always subject to erasure and reconstruction, and never adequate to recover the past in full presence." This acute formulation could also aptly describe the effect of feminist interventions on social or historical or canonical certainties. The Shakespearean institution creates the risk of a static center; our approaches might become strategies in the sense Michel de Certeau develops in *The Practice of Everyday Life*. Strategy, de Certeau writes, operates from "the establishment of a place of power (the property of a proper)"; it is "an effort to delimit one's own place in a world bewitched by the invisible powers of the Other." But unless we succumb to the bewitchment of predictable and uniform modes of praxis, we are not the tenants who hold "the property of a proper." Dynamic and schismatic, vectored and edged, feminism remains a heterogeneous set of tactics, and a tactic, by contrast, "is a calculated action determined by the absence of a proper locus ... This nowhere gives a tactic mobility, to be sure, but a mobility that must accept the chance offerings of the moment" (de Certeau). This aggregate we call "Shakespeare" can still (I hope) be recognized less as an institution than as a constellation of skepticisms, improvisations, ambiguities, and fugitive propositions, open both to the efficacy and to the ethics of the fluid methodologies such capaciousness invites.

Letters, Characters, Roots

Wendy Wall

He cut our roots in characters.

CYMBELINE 4.2.49

Belarius's casual statement about Fidele, the cross-dressed Imogen in *Cymbeline*, seems an unlikely place to start a meditation on feminism and Shakespeare. After all, it is a fairly minor line that doesn't self-evidently point to any serious negotiation of gendered agency. It appears at a moment when Belarius, Arviragus, and Guiderius marvel over the gentle quality of the mysterious guest who serves as their boy-housewife. Not knowing that Fidele is Imogen, these men praise his/her exquisite singing, nourishing broths, beautiful melancholy, and divine cookery. While the gender complications of the scene raise expectedly provocative issues about what the pronoun "he" references in the case of a cross-dressed female character (played by a boy actor), the fact that the illegible woman's seemingly "essential" characteristics are so thoroughly domestic might seem to neutralize the passage's feminist possibilities. In fact, we might think that critics would rush past this conventional characterization to moments in which highly charged gender struggles are more clearly on display.

But we would be overhasty. In fact, the operation of cutting and the status of character have been central to materialist, deconstructive, ideological, historical, and feminist critiques in recent decades. I'll return to consider cutting and character in this passage, but first let me think about methodology. This line in *Cymbeline* suggests to me that audience members might have thought it routine for cooks to shape alphabetic letters out of food, despite the fact that such craftwork has not survived for our inspection. My initial response is to launch a scholarly quest to identify historical materials for corroboration; after all, these sources might have much to say about the scope of women's work and their contributions. Yet, as I turn to the archive, I am weighed down by nagging questions about what I will do with this knowledge: should *The Tragedie of Cymbeline*—a material book associated with a performance shaped by literary conventions—be used to "evidence" acts (by women or men) carried out in other institutional settings in the culture? If we conscript these lines, or even the nonfictional sources that I find in the archive, as part of the project of historical recovery, do we risk positing texts as naively transparent about the gendered "experience" they represent? Do we make "history" a reified category? How might we square the impulse to use textual sources to document a history of women's lives with full appreciation for the semiotic instability that qualifies distinctions between "female" and "male," or that erodes the concept of history itself? Bearing in mind Phyllis Rackin's call for a revivified feminist practice that is historically attuned, not over-reliant on master narratives about misogyny, and aware of the presentist investments of historiography, how, we might ask, can critics process textual signs of gendered acts while appreciating textuality as itself inscriptive?

These long-standing (if here necessarily abbreviated) questions have haunted my research as I have grappled with the cultural functions of manuscript and printed recipe books in early modern England. In *Cymbeline*, Belarius and the two brothers are astonished to find a wandering youth in their cave who possesses the civilized skill of "kitchen literacy," the ability to fashion or "cut" alphabetic letters out of even cheap root vegetables. More than 140 extant early-modern English manuscript recipe collections and dozens of printed manuals indicate that aspiring non-elite women of means did indeed create food-letters and etch words onto tarts, often displaying their knowledge of socially meaningful fonts and penmanship styles (and here we might note that handwriting was commonly called "the cutting of letters"). The kitchen emerges as a place not only of arduous labor but also of imaginative license and intellectual wit, a site where concepts such as "nature," "literacy," and "art" could be held up to witty scrutiny.

The modern world has retained traces of consumable letters, chiefly in the form of alphabet soups, fortune cookies, and birthday cakes. In the age of Shakespeare, however, edible words played a role in elegant dining and the cultural capital it secured. They were a component of the domestic arts that comprised the scene of pleasure as well. One recipe writer named Lettice Pudsey tossed off a command about her gooseberry cakes: "[D]oe som[e]what on them: e[i]ther letters or what you please." Finding what pleased you was an intricate part of the fused manual and mental work undertaken in the household. Imogen's homely but literate fare is thus made meaningful by recipes that speak of domestic artifacts that could be interpreted as well as swallowed. Yet these sources go far beyond a documentary function, since they expand our understanding of the sensory range that attached to materials in the period. They suggest that women trafficked in crisp, doughy, gooey, sweet, and spiced tactile signifiers, letters whose meaning could not be abstracted from their consumable medium; letters whose ephemerality made them available for citing "substantial" signifiers of taste and knowledge. If women were insistently charactered (inscribed, constrained) through gendered ideologies projected through media, they were also makers of lettered worlds that allowed them to negotiate the personalities, dispositions, and norms attached to inscription itself. And so we move from lettered texts to lettered pastries, and back.

Rather than using recipes as the historical backdrop for interpreting the Shakespearean text, I conscript Imogen's tasty writing to thicken my understanding of the already textualized world of recipe work. Through what discourses and rhetorics were cut characters or transformed roots made legible? And here we return to Belarius's line—"He cut our roots in characters"—armed with the deconstructively informed historicist work on "character" (by Peter Stallybrass, Jonathan Goldberg, and Margreta de Grazia among others) that foregrounds its materiality. The manifold possibilities of "charactering" come to the fore in the men's characterization of the idealized youth they deem their cook and "housewife":

BELARIUS   This youth, howe'er distress'd, appears he hath had
   Good ancestors.
ARVIRAGUS   How angel-like he sings!
GUIDERIUS   But his neat cookery! he cut our roots in
      characters,
   And sauced our broths, as Juno had been sick,
   And he her dieter.
ARVIRAGUS   Nobly he yokes
   A smiling with a sigh; as if the sigh
   Was that it was, for not being such a smile;
      …
GUIDERIUS   I do note
   That grief and patience, rooted in them both,
   Mingle their spurs together.
ARVIRAGUS   Grow, patience!
   And let the stinking-elder, grief, untwine
   His perishing root, with the increasing vine!

                                    (4.2.47–53, 56–60)

We see at least two operations at work in this passage: the men
characterize Fidele and they acknowledge his/her skill in making
letters. When Guiderius describes twin outgrowths of Fidele's happy
angst—grief and patience—he repurposes the medium of Fidele's
culinary art (the root) as a figure, deploying it to mean "anchored"
or "basic." Arviragus then repeats the word when worrying that
an organism's foundation might be destructive or subject to threat.
Fidele's *rootedness* is thus associated with outward skill (the
ability to incise meaning in food) and personhood, those essential,
ancestral, and yet evolving characteristics that are the subject of
discussion. Shakespeare's penchant for verbal play, I begin to see,
prompts an inquiry into the making and inhabiting of characters,
both letters and persons. While one might write volumes on how
Fidele is assessed through particular and granulated gendered
discourses and conventions (or on how the text is itself a charactered lettered form), I can here simply observe that the repetition
of the material signifier, "root," charts a field of associated
meanings in which literate cookery fuses into the struggle to secure
essences. Fidele can transform roots into alphabets even as s/he is
the product of more abstract charactering. From the interplay of
Shakespearean text and everyday technical writing, I glimpse the

conditions of possibility for intellectual productions that are not, to my mind, sufficiently accounted for in the period's prescriptive orthodoxies about gender and domesticity.

In my reading—here and elsewhere—I attempt to negotiate the difficulty of seeing the textual record as testifying to female "experience" without being unsophisticated about semiotic instability, the provisional nature of the category called "female," or the modern investments that inflect my use of history. The marks of early modern women's textuality—figurative, material, and cultural—are internally disordered, excessive, and messy; but they are not so indeterminate as to escape the claims of ideology. Although cast in the languages of an often estranging past, they signify recognizable struggles over status, pleasure, power, and representability.

I offer this modest reading to indicate my investment in a feminist practice that resists reducing gendered subjects to the regulatory ideologies that may unwittingly be consolidated in their present articulation. I find the archive a revitalizing way to test the validity of the master narratives we deploy about gender—as a politically invested and textual field of meaning. We are only beginning to appreciate the ideologically capacious spectrum of literacies and writings in which female subjects participated—as makers of letters as well as their excessive and excluded effects.

2

Sexuality

Deeds, Desire, Delight

Bruce R. Smith
President, SAA 1994–95

X marks the spot. SeXuality is situated at the interface between observable behavior on the one hand and subjective experience on the other. "Sexuality" as a concept may not have existed in Shakespeare's time (it is a coinage of the early nineteenth century), but Shakespeare and his contemporaries recognized a category of physical acts that involved genitals and orifices just as they recognized the sensations produced by engaging in those acts. Over the acts the law kept strict surveillance. The sensations were more amply addressed in visual images, sounds, movements, smells, tastes, touches, and words having to do with what Shakespeare and his contemporaries knew as "venery." With respect to venery, acts *re*-presented to the imagination might be experienced no less intensely than the acts themselves, perhaps even more so.

Our own ways of dividing up knowledge consign observable behaviors and subjective experiences to different epistemological, verbal, and political regimes. Behaviors come under the aegis not just of legal codes but of religious dogma and ethical philosophy; experience, under the aegis of aesthetics, psychology, and neuroscience.

Beyond binaries

The X reminds us that in sexuality we are not dealing with a simple dichotomy between objective acts and subjective feelings. SeXuality embraces both. Valerie Traub confronts this challenge in her book *Thinking Sex with the Early Moderns* (2015). In critical practice across the past thirty years, Traub observes, sexual knowledge has been located within three distinct "field formations," each with its own modes of questioning, standards of evidence, and forms of argumentation. History, literary criticism, and Queer Theory converge, in Traub's view, in a Venn diagram with only small overlaps. Sexual knowledge, particularly sexual knowledge as it existed in the past, shapes up to be a difficult, if not impossible, object of inquiry.

With grateful acknowledgment of Traub's visualization, I am proposing in this essay to conceptualize Shakespeare's ways with sexual knowledge as a continuum. Surprisingly capacious and habitable, a continuum leaves room for all sorts of interplay between behaviors on the one hand and feelings on the other. A continuum presents not just polar opposites but a middle. It is in that mid position that I would locate desire, compounded in varying degrees of sensations and acts. In this move I might seem to be doing no more than to reaffirm the centrality of desire in scholarship on sexuality in the late twentieth century. This move was encouraged on several fronts: by Michel Foucault's *Introduction* (1976) to *The History of Sexuality* (1976–86), in which the erotic desires of individuals were demonstrated to be constructions of the culture in which the individuals (in more ways than one) "found themselves" and by desire for "the other" in Jacques Lacan's psychoanalytical theory (*Écrits*, 1966). No less powerful, it seems in retrospect, was the repression of desires deemed invisible if not illicit until "the sexual turn" took hold in the 1990s. In *Homosexual Desire in Shakespeare's England* (1991) I, like other writers at the time, was attempting to give intellectual and political legitimacy to those formerly hidden and repressed desires. The place of desire in the continuum I am proposing now is more equivocal.

The accompanying table allows us to appreciate the variety in Shakespeare's representations of sexuality and at the same time see affiliations between plays and poems that might otherwise escape us, particularly affiliations between earlier plays and later plays

← deed			← desire →				delight →
TA	*1H4*	*MND*	*VA*	*AYL*	*WT*		*LLL*
R3	*MWW*	*RJ*	*Luc*	*TN*	*Tem*		
KL	*2H4*	*MV*	*Son*				
Per	*MM*	*MA*					
	Oth	*TC*					
	AW	*AC*					
		Cym					
		TNK					

and among comedies, histories, and tragedies. Most important of all, in my view, is the invitation to consider the different kinds of responses that the representations seem designed to engage. As reference points in this enterprise we can use three Ds: deeds, desire, and delight.

There are other possible terms, of course, for the three Ds—"acts" for "deeds," "want" for "desire," "affect" for "delight"—but the three Ds have early modern usage to recommend them. Lysimachus in *Pericles* voices a common idiom when he wishes Marina would "do the deeds of darkness" (4.5.37). "Desire" finds its most high-strung spokesman in Troilus, who declares to Cressida: "This is the monstruosity in love, lady, that the will is infinite and the execution confined; that the desire is boundless and the act a slave to limit" (3.2.77–80). As for "delight," we have Hamlet's quip to Rosencrantz and Guildenstern, "Man delights not me — nor women neither, though by your smiling you seem to say so" (2.2.274–5).

"Delight" has the added advantage of being a common word in early modern English for aesthetic pleasure. Sir Philip Sidney in *A Defence of Poesy* (written ca. 1579, published 1595) speaks for most critical commentators of the time when he defines the art of making things out of words as "a representing, counterfeiting or figuring forth — to speak metaphorically, a speaking picture— with this end: to teach and delight." As an example of delight in connection with comedy Sidney cites the view of "a fair lady" and, as an example of delight mixed with ridicule, the painted image of Hercules spinning in women's clothes: "so strange a power in love procureth delight, and the scornfulness of the action stirreth laughter."

Along the continuum that links deed, desire, and delight there are, of course, slippages. Hamlet's use of "delight" as a verb—as an action, not a state of being—serves as a reminder that deeds are mediated by delight just as delight is mediated by deeds. A famous example of such slippages can be found in *Shakespeare's Sonnets* 135 and 136, where the repeated and italicized word "will" signifies, among other things, all three Ds, all at the same time: (1) desires of "thou" and "I," (2) deeds involving both male and female sexual organs ("thy will" and "my will"), and (3) exuberant delight in the verbal play with those deeds and desires. When it comes to sexuality, the points on the continuum are not static but dynamic. In the literal sense of the word, they *imply* one another.

Representing sexuality

In the table I have indicated my own estimate of where on the continuum some of Shakespeare's best-known works might be placed. To be sure, laying the works out in this way neglects the subtleties of individual plays and poems. It may seem incontestable that sexuality in *Titus Andronicus*, *Richard III*, and *King Lear* on the left end of the continuum is represented as deeds; with *Love's Labour's Lost, The Winter's Tale*, and *The Tempest* on the right end the case for delight is more qualified. In each of the latter three scripts the experience of delight on the part of young protagonists predominates, but each script balances this youthful delight with countenancing sexuality as deeds: the exploits of Jaquenetta and her suitors in *Labour's*, Leontes's obsession with Hermione's supposed adultery in *The Winter's Tale*, Caliban's alleged attempt to rape Miranda in *The Tempest*. For each work on the continuum I have tried to locate the *primary* focus in representations of sexuality, recognizing all the while that the power of these plays and poems on the imaginations of spectators, listeners, and readers across the past four hundred years has much to do with the multiple focuses in each script. Closer attention to several particular places on the continuum can let us observe three factors in action.

Starting from the left, we find ourselves confronted with six quite diverse scripts: in presumed chronological order they are *Henry IV, Part 1* (1596–7), *The Merry Wives of Windsor* (1597–8), *Henry IV, Part 2* (1597–8), *Measure for Measure* (1603–4), *Othello* (1603–4), and *All's Wells That Ends Well* (1607–8). In all of them sexuality as deed looms larger than sexuality as desire, and sexuality as delight remains a distant prospect. Falstaff's corporeality, his imagination of sexuality as physical acts, largely accounts for the position of *Henry IV, Part 1*, *Merry Wives*, and *Henry IV, Part 2* in this group. The Prince's opening taunt to Falstaff in *Henry IV, Part 1* establishes the fleshly mode of representation: "What a devil hast thou to do with the time of the day? Unless hours were cups of sack, and minutes capons, and clocks the tongues of bawds, and dials the signs of leaping-houses, and the blessed sun himself a fair hot wench in flame-coloured taffeta, I see no reason why thou shouldst be so superfluous to demand the time of the day" (1.2.5–11). Even the witty sparring of Hotspur and Lady Percy turns on the lady's question "For what offence have I this fortnight been / A banished woman from my Harry's bed?" (2.3.37–8).

The inclusion of *Measure* and *All's Well* in this group is occasioned by the bed-tricks that have proved so problematic to our own sensibilities. In fact, no fewer than forty-four surviving scripts from 1594 to 1630 deploy some form of bed-trick, and the device even has its own number in Stith Tompson's *Motif-Index of Folk Literature* (1955–8): number K1843.2. Perhaps the bed-tricks were, in the eyes of Shakespeare and his contemporaries, no less delightful than ridiculous. If so, delight is more implicated in *Measure* and *All's Well* than modern criticism usually recognizes. In this grouping of representations of sexuality as deed, *Othello* finds a place despite the protestations of desire expressed by Othello and Desdemona. Iago's opening image "an old black ram / Is tupping your white ewe" (1.1.87–8) reduces those desires to a brute physical act. Just such a deed becomes Othello's obsession, turning his smothering of Desdemona in 5.2 into an act of sexual consummation.

Moving further along the continuum, we encounter another interesting cluster in the generically and chronologically diverse group *A Midsummer Night's Dream* (1595), *Romeo and Juliet* (1595), *The Merchant of Venice* (1596–7), *Much Ado about Nothing* (1598–9), *Troilus and Cressida* (1602), *Antony and Cleopatra* (1606), *Cymbeline* (1610–11), and *The Two Noble Kinsmen* (1613). In this group, declarations of desire and expressions of delight are conspicuous but sexuality as physical act remains persistent. Bottom's tryst with Titania in *Dream*, 3.1 and 4.1, the Nurse's bawdy jokes in *Romeo*, 1.3, and Mercutio's reduction of Juliet to "An open-arse" in 2.1.38, the witty exchanges about rings in *Merchant*, 5.1.300–7, the charade of Hero's unfaithfulness in *Much Ado*, Pandarus's knowingness and Thersites' rant "Lechery, lechery, still wars and lechery" (*Troilus*, 5.2.201–2), the frankly acknowledged physicality of Antony's and Cleopatra's passion for one another, Iachimo's blazon of Imogen's body in *Cymbeline*, 2.2, Arcite's blunt declaration about Emilia, "I love her as a woman, to enjoy her" in *Kinsmen*, 2.2.165: all of these keep sexuality as a physical act seething beneath the surface even as the protagonists profess high-sounding desires.

Three works of poetry that strike me as being precisely poised on desire—*Venus and Adonis*, *The Rape of Lucrece*, and the *Sonnets*—I will defer until the final section of this essay. In the meantime, three other congeries of plays await our attention along the continuum between desire and delight. Though they vary in likely date of composition, all of them are classified in the First Folio as comedies. The desires that are given suasive voice and seductive visuality in *As You Like It* (1599–1600) and *Twelfth Night* (1601) open out into deeds in one direction and delight in the other, but it is the delight of being in love that has the stronger pull. *As You Like It* includes Touchstone's low pun about how he gave two "cods" (testicles as well as pea husks) to Jane Smile (2.4.48–50), Maria may invite Sir Andrew to "bring your hand to th'buttery bar, and let it drink" and perhaps gesture at the same time to her breasts (*Twelfth Night*, 1.3.68), Malvolio may fantasize about rising from "a day-bed where I have left Olivia sleeping" (2.5.45–6) and "play with my … – some rich jewel" (2.5.57–8), but it is Rosalind and Orlando's swoons and Orsino's synesthetic delight at being in love that set the dominant tone in each play. Prompted by Sidney, we may laugh at Touchstone's puns and Malvolio's delusions, but the language of both scripts seems calculated to elicit an imaginative sympathy that leaves us in the place of Sidney's reader, in an equipoise of laughter and delight.

That position perhaps gives us a cue for responding to the homoeroticism that scholars, actors, and directors have found since the 1970s in *As You Like It* and *Twelfth Night*. The delicious balance between ridicule and delight that Sidney finds in an image of Hercules spinning is set up by Sidney himself in Mucidorus's amorous blazon of the body of an Amazon warrior in 1.12 of *The Countess of Pembroke's Arcadia* (published 1593)—a figure that turns out to be Mucidorus's friend Pyrocles. Sidney in his observation about the delightful ridiculousness of cross-dressed Hercules can help us get our bearings on the cross-dressed female protagonists of *Merchant, As You Like It, Twelfth Night*, and *Cymbeline*: "so strange a power in love procureth delight, and the scornfulness of the action stirreth laughter."

The subjective experience of delight looms larger still in a chronologically diverse group of plays on the far right of the continuum. Leontes's jealousy may impel the plot of *The Winter's Tale* (1609–10) on its course toward tragedy, but the play is rescued by the delight communicated so exuberantly by the young lovers. Sexual violence may haunt *The Tempest* (1610–11) and Prospero may be anxious for his daughter's virginity even with Ferdinand, but the delight of the young lovers is represented not only subjectively, in their professions to one another, but objectively in the masque that Prospero conjures for them, complete with the images of sexual consummation and fecundity common to epithalamia. For sexuality as unadulterated delight, however, we must look to one of Shakespeare's earliest scripts, *Love's Labour's Lost*.

Presenting sexuality

A further benefit of the concatenation of deed, desire, and delight is to make us think afresh about the claims of Puritan polemicists like Philip Stubbes that play performances not only represent sexual acts but incite sexual desires in the here-and-now. For the spectator/ listener, or so Stubbes imagines in *The Anatomie of Abuses ... [in] Ailgna* (1583), the experience of watching and hearing a play begins in flirtation, passes through foreplay, and ends in *emissio seminis*: first "wanton gestures," "bawdy speeches," "laughing and fleering," then "kissing and bussing," "clipping and culling," "winking and glancing of wanton eyes," and finally the departure of spectators homeward in twos, where "in their secret conclaves they play the Sodomites, or worse." Rhetorically at least, Stubbes enacts the ejaculation that disturbs him.

Stubbes reminds us that, *pace* Sidney, object lessons and delight are not the only factors involved in seeing, hearing, and reading fictions made out of words. At the very center of these transactions is a desire to enter into the imagined world created out of words and personally to own the sexual knowledge on offer. In my estimation the works by Shakespeare that engage desire most insistently are the third-person narrative poems *Venus and Adonis* (1592–93) and *The Rape of Lucrece* (1593–94), and the first-person poems collected in *Shakespeare's Sonnets Never Before Imprinted* (written c. 1593–1603, published 1609). The intensity of the desires represented in the two narrative poems may account for the fact that both of them were Shakespeare's most frequently reprinted and presumably most frequently read works in his own lifetime. More elusive is the reading history of the *Sonnets* while they circulated in manuscript among the author's "private friends," as Francis Meres describes in 1598.

All three of these nondramatic works center on desire focused explicitly on particular sexual deeds at the same time that they inspire delight through the exercise of the reader's imagination. The scenario in both *Venus and Adonis* and *The Rape of Lucrece* follows just the trajectory that Stubbes insinuates with respect to stage comedies: first flirtation (the narrator's descriptions of Adonis's beauty, Tarquin's blazon of the sleeping Lucrece's body), then foreplay (Venus's wrestling Adonis to the ground, Tarquin's venturing to touch), finally the deed itself (the boar's rape of Adonis in the groin, Tarquin's rape of Lucrece). Through it all the reader is granted the privileged position of a voyeur who can both experience the desires and see the deeds, all without any personal consequences.

In terms of the continuum, Shakespeare's collected *Sonnets* occupy a particularly expansive space, stretching from brute physicality on the one hand to finely nuanced representations of interior experience on the other—sometimes in the space of fourteen lines or less. Consider the transition in Sonnet 129 from "lust in action" in line two to "A bliss in proof" in line eleven to "Before, a joy proposed; behind, a dream" in line twelve. By now many critics would agree that the *Sonnets* do not enact a through narrative, however hard some commentators (myself included) have tried to find one. What *does* continue through all the *Sonnets*, what carries over from one poem to another, is the position accorded the reader: a knowingness about sexuality that includes penis, anus, and vagina, varyingly intense degrees of desire, and delight in the words that express that plenitude. In this respect the *Sonnets*, like the narrative poems, can be said not just to represent sexual knowledge but to *present* it to the reader, to make it available for the reader's own possession. In some respects Stubbes was discerning. What he and his kind always miss, however—and what Sidney understands perfectly—is the irony that accompanies the experience of delight when sexuality is "figured forth."

My personal experience with reading, seeing, hearing, and thinking about early modern fictions for more than forty years suggests that Sidney's desire, tempered by detachment and delight, is in fact the position that all of Shakespeare's engagements with sexual knowledge, the *Sonnets* most of all, invite us to assume. In early modern texts passionate irony is, as we say now, the sweet spot. X marks the spot.

Rethinking Sexual Acts and Identities

Mario DiGangi
President, SAA 2015–16

In Fall 2014, Will Fisher and I cotaught a PhD course at the CUNY Graduate Center on "Histories and Theories of Early Modern Sexuality," one aim of which was to take stock of the wealth of historical, literary, and interdisciplinary scholarship that has rejuvenated the field during the past decade. For all the variety of this work, it struck me that many of the critics we were reading continued to make recourse to some version of the "acts versus identities" debate that has structured historical sexuality scholarship ever since Foucault posited (in Robert Hurley's problematic English translation of *The History of Sexuality* [1978]) that where the Renaissance sodomite had been a "temporary aberration," the modern homosexual "was now a species." As Carla Freccero, David Halperin, Lynne Huffer, Ruth Mazo Karras, Eve Sedgwick, and others have observed, this notorious passage has been used to authorize some debatable assumptions and claims: that we cannot speak of sexual proclivities, styles, or subjectivities in premodern cultures, which only criminalized certain sexual acts; that we can determine the date of an epistemic shift after which the performance of homosexual acts constituted a homosexual "identity" (a word that does not appear in Foucault's original French); that we can measure the incoherence of past sexual regimes against the coherence and legibility of the modern concept of homosexuality. If the "acts versus identities" paradigm is no longer tenable, it is because a large body of scholarship has nuanced and complicated our understanding of the ways in which the performance of particular sexual acts might have informed subjective experiences and social perceptions in premodernity. While some early modern scholars continue to use "identity" as a touchstone for describing how sexual practices shape experiences of selfhood, others reject the concept of identity entirely, and still others have explored alternative concepts of personhood and social role. In what follows, I concentrate on how particular questions around acts and identities came to inform our class discussions about nonreproductive sexual practices, race, prostitution, bestiality, and affect.

An inherent limitation of the "acts versus identities" debate is its Foucauldian origin in a discussion about a particular act (sodomy, in the form of male anal intercourse) and a particular identity (male homosexuality). Recent scholarship has productively expanded and complicated our knowledge of early modern sexual acts by looking beyond the most familiar practices—male–female vaginal intercourse and male–male anal intercourse—and by interrogating the epistemological foundations of such knowledge. For instance, in "Making Sexual Knowledge" Valerie Traub explores how sex is fundamentally "opaque, inaccessible, and resistant to understanding." Will Stockton and James Bromley, editors of *Sex Before Sex: Figuring the Act in Early Modern England* (2013) cite the influence of Foucault when observing that contemporary discourses of "gay, lesbian, and heterosexual identity" have guided analysis of sex in early modern texts, thus leading to the neglect of non-identitarian sexual acts such as chin-chucking, anilingus, drinking, and bestiality, all of which are explored in the volume.

Nonetheless, in the introduction to his forthcoming book on early modern sexual practice, Will Fisher suggests that research on sex acts "should not be seen as incommensurate with research about sexual identity." Late seventeenth-century pornographic texts, he notes, evince an "associational logic" that attributes a kind of sexual preference or proclivity to men who habitually become aroused by acts such as flogging. Fisher advocates further exploration of the connection between the habitual performance of particular sexual acts and notions of personhood that do not correspond to contemporary identity categories such as "lesbian" or "gay," which for all their ideological incoherence, I would add, still exert a normative force on present configurations of sexuality. Similarly, in *Sexual Types* (2011) I argue that in early modern England the sodomite is defined not only by the criminal act of anal intercourse but also by the habits of drunkenness and luxurious consumption that are associated both with the sins of Sodom and with the familiar practices of male fellowship. The concept of a sexual type allows us to identify culturally resonant figures that articulate the linkages between sexual transgressions and other forms of social disorder, without requiring that we conform such figures to present-day gender- or sexual-identity categories.

Approaching figures such as the sodomite and tribade not as fixed sexual identities but as recognizable sexual types also encourages an intersectional analysis that can account for the way that categories such as gender, status, and race inform sexual meaning. For instance, I argue that the ambiguities that frequently surround descriptions of the tribade's sexual acts—does she use her clitoris to rub or penetrate her partner? is her partner gendered as feminine or masculine?—derive in part from racial fantasies about the strange bodies and customs of African, Turkish, and Indian women (including Titania's votaress in *A Midsummer Night's Dream*). In his essay on "Western Encounters with Sex and Bodies in Non-European Cultures, 1500–1750" (2013), Jonathan Burton uses the category of race to provide an important corrective to the Eurocentric bias of *The History of Sexuality*. Taking issue with Foucault's claim that sexual identities first emerged in modern Western societies, Burton posits that "European notions of sexual identity may have also formed through encounters with non-European cultures," members of which sometimes exhibited gender traits or sexual habits that Western observers interpreted as constituting a distinct social role. According to Burton, European descriptions of Moroccan innkeepers and American berdaches seem to recognize them as representatives of a "distinct community," "minority," or "subculture": the detailed descriptions of their transgressive sexual and gender behaviors coalesce around an ascription of "categorical identity."

In a course unit on prostitution and "whoredom" (an early modern term conveying various sexual offenses), we also explored how sexual acts might produce, appropriate, or express a particular gender or status identity. Analyzing sexual slander in *Domestic*

Dangers (1996), Laura Gowing concludes that whereas men could commit fornication or adultery without suffering a radical decline of reputation, for a woman to commit such acts "signified the loss of the whole character; it led to a permanent state of whoredom." Gowing's account of the personal, familial, and communal importance of a woman's sexual "character" illuminates the severity of the crisis faced in Shakespeare's plays by slandered women such as Desdemona (*Othello*) and Hero (*Much Ado about Nothing*). Whereas discussion of cross-dressing in Shakespeare usually focuses on women who adopt male disguises, Cristine Varholy's essay on "Cross-Class Dressing" (2008) in London brothels and theatres examines Bridewell court cases concerning prostitutes who dressed like gentlewomen in order to attract clients with a taste for "respectable" women. In such instances, Varholy argues, dressing up constituted a theatrical "manipulation of identity" that enabled or enhanced a particular sexual encounter; I would emphasize, however, that the male client's fantasy seems to depend upon reifying and eroticizing the identity of "gentlewoman." The relation between sexual performance and social status is also central to Jennifer Panek's exploration of "He-Whores and Male Sexuality on the Early Modern Stage" (2010). Although Panek does not use the language of identity, she demonstrates that two kinds of men—physical laborers and men with a sanguine temperament—were believed to possess exceptional sexual stamina. For such men, performing multiple sex acts would not bring about the effeminizing debilitation often associated with male sexual expenditure, but would instead testify to a kind of inherent masculinity, a quality expressed in the familiar term "stallion."

In discussions of masochism, bestiality, and affect, we explored the ways that certain sexual practices and queer spatial "orientations" (to use a term from Sara Ahmed's *Queer Phenomenology* [2006]) might blur or trouble identities. Karen Raber, in *Animal Bodies, Renaissance Culture* (2013), argues that human–animal intimacy can facilitate affective, visceral agencies and pleasures that are not reducible to the act of bestiality. Defining eros as a "drive to union" that "transcends the genital expression of that union," Raber points to the corporeal melding between rider and horse celebrated in Renaissance horsemanship manuals, as well as *Venus and Adonis*'s way of rendering "species categories" untenable through the fluid, shifting identities it attributes to its human, animal, and divine figures. My own essay on "Shakespeare's 'Bawdy'" explores how several of Shakespeare's characters (including Hamlet, Othello, Leontes, and Mercutio) use the word "bawdy" to ascribe sexual agency to non-human or part-human "bodies" such as blood, wind, planet, or hand. Borrowing from Jane Bennett's *Vibrant Matter* (2010) the notion of "impersonal affect," I argue that "bawdy" conveys an anxious belief about the contaminating eroticism of things, which threatens to violate both the physical boundaries and the conceptual distinctness of the human body. If, as I have suggested above, early modern culture recognized that the performance of sexual acts, under certain circumstances, might define a particular kind of character, type, or person, then the notion of a person-less sexual agency occupies an antithetical conceptual pole that can help us to rethink the complex relationship between sexual acts and identities in Shakespeare's time.

HexaSexuality

Madhavi Menon

Sexuality demands an identity

Stanley Wells does it. So does Joseph Pequigney. Many critics do it: they call Shakespeare gay. The most recent version of the debate about Shakespeare's sexuality has been played out on the pages of the *Times Literary Supplement*, with Brian Vickers claiming that Shakespeare was not gay and Stanley Wells riposting that he was. I am not here to judge whether or not Shakespeare was gay. My stand on this is identical to that of Eve Kosofsky Sedgwick in *Epistemology of the Closet* when she asks: "Has there ever been a gay Socrates? Has there ever been a gay Shakespeare? Has there ever been a gay Proust? Does the Pope wear a dress? If these questions startle, it is not least as tautologies. A short answer, though a very incomplete one, might be that not only have there been a gay Socrates, Shakespeare, and Proust, but that their names are Socrates, Shakespeare, and Proust." But the interesting thing is that sexuality, not least between Vickers and Wells, is raised as a question of identity: Was Shakespeare gay? The texts most commonly adduced in such a debate are the *Sonnets*, bountiful as they are in praising masters who are also mistresses, and in comparing male patrons' loveliness to that of a summer's day. But whether Sonnets 18 and 20 suggest Shakespeare was or was not gay, the fact remains that we cannot think of sexuality outside the rubric of identity. Sexuality, *pace* Michel Foucault, is not that which creates identity but that which is created by identity as its "natural" core. The sex of the person with whom one has sex becomes the determinant of one's own sexuality. And that sexuality becomes one's identity. Thus the demand to know to whom *Shakespeare's Sonnets* are addressed becomes a demand to know with whom Shakespeare had, or might have imagined having, sex.

Desire refuses identity

One of the things on which we can agree, even if we do not care whether Shakespeare was gay, is that sexuality has an intimate relation with desire. But, and here is the rub, the feeling is not mutual. Desire tends not to reciprocate sexuality's longing for it. Instead, desire plays fast and loose, rarely plighting its troth, wandering at will and with abandon. It is this wandering desire that provides the Shakespearean corpus with the bulk of its matter. Thus Viola is able to throw her hands up in the air in *Twelfth Night* when she discovers that Olivia is in love with her in male disguise as Cesario. Indeed, Olivia's longing begins at precisely the moment when she hears a description of Viola/Cesario that suggests she is *indecipherable* in terms of identity categories:

OLIVIA   Of what personage and years is he?
MALVOLIO Not yet old enough for a man, nor young enough for a boy, as a squash is before 'tis a peascod, or a codling when 'tis almost an apple. 'Tis with him in standing water between boy and man.
      ....
OLIVIA   Let him approach. Call in my gentlewoman.
                                                    (1.5.151–5, 158)

A woman falls in love with another woman in disguise as a man who is her/himself in love with a man. It all turns out hetero in the end, but the thrust of the play is on desire rather than on the identity imposed at the conclusion. Indeed, the text tries to fix the dilemmas of desire but fails to erase the eros in which the play is drenched.

Desire is subtractive

Desire in Shakespeare is not only erotic, but it is also bad at mathematics. Where it should add, it subtracts, and where it should divide, it multiplies. Take *Macbeth*, for instance. The play has a perfectly good set of witches but they refuse to let their attributes add up to an identity. "You should be women," Banquo says with a touch of peeved grievance, "And yet your beards forbid me to interpret / That you are so" (1.3.45–7). For Banquo, a hag with a beard doth not a woman make. Yet the text is perfectly comfortable presenting these characters as putting a hex on identity (the German *hexe* means "witch"). Thus it is that *Macbeth* ceaselessly serrates the borders of what is considered natural. A man not of woman born saves the day, while the Witches not to be distinguished from men or women set the scene. Far from coalescing into sexed identities, characters in this play flaunt attributes that simply do not add up.

Desire travels

Anticipating Alain Badiou's claim in *Saint Paul: The Foundation of Universalism* (2003) that universalism is subtractive—it disallows individual attributes from leading to a preordained identity—Shakespearean desire too takes shape across bodies, spaces, and times without cohering into any one specificity. In other words, a set of desires do not automatically lead to an identity. Man can desire man without being homosexual or gay or a sodomite, woman can desire man without being heterosexual or reproductive or a sodomite, and so on. An amazing number of these nondetermining desires attach to the person of Titania in *A Midsummer Night's Dream*. She falls in love with an ass and falls out with her husband over a changeling Indian boy, but in the play these events make her neither a zoophile nor a basmati rice queen. Titania "steals" the boy from an Indian king, and Oberon in turn steals the boy from her; she claims her desire is in memory of her votaress who has died in childbirth, while Oberon gives no reason whatsoever. Titania's longing for her votaress does not make her a lesbian and, equally, Oberon's desire for the boy does not in the play make him a pederast or a homosexual. Desires swirl from India to Athens, from male to female, but we do not get a sexual identity at the end of all those travails.

Universal travails

In Badiou's Pauline universe, the primary tendency of the self is to go beyond its self. Such a tendency has a one-word title in the Shakespearean universe: Desire. Whether it be for otherness, movement, sex, love, or death, Shakespeare's texts focus on a desire whose subtractive tendency militates against a fixable identity. Not only is this true for people alive in the world, but it is also true of the dead. In *As You Like It*, the idea that people can be fixed by their desire is laughable even in death—"Men have died from time to time and worms have eaten them, but not for love" (4.1.97–9). The play stages an extended wooing session between two men, and names one of them Ganymede, the mythological character kidnapped by Zeus to be the male cupbearer of the gods; Ganymede's Latin name is Catamitus. Either no character in the play, including Ganymede's lover, knows anything about mythology, or else they are not bothered by the play's allusion to the often violent travails of desire. This play, like others, is at home with desire's flights of fancy. In Shakespeare, desire travels, universally.

Such a universal desire might best be termed queer

Is itinerancy the universal currency of desire? Does all desire always travel? When Antony is traveling in Italy, away from Cleopatra, the queen of Egypt reminisces about their lovemaking:

That time? O times!
I laughed him out of patience, and that night
I laughed him into patience, and next morn,
Ere the ninth hour, I drunk him to his bed,
Then put my tires and mantles on him, whilst
I wore his sword Philippan.

(2.5.18–23)

Cleopatra and Antony trade places during this extended session of
sex. She takes on his phallic authority and bestows her petticoats
on him. Sexual travel in this scene mirrors the travel between Rome
and Egypt throughout the play. And this travel is specifically that
of *desire*. No sexuality here, despite and because of the plentiful
sex. Instead, we have a desire that refuses to settle in a country
or language or dress or gender; a desire that does not pretend any
resting place is ontologically fixed or epistemologically permanent.
This Shakespearean desire is not an additive concept that generates
a sexual identity. Rather, the queerness of desire is that it resists
identity in the singular while simultaneously occupying several
identities at once. The queerness of Shakespearean desire resides in
its not being resident in any single act or identity. A queer desire
can only complicate the identities that we attach to it. As such, it
pushes at the boundaries of a sexuality that presumes stable subject-
formation. In Shakespeare, this pushy desire is universal—it crosses
boundaries of genre and gender alike—and it is queer—it militates
against both identities and endings. Not hetero- or homo-sexuality,
then, in Shakespeare, but hexasexuality. Desire is the universal
solvent that refuses to resolve itself into identity.

3

Teaching

The Classroom

David Bevington
President, SAA 1976–77, 1995–96

Although the educational revolution of the past thirty-five years or so has often sought to replace dead European white male authors in the traditional curriculum of high school, college, and university with writers arguably closer to the concerns of today's students and readers, Shakespeare has generally survived this trend and seems even to have profited from it. Why? Shakespeare is indisputably dead, European, white, and male. So are Milton and Spenser and Pope, who are in decline as authors to be read and studied, while Maya Angelou and Virginia Woolf and Gabriel García Márquez thrive. Bucking this trend, Shakespeare enrollments are generally doing well across the board. This is true not just in terms of student numbers, but in the world of criticism as well: New Historicists, feminists, and deconstructionists alike are less and less inclined to illustrate and test their theoretical claims by reading Shelley and Tennyson, whereas those same contemporary critics find Shakespeare simply irresistible. Think of Terry Eagleton, for example, or Stanley Cavell, or Germaine Greer. Shakespeare has a way of throwing new questions back at us, adding a rich complexity to the process of reading texts closely. Books on Shakespeare pour forth, at the rate of more than one a day, many of them quite fascinating. Shakespeare seems to provide what Matthew Arnold once called a "touchstone" of literary criticism, a way of answering why some texts survive over the centuries and become immortal. Arnold preferred Homer as his example; today's touchstone tends to be Shakespeare. He survives and prospers not because of being traditionally the subject of teaching in schools and colleges, but really in spite of that: students and teachers and critics alike find that no other writer can go beyond his ability to challenge, to interrogate, to illuminate, and to insist that we rethink ourselves and our cultural heritage.

How can teaching help to foster this constructive way in which Shakespeare appears to be God's gift to the humanities classroom? Let me start with what is sometimes called the New Liberal Arts Curriculum, a program designed primarily for the teaching of advanced placement classes in high school and of core humanities classes at the college level. A seminar entitled "Shakespeare and the Liberal Arts Curriculum" at the 2014 Shakespeare Association of America meeting in Saint Louis, chaired by Jeff Rufo and Elizabeth Hutcheon, addressed this very subject. One participant, Mary Janell Metzger of Western Washington University, adroitly suggested in her paper that Shakespeare addresses perfectly the need for coherence in the New Liberal Arts. As that curriculum changes and experiments with new materials at a host of widely differing institutions, how is the potential reward of ever-greater diversity to be balanced by some pattern of coherent literary form? Her answer is that Shakespeare provides exactly this needed value. His work offers various models of poetic form and genre: lyric poetry, genial satire, colloquial prose, blank verse description, peppy dialogue, tragic soliloquy, and much more. In the process of close reading in class, a teacher can explore the potentials of prose and verse, of comic rhymes, of introspective meditation, and of sharply engaged debate.

A chief aim of teaching literary texts is to improve skills in close reading. Many students in our classes have had little practice in this, at least at the level of intellectual sophistication that will enable them to become better at interpreting, reasoning, and arguing—skills that apply to whatever profession they may ultimately enter. What better text for this than Shakespeare? He is, admittedly, hard to read. But that is a positive challenge, not a reason to shift over to teaching *To Kill a Mockingbird* instead. Shakespeare is hard, to begin with, at the expository level. I remember a student who came in during office hours to ask if we could talk about the opening scene of *Henry IV, Part 1*. Good, I replied, are you puzzled about why King Henry is so anxious about civil strife in his country? Should we discuss what his relationship is like with the Earls of Northumberland and Worcester, and how his former partnership with the Percy clan in *Richard II* seems now to have deteriorated? No, she said, I just don't understand a word of what is being said. What does this mean, "the thirsty entrance of this soil / Shall daub her lips with her own children's blood" (1.1.5–6)? What are these "meteors of a troubled heaven" that somehow resemble "the intestine shock / And furious close of civil butchery" (1.1.10; 12–13)? Clearly it was time to slow down and read closely, image by image. And, once these first difficulties of clarifying plot situation are at least partly resolved, we can go on to the dense complexities of interpretation that we all struggle with in this remarkable writer. Shakespeare is for all seasons. In courses from entry-level humanities core up to PhD seminars, we can hope to assist students in moving on from improving reading skills to becoming sophisticated critics.

One huge benefit of choosing Shakespeare as a text to be read with astute care is that he is a dramatist. He is a poet too, of course, but for the most part that great achievement takes dramatic form. Drama is a challenging genre to teach, and especially so in Shakespeare. Students need to get used to speech prefixes, lines of verse, lines of dialogue often divided between two or more speakers, stage directions both original to the early printed text and added by editors, indications of scene breaks and of scenic location, and shifts between verse and prose, as well as glosses and footnotes added in modern editions. Here again the difficulty is a positive challenge. A teacher needs to encourage students to stage in their minds the scene being presented on the page. They should learn to play the role of director. Prose fiction customarily tells the reader what he or she needs to know about location, time of the day and of the year, costuming of the characters, and what they are thinking. A dramatic text throws a beneficial burden on the reader to "Piece out our imperfections with your thoughts" (Prologue 23), as the opening Chorus of *Henry V* puts it, speaking on behalf of his acting company and of the dramatist. "Think, when we talk of horses, that you see them / Printing their proud hoofs i'th' receiving earth" (Prologue 26–7). Spoken dialogue and printed text alike challenge the reader in ways that even a film cannot hope to do, since film, like prose fiction, tells where we are and whom we are beholding. Drama is the genre of imaginative re-creation.

Shakespeare is of course a powerful thinker. That, however, should not encourage us to teach him as if he were presenting a philosophical treatise. Good philosophers can certainly do splendid things with Shakespeare, but in my view we should never lose track of the fact that he was a professional dramatist, taking parts onstage with his acting company for at least some of his career and writing plays that he knew would suit the capacities of his fellow actors and the tastes of their socioeconomically diverse audience in a theatre like the Globe. Some twelve years ago I was asked by Steven Nadler, editor of Blackwell Great Minds, if I would like to contribute a study of Shakespeare to that series of books about great thinkers: Kant, Augustine, Descartes, Sartre, Schopenhauer, and the like. I said I'd be delighted so long as the publisher wouldn't object if I came to the conclusion that Shakespeare isn't a philosopher in the usual sense of that term. This was agreed to and I set to work. When I submitted my text and it was sent off for peer review, the answer quickly came back: who is this Bevington guy and why is he arguing, in our series, that Shakespeare is not a philosopher? We straightened out this disagreement, and *Shakespeare's Ideas* duly appeared, arguing that Shakespeare is what he might himself have called a "natural philosopher," like Corin in *As You Like It*, who, when asked by Touchstone, "Hast any philosophy in thee, shepherd?" (3.2.21) replies that he knows "that the property of rain is to wet and fire to burn," that "a great cause of the night is lack of the sun," and so on (3.2.24–5, 26–7). Touchstone concludes this delightful colloquy with the observation that "Such a one is a natural philosopher." My point was, and is, that Shakespeare wears his learning lightly. He seldom alludes to philosophers by name, and tends to do so on those rare occasions in a wryly jesting way, as when he mentions Socrates as the henpecked husband of Xanthippe in *The Taming of the Shrew* (1.2.70). Shakespeare was a dramatist.

In the classroom, I like to encourage students to minimize the presumed distinction between "literary" and "theatrical" approaches to dramatic texts. English departments and theatre departments are too often hostile toward one another in American higher education. I contend that one should expect to find no important difference between the careful reading of a scene in class and a first reading of a playtext by an acting company gathering for the first time with the director to explore the work they are about to enact. In both cases, the questions are basically theatrical and at the same time analytical. Why, in the opening scene of *Antony and Cleopatra*, are two essentially anonymous soldiers given the opening and closing speeches of an action that focuses mainly on the play's famous lovers? Who are these soldiers? The Folio text identifies them as Demetrius and Philo, but on stage their names are never mentioned. Why? Where are they to be located on stage? Downstage as a kind of framing device, or elsewhere so as not to obstruct the audience's view of Antony and Cleopatra? How, in the Elizabethan theatre with its general absence of sets, do we know we are in Egypt? How are Cleopatra and Antony costumed? What about costuming for the ladies, eunuchs, servants, soldiers, and others in attendance? What theatrical signals are embodied in the dialogue or stage directions? Why is Enobarbus seemingly absent, or is he? Does the Messenger who enters with news from Rome wear Roman garb? What are Cleopatra and Antony quarreling amorously about? Why is Cleopatra teasing him? What does Antony mean when he boasts that "The nobleness of life / Is to do thus" (1.1.37–8)? Does he embrace Cleopatra as he speaks? Is he appealing to an inspiring idea of putting personal relationships above the petty claims of politics, or is he drunkenly flattering Cleopatra and fooling himself into thinking that his life in Egypt is somehow ennobling? To begin to answer such questions, students need to learn how to stage the scene in their minds and imagine how, as director, they would offer ideas to the actors taking the various parts in this scene.

This kind of exercise can be energizing in class. Sometimes I begin with a reading out loud by members of the class. Shakespeare often provides a generous number of parts. This way of beginning can require that students open their mouths and say something. They can be encouraged to put some expression into what they are saying. In the ensuing discussion, they can be asked to explain individually why their characters have said what they have said. In what way is a particular utterance a response to what preceded it? Which character or characters take leads in directing the conversation? The advantage of a dramatic text is that it can put readers into the picture directly. If course assistants are available to conduct discussion sections, one can encourage them to try this method; a fifty-minute hour is often just about right for one juicy scene, explored in this kind of theatrical detail. And beginning with a specific text can, if adroitly managed, then open out into larger questions about the play and its characters. What do students think of Cleopatra? As a woman who has known more than one man, is she prepared to be loyal to Antony, or would she, as Antony fears, pack cards with Caesar? Has Antony's infatuation with Cleopatra subdued his judgment?

Let me suggest another teaching venue to test the proposition of how one can teach a difficult text like Shakespeare to students unfamiliar with Elizabethan English and with the complexity of Shakespeare's thought. Increasingly, teachers interested in our burgeoning prison population are discovering that Shakespeare's texts can be both illuminating and therapeutic. My own experiences in this venture have been with Laura Bates, a Comparative Literature PhD from the University of Chicago now teaching at Indiana State University in Terre Haute and actively involved in teaching Shakespeare at the Wabash Valley Correctional Facility just south of Terre Haute. While she was still in Chicago I attended some sessions that she conducted in a closed, securely locked room with perhaps nine African American inmates, mostly in their late twenties or early thirties, all of them incarcerated for murder. Among the plays of Shakespeare that can work well in such an environment, like *Macbeth, Julius Caesar,* and *Hamlet,* Laura chose what might be called the "rumble" scene in *Romeo and Juliet,* in which a street brawl ends with Tybalt slaying Mercutio and then Romeo taking revenge on Tybalt. The inmates were asked to stand and read aloud, going for expression in their individual parts as much as they could. They stumbled over proper names and other difficult words, but without embarrassment. Then followed a discussion, line by line, of what the characters on stage were saying to one another. Finally, the members of the group were asked to restage the scene in their own words. The dialogue began with Benvolio saying "Hey, man, it's hot, man, those Capel dudes are all over the place. There's going to be a fight, man." The focus of attention was inevitably and properly on the way the men dared each other, jockeying for position to see who would go first, and then most importantly on Romeo's decision to challenge Tybalt even though Romeo has just vowed to Juliet to love her and honor her family. The intense peer pressure goading Romeo on to show his friends his macho resolution made perfect sense to these inmates, and provoked a really interesting conversation on how they individually had experienced the way in which gang mentality had all too easily led them into a fatal wrong choice. I was deeply moved by their readiness to admit their own criminal guilt and to seek to understand how they had let this happen to themselves.

The use of film is inevitably attractive in the teaching of Shakespeare since, along with Jane Austen, he is among the most extensively filmed writers of all time. Caveats are in order. Many Shakespeare films are so flawed that great care is required in choosing illustrations for classes. Too many of the BBC/Time-Life Shakespeare series filmed in the 1980s commit the unpardonable sin of making Shakespeare seem dull. I think of *The Winter's Tale*, for example, or *All's Well That Ends Well*. The series' *As You Like It* employs Masterpiece Theatre scenic realism to such an extent that all the magic is drained out of the Forest of Arden; it is a place where Duke Senior and his foresters sit under real trees, dismally swatting at midges, instead of being a place of imagination. Plays like *A Midsummer Night's Dream* and *The Tempest* show how easy it is to play visual tricks with the camera that explain away and trivialize all that is mysterious. But there are several fine versions of *Hamlet*, including Michael Almereyda's 2000 production set in modern-day Manhatten, Grigori Kozintsev's 1964 Russian production, David Tennant's RSC production of 2008–9, and, less well known, Kevin Kline's *Great Performances* production for television in 1990. (I leave out here, as useful but partly disappointing, Franco Zeffirelli's 1990 production and the four-hour complete *Hamlet* by Kenneth Branagh in 1996.) Multiple screen versions enable one to compare different versions of a given scene, a method well employed using Branagh's *Much Ado about Nothing* of 1993 in tandem with Joss Whedon's marvelous black-and-white, modern dress version of 2012 with Alexis Denisof and Amy Acker as Benedick and Beatrice. The list could go on. I avoid showing long stretches or complete showings during class time, which is too precious for that, but film clips in class can generate fine discussion, and it's a very good idea to schedule complete showings out of class time. Shakespeare films in other languages, not simply translated but rewritten in other languages, can demonstrate the limitless range of Shakespearean production across different cultures; here,

Grigori Kozintsev's versions of *King Lear*, *Korol Lir* (1971), and Akira Kurosawa's *Ran* (1985) and *Macbeth* (*Throne of Blood*, 1957) are especially effective.

Watching a good film version is often a way to show students that Shakespeare is not so difficult after all, at least not in performance. Students will discover that a play makes perfectly good sense when skilled actors provide a theatrically lively presentation, whether in the theatre or film. The voice and gestures offer interpretation that can get students started in reading more closely. I remember a fine production of *Love's Labour's Lost* at the Chicago Shakespeare Theatre, 2002, in which Scott Jaeck as Armado and Ross Lehman as Costard were not merely hilarious; they grimaced and gesticulated as though the often contrived and artful wordplay assigned to their parts were as clear and meaningful as is the summer's day.

But we mustn't forget that the play's the thing (someone must have said that), and that film versions must not displace repeated and detailed encounters with the text. At a certain point, films make interpretation all too easy. We want students to recreate the play in stage settings of their own imagination. This is the sense in which Shakespeare becomes a man of the theatre even when, or especially when, we read and visualize his words.

Money for Jam

Marjorie Garber

"Teaching Shakespeare," said R. W. B. Lewis to me, in or around 1970, "is taking money for jam." I was a beginning assistant professor at Yale, where I had done my graduate work. Lewis, one of the founders of the field of American Studies, was already celebrated as the author of *The American Adam* (1955). He would shortly gain wider international fame as the prize-winning author of biographies of Edith Wharton and the James family. "Taking money for jam." I had no idea what this idiom meant but the implication was clear (and later substantiated by the *OED*): "a profitable return for little or no trouble; a very easy job." Chatting casually over tea with a young colleague, Dick Lewis meant to be kind, or at least kindly. He wasn't disparaging my chosen field, or my course assignments. He was merely reassuring me that—not to worry—teaching Shakespeare was easy.

As compared to what, he didn't say. Maybe American Studies, maybe the kind of Renaissance scholarship then being done at Yale by scholars like Thomas M. Greene and Richard Sylvester, many of whose courses were for graduate students. Undergraduate Shakespeare at Yale at the time was being taught, very successfully, by two distinguished professors whose major work, up to that time, had been in the eighteenth century: Maynard Mack and Alvin Kernan. Both would go on to publish influential essays based on their undergraduate Shakespeare lectures. But both were in the most admirable sense initially gifted generalists, teaching Shakespeare as part of the heritage of literary and cultural literacy that was, at the time, pretty much unquestioned.

The noun "Shakespearean," often used these days to describe a scholar who specializes in Shakespeare, has also encompassed, in its variegated history since the early nineteenth century, Shakespeare enthusiasm or fandom on the one hand and, on the other, the belief that William Shakespeare, rather than Bacon or Oxford or anyone else, wrote the plays. Sir Walter Scott's biographer observed in 1837 that Scott's aunt was "about as devout a Shakespearian as her nephew"; a writer in the *New York Herald* in 1874 opined that "considerable blank ammunition has been wasted in this ridiculous war between the Baconians and the Shakespearians." In 1971 the *Daily Telegraph* was still using "Shakespearean" to mean "buff" or "fan" ("One of those devoted Shakespeareans who knows his author backwards") but by 1979—I'm tracking the word through the *OED*—Frank Kermode, definitely a "Shakespearean" in the academic sense, could write "Shakespearians may find explanations of the mysteriousness ... of *Hamlet*, by considering instead the *ur-Hamlet*" (Kermode, *The Genesis of Secrecy*, 1979). The context is a discussion of narrative, biblical scholarship, and literary analysis; the "Shakespearians" here are assumed to be professional scholars.

"Shakespearean" now of course functions routinely as a back-formation, used to describe Shakespeare adepts and Shakespeare critics from the eighteenth century to the present day. A series called "Great Shakespeareans," published now by Bloomsbury, includes Dryden and Pope, Garrick and Siddons, Marx and Freud, Empson and Wilson Knight, Brecht and Joyce, and many more.

But this is a twenty-first-century series and perspective, from which vantage point "Shakespearean" is not only a legible category but also an all-encompassing one. For at a certain point in the mid-to-late twentieth century, just around the time that Dick Lewis was telling me that teaching Shakespeare was taking money for jam, the designation "Shakespearean" was shifting (as the modulation in *OED* usage implies) to describe a class of academic scholars whose research, publications, and teaching were centrally focused on Shakespeare. Positions for scholar-teachers who specialize in Shakespeare are advertised regularly, as such. The members of the Shakespeare Association of America, whether they are graduate students or tenured professors, are "Shakespeareans." Shakespeare today is not only an author but a field. And not only a field but a profession.

Here are a few indicative dates: The Shakespeare Association of America was founded in 1972. The International Shakespeare Association was founded in 1971. The first World Shakespeare Congress was held in 1976. The Australian and New Zealand Shakespeare Association was founded in 1990. The British Shakespeare Association was founded in 2002. The Shakespeare Association of India was founded in 2008. The Asian Shakespeare Association was founded in 2012. These are organizations for professional Shakespeareans, dedicated to scholarship, teaching, and the study of performance. Like analogous professional organizations for medieval, eighteenth century, Victorian, or modernist studies, most have dues-paying members, are linked to journals, and hold conferences that provide networking opportunities as well as intellectual exchange.

What does all this mean for the teaching of Shakespeare?

For one thing, it means that "the Shakespeare course," the one all undergraduates were urged to take (by advisers, by their parents, by their peers, by the English department, by their own inclination) has now often diversified, or multiplied, into a range of courses with more specific or specialized themes and aims. Small colleges and large research universities alike now regularly offer undergraduate courses in Shakespeare and Gender, Shakespeare and Performance,

Shakespeare and Race, Shakespeare and Politics, Shakespeare and Colonialism, Shakespeare and Religion, Shakespeare and Film, Shakespeare and the Archive, Shakespeare and Adaptation, and Queer Shakespeare, as well as courses organized by genre, period, or author (Shakespeare and Marlowe, Shakespeare and Stoppard). Further options in media (film clips, YouTube, digital texts, etc.) have likewise changed the way "Shakespeare" is taught.

The expansion of Shakespeare into Shakespeare studies is a good thing, without doubt. It's great for students and faculty, and a fabulous opportunity for teaching at all levels (happily remunerated, in most cases, with a little more than "jam"). But with every gain there is a certain loss, and what is sometimes at risk is what might be described as either "Big Shakespeare" or "Town Meeting Shakespeare": students (from many fields and in many majors) and auditors (from the community and sometimes from the faculty and staff), gathering in a large lecture hall to experience, together, a lecture-as-performance, an exhilarating and provocative collective hour of Shakespeare, twice or three times a week. Such Shakespeare lectures (by Kittredge, by Auden, and by numerous modern and recent practitioners) often became legendary. They brought together diverse segments of the college or university population; they spurred discussion outside the lecture hall; they provided memories and "glue," as well as inspiration, for students many years after graduation. When I spoke to the sixtieth reunion class at Harvard commencement several years ago, virtually all those present had stories to tell about, and sharp memories of, the Shakespeare course they took in the 1940s. This is one specific and historic role for the teaching of Shakespeare that it's useful to remember as we move forward. The present-day public humanities event, meant to bring together what used to be called town and gown, is a version of "the Shakespeare course" as it functioned, for many years, both within colleges and universities and adjacent to them.

The way Shakespeare is taught in schools today owes not a little to various approaches to the novel, and to lyric poetry, that emphasize the agency, identity, and "intention" of the author, rather than the collaborative mode of the early modern theatre. The celebrity of Shakespeare exacerbates this tendency, leading to questions about the writer's personal history and internal thought processes, as if literary craftsmanship and the creative imagination could be traced to, and explained by, an origin. Like the "tragic flaw," this obtrusive concept, asserted as a matter of both faith and fact, often gets in the way of teaching. Let me close, therefore, with a classroom practice based upon my own particular resistance to intentionalism, a habit of mind that Shakespeare seems particularly to provoke.

I'm often asked by students why Shakespeare does X or Y or Z, to which of course there is no answer, since even if teachers were psychics or time-travelers or investigative journalists, we could not know what was in an author's mind. Moreover, even if Shakespeare had left us a signed document explaining an "intention," that intention might be at considerable variance with the achievement or perceived effect. What I try to do in class is to get students to think in terms of the effect rather than the intention, and of the play rather than the author: "what is the effect of X or Y or Z on the play?" I've found that getting students to replace "why [does the author]" with "how [does the play]" makes for clearer thinking, as well as for responses that are more satisfying to the student and more creative and illuminating about the play.

When I did this with a group of freshmen studying "Shakespeare and Magic" they learned incredibly fast. On one occasion when a student began to ask "Why did Shakespeare ..." she paused and then reframed the inquiry in terms of the play rather than the playwright. Her question was pertinent and interesting. The responses from the class were imaginative and thoughtful. A new generation of Shakespeareans had begun their work.

Extension Work

Patricia Cahill

Recalling a moment before our field became professionalized, and our classes so specialized, Marjorie Garber reminds us that, historically, the typical university or college Shakespeare course appealed to a much wider audience beyond the English majors who these days congregate in our classrooms. Garber's lament for the passing of what she wittily terms "Big Shakespeare" immediately resonated with me, and I found myself thinking of Adrienne McNeil Herndon.

A remarkable woman of color, Herndon more than a century ago galvanized the study of Shakespeare at Atlanta University (the historically black college founded in 1865 and now consolidated as Clark Atlanta University). Equally impressively, she employed Shakespeare to accomplish what her contemporaries characterized as the university's "extension work," finding in Shakespeare what Garber would describe as a kind of "glue": a means to bond some of the diverse members of Atlanta's African American community.

Born in 1869 to an unmarried former slave, Herndon graduated from Atlanta University's Normal School and briefly worked as a public school teacher until 1893, when she began teaching elocution (and, under the guise of that subject, Shakespeare) at her alma mater. Supported by her husband Alonzo—a former slave and sharecropper whom she married in 1893 and who amassed a fortune through business enterprises, becoming one of the country's first African American millionaires before his death in 1927—Herndon tirelessly pursued a career on the stage until her early death in 1910. Spending her summers studying "general culture" and "public reading" at the Boston School of Expression, she made her professional debut in that city in 1904 in a one-woman show based on *Antony and Cleopatra*, which she performed under the stage name Anne Du Bignon, daughter of an old South Carolina family of French and Creole origins. She received rave reviews and later went on to win prizes while studying at New York City's School of Dramatic Arts. Nevertheless, she failed to secure any more acting work, most likely because the entrenched racism of the professional theatre world proved impossible to navigate.

One of the first people to teach Shakespearean drama at a historically black college, Herndon clearly set her sights on Big Shakespeare. She thus instituted what turned out to be the extremely popular tradition of an annual class-day dramatic performance. Open to all, these productions were celebrated not only for the quality of both her direction and the student acting but also for their opulent costumes and properties, likely made possible by her New York theatre connections. For her first foray in spring 1905 she directed *The Merchant of Venice* to a packed house. A year later she followed up with an even more popular production of *The Taming of the Shrew*. Remarkably, despite Atlanta's bloody race riot of September 1906—after which she remarked in a 1907 letter to Booker T. Washington that she sometimes "doubt[s] if there is any spot in this country where one with Negro blood can plant a home free from prejudice, scorn and molestation"—she subsequently directed *As You Like It* (1907) and *Twelfth Night* (1908). Moreover, Herndon was in the midst of directing *The Tempest* when she succumbed to Addison's disease at the age of forty. Shakespeare, as Herndon made clear, deserved the deepest devotion (according to her husband, she had loved him since infancy). Occasionally, however, she found inspiration for her extension work elsewhere in English literary history. Most notably, in 1909 she directed and starred in *Everyman,* a role that, tragically, proved to be her last. Acting alongside her students as well as her dear friend and university colleague W. E. B. Du Bois, she enthralled spectators in the 1000-seat auditorium of Atlanta's social-minded First Congregational Church, a fund-raising event later lauded in the *University Bulletin* for "bring[ing] to the people without the walls of the University the educational advantage of witnessing a good dramatic performance."

Herndon's work outside Atlanta University classrooms suggests a complex alchemy of practical pedagogy and visionary politics. Writing in the national literary journal *The Voice of the Negro* in July 1906, she makes it clear that her pioneering Shakespeare productions were not intended as a diversion from the violence and injustice of the Jim Crow South. On the contrary, she frankly acknowledges the exclusionary policies of white theatres and calls for the construction of new performance venues, a popular theatre "circuit" to serve the South's burgeoning African American population. Moreover, in what strikes me as a radical move, she boldly claims Shakespeare for African American culture. She notes that African Americans were "unmarred by the conventional training of the highly cultured races" and thus had the potential to become truly superior dramatic artists, capable of the vernacular expression demanded by Shakespeare's language. More audaciously, she avows that African Americans, precisely by dint of the afflictions they have suffered, are far better positioned than whites to grasp Shakespeare's genius. "To interpret the depth of the human heart and to bring it into another's consciousness," she wrote, "one must have lived and suffered, and striven—and who among the Negro race has not received this sympathetic touch and insight as a birth-right? A more dramatic life than the one given the American Negro can hardly be imagined." In short, while

Herndon affirmed Shakespeare's universal appeal, her pedagogy was profoundly mindful of the historical particulars of African American disenfranchisements.

As the 400th anniversary of Shakespeare's death approaches, I find myself increasingly pondering the Atlanta tercentenary celebrations in spring 1916 when, not surprisingly, Big Shakespeare was the order of the day. One imagines that Herndon was sorely missed at Atlanta University, where, one day in April, as its *Bulletin* records, "the rhetorical exercises took the form of a Shakespeare anniversary celebration, different students giving essays and orations on the life and works of Shakespeare and presenting scenes from some of the best known plays." A month later, on a Saturday afternoon, thousands crowded into an Atlanta park to see an enormous Shakespeare pageant including dances, an orchestra, a chorus, and a procession of thousands of costumed schoolchildren. While the newspapers highlighted the diversity of these events, which were organized mostly by socially elite women but included "twenty-eight little school children whose mothers were at work in cotton mills," we can be sure that Atlanta's racial exclusions were writ large. As the *Atlanta Constitution* noted, a highlight of the pageant was the appearance of one of the stars of D. W. Griffith's 1915 *Birth of a Nation*, Henry B. Walthall, who was hailed as "a man who has rendered the south a distinguished service in portraying her sufferings in the days of reconstruction." Linked with the sufferings of white folks and a film that inspired the refounding of the Klan in Georgia in 1915, this Big Shakespeare turned Herndon's radical dream upside down.

Moving away from that segregated context of Herndon's Big Shakespeare, I'd like to conclude by way of my own experience as a white woman teaching Shakespeare to students from Atlanta's Emory University. After more than a decade in the classroom, I decided last year to venture beyond the university's walls and try out a little "extension work" in the form of a pedagogical project I now think of as Small Shakespeare. Specifically, inspired by the work of Joe Winston and Miles Tandy, British teaching artists who advocate a play-based Shakespeare pedagogy for young people, I'm forging a collaboration between my predominately white and middle-class students and the mostly African American children who attend an underresourced elementary school in Southeast Atlanta, just a few miles away from where Herndon taught

Shakespeare and elocution. With the assistance of a teaching artist in the Atlanta Shakespeare Company, I aim to foreground the theatricality that David Bevington eloquently urges us to place at the center of Shakespeare pedagogy. But I also want to revisit, however modestly, the link that Adrienne Herndon forged between Shakespeare and Atlanta's African American communities. Thus last spring, my fifteen students and I introduced some forty-five second-graders to a dozen scenes from *The Tempest*, a play chosen in honor of Herndon, via a semester-long series of acting workshops. This spring, with a new group of Emory students, those same children, now third-graders, are engaging scenes from *Much Ado About Nothing*. As an educator in this extended classroom, I increasingly see Shakespeare through the eyes of school children whose material histories differ markedly from those of my Emory students. Moreover, these encounters across all our differences are, I think, at the heart of the best experiences with both teaching and drama. We're finding that as these schoolchildren connect with Shakespearean language through their voices and bodies, they gain a profound ownership of Shakespeare. That is, we're hoping that Shakespeare will be the vehicle for what—following Herndon—I would call a more dramatic life.

4

Editing

Facts, Theories, and Beliefs

Barbara A. Mowat
President, SAA 1996–97

Few moments in the history of editing Shakespeare's plays have been as explosive as that in which the *King Lear* text known and loved by Shakespeare scholars, directors, and readers alike was condemned, characterized by Stanley Wells as "a wraith born of an unholy union" (1983). For those too young to remember those heady days, the initial confrontation between the editors who believed in what René Weis now calls the integral *King Lear* text and the revisionists for whom that text had become anathema, believing as they did that quarto *Lear* was Shakespeare's original version and Folio *Lear* his revision, occurred in 1980 in a seminar at the annual meeting of the SAA. Ron Rosenbaum, in *The Shakespeare Wars*, quotes Gary Taylor's description of that seminar as a "palace coup" pulled off by "upstart revisionists," while two "respected senior scholars [announced] their conversion to the revisionist cause" and G. K. Hunter, "champion of an orthodoxy that [had] lasted for centuries, [found] himself surrounded and embattled." Rosenbaum goes on to note "the shock, the veritable earthquake reverberations (within the profession, anyway)" caused by the revisionists' challenge and the subsequent publishing of separate quarto and Folio *Lear*s in the 1986 Oxford *Complete Works*.

This explosive moment is memorable in itself and is, at the same time, a brilliantly illustrative example of how a shift in beliefs about early printed Shakespeare texts can alter the course of editorial practice. The first time such a shift occurred was in the late eighteenth century. Until that moment, Shakespeare editors accepted Heminges and Condell's claim that the Folio texts were far superior to any of the quartos, and they therefore used the Folio as copytext for every play. After all, if, as Heminges and Condell wrote, the Folio was printed from Shakespeare's own papers and the quartos from texts that were "stolen, … surreptitious, … maimed, … and deformed," an editor would be beyond quixotic to base his text on a quarto printing, and would think carefully before preferring a quarto reading to one from the Folio. However, when Edward Capell demonstrated in the 1770s that nine of the Folio texts had been printed not from Shakespeare's manuscripts but from the hitherto despised quartos, beliefs about both the quarto and Folio texts shifted. As A. W. Pollard put it in 1909, if Heminges and Condell provided as printer's copy the very maimed and deformed quartos they attacked, then "we have no proof of the exercise of any editorial care" for any text in the Folio. The result was a long nineteenth century of somewhat cynical evaluation of quarto and Folio texts alike. On the practical level, editors began to examine their options for copytext, gradually settling into using quarto printings at least for the nine plays reprinted in the Folio, but, with both kinds of texts under suspicion, they felt free to pick and choose among readings.

This 1770s shift in editorial beliefs about the authority of the early texts was triggered by a "novelty of fact," to use Thomas Kuhn's terminology. In other words, it came about because of an actual discovery of facts about the printing of Folio texts. The next major shift, which occurred in 1909, was, in contrast, brought about through "novelty of theory." A. W. Pollard simply reinterpreted the words of Heminges and Condell, explaining that their attack on the quartos must have applied only to certain "bad" quartos, not to such as the nine that served as printer's copy for Folio plays. Pollard's imaginative leap brought to an end the "bibliographical pessimism" that had descended in the 1770s. As W. W. Greg wrote in 1955, Pollard's reinterpretation of Heminges and Condell's language not only led scholars out of the "quagmire of nineteenth-century despondency," but also afforded a "great stimulus to research."

This research, famous now as the New Bibliography, produced in very short order the third major shift in editorial beliefs about the early printed texts. By the mid-twentieth century, editors had learned to believe that the "bad" quartos were printed from memorially reconstructed or reported manuscripts, that the "good" quartos were printed from Shakespeare's own holographs, and that at least some of the Folio texts were printed from theatrical "promptbooks" which had themselves been created from Shakespeare's holographs. Suddenly, instead of working with highly suspect quarto and Folio texts, editors found themselves in possession of printed texts only one or two removes from Shakespeare himself. Many editors would doubtless have attributed this remarkable shift to "novelty of fact," since the New Bibliographers believed they could almost scientifically identify texts that were printed from Shakespeare's holograph and those printed from theatrical documents.

Which brings us to that explosive moment in 1980. While editorial beliefs about quarto and Folio texts were changing and Shakespeare editions changing with them, the text of *King Lear* had remained largely unaffected by shifting editorial beliefs until the coming of New Bibliography. The earliest editors, noting passages present in one *Lear* text but not the other, considered most of the quarto-only passages as Shakespeare's, and they assumed that these passages were missing from the Folio because either Shakespeare or Heminges and Condell had removed them, though they could rarely find a reason for them to have done so. In the notes to his 1725 edition, Alexander Pope, the first editor to have obtained a 1608 quarto, wrote, for instance, that early in the third act of *Lear* are lines found only in the quarto "which seem necessary to the plot": "How both these [lines], and a whole Scene ... in the fourth Act, came to be left out in all the latter editions [i.e. the Folios], I cannot tell: they depend upon each other, and very much contribute to [making] clear [the] incident [of 'the arrival of the French army']."

Occasionally he approved of such a cut. For example, in the scene in which the mad Lear puts an invisible Goneril and Regan on trial, Pope found passages in the quarto missing from the Folio. He places an asterisk in his text before Edgar's "The foul fiend bites my back," and writes, "There follow in the old edition [i.e. the quarto] several speeches in the mad way, which probably were left out [of the Folio] by the players [i.e. Heminges and Condell], or by Shakespear himself. I shall however insert them here, and leave 'em to the reader's mercy." But he considered most of the quarto-only passages necessary to the action or characterization. He discovered, for example, that the Folio omits thirty lines from Albany's back-to-back speeches that make up the bulk of his powerful Act 4 attack on Goneril. Pope includes them in his text, he writes, because "These [lines] … are in the edition of 1608, and are but necessary to explain the reasons of the detestation which Albany expresses here to his wife"; again, commenting on the Folio omission of the quarto scene immediately following this one, he writes, "This Scene, left out in all the common books [i.e. the four Folios], is restor'd from the old edition; it being manifestly of Shakespere's writing, and necessary to continue the story of Cordelia, …"

Pope left it to Lewis Theobald, editor of the 1733 edition, to fully incorporate quarto-only material and to discuss the speech-prefix variant so important to the 1980s revisionists, that which determines whether the last speech of the play is spoken by Albany, as in the quarto, or by Edgar, as in the Folio. Theobald, like Pope, was very snobbish about the "Players" who had put together the Folio, and his amusing note on the final speech prefix, which he, like Pope, changes from Edgar to Albany, reads: "This speech from the Authority of the Old Qto is rightly plac'd to Albany: in the Edition by the Players [i.e. Heminges and Condell] it is given to Edgar, by whom, I doubt not, it was of Custom spoken. And the Case was this: He who play'd Edgar, being a more favourite actor, than he who personated Albany; … it was thought proper [that] he [who play'd Edgar] should have the last Word."

As the decades passed, the *King Lear* text established by Pope and Theobald was, as I noted earlier, largely unaffected by the shifts in editorial beliefs about Shakespeare's early printed texts. Samuel Johnson's 1765 assumption that Folio *Lear* was Shakespeare's revision of the quarto text—although Johnson noted that Shakespeare did a very poor job of it through haste or carelessness—was generally accepted by succeeding editors, who continued to use the quarto to supplement or replace words in the Folio text. Neither the Capell nor the Pollard shifts affected *Lear* texts—after all, the *Lear* quarto was not one of the nine deter-mined by Capell to have been reprinted in the Folio, and Pollard's classification of the *Lear* quarto as "good" did not disturb existing editorial beliefs. It was only when New Bibliographical scholars asserted that quarto *Lear* was not Shakespeare's but was instead a "bad" quarto, either memorially reconstructed or a shorthand report, that *Lear* editions were suddenly affected.

W. W. Greg, preeminent among the New Bibliographers, was certain that the quarto was printed from an unauthorized manuscript acquired surreptitiously by the publisher. Writing in 1942 that quarto *Lear* was "of small textual value," he bemoaned its effect on *King Lear* editions. There were, he noted, more than 400 quarto readings in the *Lear* text printed in the canonical 1864 Globe edition of Shakespeare's works. Greg's hope was that in future editions of the play 300 of those readings would be replaced by readings from the Folio. When we compare the opening 200 lines of *King Lear* in the *Globe* edition with those in G. B. Evans's 1974 Riverside edition (a stellar product of New Bibliographical theory), we see that Greg's hope was close to fulfilled: the 30 quarto readings in the opening 200 Globe lines have shrunk to six such readings in Evans.

To realize that the Riverside edition was published only six years before the palace coup in 1980 is to begin to understand why the revisionist challenge should have so shaken the Shakespeare world. Editors had in general accepted the New Bibliographical determination that quarto *Lear* was of no authority, and while continuing to include quarto-only passages, they had increasingly shaped their editions of *King Lear* to reflect the primacy of the Folio. Suddenly the "upstart revisionists" were insisting that quarto *Lear* was Shakespeare's original text, carefully revised by the author himself to create what we know as Folio *Lear*. The chutzpah itself is almost enough to account for the "earthquake reverberations" noted by Rosenbaum. Yet clearly there was (and is) something more than chutzpah at issue here, since the revisionist claims about the early printed texts had an immediate and ongoing impact on the editing of *King Lear*—this despite the fact that the shift in beliefs was triggered neither by "novelty of fact" nor, arguably, by "novelty of theory."

To think first about "novelty of fact": the pertinent evidence presented by the revisionists had been available and discussed since the early eighteenth century. Recently discovered facts about the printing of the texts—that, for example, the 1608 quarto was printed in the shop of someone who had never before printed a play and was set into type by woefully inexperienced compositors, and that the printing of the second quarto of *King Lear* in Jaggard's print shop in 1619 may well have had an impact on the printing of the Folio in the same print shop very soon thereafter—were not to the point. As the late Trevor Howard-Hill made clear in 1985, such discoveries about the printing of quarto and Folio *Lear* are marginal to the controversy over whether or not the Folio represents Shakespeare's revision.

As for "novelty of theory": revisionist theorizing—i.e. that the quarto represents Shakespeare's original text and that the Folio text was Shakespeare's revision—rather than being a novelty, harks back to 1765. What, then, was so galvanizing about the revisionists' claim that Folio *Lear* represents Shakespeare's "full-scale imaginative reshaping of the play" (René Weiss, 2010)? I suggest that it was what we might name a "novelty of narrative." Michael Warren first sketched out this narrative in a 1976 presentation published in 1978. Editors seeking explanations for the lines and passages that appear in one text and not the other had proposed (and continue to propose) that passages missing from the Folio were likely cuts ordered by the Master of the Revels or were the victims of theatrical abridgment for performance. They tended (and still tend) to explain Folio lines not present in the quarto as later additions, possibly for theatrical revivals—some of them added perhaps by an interpolator after Shakespeare was no longer around, as seems to have happened with *Macbeth*. Michael Warren and his fellows, looking at exactly these same variations between the texts, saw instead a pattern, and behind the pattern they saw a creator of that pattern.

As Warren laid it out, the cuts and additions were not random, nor were they produced by several hands. The trimming of thirty lines or so from Albany's speeches attacking Goneril, for example, was not done for the sake of abridgment, but was one of several cuts designed by Shakespeare to make Albany a "weaker character." Correspondingly, other changes, and especially the cuts in and additions to Edgar's lines, were Shakespeare's deliberate "strengthening of Edgar's role." For Warren, these Shakespearean alterations led to and climaxed with the speech prefix for the play's final speech, changed from "Albany" in the quarto to "Edgar" in the Folio. This and other alleged patterns of Shakespearean revision yielded a narrative that quickly captured the imagination of much of the Shakespeare world. The plot of this narrative, as Warren expressed it, is that "Q and F embody two different artistic visions," both of them Shakespeare's.

But why should a narrative have such power? According to Roland Barthes, the human need for story is part of our very humanness: narrative "is simply there like life itself"; it "ceaselessly substitutes meaning for the straightforward copy of the events recounted" ("Introduction to the Structural Analysis of Narratives," 1977). If we substitute "textual differences" for "events," we can say, with Barthes, that narratives about the *Lear* quarto and Folio texts "ceaselessly substitute meaning for the straightforward listing of textual differences." Once the revisionists put their story up against that told by those who believe in an integral text, the revisionists' story, as story, won hands down. The narrative presented over the years by the traditionalists is a bit complicated, a bit liable to change, filled with perhapses, and more than a bit dependent on the listener's knowledge of rather arcane matter. The revisionist story, in contrast, is easily understood and engaging; it has a celebrated author as its protagonist, it focuses primarily on dramatic characters about whom we care, and it depends on evidentiary facts which are not in dispute: i.e. everyone agrees that the cuts and additions exist. As stories go, the revisionist narrative is a captivating one. No wonder the Shakespeare world sat up and took notice, and that editors rushed to turn out variations on two-text *King Lear*s.

And no wonder the conflict, though muted, continues. How does one prove the relative truth of stories that assign conflicting meanings to the same set of data? At the moment, almost any scholar who writes about *King Lear* acknowledges the difference between the two texts and usually mentions revision. On the other hand, editions of *King Lear* that aim at presenting the traditional originary text continue to be published. René Weis (2010) points to the publication in 1997 of the single-text Arden 3 *King Lear* as marking "a shift away from the intellectual certainties of two-text scholars and critics back to the doubters, who had argued all along that the fact that *Lear* survives in two different printed texts might not be best explained as rewriting by Shakespeare."

In the past few decades, facts about the printing of the early texts of *Lear* have begun to be assimilated into our thinking about the play, and it is not impossible that a novelty of fact or of theory will at some point significantly shift our beliefs about the two texts. The forthcoming publication of the MLA New Variorum *King Lear,* for which the editor, Richard Knowles, deeply distrusting the Folio text, uses quarto *Lear* as his foundation, will inevitably provide information that to us is novel. In the meantime, as the implications of Paul Werstine's demonstration of the facts about extant manuscript playbooks are absorbed (*Early Modern Playhouse Manuscripts and the Editing of Shakespeare*, 2012), New Bibliographical certitudes about texts printed from holograph versus texts printed from playbooks will almost certainly be discarded and beliefs about the early printings will surely shift.

But whatever the fate of the two-text narrative and whatever the future of *King Lear* editing, that explosive moment in 1980 and its aftermath have had a markedly salutary effect on Shakespeareans' relationship to the texts they study and teach. I would think it impossible for any such scholar today to be unaware of the basic facts about the kinds of choices editors make and the beliefs about the early printed texts that lie behind such choices. Shakespeareans now know that when they select an edition, they are deciding to trust its editor and his or her editorial beliefs and assumptions. We editors, too, have been sharply reminded that our assumptions about the quartos and the Folio have a powerful influence over our editorial practices. Instead of waiting for another paradigm shift, we can ourselves ponder the validity of what we have been taught and what we believe, and we can subject every textual narrative to clear-eyed analysis. Such skeptical awareness may be the ultimate gift of the revisionists' coup; if so, it is a gift worthy of every Shakespearean's gratitude.

What We Owe to Editors

Lukas Erne

It is easy to complain about editors. They waste time and energy on commas, collation, and compositors. Their work is cumulative and mechanical, not worthy of the recognition that comes with essays and monographs. It is also derivative, and so editors embed in their editions the oppressive ideology of their predecessors and thereby perpetuate it. They misrepresent the original text, impose artificial clarity upon it, close down its openness. They add to the original text. They rewrite the author in their own image. Editors do not annotate enough, or they drown the text in commentary. They write incomprehensible collation notes that no one cares about. They base their editorial decisions on unverifiable hypotheses about the provenance of texts. There are also far too many Shakespeare editors. They repeat each other, and themselves. They are only in it for the money. All these complaints are well known. Some of them are even justified, sometimes.

What may be more difficult than complaining about editors is to appreciate what we owe to them. There is a simple reason for this, which is that much of their work tends to be invisible. When we buy Shakespeare's *Hamlet*, we assume the text we read to be Shakespeare's, not the editor's. When readers acquaint themselves with the plays, much of what they know and think about them is derived from editions, yet once they have acquired that knowledge and those opinions it is easy to take them for granted. Editors are the unacknowledged mediators of the word.

Take Shakespeare's dramatic language. Almost all the plays are written in prose and verse, but the early editions are not always a good guide to which bits are prose and which ones verse, nor do they always correctly lineate the verse. Early modern compositors sometimes disrespected the lineation in the manuscript from which they set the text, partly to save or waste space when it suited their purpose. Therefore, it is often up to the modern editor to fix the verse. The recent Arden *Coriolanus* (2013) is a case in point. Even though Peter Holland warns us that the lineation adopted by Shakespeare's eighteenth-century editors is not always satisfactory, and even though he refuses to follow such unsatisfactory relineation and often reverts to that in the First Folio, he nonetheless prints many passages as they were first lineated by eighteenth-century or later editors, drawing seven times on Nicholas Rowe (1709–14), sixty-one on Alexander Pope (1723–5), six on Lewis Theobald (1733), four on Thomas Hanmer (1743–4) and Samuel Johnson (1765), fifteen on Edward Capell (1767–8), four on George Steevens (1773), three on Edmond Malone (1790), and one each on Alexander Dyce (1857), David Bevington (1980), and the Oxford *Complete Works* (1986). The verse we read today

SHAKESPEARE IN OUR TIME

as Shakespeare's *Coriolanus* in the Arden series thus consists of a transhistorical editorial collage, with more than three hundred lines whose lineation have their origin in the eighteenth century or later. Nor is the Arden *Coriolanus* a special case. Modern editors are essentially in agreement that the lineation proposed in the course of the editorial tradition is often superior to that in the sixteenth- and seventeenth-century quartos and folios, and therefore adopt it. Yet many modern readers fail to realize that what we think of as Shakespeare's verse is often a skillful editorial (re-)construction.

It is equally easy to miss how much of the actual text is editorial. Some emendations are well known. Mistress Quickly's description of the dying Falstaff—"his nose was as sharp as a pen, and 'a babbled of green fields" (*Henry V*, 2.3.16–17)—goes back to Theobald, who emended the Folio's "and a Table of green fields." "What's Montague?" Juliet famously asks, and goes on to say, "It is nor hand nor foot, / Nor arm nor face nor any other part / Belonging to a man. O be some other name!" (*Romeo and Juliet*, 2.2.40–2). The passage can be found in no early text but goes back to Malone, who drew on the first and the second quarto to produce it. The nicely chiastic line "A bliss in proof, and proved, a very woe" in Sonnet 129 is also Malone's, who emended "proud and" to "proved, a." Yet most editorial readings are less well known. In *Antony and Cleopatra*, Octavius Caesar, receiving news of Pompey's growing popularity, says:

It hath been taught us from the primal state
That he which is was wished until he were,
And the ebbed man, ne'er loved till ne'er worth love,
Comes deared by being lacked. This common body,
Like to a vagabond flag upon the stream,
Goes to and back, lackeying the varying tide,
To rot itself with motion.

(1.4.41–7)

The passage contains two readings first adopted by Theobald, "deared" in line 44 and "lackeying" in line 47, where the Folio has "fear'd" and "lacking." Not only John Wilders's Arden edition (1995), from which I have quoted, adopts it, but so do many others. The quoted speech is no exception: sixty-nine readings in the dialogue text of *Antony and Cleopatra* in the Oxford *Complete*

Works are post-1700 emendations. Today's editors by and large agree that these readings improve on the text in the First Folio and make sense of passages which would otherwise remain obscure. Yet for many modern readers, these editorial improvements pass unnoticed.

Likewise, we easily forget how much of the Shakespearean text we would struggle to understand if editors did not provide notes that conveniently explain it. The early quartos and folios had no annotation, and the editions by Rowe and Pope little of it, but starting with Johnson, editors have undertaken Herculean labors to illuminate the countless words and passages that are far from self-explanatory. If our engagement with Shakespeare today can start from a good level of understanding of the primary text, then that is because modern editions digest in their commentary the scholarly insights of several centuries.

We not only want the dramatic text we read to make sense; we also want to understand the dramatic action with which it goes hand in hand. To help us do so, modern editors add stage directions that allow us to visualize what happens when, who speaks to whom, which characters are present, and when they leave. To choose an edition at random, A. R. Braunmuller (1997), in his New Cambridge Shakespeare *Macbeth* (a short play) adds about fifty stage directions and significantly alters many more. Without these editorial stage directions, readers might appreciate the text as a dramatic poem, but they would find it much more difficult to understand how it works as a play. Whether we realize it or not, modern editors play a vital role in alerting us to how Shakespeare's dramatic texts relate to performance.

Apart from decisively shaping our reading of Shakespeare's plays, the careful work of editors also helps delimit the canon. Giorgio Melchiori's well-informed edition of *Edward III* in the New Cambridge Shakespeare series in 1998 heralded the play's canonization, now confirmed by its inclusion in the Arden series, the Riverside, and the Oxford *Complete Works*. Brean Hammond's Arden edition of *Double Falsehood* (2010) has been at the heart of a heated debate about the play's Shakespearean credentials. And *The Funeral Elegy for William Peter* briefly rose to fame in the late 1990s, when Donald Foster and Richard Abrams argued for Shakespeare's authorship, until Gilles Monsarrat and Brian Vickers, who have recently included the poem in their edition of

The Collected Works of John Ford (2011), exposed the invalidity of their claims. We may be tempted to think of the contents of a Shakespeare series or "complete works" as a given, but it is not. It is determined by editors.

In recent decades, editors have also done much to help us understand what is at stake in Shakespeare's multitext plays. Not that a consensus has been reached as to the relationship of the texts of, say, *King Lear*, *Hamlet*, and *Othello*. But the terms of the problem have been clearly defined, and no new scholarly edition now pretends that there is simply one play, and that we all know what its text is. Whether they edit all three texts (the Arden *Hamlet*), both texts (the Oxford *Complete Works Lear*), a subseries of "early quartos" (the New Cambridge series), or a single conflated text that marks quarto/folio differences with superscript Qs and Fs (the Arden *Lear*), editions now outline what the options are and which one they have chosen. Nor is there any sign that the importance of Shakespeare's editors will diminish in the near future. At present, many of them are thinking hard about how best to mediate Shakespeare to readers and users in the age of digital reproduction. How exactly the works will reach us in the future we do not currently know, but if the experience of the past four centuries is anything to go by, we can be confident that—whether readers will notice it or not—the editors' mediation will be decisive and enabling.

What's Next in Editing Shakespeare

Sonia Massai

Editing generally features less prominently among the activities organized to celebrate a Shakespeare anniversary than do public performances, exhibitions, or civic displays, but anniversary celebrations certainly seem to catalyze editorial efforts and critical thinking about the principles that inform the re-presentation of Shakespeare to new generations of readers. The monumental Cambridge edition of 1863–6 and its 1864 single-volume Globe Shakespeare companion edition are a case in point. So what kind of landmark is 2016 in relation to the editing of Shakespeare?

In his contribution to *Shakespeare in Our Time*, Lukas Erne has perceptively captured a renewed sense of optimism in the achievements of the editorial tradition. This optimism is refreshing after post-structuralism and digital technologies in the late twentieth century had called into question the viability, or even the desirability, of methods seeking to recover authorial readings by lifting the veil of print from the early quarto and folio editions of Shakespeare's works. In fact, the combined impact of a post-structuralist critique of the "author" and of the "work" as stable sources of meaning, the unprecedented availability of facsimiles of the early editions of Shakespeare's works online, and the forcible rejection of textual narratives about "good" and "bad" quartos, or "foul papers" and "promptbooks," led late twentieth-century editors and textual scholars to make influential pronouncements about the "End of Editing."

The past few years, leading up to the quatercentenary of Shakespeare's death, have shown that these challenges, rather than the "End of Editing," have actually produced a clearer sense of what editors can and cannot claim to be doing when they edit Shakespeare for twenty-first century readers. The received text of Shakespeare produced by the editorial tradition is no longer understood as a repository of original authorial or theatrical intentions, but it is nevertheless celebrated with renewed enthusiasm as a textual artifact endowed with a vast amount of cultural capital in its own right. As Barbara Mowat shows in this volume, the "End of Editing" can also be said to have produced a salutary amount of "skeptical awareness" toward the changing assumptions and beliefs that have shaped and continue to inform the editorial tradition.

"Shakespeare [editors] in Our Time" have not only become more skeptical about the textual narratives that shaped the editing of Shakespeare in the twentieth century, but they have also started to edit according to principles that diverge quite significantly from those narratives and from the editorial method most influentially theorized by Walter Greg in his "Rationale of Copy-Text" (1950). Instead of editing their copytext critically and eclectically, in light of its assumed provenance ("foul papers" or "promptbook") and the editor's own sense of what may constitute an authorial reading, editors in our time are increasingly practicing "single-text" editing, which involves editing one (or more) early form(s) of a play as discrete textual artifact(s) by focusing mostly on the quality of the press work and on those aspects of the transmission of copy into print that may have altered it. Single-text editing is becoming established as a desirable alternative not only to the Gregian editorial method that produced conflated and/or eclectically emended editions but also to the "synoptic" approach championed with great ingenuity by some Shakespeare editors at the turn of the last century, when variation and instability in the early versions of the same play were re-presented through a single, but typographically composite, text (see, for example, R. A. Foakes's Arden 3 edition of *King Lear*). However, single-text editing embraces quite a wide range of editorial practices and it has not affected the editing of Shakespeare as thoroughly as one would expect, given the increasing scholarly popularity it currently enjoys.

The most uncompromising version of single-text editing is the direct descendant of diplomatic editions and re-presents early modern playbooks as digital images or in photo-facsimiles. Images and facsimiles, far from offering unmediated access to the early editions they reproduce, are nevertheless effective at foregrounding their collaborative quality as composite textual artifacts. Responding to David Greetham, who has argued that one cannot practically "*produce* a social textual edition" that can fairly represent the thoroughly collaborative conditions of textual (re)production in the early modern period, H. R. Woudhuysen has hailed the photographic facsimile editions published by the Malone Society since the mid-1980s as the closest realization of "exactly such ... 'social textual edition[s]'" (*Textual Performances*).

Single-text editing, when applied to multiple forms of an early modern text, can also represent an important corrective to "versioning," which is generally understood as an editorial approach aimed at recovering first and second authorial intentions and/or different theatrical incarnations of the "work." Ann Thompson and Neil Taylor, for example, decided to edit the three main early texts of the play for their Arden 3 edition of *Hamlet*, not because they believe that "William Shakespeare was necessarily the sole author of every word" in all three or because they claim to know "how it was that they came to be in print," but because they regard them as "remarkably distinct entities."

One other important approach to single-text editing is the "empirical" method proposed by Paul Werstine. According to

Werstine, editors should go back to the archive in order to establish how the (re)setting of the printer's copy into print may have gone wrong in ways that are distinctive of early modern scribal and/or printing practices. Given the scarcity of surviving documents, it would of course be too restrictive to emend only when editorial intervention is supported by archival evidence. But limiting editorial intervention to rectifying manifest errors that are *likely* to have occurred during scribal transcription or in the printing house would have the major advantage of producing a version of Shakespeare's texts which is not currently commercially available and which would appeal to both specialist and non-specialist readers.

Even editors fully committed to single-text editing often defer to the authority of the received text, as illustrated, for example, by Othello's first speech at the beginning of Act 5, scene 2. In both the 1622 quarto and the 1623 Folio, Othello reminds himself that, while he has the power to "put out" Desdemona's "light" (l.7) (i.e. to take her life) as easily as he can quench his torch, he can relight his torch but he cannot revive Desdemona. As is often the case in Shakespeare, Othello then reconsiders this same insight by using a different set of images. In the quarto (M1), Othello reminds himself that, having "pluckt the rose" (l.24), the latter "must needes wither" (l.26). He therefore considers smelling "it on the tree" instead (l.26) and remarks that the rose's "balmy breath" has such power on the senses that it "doth almost perswade / Iustice her selfe to breake her sword" (ll. 27–8). The generic quality of Othello's references to "the rose" and to smelling "it on the tree" distances him from the immediacy of the sensorial experience his words evoke. A quarto-only stage direction opposite lines 30–1—"*He / kisses her.*"—suggests that Othello finally takes his leave of Desdemona by kissing her, probably starting with a kiss in line 28, immediately before "once more," and ending with a valedictory kiss, "and this the last," in line 30. In the Folio (Vv4), no stage direction prompts Othello to kiss Desdemona. Othello seems in fact more immediately enthralled by his sense of smell: the quarto's "the rose" becomes "thy Rose" (TLN 3660) in the Folio, where the deictic pronoun foregrounds Desdemona's physical proximity to Othello, who is in turn overwhelmed by the sweetness of her breath ("Ile smell thee on the Tree. / Oh Balmy breath," TLN 3662–3). Although "one more" (TLN 3664, 3666), a Folio-specific alternative to the quarto's "once more" (ll. 38, 30), is normally taken to suggest the discrete, and culturally more discreet, act of kissing, as opposed to the indiscreet and oddly unquantifiable act of smelling, it may instead refer to "one more" *breath*, which is countable elsewhere in Shakespeare (see, for example, *Richard II*, 3.2.164–5 or *Henry VIII*, 1.4.29).

Modern editions, even when based on the Folio, reproduce the more familiar stage action supported by the quarto or a conflated version of the stage action supported by each version, presumably because the act of kissing Desdemona's lips, as opposed to the act of smelling her "balmy breath," coheres more readily with our *cultural* (as opposed to our *textual*) narratives about what Othello should do at this crucial moment in the play. Current editorial practice therefore imposes the act of kissing called for by a stage direction in the quarto onto the Folio, thus obscuring the eroticism commonly associated with the sense of smell in other early modern texts (one fitting example is Robert Armin's quip upon the question "What smels sweete?"; see *Quips upon Questions*, 1600). Conversely, single-text editing, whether in photo-facsimiles, in parallel-text editions, or in empirical editions, is bound to lend fresh insights into similar moments of great textual and cultural interest.

5

Mortality

Suicide as Profit or Loss

Mary Beth Rose
President, SAA 1997–98

Shakespearean tragedy embodies and enacts loss, which it attempts to frame and give meaning through the powers of definition and representation. When, at the end of folio *King Lear*, Edgar observes that "The oldest hath borne most; we that are young / Shall never see so much, nor live so long" (5.3.324–5), he assigns to the horrific series of murders and betrayals that constitute the play's action an elegiac meaning: the best, was; the future by implication will be a diminished thing. Shakespearean tragedy destroys the past and then turns around and mourns the loss and destruction. I want to explore the ways in which the heroic action of suicide in two of Shakespeare's Roman tragedies intervenes counterintuitively in the process of tragic meaning-making. I will suggest that when protagonists in *Julius Caesar* and *Antony and Cleopatra* choose to commit suicide, they are seeking to reconstitute mourning as a kind of victory. An unlikely consolation, suicide nevertheless serves in these two plays not only as a bulwark against loss but as an attempt to reconceive loss as profit. In the earlier play, *Julius Caesar* (1599), the suicidal effort to defy loss fails, while in the later play, *Antony and Cleopatra* (1606–7), the heroic endeavor to refigure loss as profit through the act of suicide partially succeeds.

At the end of *Julius Caesar* Mark Antony and Octavius find their defeated enemy Brutus dead by suicide. "For Brutus only overcame himself, / And no man else hath honour by his death," his companion Strato explains (5.5.57–8); and Lucilius confirms the grim triumph: "So Brutus should be found," he informs the victors, defying their claims to conquest (5.5.59). But Brutus's allies fail in their attempt to characterize his suicide as victorious: instead, Mark Antony immediately usurps the power that proves so critical throughout the play, the dangerous glory of the last word. Establishing his political right to create meaning, Antony delivers Brutus's epitaph:

> This was the noblest Roman of them all:
> All the conspirators save only he
> Did that they did in envy of great Caesar.
> He only, in a general honest thought
> And common good to all, made one of them.
> His life was gentle, and the elements
> So mixed in him that nature might stand up
> And say to all the world, 'This was a man!'
>
> (5.5.69–76)

It is of course not the first time in the play that Antony has unleashed his brilliant rhetorical power to transformative effect. His words are stirring, gracious: but, as often happens in *Julius Caesar*, the lofty tone of that which is spoken as oracular pronouncement proves neither lucid nor accurate as an account of actual circumstance. Brutus's nobility, according to Antony, lies not in his deeds but in his character and intentions, his gentleness, his lack of envy and his "general honest thought." While high-minded, Brutus's intentions have in fact failed to result in successful actions. He meant well; but his actions by implication were misconceived: the conspiracy that toppled Caesar was not a good thing. The irrefutable historical irony of hindsight reveals what Antony cannot know: that the assassination of Julius Caesar, meant to restore the Roman Republic, in fact hastened the beginnings of empire, introducing decades of tyrannical Caesarism. Sympathetically evoking Brutus's honorable character, Antony's epitaph—so dignified in tone, and so beautiful—manages to deprive Brutus's suicide of any possibility of triumphant meaning.

The contest between Brutus's construction of his own suicide as a victory and Antony's trumping redefinition of it as tragic defeat point to the ways in which suicide becomes the focus of the play's negotiations between profit and loss. Cassius kills himself; then his devoted henchman Titinius kills himself. We learn that Portia has destroyed herself by swallowing fire; Brutus's suicide is the climax of the last act. In *Antony and Cleopatra*, Enobarbus takes his own life, followed by Eros, Antony, Iras, Cleopatra, and Charmian. There are of course suicides in Shakespeare's non-Roman tragedies: Othello, Romeo and Juliet, the Goneril-Regan debacle in *King Lear*, and possibly Lady Macbeth and Ophelia. Each is an individual reaction to remorse or to bereft and betrayed love. In contrast, suicide in the Roman plays seems almost a consensual collective process, an agreed-upon social response to dishonor and defeat. Suicide in the Roman plays represents the endeavor to turn loss into profit.

A combination of classical and Renaissance conceptions of suicide inform Shakespeare's Roman plays. *Sleepless Souls*, by Michael MacDonald and Terence R. Murphy, traces what these scholars see as a gradual hardening of attitudes toward suicide in the Middle Ages and early modern Europe—in comparison to the relatively permissive practices of Rome. MacDonald and Murphy cite Augustine's emphatic denouncing of self-murder, pointing out that in the year 1000 the Church, roundly reiterating a seventh-century finding, decreed that suicides could not have normal burials but instead what Shakespeare refers to as "maimed rites" in the funeral of Ophelia; indeed those who killed themselves might be buried at crossroads, or with a stake through their hearts. By the late Middle Ages, suicide was condemned by religion, folk belief, and common law. In Tudor England government regulations against suicide became increasingly rigorous and, after the Reformation, theologians insisted that suicide was both a crime and a sin. Suicide was an expression of despair, the dangerous antithesis of Christian hope.

Although laws against suicide did not change until the nineteenth century, more liberal and tolerant attitudes prevailed in England after 1660. Despite the rigors of spiritual, legal, and popular condemnation, ambivalence about suicide existed in the Renaissance as well. With the study of classical writers, Humanism fostered awareness of more tolerant attitudes to suicide. Early modern writers such as Sidney, Bacon, Montaigne, and Donne wrote defenses of, or extended debates about, suicide. In addition, just as today, acts of honorable sacrifice and religious martyrdom were difficult to distinguish from the alienated rejection of human life implied in self-slaughter. Yet the prevailing attitude toward self-destruction in sixteenth and seventeenth-century England was condemnatory. MacDonald and Murphy show that punishment of suicide was unprecedented and unparalleled in severity.

The most famous Shakespearean association of suicide with sin remains Hamlet's wish that "the Everlasting had not fixed / His canon 'gainst self-slaughter" (1.2.131–2). Cleopatra briefly considers the conjunction: "[I]s it sin / To rush into the secret house of death / Ere death dare come to us?" she asks (4.15.84–6); but she quickly dismisses the thought: "Let's do't after the high Roman fashion" (4.15.91) she concludes. Written in the same year as *Hamlet*, *Julius Caesar* is equally preoccupied with suicide. Yet the self-destructions in the latter play carry no taint of sin: indeed, to be or not to be is never precisely the question, at least not in spiritual terms. What brief debate there is in the play about suicide revolves around the issues of manliness and courage; and those dilemmas of honor and heroism are quickly resolved in favor of self-destruction when defeat inevitably looms.

Although not represented in terms of sin, suicide in *Julius Caesar* is riddled with, indeed almost defined by, error: errors of logistics, judgment, miscommunication, delusion, and fear. Further, the tactical and psychological mistakes that generate the suicides of Brutus and Cassius characterize their actions in life as well as death, permeating their heroic dignities with irony, futility, and waste.

"Indeed it is a strange-disposed time. / But men may construe things after their fashion / Clean from the purpose of the things themselves" (1.3.33–5), Cicero tells Caska, pointing to the crisis of meaning that characterizes the play. First, Brutus's idealism not only prevents him from thinking of "the things themselves," but causes him actively to reject them. "I know no personal cause to spurn at him / But for the general," he reflects when deciding whether Caesar should be assassinated. "He would be crowned," he continues with no proof (2.1.12); in fact there is evidence to the contrary, since Caesar has just three times publicly turned away Antony's offer of a crown. But Brutus rejects his knowledge of empirical reality in favor of abstract thought. Turning away from his own observations, choosing to create, and then prefer, his own meaning, despite what he has seen: these are the mechanics of Brutus's delusion. Joining with the conspiracy, Brutus attempts to redefine the bloody mutilation of Caesar's assassination as a sacrifice, a sculpture "fit for the gods" (2.1.172). But the repeated rejection of actuality leads to fatal errors of judgment: the decision not to include Cicero, whose age and eminence might have loaned greater authority to the conspiracy; the decisions, against the advice of Cassius, to let Antony live and speak last at Caesar's funeral; the military blunders at Philippi that lead ultimately to defeat.

In the instance of Antony's epitaph for Brutus, Cicero's sense of the anarchic potential of individual interpretation is correct. *Julius Caesar* is replete with some of the most stirring rhetorical pronouncements in Shakespeare, none of which proves accurate. "Countrymen: / My heart doth joy that yet in all my life / I found no man but he was true to me," Brutus states movingly, before his suicide (5.5.33–5). Yet this assertion is not accurate, not in the least. Cassius has seduced him into joining the conspiracy by pitching forged anonymous letters allegedly from the Roman populace in at Brutus's window, letters that demand that Brutus take the lead in restoring the republic. Antony lies to Brutus when promising that he will not attempt to stir the populace against the conspirators if he can speak at Caesar's funeral. In direct contradiction to his own observation that men consistently have been true to him, Brutus himself accuses Cassius of deceiving and shortchanging him during the alarming and vicious quarrel in which the two engage before Philippi. "There is a tide in the affairs of men / Which, taken at the flood, leads on to fortune," Brutus intones with impressive, irresistible eloquence when recommending aggressive action in the march to Philippi (4.3.216–17). Again, the rhetoric is stirring, but the recommendation is wrong; events prove that he should have listened to Cassius's more experienced advice to let the enemy seek them. "I shall have glory by this losing day / More than Octavius and Mark Antony / By this vile conquest shall attain unto," Brutus magnificently assures his companions before his suicide (5.5.36–8). But Antony and Octavius take over the world; the republic is not restored, and an empire that takes the shape of Brutus's worst nightmares is established instead. In addition, as the audience knows, Brutus's historical legacy is at best mixed. Although successive generations frequently regard him as noble if misguided, Montaigne (to cite one example) argues that Brutus and Cassius would have provided a more effective defense of Roman liberty had they remained alive; and Dante (to cite another) places them in the innermost circle of Hell, where traitors languish, freeze, and burn.

The tragic failure to create stable meaning is distilled in the suicides themselves. Cassius destroys himself because he wrongly thinks Brutus is defeated and Titinius taken. Titinius, viewing Cassius's dead body, devotedly follows suit, acknowledging it all as a mistake but finding no alternative, pronouncing what could be an epitaph for both Cassius and Brutus: "Alas, thou hast misconstrued everything" (5.3.84). Brutus's suicide can in turn be conceived as a result of these same, devastating errors.

The self-inflicted deaths in *Julius Caesar* can be characterized by what A. Alvarez in his book *The Savage God* describes as a "constant impurity of motive." Considering suicide as a move in the deadly, competitive political games of ancient Rome, Paul Plass, in *The Game of Death in Ancient Rome,* observes that suicide could be a triumphant last move with an articulate political agenda: a defiant gesture of resistance to power, suggesting the achievement of freedom in accepting and controlling death.

I began my discussion citing Lucilius's intention to defy Mark Antony and Octavius by defining Brutus's suicide as a profitable act of liberation; an effort which, I argued, fails, when Antony as military victor simultaneously seizes the rhetorical powers of meaning-making. In *Antony and Cleopatra* suicide as a freely chosen countermove in a deadly power struggle is more explicitly recognized and successfully executed. Cleopatra, briefly considering and rejecting the idea of self-destruction as sin, moves on: "[I]t is great," she declares, "To do that thing that ends all other deeds, / Which shackles accidents and bolts up change" (5.2.4–6). But the "high Roman fashion" turns out not simply to involve accepting death bravely, escaping by choice from defeat, dishonor, and the humiliation of being paraded in triumph and parodied by "Some squeaking ... boy" (5.2.219); equal importance inheres in Cleopatra's impudent thwarting of Caesar's desire to demonstrate his magnificence by granting clemency to the conquered queen. Octavius is so clear about his need not only to assert, but to be seen to assert, this power over Cleopatra, that he threatens to kill her children if she should defy him by taking her own life. But

Cleopatra views these threats and promises for what they are, a means to subdue and humiliate her so "that I should not / Be noble to myself" (5.2.190–1). The multiply motivated theatrics of her suicide include among their salient components the defiant aim of making Caesar "ass / Unpolicied!" (5.2.306–7). Just as Antony does in *Julius Caesar*, Octavius as military victor has the last word in *Antony and Cleopatra*. But it is debatable whether, in eulogizing the lovers as a "pair so famous," he is forced to accept and perpetuate their positive self-conceptions of their own suicides, rather than depriving their legend of triumphant meaning, as Antony does to Brutus with such ruthless success (5.2.359).

Plass clarifies the ways in which the intended meanings of political suicide—the dynamics of freedom of choice versus compulsory death—can always be inverted. This insight points to the quandary with which I began: is suicide in the contexts of these plays profit or loss? Is it an act of freedom or compulsion, self-determination or despair? Plass's connection of suicide with interpretation—as well as with the devious possibilities of meaninglessness—therefore brings us back to the vexed relation of self-destruction to loss and defeat in the Roman context. Clearly suicide has the simultaneous, self-contradictory potential for hypersignificance—an excess of meaning—as well as for incoherence—inaccessible, unstable meaninglessness. To put the question simply, is suicide in Shakespeare's plays a passive or an active deed: a submissive willingness to endure death itself as suffering, an affliction, an inevitable loss: or a deed of aggressive self-ownership, committed profitably to prevent suffering by actively taking one's life?

The startling, focused energy with which Antony and Cleopatra strategize and execute their suicides contrasts vividly with the waning and fragmented vigor of Brutus and Cassius. Within the indeterminate political logic of suicide, the pair achieves partial success. But in the deadly game of Roman power, Antony and Cleopatra (particularly Cleopatra) demonstrate considerably more self-consciousness and savvy than their immediate suicidal predecessors. Cleopatra manages with cunning theatricality to outmaneuver Caesar's devious and self-aggrandizing clemency. And, choosing to bury the lovers together, Octavius creates their epitaph in the terms Antony and Cleopatra might have chosen for themselves.

For Brutus and Cassius suicide is about avoiding, or possibly transcending, the occasion of present dishonor that has arisen in relation to the past: "Caesar, now be still" (5.5.50). Strikingly, Antony and Cleopatra each strive to construct their suicides in terms of the future: "I come, my queen," Antony says, thinking Cleopatra is dead, "Where souls do couch on flowers we'll hand in hand / And with our sprightly port make the ghosts gaze" (4.14.51–3). "Husband, I come," Cleopatra echoes him later (5.2.286). In applying the asp/baby to her breast and redefining its lethal power as life-nurturing, as well as referring to Antony as her husband, Cleopatra assumes the positions of wife and mother; and, by insistently, as she puts it, imagining Antony, she defines herself in relation to the future, rather than the past. It is this relation of the heroes to the future that distinguishes *Antony and Cleopatra* from Shakespeare's other late tragedies: even Caesar's epitaph emphasizes their perpetual and forthcoming legend, rather than the lost glory of their past achievements. Consider in contrast the epitaphs of other Shakespearean tragic heroes. Hamlet, a prince nipped in the bud, "was likely, had he been put on, / To have proved most royal" (5.2.381–2). Othello, a thwarted lover, was "great of heart" (5.2.359); the last words of *King Lear* look only backward.

Like other scholars, I argue that the later play, *Antony and Cleopatra*, begins to move out of the tragic sphere, to reconfigure the dynamics of profit and loss away from mourning. But I would add that the earlier play, *Julius Caesar*, points more firmly in the direction of Shakespeare's extended and profound treatment of tragic meaning-making as elegiac. Distilled in the representation of suicide in *Julius Caesar* are the delusions, errors, and ambivalence of the protagonists; the emptying out of meaning from stirring and beautiful rhetoric; the ironic and overwhelming force of historical events as the past inexorably diminishes the present and future; the grandeur and failures of heroism itself. All of these issues and their implications, which Shakespeare is to develop so relentlessly in his late tragedies, are already present in *Julius Caesar*, whether as profit, loss, or both.

Death and *King Lear*

Michael Neill

It is nothing.

ARCHDUKE FRANZ-FERDINAND (1914)

In my *Issues of Death* (1997), *King Lear* receives less attention than any of Shakespeare's major tragedies. Looking back, this seems an inexplicable mistake; yet the play is similarly disregarded in Michael Andrews's *This Action of Our Death* (1989) and William E. Engel's *Death and Drama in Renaissance England* (2002); while in Robert N. Watson's *The Rest is Silence* (1994) it is only "the brooding absent presence of my argument." Yet as long ago as 1966, William Elton's *King Lear and the Gods* addressed the play's nihilism, exploring the theological implications of the protagonist's "[N]othing will come of nothing" (1.1.90) to show how "the devastating fifth act shatters ... the foundations of faith itself." Anticipating Donne's description of death as "the most inglorious and contemptible vilification, the ... peremptory nullification of man," *Lear* shows a king forced to recognize the "smells of mortality" upon his own sanctified hand, a man reduced to a mere "ruined piece of nature" in an "image" of the "promised end" when "this great world / Shall ... wear out to naught" (4.6.129–30; 5.3.261–2). This is a play whose entire action is triangulated around three great negatives: "nothing," "no cause," and "never." Turning its back on both traditional moralization and the consolations of memorial artifice, it confronts death as mere blankness, the utter abjection of "nothing."

If, as I argued, early modern tragedy is about "the discovery of death and the mapping of its meanings," then *Lear* is perhaps the single most striking contribution to that atlas of mortality. Lear's opening declaration of his "darker purpose" is ostensibly about practical matters of inheritance; but the ironic self-deprecation with which he attempts to preempt the issue of his own frailty marks out the play's fatal direction by drawing attention to the implicit significance of the map on which a monarch is about to chart his own undoing: recalling the conceit of Elizabeth's Ditchley Portrait, in which the queen's body is set against the map of her body politic,

Lear's ceremonious division of the kingdom begins to resemble a dangerous exercise in self-dissection. What results is a vividly pictorial version of the "woeful pageant" (4.1.321) in *Richard II*, where another king undertakes to "undo [him]self" (203) in a formal surrender of authority that strips him of the very "name was given me at the font," reducing him to a mere "nothing," a histrionic "shadow" divorced from his own substance (255, 201, 292–9). In his prison cell Richard will imagine himself as an empty role-player, who may be "kinged again" only to be "unkinged" once more, becoming in the process so much a "nothing" that only the final annihilation of death can soothe his distress:

> But whate'er I be,
> Nor I nor any man that but man is
> With nothing shall be pleased till he be eased
> With being nothing.
>
> (5.5.31–41)

Richard's incantatory "nothings" can help to explain the extraordinary violence of Lear's reaction to Cordelia's "nothing" in the love test (1.1.87–9): it is not simply that her stubborn refusal to play her assigned part reduces her father's theatre of royal bounty to humiliating anticlimax; the pausing enforced by the word's stark rhetorical and metrical isolation makes their repeated "nothings" hang in the air like portents of the very end which the mock-abnegation of "crawl[ing] towards death" had sought to buy off; and Lear can resist it only by a gesture of counter-annihilation. "Nothing will come of nothing." On the face of it, this seems like a simple monitory application of the old proverb *nihil ex nihilo fit*, warning Cordelia that she can expect to gain only the contemptuous "Nothing" of his subsequent offer to Burgundy (247). But to a contemporary audience Lear's proverb will have been complicated by its ironic echo of the Christian orthodoxy which insisted that God had fashioned his entire creation out of nothing, and by the corollary of which Thomas Nashe reminds us: "This world is transitory; it was made of nothing, and it must to nothing" (*Works*, III).

Stripped of the "Propinquity and property of blood" that, in her father's eyes, define her being (1.1.115), Cordelia herself is reduced to nothing, since "we / Have no such daughter" (264–5). But it

is the king himself who—as the Fool points out—will be subject
to a more absolute nullification: in the repeated negatives of an
exchange that becomes an extended riff on Hamlet's "The King
is a thing ... Of nothing" (4.2.26–8), even the Fool's affectionate
"nuncle" can seem charged with its own punning negativity:

KENT   This is *nothing*, fool.

FOOL   ... you gave me *nothing* for't. [*to Lear*] Can you make
no use of *nothing*, *nun*cle?

LEAR   Why *no*, boy; *nothing* can be made out of *nothing*.

        *   *   *   *   *   *   *

FOOL   ... I would *not* be thee, *nun*cle. Thou hast pared thy wit
o'both sides and left *nothing* i'the middle .... I am better than
thou art now. I am a fool, thou art *nothing*.

        *   *   *   *   *   *   *

LEAR   Does any here know me? Why, this is *not* Lear
...

     Who is it that can tell me who I am?

FOOL   Lear's shadow.
           (1.4.126–30, 177–85, 217–22; all italics in quotations
                                      are the author's)

A "shadow" is a thing of no substance—a mere actor, in one of the
word's contemporary meanings, but also a ghost, a "nothing" like
the dead king in *Hamlet* (3.4.132–5).

Just as Richard II performs his self-undoing by renouncing the
symbolic accoutrements of royalty, so Lear's is acted out through
successive literalizations of the metaphor with which he first
imagined his surrender of authority: "Since now we will *divest*
us both of rule, / Interest of territory, cares of state" (1.1.49–50).
The idea of royal identity as a kind of dress, though admitted
here in an almost offhand parenthesis, is one to which the play
repeatedly returns. Coronation, of which we are reminded by
Lear's offer of "this coronet" to his sons-in-law (140), was
a sacramental act of formal *investiture* that transformed the
nature of its recipient: so that to "undeck the pompous body

of a king" (*Richard II*, 4.1.250) was in some profound way to annihilate his identity—as Cordelia's is proximately undone by the "dismantl[ing]" of her father's favor (1.1.218). The paradox of Richard's gesture, however, is that for his ceremony to have meaning, credence must be given to the king's quasi-sacerdotal powers. Something even more radical is involved in *Lear*; and the clue is to be found in the "presented nakedness" of Edgar— "Edgar I *nothing* am" (2.2.182, 192). Turning himself into Poor Tom, identified by his own father simply as the "naked" fellow (4.1.42, 46, 54), he appears to Lear as a mirror for his own sense of nullification: "Couldst thou save *nothing*? ... *Nothing* could have subdued nature / To such a lowness but his unkind daughters" (3.4.63, 69–70). Out on the heath, even before Lear calls down annihilation upon the world, the king pitches his own "little world of man" against a storm that threatens to "make *nothing*" of him (3.1.9–10). Confronted by the nullity of Edgar's "Unaccommodated man" (3.4.105), Lear is driven to act out his own undoing, repudiating what he comes to see as the vacant guise of "Robes and furred gowns" (4.6.161): "Off, off you lendings" (3.4.106). He then passes through the judgmental purgatory of 3.6 before being carried unconscious from the stage.

What follows this symbolic death is a resurrection—the so-called "restoration scene" in which the king appears in "these garments" that are meant to re-invest him with his royal identity—even though he himself cannot recognize them (4.7.22, 66–7). This scene climaxes in an extraordinary declaration from Cordelia that simultaneously paraphrases her fatal "nothing" and cancels out all that followed from it: "No cause, no cause" (75). But the cruelty of Shakespeare's design is that, in theatrical terms, this moment of sublime nullification turns out to be a deceit; for the play is headed towards a very different end—one in whose incantatory negatives "nothing" is again paraphrased, but this time with a finality that exposes its earlier translation as empty wish fulfillment: "No, no, no life! ... thou'lt come no more, / Never, never, never, never, never" (5.3.304–7). As if this weren't enough, Lear's cry is followed by a piece of stage business that faces the audience with nullification of the most peremptory kind: "Look on her:" cries the dying old man, "look, her lips, / Look there, look there!" (Folio, 309–10). It is, I think, the only moment in Shakespeare where the audience's gaze is directed onto a face without their being told what to see;

and that is because on those cold lips there is, in the absolute sense, nothing. Somewhere in the back of Shakespeare's mind must surely have been the terrible lines from the second act Chorus of Seneca's *Troades* (*post mortem nihil est ipsaque mors nihil* ...)—which he had recently remembered in *Measure for Measure* (3.1.117–31). I quote it here in the superb version by the Earl of Rochester, which moves towards its own, equally conclusive, gesture of silent nullification:

> After Death nothing is, and nothing Death ....
> Devouring Time swallows us whole,
> Impartial Death confounds Body and Soul.
> For Hell, and the foul Fiend that rules
>   The everlasting fiery Gaols,
> Devis'd by Rogues, dreaded by Fools,
> With his grim grisly Dog that keeps the Door,
>   Are senseless Stories, idle Tales,
> Dreams, whimsies, and no more.

Shakespeare's Here

Scott L. Newstok

Identity has always entailed a shuttling back and forth between the physical body and how it is conceived. This interplay between the actual/physical and the imagined/mental requires memory to put what was in touch with what is. A literary object enacts this tension between the physical and the imagined; Shakespeare relished the subtle modulations of playing within this space. Four centuries of desiring to speak with the dead can be traced through Shakespeare's lyric remembrancers back to his own verse: "FORBEARE / TO DIGG THE DVST ENCLOASED HEARE."

The 1632 Second Folio includes the following anonymous poem:

> "An Epitaph on the admirable Dramaticke Poet, W. SHAKESPEARE"
> What neede my *Shakespear* for his honour'd Bones,
> The labour of an age in piled Stones,
> Or that his hallow'd reliques should be hid

Under a Star-ypointing *Pyramid*?
Dear son of memory, great heir of Fame,
What need'st thou such weak witnes of thy name?
Thou in our wonder and astonishment
Hast built thy self a live-long Monument.
For whilst to th' shame of slow-endeavouring art,
Thy easie numbers flow, and that each heart
Hath from the leaves of thy unvalu'd Book,
Those Delphick lines with deep impression took,
Then thou our fancy of it self bereaving,
Dost make us Marble with too much conceaving;
And so Sepulcher'd in such pomp dost lie,
That Kings for such a Tomb would wish to die.

We know the poem's later attribution from John Milton's 1645 *Poems*, where it was titled "On Shakespeare. 1630." The "On" preposition conveys the quality of an epigram *on* a subject. "On" also hints at the material origin of the epi-gram (*writing on*): this almost-sonnet purports to be *on* (as in, on top of) Shakespeare, as well as *on* (about) Shakespeare. The poem's ambition suspends an incertitude about whether verse can adequately memorialize, or whether a predecessor's work rather paralyzes us with its monumentality ("Dost make us Marble with too much conceaving"). Paul de Man, via Wordsworth, found *prosopopeia* (or, in George Puttenham's translation, "counterfeit impersonation") here to enact a fundamental anxiety about making the dead speak (and making ourselves dumb).

This poem's backward glance, like that of Lot's wife, is just as intriguing as its legacy. As many have noted, Milton was already subsuming his predecessors in constructing his first published poem as a verbal monument. There are shrewd nods to the First Folio, including to the commemorative verse by Leonard Digges (and in bold here):

Shake-speare, at length thy pious fellowes give
The world thy Workes : **thy Workes, by which, out-live
Thy Tombe,** thy name must when that stone is rent,
And Time dissolves thy Stratford Moniment,
Here we alive shall view thee still. This Booke,
When Brasse and Marble fade, shall make thee looke

Fresh to all Ages: when Posteritie
Shall loath what's new, thinke all is prodegie
That is not Shake-speares; ev'ry Line, each Verse
Here shall revive, redeeme thee from thy Herse ...

"Here," that speaker-specific deictic points not only to the book (*here*, *this* book, in which *this* verse appears), but also the formulaic epitaphic invocation "*Here lies*." The words here "shall revive" thee, who we "Here all alive shall view."

The ritual lament marks a similar pivot within Ben Jonson's longer commendation:

My Shakespeare, rise; I will not lodge thee by
Chaucer, or Spenser, or bid Beaumont lye
A little further, to make thee a roome :
Thou art a Moniment, without a tombe,
And art alive still, while thy Booke doth live,
And we have wits to read, and praise to give.

While this last line echoes the close of Shakespeare's Sonnet 106 ("[We] Have eyes to wonder, but lack tongues to praise"), it more overtly invokes William Basse's elegiac lines:

Renowned Spencer lye a thought more nye
To learned Chaucer, and rare Beaumond lye
A little neerer Spenser, to make roome
For Shakespeare in your threefold, fowerfold Tombe ...

Milton also likely thought the verse on the Stanley tomb at Tong was written by Shakespeare, as did other contemporaries:

   Not monumental stone preserves our Fame;
Nor sky-aspiring Piramides our name;
The memory of him for whom this standes
Shall outlive marble and defacers hands
When all to times consumption shall be given
   Standly for whom this stands shall stand in heaven.

These lines in turn trope the Horatian *Exegi monumentum aere perennius* that opens Sonnet 55:

> **Not marble, nor the gilded monuments**
> **Of princes, shall outlive this powerful rhyme;**
> ...
>   So till the judgment that yourself arise,
>   **You live in this, and dwell in lovers' eyes.**

You live in this: these words, here, rehearsed by being read again. Lyric immediacy emerges in part from keen awareness that something absent (even if in anticipation) can be only partially recuperated by a text "here." Many sonnets ring the changes on this mortal theme: "And thou in this shalt find thy monument" (107); while the speaker's verse "is but as a tomb, ... You should live twice: in it, and in my rhyme" (17).

What might be called the temporality of the "future imperfect" is ingeniously dramatized in Sonnet 81:

> Or I shall live, your epitaph to make;
> Or you survive, when I in earth am rotten;
> From hence your memory death cannot take,
> Although in me each part will be forgotten.
> Your name from hence immortal life shall have,
> Though I, once gone, to all the world must die;
> The earth can yield me but a common grave,
> When you entombed in men's eyes shall lie.
> Your monument shall be my gentle verse,
> Which eyes not yet created shall o'er-read,
> And tongues to be your being shall rehearse,
> When all the breathers of this world are dead.
>   You still shall live, such virtue hath my pen,
>   Where breath most breathes, even in the mouths of men.

An initially balanced set of outcomes—either the speaker or the addressee will die first—soon tip into asymmetrical destinies: for the addressee, *an epitaph, memory, an immortal name, lying entombed in men's eyes in my (this!) verse monument*; for the speaker, *decay, oblivion, an unmarked grave*, culminating in the aggressively buried absence of the speaker in the sestet (but for "my pen"). It's of course the deliberate irony of the *Sonnets* that the addressee of this poem is re-hearsed (un-hearsed) through nothing other than the "virtue" of the poet's words.

Both plays and epitaphs depend upon the problematically deictic reference to something "Here." The recourse to a declarative "here" across print and stage media has as its common reference point the body—a body that is in a peculiar way *not quite present*, and thus needing proclamation of its presence. Shakespearean characters acknowledge their ghastly semi-absence onstage, where there is no "here" *here*. When Romeo avers "I have lost myself. *I am not here. / This is not Romeo, he's some otherwhere*" (1.1.195–6), or when Othello laments "That's he that was Othello? *here I am*" (5.2.281), we sense Shakespeare intuiting a subtle insight about performed presence. He took the Epicurean solace—"When we exist, death is not present, and when death is present, we do not exist"—and sought to step outside of it, making Hamlet's death sentence "*I am dead*" possible, albeit within quotation marks.

Speaking of one's self in the past tense, or of one's death in the present tense, entails the imaginative scope of fictive work: crafting absent things to appear present; making the dead legible to us again. Recall Cicero's account of Simonides, who was fabled to have invented the art of memory and its method of *loci* in response to identifying unrecognizable deceased bodies by their spatial placement. This coincidence of time and space through the deictic center would later be elaborated in the mnemonic theatre of Giulio Camillo (1480–1544).

Part of Shakespeare's dramaturgical ingenuity entailed working imaginatively with his many theatrical collaborators (both playwrights and players). Yet another mode of collaboration characterizes the staging of the statue scene in *The Winter's Tale*, one that traverses arts, time, and geography. Here he worked not only with the named "rare Italian master" Giulo Romano for the multimedia (sculpture, painting, music, words) final performance, but also with a mute Giulio, hinted at through the character of Camillo, whose name obliquely alludes to this tradition of memory practices, or tools for thinking and inventing.

How do we revivify the past, verbally? By sacralizing space, by marking it out "here." The stage and page alike make creative use of negative space—what in Japanese aesthetics is called "*ma*," or what the design theorist Christopher Alexander terms "the void."

Sacred space (in Hebrew: *makom*) emerges from shaping what's around us to help us stand upright: "I am ashamed. Does not the stone rebuke me / For being more stone than it?" (5.3.37–8). Milton—we—hear Shakespeare's audacious triumph over death:

> 'Tis time; descend; be stone no more; approach.
> Strike all that look upon with marvel. (5.3.99–100)

What ceremony else?

6

Media

Spectatorship, Remediation, and One Hundred Years of *Hamlet*

James C. Bulman
President, SAA 1998–99

Let's imagine ourselves in the New Gallery Kinema on Regent Street in 1913, members of an audience gathered to watch the first feature-length *Hamlet* in an emergent if slightly disreputable medium called moving pictures. At fifty-nine minutes, the film captures the performance of Sir Johnston Forbes-Robertson, called the greatest Hamlet of his generation, who, at sixty, may be a little long in the tooth to play a university student but nevertheless is still capable of bringing to the role a nervous energy tempered by princely self-restraint for which his stage Hamlet was prized. As the projectionist begins to crank, our experience to a degree replicates watching a stage play: a stationary camera, as if placed a few rows back in the stalls, offers, as Judith Buchanan observes, "an unwavering, frontally placed, point of view" with "almost no attempt to edit a scene by breaking it up with cut-ins of differing focal lengths or shots taken from different perspectives" (*Shakespeare on Silent Film*, 2009). The acting style, too, seems to be locked in the late nineteenth century, with grand theatrical gestures, exaggerated grimaces, and eyes rolling heavenward.

Drawn from Forbes-Robertson's 1897 acting text, the script has been radically cut. Title cards announce what will be enacted in the frames that follow, at times unnecessarily, as when we are told that "The king and Polonius hide behind the curtain" just before we see them do so. Sometimes title cards bearing heavily edited speeches alert us to what characters are saying. Oddly, these cards often include ellipses, as if in deference to those who can tell what lines have been omitted. The one bearing Polonius's advice to Laertes selects only his most famous clichés, as if assuming the audience is familiar with the speech: "Give every man thine ear but few thy voice ... Neither a borrower not a lender be ... To thine own self be true." Even more oddly, while characters mime the action, they are often shown to be speaking their lines at great length, as if the film-makers were oblivious to the fact that for the audience in the dark, the rest was silence. If, as Alan Galey writes in his essay for this volume, Shakespeare is often recruited to validate the capacity of an emerging technology to supplant older technologies—to trumpet a new medium's remediation of another—then Forbes-Robertson's silent *Hamlet* remains too wedded to the conventions of theatre and print to remediate them effectively.

True, portions of the film break away from its textual and theatrical origins to offer something more cinematic. Outdoor scenes such as Hamlet's confrontation with the Ghost or his conversation with the Gravediggers could be shot on location rather than in a studio because recording sound was not an issue. The Ghost appears as a transparent figure who dissolves in a technique invented by stop-trick photographer Georges Méliès; and director Cecil Hepworth uses crosscutting effectively when glimpses of the mad Ophelia walking along a river bank, picking flowers, are interspersed with shots of the King conspiring with Laertes. Spectators are thus alerted to Ophelia's imminent death without having to see it: the film "opens up" a scene which in the play is only narrated by Gertrude. Moments like this hint at what cinematic artistry could eventually bring to Shakespeare.

But the potentials of film were slow to be realized by Shakespeare directors. When sound was introduced into film, directors could seize the opportunity to foreground his language again; yet unlike theatre, film is primarily a visual medium, so a tension between language and spectacle has characterized Shakespeare "talkies" from the outset. Laurence Olivier, the chief exponent of Shakespeare on film in midcentury, is often credited with translating theatrical speech and action into cinematic terms. His 1948 *Hamlet*, filmed in black and white and often in deep focus, employs what Samuel Crowl calls "deliberately obtrusive camera work" to make spectators aware of the camera as an interpretive lens, a "visual accomplice" to Hamlet's probing, covert intelligence (*Shakespeare and Film*, 2008). The film opens with a "roving camera on a crane that peers everywhere," observes Kenneth Rothwell, guiding the spectator's eye from the turret overlooking the sea, down a circular staircase and past Ophelia's bedchamber, prying into Claudius's closet, lingering at the door of the Queen's chamber with the bed on which Hamlet will accost his mother, and finally moving into the great hall where he will catch the conscience of the King (*A History of Shakespeare on Screen*, 2004). Such cinematography finds a visual language for Olivier's Freudian interpretation of Hamlet's indecision and demonstrates how camera work could remediate a play that had hitherto been understood in largely theatrical terms.

Yet as Robert Shaughnessy argues, those who assert "the aesthetic independence and purity of the [film] medium" ignore the pervasive theatricality of Shakespearean cinema in the first half of the twentieth century, which makes the medium a complex hybrid of stage and screen techniques (*A Concise Companion to Shakespeare on Screen*, 2006). Olivier's film reveals its theatrical origins in multiple ways. He had acted Hamlet at the Old Vic in 1937, in a production by Tyrone Guthrie that foregrounded Ernest Jones's theory of Hamlet as a neurotic Oedipal figure. The film's cinematic mise-en-scène, too, seems to have been inspired by the Old Vic's uncluttered abstract expressionist set. Olivier often plays Hamlet theatrically, addressing soliloquies to an unseen audience as he gazes off screen and even recreating a crucial moment from his own stage performance when Hamlet, cued by the exit of the visiting players, runs to the platform where their trunk of props beckons him, stands in a spotlight that illuminates only him and, pirouetting theatrically with outstretched arms, shouts, "The play's the thing / Wherein I'll catch the conscience of the King!" at which point the light fades to black. The players' performance makes even greater use of theatrical artifice. Hamlet gathers the court audience to watch "The Murder of Gonzago" not as Shakespeare wrote it, but only as the dumb show that precedes it, the action mimed with a gestural overacting which makes oblique reference to the style of silent Shakespeare films of the previous generation—a subtle reminder of how the technology of sound reproduction has effectively remediated the filming of Shakespeare.

If films such as Olivier's employed cinematic techniques to translate Shakespeare's language into images, the new medium of television, which originated in radio, reverted to prioritizing the text. Television worked best with talking heads, framing scenes in medium close-up shots with at most two or three actors in range. Televising Shakespeare's plays was seen as a way to legitimize the new medium by bringing high culture to the masses, precisely as it was by cinema in 1913. In the 1950s, director George Shaefer launched a daring project to broadcast performances of six of the most popular plays; and in them, he cast in lead roles his friend Maurice Evans, a British stage actor who had emigrated to America in the 1930s and become a notable Shakespearean actor in New York before enlisting for military service during World War II. The first of Shaefer's broadcasts was *Hamlet* (1953), an adaptation of the play which he and Evans had performed for soldiers in the Pacific. The surprising popularity of this *G.I. Hamlet*, as it came to be called, augured well for the future of televised Shakespeare.

Before the advent of video, televised Shakespeare had to be broadcast "live," a concept which, as Philip Auslander argues in *Liveness: Performance in a Mediatized Culture* (2008), is historically contingent, having evolved only when the reproduction of a live performance in another medium such as film became possible. Television offered viewers liveness at a distance, but in real time. The broadcast was subject to the same unpredictability and risk in the studio as a performance on stage. Multiple cameras had to be precisely calibrated to ensure a continuity of action; actors had to get in place for each scene, often with costume changes made in seconds; and there was no opportunity to do another take. Furthermore, Evans was a mannered, declamatory actor of the old school, his performance not modulated for the medium; and the quasi-realistic sets tended to compete with actors for attention on the small screen. In a sense, early televised Shakespeare did what silent films had done: memorialize theatrical productions with a rather primitive technology that occasionally replicated too closely what could have been seen on stage, and, with some exceptions, restricted rather than realized the potentials of the new medium.

Watching television at home, of course, is a very different experience from watching a film in a theatre. While, for those who tuned in, seeing Shakespeare performed "live" on television was still an event, it no longer served a social function, and responses were not collective. With lights in the living room on and the screen too small to show much detail, spectators may have been as susceptible to distraction as they are today when watching Shakespeare on digital media. The development of two new technologies, the videotape in the 1970s and the DVD in the 1990s, created more possibilities for watching Shakespeare at home or at school by appropriating for film the characteristics and accessibility of a printed text: one could start and stop a film at will, view it repeatedly, replay scenes out of sequence, and even divide the film into chapters. The BBC was quick to capitalize on video technology by filming all thirty-six Shakespeare plays over a seven-year period, 1978–85, ostensibly for television broadcasts, but in fact to disseminate them for profit as videos. Furthermore, those films that had once been the exclusive domain of wide-screen cinemas now could be viewed on smaller screens, thus complicating distinctions between film and television and calling into question the very nature of what one was watching. Was a video of Olivier's *Hamlet* viewed on television still a film? If it was reformatted to fit the differently shaped television screen, were spectators viewing a hybrid less inherently cinematic than what they would view in a theatre?

The digital revolution has further complicated the idea of what a Shakespeare film is. With a PC and other digital devices, one can view a film not only as a solitary spectator, but interactively; one can select images and move them about, juxtapose scenes, view the same scene from different film versions, even introduce material from external sources to create one's own personal film, as Pascale Aebischer explores in her essay for this volume. This, in essence, is what Hamlet does in Michael Almereyda's *Hamlet*, set in New York City in 2000, a film which, in the words of Thomas Cartelli and Katherine Rowe, "probes the strengths and limitations of different memory technologies, including photography, film, video, and digital video," each of which absorbs and remediates those technologies that preceded it (*New Wave Shakespeare on Screen*, 2007). The film opens with Hamlet gazing at a computer screen on which he is editing a montage in PixelVision, an outdated technology which he adapts to his own purposes. The black-and-white images he has assembled, from dinosaurs to stealth bombers, fill the screen as Hamlet meditates on man as the "quintessence of dust," revealing an existential despair that explains his use of digital media as a bulwark against engagement with others. His reality never more than virtual, this Hamlet frames most of his soliloquies as video sequences. The final product of his editing is "The Mousetrap," a bricolage of filmic devices and cinematic tricks that creates a narrative resembling the play-within-the-play it replaces. Stitching together black-and-white images and clips culled from silent films, home movies, and hardcore porn, Hamlet foregrounds his obsession with his lost childhood, his mother's sexuality, and his uncle's guilt. In so doing, he pays homage to the history of film; yet Almereyda's stance is oppositional. The grainy texture and artless cutting of Hamlet's silent "Mousetrap" aggressively confront the illusion of invisible technology sought by realist filmmakers such as Franco Zeffirelli and Kenneth Branagh who made *Hamlets* (1990, 1996) for the cineplex.

Hamlet's showing his home video to the assembled court in a private screening room is itself a throwback to the era of collective audition. Unlike his court audience, however, most viewers have seen Almereyda's film not in a theatre but as a DVD or as streaming video on their laptops or tablets; for, as Richard Burt writes, "the horizon of reception" is now "composed of multiple viewing possibilities that reframe the initial theatrical viewing, if it occurred at all" (*Shakespeare, The Movie II*, 2003). Viewing Shakespeare on film, it would seem, will never again mean what it once did: a gathering of spectators at a cinema to watch on a large screen a performance that will not be available to them in any other medium.

Yet a recent phenomenon—live cinema relays of stage performances to audiences in theatres remote from the site of origin—has brought the history of filmed Shakespeare full circle. The release of a "live" performance of Richard Burton's popular modern-dress *Hamlet* to 976 cinema screens in 1964, for two days only, was an instructive precursor of this phenomenon. Responding "to the widespread anxiety that television would prove the demise of both theatre and film," producers attempted to woo back audiences by filming the play on the stage of the Lunt-Fontanne Theatre before live audiences over a three-day period, striking prints from the film

negatives quickly and then advertising Theatrofilm as a transformative new medium which would replicate the ephemeral theatrical
experience on a national scale. The experiment did not succeed:
Burton's *Hamlet* resembled live 1960s television too closely, its
mediation "not virtual enough to capture the peculiar *thereness* of
the stage or of film" (W. B. Worthen, "*Hamlet* at Ground Zero,"
2008).

Digital technology has made all the difference. Now, fifty years
later, spectators interested in seeing current productions by the
National Theatre, the Royal Shakespeare Company, Shakespeare's
Globe, and the Stratford Festival in Canada gather in large
numbers to watch "live" film relays. For each relay, six or seven
cameras, mobile and stationary, provide a mix of live feeds to
ensure a range of points of view on the performance, while the
subsequent editing of shots makes the final product more cinematic
than live broadcasts on television ever are. Digital technology
thus offers remote spectators an experience potentially more
immediate than that enjoyed by the theatre audience attending the
live performance. High-angle establishing shots define the theatre
space for spectators in the cinema; close-ups allow them to see
actors' faces in minute detail and to observe subtle interactions
among actors that might not be detectable to those attending; and
staging can be viewed from multiple perspectives, with cameras
acting as performer–observers, taking spectators into the frame,
"satisfying the often unconscious desires of an audience though a
shifting gaze continually responding to the emotional dynamics of
the performance unfolding on the screen" (Susanne Greenhalgh,
2014). Paradoxically, such intimate access to the stage often makes
the cinema relay feel less mediated than viewing the performance
in a theatre.

The question of the "liveness" of a cinema relay is vexed,
however, for if spectators are not watching the stage performance
in real time, if it has been prerecorded and camera feeds edited as
they are for film, and if the relay eliminates the unpredictability,
risks, and spontaneity that characterize stage performances, can the
experience of the cinema audience ever feel as authentically "live"
as that of the theatre audience? This question may be moot in a
digital age when, as Auslander points out, the concept of "liveness"
has broadened to include a sense of copresence among Internet
users or a connectedness to others afforded by social media. Yet

the question becomes insistent when cameras, in most live cinema relays, pan to the theatre audience, showing them taking their seats, laughing, applauding, or silently looking on. Such focus on the "live" theatre audience can make the remote cinema audience acutely aware of how their own responses may differ from those of the audience on screen, disconcertingly conscious of their roles as spectators at a hybrid event, not quite film, but not quite theatre.

The 2010 broadcast of Nicholas Hytner's *Hamlet* for NT Live posed the problem of spectatorship most directly in its filming of "The Murder of Gonzago," performed just before the interval. In the cinema relay, as lamps are brought onto the stage to illuminate the players about to perform the play-within-the-play, the camera pulls back to reveal the scaffolding and lighting rig of the vast Olivier stage, acknowledging the meta-theatricality of the event. As they watch the court audience gather for the play and then watch the players enter and begin their performance, cinema spectators are privileged to have on the large screen a much closer view of the action than the Olivier audience enjoys; and as the court audience reacts to the play, the camera focuses the cinema spectators' attention on reaction shots, especially on a close-up of Hamlet as he shines a stage light on Claudius and exclaims, "You shall see anon how the murderer gets the love of Gonzago's wife" (3.2.256–7). Yet as their attention is turned to the audience sitting in the Olivier theatre, spectators are forced to recognize their own position as remote observers, watching a "live" theatre audience reacting to an onstage audience reacting to a troupe of players performing a play. And when the remote spectators applaud at the end of the performance, as audiences at live cinema relays nearly always do, they do so with an ironic awareness that their applause is meaningless, for the actors cannot hear them. They are responding to a theatrical event for which they are, yet are not, present. Live cinema relays of Shakespeare thus alert us to how complexly remediated film has become—and how compromised our position as spectators.

Performing Shakespeare through Social Media

Pascale Aebischer

The 400th anniversary of Shakespeare's death is also the birthday of the SAA's annual digital salon, which recognizes the impact constantly evolving new technologies have had on Shakespeare's afterlives. Digitized texts, historical documents, and performance records encourage, as Alan Galey points out, our faith in accessibility and "authentic" remediation. At the same time, our critical instincts prompt us to question the accuracy of such heavily mediated and encoded texts, to point to the fragmentary nature of the performance record and, following Peggy Phelan's lead, to debunk the notion that digital video recordings can ever be an adequate surrogate of live performance. A database such as the MIT *Global Shakespeares* can have the paradoxical effect of making its user keenly aware of the *inaccessibility* of archived performances as live events: even as they are only one click away, digitized performances are marked by their geographical, historical, and linguistic remoteness, opening a window onto an event that cannot be experienced in real time and space.

Such distance from the digital object is counter to our everyday experience of the immediacy, immersion, and participatory logic of social media. Away from scholarly databases, Shakespeare and Marlowe's Twitter avatars spout 140-character opinions; social-shakespeare.tumblr.com connects amateur performers across the globe for online play-readings; and girls post their Ophelia-inspired memes on Flickr and YouTube. It is this (a)liveness of social media and its ability to turn users into coproducers of Shakespearean content that I want to focus on as I consider the Royal Shakespeare Company's 2013 production of *A Midsummer Night's Dream*.

With "a little bit of help from" Google Creative Lab, the RSC's fortieth staging of this play, #Dream40, harnessed the social media of Google+ to explore how theatre and social media might come together to embed a theatrical performance in an immersive digital environment. As "a digital theatre project," #Dream40 consisted only in part of the performance of Shakespeare's comedy, by a troupe of RSC actors, across three days of the midsummer solstice in 2013. Starting in a rehearsal space for the opening court scenes, Gregory Doran's site-sensitive staging moved outdoors for the forest scenes, ending in the Dell behind the Courtyard Theatre just after Holy Trinity Church's iron tongue of midnight had told twelve. While the rehearsal costumes drew attention to the metatheatricality of Shakespeare's play, the production spatially separated actors from their audience, stuck to Shakespeare's script, and had a clear beginning, middle, and end.

In a departure from theatre etiquette, however, Doran encouraged the Stratford audience to switch on their phones and start responding to the play. Through social media, they, along with audience members sitting at their computers across the world, were able to interact with the "group of commissioned artists [who] created new characters inspired by the activity in the play." On Google+'s "online stage," these new characters generated subplots (part prescripted, part improvised in response to events over the three days of the project) that were transmitted through news feeds, dedicated websites (for the nunnery and the pub), voice podcasts, texts, video blogs (or vlogs), and photographs.

Once the live performance had concluded, the three thousand plus posts the project accrued were connected, as hyperlinked images that appeared briefly in the middle of the screen, to a voice recording of the production in rehearsal which, at the bottom of the screen, is represented by a linear timeline (http://dreaming. dream40.org/timeline). At the time of writing, viewers can still enter the performance project and follow the invitation to "Listen to the play but feel free to hit pause whenever you'd like to explore the digital world spun around it." Clicking a link does not interrupt the voice recording but opens up a new window which, more often than not, contains multiple hyperlinks that can lead the viewer ever further away from the timeline and Shakespeare's plot. It is not for nothing that one pathway ends on a reading of Robert Frost's poem "The Road Not Taken."

Pulling against the linearity of the RSC actors' rendering of Shakespeare's *Dream* "as originally written," the spectator who enters #Dream40's digital environment becomes the coproducer of a "hyperdrama" (Giannachi, *Virtual Theatres*), which challenges the boundaries of the Shakespearean text along with its authority and implicit value systems. The digital medium becomes a means of multiplying and dispersing the Shakespearean plotlines, altering in potentially radical ways the priorities and politics of the early modern play. Social media act as a means of characterization, allowing figures who don't even exist in Shakespeare's text to have access to the three-dimensional characterization Shakespeare often reserves for his male protagonists. Shakespeare's masculine soliloquies are supplanted by the interior monologues of the women of Athens transmitted through their agonizingly intimate vlogs and podcasts. In the continuous present of the Internet, the newly created townsfolk of Athens come to life with each click, making them recognizably "real" and part of the viewer–participant's world. By contrast, Shakespeare's characters "as originally written" and performed by the RSC cast lack presence, "reality," and relevance in the digital environment.

Like Lysander's sister Ophelia, who escapes from Abbess Volumnia's convent (the St. Agnes Reformatorium for Girls) to purposefully lose and find herself in the green world of the forest, the online audience members are reimagined by the Google+ environment as engaging (*pace* Guy Debord), in a virtual *dérive*, an exploratory stroll responsive to the structural boundaries and pathways inherent in the environment. Suspending their everyday activities to explore the social and environmental landscape created by the project, the users as coproducers of their individual narratives find shortcuts, use avatars to interact with characters and/ or other users' avatars, and map their own psychogeography of Google+'s digital Athens and its wood.

Only partly the effect of chance, the spectators' *dérive* requires ethical agency as they choose which voices to listen to, whose posts to read, which clips to watch, whether to post content of their own. While in their *dérive* some spectators will be enticed by the frantic preparations for Theseus's stag party by his nervous best man Hercules, and others may discover another facet of this protagonist by listening to Abbess Volumnia's increasingly hysterical SoundCloud podcasts that chart her journey from sexual repression to voluptuous abandon in Hercules's arms. Some may be stopped in their tracks by the absurdity of the "Hamster of Fate" (footage of a toy hamster choosing, e.g., a happy over a sad ending for the play) or the sheer joy of the Fairies' Flying School's YouTube clips (shot from the wobbly point of view of the hapless student pilot crash-landing while being admonished by an unseen RAF-style instructor). Others will seek out a trajectory of resistance to the politics of the play as they watch Ophelia's desperate vlogs detailing life in the nunnery, read Mrs. Egeus's embittered denunciation of her husband's oppression of herself and Hermia in *The Knight's Herald*'s "court gossip" column, and explore the antibourgeois politics of Beagle the Bellows Maker. Even as these characters oppose the value systems embodied by Shakespeare's play, they illuminate its core concern with the regulation of sexuality and sublimation of the laboring classes' anarchic impulses in the creation of festive entertainment.

The axes of #Dream40 thus return to the heart of Shakespeare's play. The very fact that the online viewers become participants in the production of #Dream40, changing the course of the hyper-drama through their journey, is fundamentally true to the play's exploration of how the medium of theatre is subject to interaction between play(ers) and audience. Like his online viewer-participant counterparts, Puck shifts from the role of "auditor" to that of "actor" to change the direction of the plot. Quince's actors need not fret that their realistic portrayal of the lion might traumatize their courtly audience, whose chatter also shapes the performance when Theseus intervenes to curtail the epilogue. Shakespeare's play represents the blurring of the roles of actor and auditor as intrinsic to his medium.

Running counter to the play's insight that audience participation is a fundamental ingredient of theatrical performance, the opposition in the #Dream40 project between the RSC actors' live performance of Shakespeare's text and the virtual digital environment in which it is embedded has the paradoxical effect of representing live performance as predictable, repetitive, and two-dimensional. By contrast, Google+'s exploitation of the affordances of social media enables the creation of a three-dimensional universe alive with non-Shakespearean content that absorbs the anarchic energy of Shakespeare's comedy, making the digital the prime site for the construction and critique of Shakespearean plotlines and politics. In #Dream40, the most engaged spectators are those who pay little attention to the RSC's live performance and who enter the production's digital environment as Puck-like, auditor–actors on a *dérive*. Their trajectories through the virtual forest of Athens create new, individual *Dream*s, whose authenticity consists not of adherence to Shakespeare's text but of the experiential liveness of participation in the Shakespearean environment.

Far from entrenching the division between live/authentic versus digital/mediated, #Dream40 highlights the fallacy of such a division for the performance of Shakespeare in our time.

Reading Shakespeare through Media Archaeology

Alan Galey

If new media share one quality across historical contexts, it is their capacity to generate stories about themselves, whether triumphal chronicle-histories or anxious prophecies of doom. The emerging subfield of media archaeology seeks to avoid both extremes, and prefers to use media artifacts from the past "as tools to excavate the present," as Paul DeMarinis puts it (see his chapter in *Media Archaeology: Approaches, Applications, and Implications*). Media archaeologists typically combine technical understanding of media with an interest in discontinuities, ambiguities, and outright failures in the neglected areas of media history. As the field's founding theorist Wolfgang Ernst tends to describe it, drawing upon the work of Michel Foucault, media archaeology takes its name from a preoccupation with the gaps, silences, and ruptures that progress-focused media histories neglect, but which also expose the invisible rule-systems that govern the stories we tell about media (see Ernst's *Digital Memory and the Archive*). Though Ernst downplays the more conventional sense of *archaeology* as the study of material traces of human societies, Shakespeare studies shares with archaeology a fascination with material culture, as well as an appreciation of the challenge of piecing knowledge together from fragments. Shakespeare's works—whether experienced as written texts, as performances, or as media-bending experiments—have migrated through different technologies and media in ways that lend themselves to what Ian Hodder, an archaeologist of Neolithic settlements, has called "interpretation at the trowel's edge" (*The Archaeological Process*).

Let us consider a dig site in the realm of Shakespearean media archaeology. Within the Folger Shakespeare Library's collections sits a volume whose annotations reveal a scholar's labors over strata of media that overlap within a single artifact. In the early 1860's, the noted chess player and Shakespeare editor Howard Staunton was preparing his facsimile edition of the 1623 Shakespeare First Folio, which would introduce many Shakespeare readers to the idea of photographic reproduction of old books. The volume at the Folger happens to be Staunton's own proof copy (Folger call no. PR2752 1866n Sh.Col., copy 4), prepared by the printer Day & Son so that Staunton could check the quality of the reproductions against the originals. (I touch upon Staunton's proofreading briefly, as part of the prehistory of digitization, in my broader study in *The Shakespearean Archive*.)

In his numerous annotated queries, instructions, expostulations, and other material traces of textual labor, Staunton inadvertently left a record of his own detailed reading of a new media artifact, as he painstakingly evaluates the capacity of one new medium (photography) to remediate another (early modern print). Staunton performs this work using yet another writing technology, manuscript pen and pencil marks, recorded on the medium of cheap late-Victorian paper.

Many of Staunton's annotations seek to arrest the proliferation of meaning that occurs as text passes through the interfaces between old and new media. Throughout his proof corrections, he struggles to keep long *s* (ſ) characters from becoming f's, and vice versa, due to the inadvertent addition or omission of the tiniest of marks—an unavoidable hazard in the photolithographic process. In *The Merchant of Venice*, for example, Staunton catches the misreading "Good sir, this ring was given me by my wiſe" (p. 180 in the Folio's Comedies section; 4.1.437 in the Arden 3 lineation), caused by the failed registration of the crossbar of the f in the final word. Immediately after, Staunton's proofing annotations rail against the opposite problem, where the printer seems to have retouched the letter c to create the nonsensical reading "Shed thou no bloud, nor eut [*sic*] thou lesse nor more." Staunton's note admonishes the printer not to retouch any other letters without his specific direction, and his frustration with the intervention is unmistakable. Perhaps the most telling annotation appears next to the Folio's mis-set line "my affaires have mad: you wait" (p. 170), where Staunton asks, as if in a moment of existential angst, "what does this mean?" One sympathizes with Staunton's desire to interrogate a compositor who has been dead for centuries.

Other, more frequent Staunton-isms among the proof corrections include "speck," "dot-i," and "clean out" (all visible, for example, on p. 178 of the Comedies), as ink, dirt, paper, and meaning take on configurations just beyond his control. Overall, Staunton's flurries of proofing notes give the impression of a man frantically sticking fingers in a dike, as though the medium of print cannot hold back the torrent of misreadings as the text interfaces with the newer media of camera lenses, photosensitive plates, and lithographic substrates.

Paper sometimes tells its own stories apart from what people choose to write upon it. Although nearly two hundred and fifty years separated Staunton's printer, Day & Son, from the printing house of William and Isaac Jaggard, they evidently shared the same instinct to recycle paper whenever possible. The proof copy that Day and Son provided to Staunton is evidently printed on reused waste paper, some of which bears the marks of other printing-house activities. On the rectos and versos of four different leaves in *The Merchant of Venice*, which apparently were part of a single sheet that had previously been used to draft up a large advertisement, one can read, in mirrored arcs of block capitals in blue drafting ink and pencil, "HER" (facing p. 177), "BERT'S" (facing p. 176), "PALE" (facing p. 180), "ALES" (facing p. 181). This kind of intermixing of Shakespeare text and advertising anticipates James Joyce's punning appropriation of Portia's song in *Ulysses*, where it gets reworked into a bit of punning doggerel recalled by Stephen Daedalus: "O tell me where is fancy bread? At Rourke's the baker's, it is said."

The world keeps getting into our texts, it seems, even through the very paper. Yet, as Joyce well knew, in desiring purity in transmission we can overlook the pleasures of contamination. (This last phrase is the title of David Greetham's 2010 book on the topic; Pascale Aebischer's chapter describes a similar interpenetration of world and text, via social media and ubiquitous computing, in an experimental performance of *A Midsummer Night's Dream*.)

An advertisement for Staunton's facsimile nevertheless tells a celebratory story about the First Folio's mechanical reproduction, and comments upon Staunton's use of photography to create an aggregate of the best Folio pages drawn from three different copies: "Thus, by the regenerative process of Photo-Lithography, the First Folio itself, as near as may be, is put within the reach of all classes, and commands a wide support in acknowledgement of the enterprise that has turned into such a current this new and invaluable art" (printed in *The Official Programme of the Tercentenary Festival of the Birth of Shakespeare*, 1864, p. 96). The same threads run through present-day fascination with Shakespeare and digital media: faith in accessibility, afforded by the new medium for the benefit of "all classes"; the recruitment of Shakespeare to validate a new technology, "this new and valuable art"; and a lingering anxiety over the object of representation and the authenticity of its surrogate. Media archaeology, as noted above, emphasizes the gaps in media history. There is a considerable gap between the advertisement's confident invocation of "the First Folio *itself*" and its immediate qualification: "as near as may be."

That very gap is where Staunton found himself struggling with the Shakespeare text's remediation. Those involved in Shakespearean new media projects today, especially the coders themselves, know the long hours, false starts, and conflicting imperatives that may leave their mark on the code, documentation, media files, data sets, and other layers of a digital project. Like Staunton, we have looked quizzically at prior layers of encoding and mediation and asked "what does this mean?"

We might also take a cue from the language of the advertisement, once again, and remember the "regenerative process" that can ensue in Shakespeare's encounters with new media of all kinds. As James Bulman shows in his chapter on *Hamlet*'s regenerations, new forms of Shakespearean liveness form a dialogue with prior media. Digital editions, as performances of a different kind, also hold some regenerative promise, but media archaeology offers a perspective which, like book history and bibliography, calls us to notice processes of mediation beyond those that determine textual accuracy, and instead take part in the social and technological afterlife (or *nachleben*) of the Shakespeare text. Given the productive difficulty of pinning down Shakespeare's dramatic works as native to one medium or another—are they print? performance? something uncategorizable?—there is much yet to learn at the trowel's edge of Shakespearean media archaeology.

7

Race and Class

Is Black so Base a Hue?

Jean E. Howard
President, SAA 1999–2000

Is the early modern racialized subject allowed to have class, in the many meanings we might give that word now, including both a place in a hierarchized social structure and dignity? This question is prompted by the somewhat odd pairing of *race* and *class* as the organizing principles for essays in this section. Most of the chapters of this book are devoted to a single word, like *biography* or *feminism,* or to two words that form a recognizable phrase, like *social context* or *source study.* Only two other entries yoke disparate things together: *text and authorship* and *the body and emotions.* One could argue, however, that in a humoral universe, the body and the emotions were considered indissoluble, and that a long history of textual scholarship has made yokemates of texts and the authors (single, multiple, or anonymous) who composed them. But *race* and *class,* do they have any inevitable or historically constructed linkage? Some critics might join them as examples of critical anachronism, employing a restrictive historicism to argue that *race* did not mean in the early modern period what it means today or that early modern England was a *status* and not a *class* society. These terms also might be arbitrarily joined as trailing unfashionable political commitments in their wake. Often, though not always, critics of race and class openly place their work in relation to contemporary struggles against colonialism and its aftermath, structural racism, and the injustices spawned by unfettered capitalism.

I am going to treat the conjunction seriously and ask: how do race and class interpenetrate and relate on the early modern stage? Can racialized figures be assigned stable class positions in early modern drama? Does race in some way determine class or does race obliterate class distinctions? These questions are important if we are to address how race gains saliency on the early modern stage and interacts with other modes of social difference. While many scholars have discussed early modern race in terms of religion, climate, or family affiliation, I will focus narrowly here on the early modern theatre's racialization of somatic difference, looking at characters clearly designated as black or Moorish and for whom a dark complexion is a notable marker of identity. For this brief essay, I will address class simply as a hierarchized system of social differentiation based on one's relationship to work, wealth, and privilege, and expressed in the early modern period through terms such as laboring man, yeoman, gentry, and nobility.

I begin with Aaron's question in *Titus Andronicus:* "is black so base a hue?" (4.2.73). Aaron asks this question of the nurse who has brought him the black child he has fathered with Tamora, Queen of the Goths. To the nurse, the child's blackness is an abomination.

> Here is the babe, as loathsome as a toad
> Amongst the fair-faced breeders of our clime.
> The empress sends it thee, thy stamp, thy seal,
> And bids thee christen it with thy dagger's point.
>
> (4.2.69–72)

This cruel speech elicits both Aaron's question—"is black so base a hue?" and eventually his assertion that "Coal-black is better than another hue" (4.2.101). I want to linger over *base* and *better,* both used to describe the baby's coal-black color. Is it possible for anyone but Aaron, the father, to imagine blackness as a "better" hue than white? Or is blackness a hue that is inevitably wed to baseness and so to what is *low, low-born, not noble, of low quality, worthless, ignoble, craven, illegitimate*—all meanings that the *OED* assigns to the term *base* in the early modern period? It is a word not only designating something worthless, but something worthless because low-born, at the bottom of the social hierarchy, perhaps so illegitimate it is not even included on that hierarchy's lowest rung. Does a figure stigmatized as black reside anywhere but on the bottom of the class hierarchy, when not placed outside it, toadlike and illegitimate?

We know that many kinds of early modern cultural productions depict black figures, men and women, who occupy the social position of servant. As Kim Hall, Peter Erickson, and others have shown, a notable genre of early modern painting depicts noble white women attended by black servants whose skin sets off their mistress's pearly whiteness. Historically, these black figures were the products of early modern mercantilism and colonial expansion with its attendant creation of new forms of unfree labor. On the stage, we find analogues in the figure of black serving women like Zanche in *The White Devil*, who participates in every sort of villainy and who mirrors in her black skin the moral blackness of the corrupt court in which she resides; or in the figure of the black male slave, like Ithamore in *The Jew of Malta*, who abets the evil of his master Barabas until he treacherously turns on that master. Whether imagined as decorative attendants or as treacherous and violent, these lower-class black figures are just that: low. When they aspire to rise, as Zanche aspires to marry the noble Flamineo and Ithamore aspires to master his master, they fail. Failure confirms the incontrovertible baseness of their natures.

The harder case is offered by seemingly socially elevated black figures like Muly Mahamet in George Peele's *The Battle of Alcazar* or Shakespeare's Othello. Muly Mahamet belongs to the Moroccan royal family. His class position is, therefore, high, even though he quickly emerges as the play's villain—in the opening dumb show Muly murders his brothers and his uncle, and that is just the prologue to his treachery. Muly is insistently racialized as a "Negro Moor" whose black skin is rhetorically foregrounded by numerous speakers. On the other hand, his good uncle Abdelmelec, also a North African, is "whitened," both in the sense of being called a "manly Moor" rather than a "Negro Moor" and by aligning himself with classical learning, good government, and temperate passions. Muly, by contrast, remains a Moorish barbarian defined by his black skin. When defeated in battle, he flees from court into the wild mountains, eats the raw flesh of lions, and dies attempting to cross a raging river, symbol of his passions. The moral baseness Muly is made to display, however, is intensified by the physical degradation visited upon him in death, a death that confirms his baseness in his blackness. The victor declares: "His skin we will be [*sic*] parted from his flesh, / And being stiffened out and stuffed with straw,/ So to deter and fear the lookers on / From any such fool fact or bad attempt" (*The Battle of Alcazar*, 5.1.251–4).

This grotesque ending hyperbolizes Muly's dark skin by reducing him to nothing but that skin. His viscera gone, Muly can be stuffed and toted about, an object and not a person, a negation. This startling stage moment sluices Muly down the species hierarchy. Tanning hides is a process that accompanies the transformation of a living animal into a carcass whose parts can be variously used: for food, for clothing, for decoration. The many kinds of leather that result from tanning the hides of goats, sheep, and cattle are one product of such a transformative process. Muly's flawed hide is less obviously useful; instead of being transformed into ornamental leather, it becomes a totem carried about as a warning. Muly has been treated like a slaughtered steer, his noble birth canceled first by his outrageous acts and then by a process of bodily degradation that renders him horrific. What remains legible in death is not Muly's noble rank, but his race, signified by his "salted" black skin. By contrast, the "Christian king" Don Sebastian gets a noble burial: "see the soldiers tread a solemn march, / Trailing their pikes and ensigns on the ground, / So to perform the prince's funerals" (5.1. 258–60). White, Christian, and noble, Don Sebastian's identity remains intact in death.

Onstage, blackness often trumps a character's other identity markers. Even though he appears to be a kind of counselor in service to Tamora and is often depicted by her side, Aaron's somewhat indecipherable class position in *Titus Andronicus* is less legible than his race. As many have noted, Aaron is seldom mentioned, either in original stage directions or in dialogue, without his epithet, "the Moor." Sometimes there are qualifiers, as when he is called "a barbarous Moor" (2.2.78) or when the term "blackamoor" is swapped out for "swart Cimmerian" (2.2.72). Even when Tamora calls Aaron her "sweet Moor" (2.2.51), Aaron's somatic difference is never forgotten, reinforced by his self-reference to his "fleece of woolly hair" (2.2.34) and by the many ascriptions of blackness to Aaron's unnamed child, a child defined almost totally by the color of his skin, whether that color is to his father a mark of beauty or to the Romans a mark of shame. Inherited and iterable from one generation to the next, blackness overwhelms distinctions. It is so powerful a signifier that when Marcus kills a fly at Titus's dinner table and says it reminds him of the Moor, Titus falls into a paroxysm of rage, striking again and again at the dead creature, the "likeness of a coal-black Moor" (3.2.79). Blackness elides differences between Moor and housefly and solicits violence aimed at the extermination of both.

Like other black stage figures, Aaron desires to ascend the social hierarchy, but is both thwarted in that attempt and punished with a death that plants him, literally, in the base earth and severs him from the rest of humanity. Aaron's soaring moment of aspiration occurs at the beginning of Act 2. Erotic mastery does not suffice. Aaron has been Tamora's lover for a while. What excites him is the political power and social elevation he can acquire through her ascendency within Rome.

> Then, Aaron, arm thy heart and fit thy thoughts
> To mount aloft with thy imperial mistress,
> And mount her pitch whom thou in triumph long
> Hast prisoner held, fettered in amorous chains
> And faster bound to Aaron's charming eyes
> Than is Prometheus tied to Caucasus.
> Away with slavish weeds and servile thoughts!
> I will be bright, and shine in pearl and gold
> To wait upon this new-made empress.
> To wait, said I? — to wanton with this queen,
> This goddess, this Semiramis, this nymph,
> This siren that will charm Rome's Saturnine
> And see his shipwreck and his commonweal's.
>
> (1.1.511–23)

Fantasizing about "mounting," Aaron would throw off base clothing (*servile weeds*) and thoughts belonging only to a slave. For a time he seems to succeed until derailed by his love for the only thing in the play's universe like himself: his blackamoor son.

Critics have recognized the sweet irony of Aaron's paternal affection. The vilified Moor has extraordinary capacity for such emotion. Yet white Rome undercuts with a vengeance any moral, social, or political elevation Aaron temporarily attains. His ending, as with so many other black characters, reveals the recurring irreconcilability of blackness and social elevation in the minds of the socially dominant race. Rather than flayed and tanned, Aaron is degraded and dehumanized in another way. Planted chest-deep in earth, he is denied food and human succor. The horror of this punishment lies partly with its denial of bodily needs. The Moor is treated as a carcass before he is dead, already half planted in earth, suspended between life and death. But like the treatment of the "tiger" Tamora's body, the horror of Aaron's fate also stems simply from exclusion from human community. Denied funeral rites, Tamora's body is devoured by beasts and birds; denied human aid, Aaron will linger on the interface between the living and the dead, the sentient and the insentient, with no relief or human approach permitted. (Writing this, I think about the black men and boys, shot by police, whose bleeding bodies, dead or alive, no one is allowed to approach). Meanwhile, Titus, Lavinia, and even the Emperor are all entombed in their family monuments, returned in death to the noble social positions their prior actions in some cases had threatened to forfeit. In death they are allowed the privilege of their class and their race. Aaron *has* no such privilege.

I am not speaking in this paper about *intentions* or about *blame*. Rather, I am looking at the logic of representation and plot. Often isolated as the only racialized black figures in their plays, the Mulys and Aarons of the early modern dramatic repertoire are overwhelmingly defined by a somatic difference that obliterates their apparent class standing and connects them with what is *low, base, bestial, illegitimate, beyond humanity's embrace*. This is how structural racism works. It is what causes a white policeman to keep a black man in a chokehold even when that black man says: "I can't breathe."

Othello, that great test case for racial thinking, seems an exception to much of what I have written here. Othello has a noble lineage: by his own account he derives his "life and being / From men of royal siege" (1.2.21–2). Within Venice Othello initially has a privileged place. He is a much respected general, Venice's bulwark against the Ottoman Turks, a man the equal of the Senators by whom he is summoned in the play's first act and at whose tables he has eaten. Though black, he seems a man whose class privilege is a secure marker of his identity: he is "the noble Moor," denominated as such by Desdemona, Lodovico, and even Iago—his nobleness a marker of elevated status and of a generous and gentle temperament.

Yet the frequent repetition of the epithet "the Moor," starting on the play's title page where Othello is identified as "The Moor of Venice," signals a homogenization of identity around blackness. Moreover, from the play's opening scene, some in Venice make that blackness synonymous with baseness and the bestial. Iago, as is widely recognized, releases the sewage of racial degradation into the play's environment. Othello is bestialized, reduced in Iago's rhetoric to an "old black ram" (1.1.87) "a Barbary horse" (1.1.110), and in Roderigo's to a "lascivious Moor" (1.1.124). Yet he is not alone. Scratch a Senator and similar thoughts erupt, as is revealed when Brabantio, who had once honored Othello as a guest in his house, now finds him repugnant when imagined as a son-in-law. The great tragedy of the play, and also its genius, is its depiction of the process by which the initially confident general, "noble Othello," begins to see himself in the terms vividly articulated by the play's acknowledged racists—as old, as black, as unworthy—a self-perception the pain of which is materially rendered when this great general falls to the ground in a seizure that temporarily renders him mute, deaf, immobile. The play vividly renders the horror of self-doubt that a racist culture can induce. The play's only black figure, Othello must absorb ever-more-blatant insinuations that he is ignorant and understands nothing about the woman he has married and the culture of which he believes himself a part. Utterly disoriented, Othello erupts into behavior that has nothing to do with his essentially "base" nature and everything to do with the effects of his social situation.

Nonetheless, as generations of critics have observed, the play represents its tragic hero's downfall in a particularly humiliating fashion. At every turn, Othello is rendered low, starting with his position as the comic butt of Iago's clever deceptions. The comic substructures of the play (the supposed cuckolding of an old man by a young wife and the duping of a master by a clever servant) implicitly lower Othello's social position. He is rendered a fool, doubting actuality and believing imaginary scenarios of seduction and infidelity. His racialization is inseparable from his imbrication in the low genres of comedy and farce. Under Iago's orchestration,

Othello cannot tell his wife from a whore, Cassio from an adulterer, Emilia from a bawd, a villain from his trusty lieutenant. In the bedroom where he has strangled his wife, Othello's misprisions are denounced by Emilia in terms that strip him of all dignity: "O gull, O dolt, / As ignorant as dirt!" (5.2.159–60). The astonishing entirety with which Othello has been led to misunderstand everything allows Emilia to describe him in language usually reserved for doltish clowns. Other indignities accumulate. In his deranged and deluded state, Othello strikes Desdemona in public, thereby removing himself from the rank of honorable men, and after Iago's evil has finally been revealed to him, Othello cannot manage to kill his antagonist.

That Othello in death is accorded Cassio's acknowledgment that "he was great of heart" (5.2.359) and that he recovers sufficiently to manage his own death are signs that Shakespeare was not content to leave Othello, as Aaron was left, outside human community. In an heroic effort of self-assertion, Othello both passes judgment on himself and attempts to re-narrate his life outside the terms in which Iago has cast it. That he cannot do so simply means that the deep racism that from the beginning has put Othello in peril continues to affect the very words he uses to construct his life story. Mobilizing the opposition of turbaned Turk and noble Venetian, Othello can only elevate himself as the latter by denigrating the former, the uncircumcised Turkish dog, and repudiating all affiliation with this racialized outsider. The baseness of the racialized subject position persists in Othello's language, denying class, status, and dignity to those who occupy it, forcing them into company with the toad, the fly, and the dog. To answer Aaron's question directly, on the early modern stage, black *is* the basest hue.

The Race of Shakespeare's Mind

Lara Bovilsky

For a good poet's made, as well as born;
And such wert thou. Look how the father's face
Lives in his issue, even so, the race

Of Shakespeare's mind and manners brightly shines
In his well-turned, and true-filed lines.

> "To the memory of my beloved,
> The Author, Mr. William Shakespeare,
> and what he hath left us"
> BEN JONSON

"The race of Shakespeare's mind": Ben Jonson's turn of phrase can still startle us. For modern readers, Jonson's link between all that seems individual and immaterial in "mind" and all that seems collective and material in "race" may appear almost paradoxical.

The image's power to jar results in part from changes in the meanings of "race," changes that were in their infancy in 1623 and that registered consequential shifts in beliefs about, and treatment of, people collectively and newly understood as racial subjects. Today, we are unlikely to use the term "race" to mean—as Jonson does—"the offspring or posterity of a person" or a family or kindred lineage, descending from a common ancestor (*OED*, race, n.6, I.2.a and I.1.a). For Jonson, these would be familiar, if relatively recent, meanings of "race," usages first recorded in 1549 and 1547, respectively. But the extension of "race" from signaling offspring and kindred groups to evoking larger groups like "tribe, nation, or people" and thence to "a group of several tribes or peoples, regarded as forming a distinct ethnic set" (*OED*, race, n.6, I.1.b and I.1.c), usages first recorded just a generation or two later, in 1572 and 1612 respectively, depended upon a momentous, generalized cultural investment in ideals of descent. The wish that the child should "breed true" the father's appearance, mind, and manners would power a belief that, collectively, groups invariably reproduced material and immaterial traits. Members of "races" would be imagined as sharing lineage, and lineage assumed to entail inherited resemblances.

The outlines and many details of this larger history will be familiar to the readership of this volume. Early modernists and Shakespeareans have done excellent work recovering the histories and metaphorics of patriarchy and of race. We have not come as far in exploring the ties *between* period understandings of kin descent and race, and, in particular, in making vivid the emergence of modern understandings of race out of understandings of rank or "degree," crudely equivalent to modern "class" and denoting social position based on lineage. Early modern understandings of degree presumed a theory of material and immaterial inherited group distinctions, including beliefs that differences of color, blood, spirit, value, and virtue distinguished people of different degrees. That is, race as we know it and class in Shakespeare's time possessed strongly similar conceptual features: we have not fully recovered this sense of degree and its ties to and transformation into race. Such work has been well begun by Jonathan Goldberg, Jean Feerick, and others, generally building on Michel Foucault's argument (mounted in *Il faut défendre la société*) that modern racial distinctions and tensions emerged from intra-European social and political distinctions and tensions. I will briefly expand on their work, focusing on the racial metaphorics of degree. Jonson's lines about Shakespeare and Shakespeare's own *The Winter's Tale* illustrate the powerful longings behind the period's hopes that descent would make ancestors live in their descendants. In both texts, the distance between the hopes and realities of descent is productive for literature, even as the fictions of descent produce damaging, linked forms of class and racial antagonisms.

In its familiar lines, Jonson's elegy unexpectedly combines an idealizing theory of parenthood, in which the child preserves and presents the father's image, and Jonson's fiercely held theory of authorial identity: the writer must work hard and knowledgeably to achieve his distinctive and memorable art. The two theories might be thought to mix uneasily, as the former posits that selves are inherited from parents ("the father's face / Lives in his issue") and the latter—spelled out at length in the poem—emphasizes the responsibilities and fruits of self-making. Jonson evidently wants them to harmonize in a kind of Lamarckian collaboration that privileges the father's self-making over the child's. This is more easily done when discussing Shakespeare's writing, in which the offspring are plays and poems fully shaped by their human parent, than when relating stories of human children, in whom paternal investments and representations are not so easily realized. Shakespeare's lines, we would assume, say only what he wishes.

Even within a single family, the fantasy of filial replication of the father stumbles (for a start) on the reality that the father is not the sole parent. (Logical stutters and halts come even more quickly when assuming uniformity within an entire clan, degree, or race, with their heterogeneous and often discontinuous lineages.) Importantly, too, lack of resemblance does not preclude true paternity. Here, the beautiful phrase, "the race of Shakespeare's mind," readily evokes Shakespeare's characteristic diction, style, characterization, and plotting. These are the "mind and manners" we hope reveal Shakespeare's parentage. Only more slowly do we recall the myriad debates over attribution, authorship, and canonicity of lines and passages that have arisen from differences of opinion about how "brightly" resemblance "shines" between William Shakespeare and the contents of his "complete works."

Resemblance and paternity, will, then, vary with the beholder. The desire that their link will be unbreachable is painful in its habitual refutation: repeatedly in Shakespeare, fathers respond to filial willfulness by bitterly punishing what they see as a lack of resemblance to themselves in the child's "mind and manners." In an elegant inversion of Jonson's optimistic observation, "Look how the father's face / Lives in his issue," the fathers' punishments regularly feature a denial of consanguinity that upholds the larger wish: there will be no paternity without resemblance. In this spirit, in *The Winter's Tale*, an outraged Polixenes responds to Florizel's "unfilial" insistence on marrying below his degree by renouncing their blood tie: "Mark your divorce, young sir, / Whom son I dare not call. Thou art too base / To be acknowledged ... we'll ... Not hold thee of our blood, no, not our kin" (4.4.411, 4.4.422–35). As this example suggests, no act is so likely to provoke lineal disowning as the child's threat to breach distinctions of birth in marriage.

In denying actual consanguinity, Polixenes's rewriting of lineal ties implicitly acknowledges that the culture's ideals of descent rely on and produce fictions. The early modern system of degree conflated social and natural distinctions in precisely the same terms that would propagate belief in racial distinctions, and it is no great distance in *The Winter's Tale* from class to race. Witness Florizel's attempts to overwrite Perdita's presumed low degree with praise of her pale and tender "hand / As soft as dove's down and as white as it" (4.4.367–8). The language of whiteness that will later resonate with fully racial discourse here attests class logics: like a noble's, Perdita's hand is unhardened by labor and untanned by the sun. As though claims for such purely noble whiteness cannot be sustained, Florizel immediately drafts racial discourse into his defense of Perdita: her hand is also "as white as ... Ethiopian's tooth, or the fanned snow that's bolted / By th' northern blasts twice o'er" (4.4.368–70). The whiteness of the Ethiopian's tooth uncomfortably alludes to Perdita's origins—her "breeding" among humble folk that sets off her virtues, as the period thought Ethiopian skin set off white teeth—and inevitably suggests limits to her transcendence, just as the African's admired teeth and dark skin belong to a single person. Florizel will later admit these limits when he cannot forbear similarly contrasting her distance from her origins with his own high birth: "She's as forward of her breeding as / She is i'th' rear our birth" (4.4.585–6). His invocation of the dark skin that glancingly both allegorizes and literalizes her low degree is perhaps nervously displaced geographically by his third comparison of the white hand to a coldly chaste symbol of refined purity, that of the twice-"bolted" (sifted) northern snow.

Shakespeare's sense of the overlap of race, class, and descent is clearest in Camillo and Florizel's choice to represent Perdita as the Princess of Libya to her unknowing father in Sicily. Shakespeare sets up a troubling equivalence here between Perdita's two false identities: as a paragon of low Bohemian birth and as a member of North African royalty, with African race again figuring low degree. Evidently, racial and class differences function as equivalent representations of birth deemed unsuitable. But to support Perdita's final turn as Princess of Sicily, the play once again calls upon parental resemblance: Perdita's "majesty … in resemblance of [her] mother; [and …] affection of nobleness … proclaim her with all certainty to be the king's daughter" (5.2.35–8). Even so, these romance transformations of shepherdess to Libyan or Sicilian princess are "so like an old tale that the verity of it is in strong suspicion" (5.2.28–9). No matter how well-turned and true-filed offspring may be, the resemblance that confirms descent in Shakespeare's mind is subject to wishful thinking, to the stories we tell about distance, difference, and sameness.

Speaking of Race

Ian Smith

The matter of speaking race is central to Othello's well-known penultimate speech that begins, "Soft you, a word or two before you go" (5.2.336) and ends with his suicide by stabbing. While this particular speech is often read as the expression of a divided self—an internal clash between the "turbanned Turk" and "Venetian" (5.2.351–2)—I would emphasize Othello's stated chief concern: "Speak of me as I am" (5.2.340). Finally grasping the horror of Iago's deception that has led to Desdemona's murder, Othello wants the world to know the full complexity of "these unlucky deeds" (5.2.339). Othello is, in effect, sensitive not just to the fact of murder that casts him in the recognizable role of reckless black killer, like Aaron his stage predecessor, but also to the perception that the black, racial stereotype of being "easily jealous" was the precipitating factor in his behavior. Additional references to himself as "the base Indian" (5.2.345) or the embodied, tear-dropping "Arabian trees" (5.2.348) multiply images of otherness to suggest how steeped Othello's language is in racial self-awareness. Official letters recounting the events will be dispatched to the Venetian hierarchy, but Othello's attendant concerns about racial stereotyping and his perceived loyalty to Venice leave him doubtful regarding the final impressions and judgments to be made. The uncertainty driving Othello's forthright request for an explanatory report of his actions is, therefore, the matter of a possibly unreliable narrator. That is, among his white, Christian auditors, whom can he trust to tell his story or speak of him in a fair, balanced way? Who among them is sufficiently free of racial bias, stemming from stereotyping, that will allow for just representation? Moreover, Othello's appeal, "Speak of me as I am," also constitutes a metadramatic invitation to audiences, readers, and literary critics alike, and recent events have illuminated further the challenges contingent on such a demand.

The fiction of a postracial America, in which race no longer matters, was abruptly exposed in the aftermath of the fatal shooting of an unarmed black teenager, Michael Brown, by a white police officer in Ferguson, Missouri on August 9, 2014. Brown's fatality, at that time the latest in a series of similar homicides, sparked nationwide, headline-grabbing protests for months and fueled wide-ranging debates about anti-black bias, state violence, and social justice. Just days earlier John Crawford III was shot and killed mistakenly in a retail store by law enforcement, and three weeks prior Eric Garner died at the hands of yet another police officer using an illegal chokehold. The months that followed saw the names Akai Gurley and that of twelve-year-old Tamir Rice added to that list of black males killed by white policemen under highly irregular circumstances. A grand jury's failure to indict the officer involved in the Brown killing further inflamed public passions, strained municipal relations, and exacerbated national perceptions of police brutality. Among the most striking findings, however, was the significant difference in the public reaction to the conversations generated around these killings, a split predicated on racial perception. On August 18, 2014, the Pew Research Center reported that, "By about four-to-one (80 percent to 18 percent), African Americans say the shooting in Ferguson raises important issues about race that merit discussion. By contrast, whites, by 47 percent to 37 percent, say the issue of race is getting more attention than it deserves." In another poll published August 25, 2014, the numbers concerning trust in the police authority show a similar divergence: "There are substantial differences in the confidence that blacks and whites have in their local police forces. For instance, whites are twice as likely as blacks to express at least a fair amount of confidence in police officers in their communities to treat blacks and whites equally (72 percent of whites vs. 36 percent of blacks)." The public's ability to speak coherently of the string of black male homicides is undermined by the fundamental racial disjunction that Othello intuits.

The troubling undercurrent to the killings is the specter of a long, shameful history of white violence and abused and slain black bodies from slavery through the Jim Crow era. It is no wonder, then, that the public response, on both sides, has been visceral, given this visitation in the form of media reports and images of a haunting history revived. The racial gap in the poll numbers attests to what Charles W. Mills in his book *The Racial Contract* (1997) identifies as the investment of a white polity seeking to maintain the security of its social and political interests through a forced agreement between races: "it is a contract between those categorized as white *over* the nonwhites, who are thus the objects rather than the subjects of the agreement." Sustaining this project of inequality, Mills explains, requires firm white denial and constant misinterpretation, arguably the mental strategies underpinning the results in the Pew polls' racial discrepancies: "One has to learn to see the world wrongly, but with the assurance that this set of mistaken perceptions will be validated by white epistemic authority." Pioneering research conducted over the past decade in the field of social psychology also corroborates the disparities in the polls' stark racial findings. In *Blindspot* (2013), Mahzarin R. Banaji and Anthony G. Greenwald have found that almost 75 percent of those tested showed "automatic White preference," and conclude that, "White preference is pervasive in American society" consistent with "racially discriminatory behavior." Additional work by other researchers on perceived black aggression and the tendency for whites to misread objects associated with blacks as weapons fills out an unstable racial picture.

Literary scholars are not immune to the cultural biases within white hegemony; as subjects working and writing under the historical and cultural influences just described, it would be nearly impossible not to be affected. Thus the pertinence and urgency of Othello's request must be restated as a major disciplinary concern. In the current state of American society, how might literary scholars reliably and responsibly tell Othello's story or, more broadly, speak and write about race? And, given race's deep historical roots, it does not appear that the subject can be avoided altogether—nor should it be. I am reminded, in fact, of Toni Morrison's insightful critique in *Playing in the Dark* (1992) about reading, American fiction, and white racial hegemony, where she suggested that readers are co-opted by the very project of reading and thus "positioned as white." With *Othello*, Shakespeare has made a brilliant and productive countermove. While the play examines a compromised black man, Shakespeare, right at the end, shifts the onus away from Othello and places it on the spectators, readers, and literary critics, challenging our own compromised abilities to speak reliably of Othello. Critics who have notoriously read Othello's end as the inevitable relapse of an innately savage black man have failed to understand or have resisted the play's dialogic demand for racial self-inquiry. Speaking of Othello, speaking about race within the discipline, requires unpacking one's white positioning, which includes making whiteness visible and an object for critical interrogation; checking privilege; and exposing the denials and misinterpretations that, too often, keep race a minority issue and race studies a faddish or questionable enterprise in the era of so-called postracial enlightenment.

Further, speaking race means positioning whiteness in relation to other social identities and classes, exchanging exceptionality for the collective solidarity of coalition building. Rather than preserve whiteness as a protected category, one understands and accepts the shared intersectional interests that speaking race requires. Framing the black killings within a renewed vision of the civil rights movement for contemporary America, the hip-hop artist and actor Common, having renounced homophobia in his own lyrics in 2007, reflects in a recent speech: "I realize I am the hopeful black woman who was denied her right to vote; I am the caring white supporter killed on the front lines of freedom; I am the unarmed black kid who maybe needed a hand but instead was given a bullet; I am the two fallen police officers, murdered in the line of duty." Speaking race enlightened by a profound intersectional identity and awareness can do justice to Othello's request, "Speak of me as I am," and inform our disciplinary endeavors as responsible, reliable scholars working in a real twenty-first century world of change for Shakespeare in our time.

8

Sources

Shakespeare and the Bible

Robert S. Miola

The closest a Shakespearean character comes to mentioning the Bible by name is a comment by the redoubtable Dr. Caius, who declares Sir Hugh Evans saved from imminent death at his hands because "He has pray his Pible well" (*Merry Wives*, 2.3.6–7). Other characters mention the Bible as a book for swearing on or (under different names) for mockery or unholy purposes: Queen Margaret sneers that King Henry's weapons are the "holy saws of sacred writ" (*Henry VI, Part 2*, 1.3.59). To the jealous, Iago gleefully proclaims, trifles light as air are strong "As proofs of holy writ" (*Othello*, 3.3.325–7). Richard clothes his naked villainy with "odd old ends, stol'n forth of Holy Writ"; he uses "a piece of scripture" to tell his enemies that God bids us do good for evil (*Richard III*, 1.3.336, 333). As if thinking of Richard, Antonio in *Merchant of Venice* appropriately warns that "The devil can cite Scripture for his purpose" (1.3.94). The Clown in *Hamlet* mentions "Scripture" twice (F, 5.1.36). In *Cymbeline* Imogen's metaphor for Posthumus's betrayal evokes contemporary theological polemic while turning out to be truer than she imagines: "The scriptures of the loyal Leonatus, / All turn'd to heresy?" (3.4.82–3). Suborning the murderers of Banquo, Macbeth asks: "Are you so gospell'd / To pray for this good man, and for his issue, / Whose heavy hand hath bowed you to the grave, / And beggared yours for ever?"

(3.1.89–92). This cynical dismissal of Christ's injunction to love one's enemies (Lk. 6:27-8; Mt. 5:44; Geneva 1599 for all Biblical references, unless otherwise noted) comes from the man who has murdered his kinsman and king and wonders why he cannot say "Amen."

Such allusions arise from the availability of translations like the Geneva and Bishops' Bibles, both of which Shakespeare used, and the shared cultural heritage of the Church of England, its Book of Common Prayer, liturgies, homilies, and readings. The Bible, its stories, and its language passed into common currency of knowing, thinking, speaking, and writing by ubiquitous reference, allusion, quotation, proverb, ballad, hymn, broadside, treatise, polemic, pictorial representation (in tapestry, stained glass, painting, and sculpture), mediation, and circulation. This ubiquity makes possible in Shakespeare and other early modern dramatists sustained allusion as well as glancing effects and surprising inversions, both comic and sinister.

On this quadricentenary anniversary, what have we learned about Shakespeare and the Bible? Early commentators such as Sir Frederick Beilby Watson (1752), like those on Shakespeare's use of classical antiquity, counted allusions and compiled parallel passages. Victorians such as Thomas Eaton (1858), Charles Wordsworth (1864), and G. Q. Colton (1888) produced lists of verbal echo, as did Thomas Carter (1905), Richmond Noble (1935), and others. This approach culminated in the labors of Naseeb Shaheen (1999), who took into account various translations of the Bible as well as prayer books, homilies, and non-Scriptural sources. This substantial body of work (Shaheen's book is over 800 pages) does not support partisan claims for Shakespeare's adherence to any religion but ably catalogs linguistic points of contact, certain and spurious, probable and possible.

These points of contact resound everywhere in Shakespeare as distant echoes. Characters often mention creation, the pains of hell, woman as the weaker vessel, the dead as worm's food or meat, the flood, the cross, the Last Judgment, the pitch that defiles, and so on. Such expressions ultimately trace back to the Bible but appear as fully naturalized elements of the language rather than as specific allusions. The same holds true for mention of various biblical names—Jesus (23 times), Christ (9 excluding related forms, "Christian," "Christendom," etc.), Mary (4, referring to the Biblical character, but not including the derived form "Marry" in popular oath), Satan (8), Adam (15), and Eve (7). More intriguing, perhaps, are the soundings of less familiar Biblical names throughout the canon: Noah, Sampson, Solomon, Laban, Jacob, Daniel, Pharaoh, Bel's priests, Judas, Job, Japhet, Herod, Jezebel, Beelzebub, Lucifer, Judas (Iscariot and Maccabeus), Golgotha, Lazarus, Jephthah, Cain, Abel, Achitophel, and others. These suggest more conscious remembrance and allusion, though other sources often influence and intermediate. Mystery play cycles at Coventry and elsewhere, for example, brought to life some of these characters (Cain, Noah, Herod, Judas). The York Cycle, and no contemporary Bible, furnished Judas's "All hail" greeting, which Shakespeare twice recalls (*Henry VI, Part 3*, 5.7.33–4; *Richard II*, 4.1.170–1). Neither Judges 11.30–40, nor the account in the Elizabethan homily "Against Swearing and Perjury" supplies the allusion to Jephthah and his daughter, but instead a once-popular but now forgotten ballad does, from which Hamlet quotes four lines (2.2.339–56). Since most Protestant Bibles did not include the books of the Maccabees, Shakespeare probably drew upon the tradition of the "Nine Worthies" or other sources for Holofernes's impersonation of Judas Maccabeus (*Love's Labour's Lost*, 5.2.582–625), whom the onstage characters cruelly mock as Judas Iscariot.

Such instances of naturalization and intermediation notwithstanding, Shakespeare's work certainly shows evidence of direct contact with the Bible. Shaheen counts 120 echoes of Psalms alone in the canon. The Psalms appeared in the popular Psalter, sung daily during morning and evening prayer, and students probably memorized them at school. Twice characters object to singing Psalms inappropriately, to tunes such as "Greensleeves" (*Merry Wives*, 2.1.54–6) or to hornpipes (*Winter's Tale*, 4.3.43–5). Falstaff refers to weavers (often Protestants from the Low Countries) singing psalms (*Henry IV, Part 1*, 2.4.126–7), and Justice Shallow recalls Psalm 89:48: "Death, as the Psalmist saith, is certain to all, all shall die" (*Henry IV, Part 2*, 3.2.36–7). Misremembering Marlowe's "The Passionate Shepherd to his Love," Sir Hugh Evans mispronounces the famous opening line of Psalm 137 (Sternhold Hopkins version), "Whenas I sat in Pabylon" (*Merry Wives*, 3.1.23). Two psalms echo in classical settings to express the anguish of imagined cuckoldry. Leontes recasts the jubilation of Psalm 28.8 ("Therefore my heart danceth for joy," Coverdale translation) into "My heart dances, / But not for joy, not joy" (*Winter's Tale*, 1.2.110–11). And Antony recalls "the bulls of Bashan" from the sonorous desolation of Psalm 22 ("My God, My God . . . why hast thou forsaken me?" Coverdale translation): "O that I were / Upon the hill of Basan, to outroar / The horned herd!" (*Antony and Cleopatra*, 3.13.131–3).

A psalm reference of another kind altogether in a classical text is a Messenger's teasing mention of psalteries, here meaning not books of psalms but stringed instruments: "The trumpets, sackbuts, psalteries and fifes, / Tabors and cymbals" (*Coriolanus*, 5.4.50–1). The Messenger here echoes the herald in Daniel 3.5, "the cornet, trumpet, harp, sackbut, psaltery, dulcimer, and all instruments of music." This odd reminiscence in ancient Rome illustrates the way Biblical phrases often appear in far-removed contexts. Supposedly from Theseus's Athens, Bottom comically misconstrues 1 Corinthians 2.9: "The eye of man hath not heard, the ear of man hath not seen, man's hand is not able to taste, his tongue to conceive, nor his heart to report" (*Midsummer Night's Dream*, 4.1.209–12). Ulysses's exclamation to Ajax—"Praise him that got thee, she that gave thee suck" (*Troilus and Cressida*, 2.3.235)— recalls the woman's cry to Jesus: "Blessed is the womb that bare thee, and the paps which thou hast sucked" (Lk. 11.27). In the same play Pandarus more suggestively adapts the Biblical phrase "generation of vipers" (Mt. 23.33; cf. 3.7, 12.34, Lk. 3.7) in his rhetorical question, "Is love a generation of vipers?" (3.1.127–8). *Antony and Cleopatra* recalls Revelation in its "new heaven, new earth" (1.1.17; Rev. 21.1), "whore" and "kings o'th' earth" (3.6.68–9; Rev. 17:1–2), stars falling into the abysm of hell (3.13.150–2; Rev. 9.1), and Cleopatra's rhapsodic praise of Antony as one whose face was like the sun and voice as thunder (5.2.78–85; Rev. 10.1–5). Beyond the re-appropriated phrase, *Henry V* features two instances of more extended and self-conscious quotation. Canterbury cites the only book of the Bible mentioned as such in Shakespeare:

> For in the Book of Numbers is it writ,
> "When the man dies, let the inheritance
> Descend unto the daughter."
>
> (1.2.98–100; Numbers 27.8)

And the Dauphin quotes almost exactly the standard French Protestant version of 2 Peter 2.22: *Le chien est retourné à son propre vomissement, et la truie lavée au bourbier* (3.7.65–6, The dog is returned to his own vomit, and the washed sow to the mire).

Tracking indirect echo or direct quotation does have certain limitations. The Bible functions not merely as a verbal source but as myth, as the great ur-text of sacred stories and of Christian redemption. Consequently, echoes and allusions stretch beyond their linguistic markers to shape in nonverbal ways action, character, and theme. Many imaginative studies of individual plays, as well as the more comprehensive attempts of Stephen Marx (2000), Piero Boitani (2009), and Hannibal Hamlin (2013), take this approach to explore Shakespeare's subtle and sustained encounters with the Bible.

Of such encounters Richard II most self-consciously fashions his story after Christ's betrayal and death. Shakespeare frames the elaborate self-dramatization by having Bolingbroke speak of washing "blood / From off my hands" (3.1.5–6) in public before and after the murder (5.6.50). Richard himself supplies the Biblical gloss:

> Though some of you, with Pilate, wash your hands,
> Showing an outward pity, yet you Pilates
> Have here delivered me to my sour cross,
> And water cannot wash away your sin.
>
> (4.1.239–42)

Hearing of the betrayal of Bushy, Bagot, and Green, Richard exclaims: "Three Judases, each one thrice worse than Judas!" (3.2.132). Dethroned, Richard again declares himself more grievously betrayed than Christ:

> Did they not sometime cry 'All hail' to me?
> So Judas did to Christ, but He in twelve
> Found truth in all but one; I, in twelve thousand, none.
>
> (4.1.170–2)

Alone, he speaks Christ's words, paraphrasing two Gospel passages: "Come, little ones," and "'It is as hard to come as for a camel / To thread the postern of a small needle's eye'" (5.5.16–17; Mk. 10.14-25). Though Carlisle predicts that the land shall be called

"Golgotha" (4.1.145), no one onstage or off can accept this presumptuous self-fashioning. Richard's egotism, self-pity, and pretension, more theatre than theology, expose the very flaws that led to his downfall. Shakespeare may hint at the colossal irony of Richard's self-identification with Christ by having him echo the devil in Matthew 8.29, whom Christ cast out: "Fiend, thou torments me ere I come to hell!" (4.1.270).

This irony is more comic than tragic in the *Henry IV* plays, where Falstaff often uses Biblical phrasing and Scriptural allusion. Before he met the Prince, he protests, he "knew nothing" but now is "little better than one of the wicked" (*Part 1*, 1.2.90–1). After the Gad's Hill episode he more directly evokes the Fall to excuse himself: "Thou knowest in the state of innocency Adam fell, and what should poor Jack Falstaff do in the days of villainy?" (3.3.163–5). Falstaff mentions knowing a tree by its fruit (2.4.415–17; Lk. 6:44), "Pharaoh's lean kine" (2.4.461; Gen. 41.1, 3), Achitophel (*Part 2*, 1.2.35; 2 Sam. 16), and finally, as the Hostess reports of his dying words, "the Whore of Babylon" (*Henry V*, 2.3.36–7; Rev. 17.5). He declares himself "as poor as Job ... but not so patient" (*Henry IV, Part 2*, 1.2.125). Three times he alludes to the parable of Lazarus and the rich man (Lk. 16.19–31), first, to envision Dives (the rich man) burning in hell (*Part 1*, 3.3.31–3), then to compare his ragged army to Lazarus, "where the glutton's dogs licked his sores" (4.2.25–6), and finally to excoriate Bardolph: "Let him be damned like the glutton! Pray God his tongue be hotter!" (*Part 2*, 1.2.34–5). Damning his drinking companion to hell for misuse of money and gluttony, Falstaff summarily condemns himself. Twice he evokes one of Shakespeare's favorite parables, the Prodigal Son (Luke 15:11–31), once to describe his army as "a hundred and fifty tattered prodigals lately come from swine-keeping, from eating draff and husks" (*Part 1*, 4.2.33–5), and later to recommend to the Host a tapestry depicting "the story of the Prodigal" (*Part 2*, 2.1.142–3). These evocations resonate in the play, which deeply reworks Prodigal Son dramatic traditions in the story of the King and madcap Prince Hal.

Of the many possible Biblical echoes and allusions in *Hamlet* (Shaheen discusses over seventy passages), references to Genesis and Matthew most hauntingly resound. Claudius confesses the regicide as fratricide, as a reenactment of Cain's murder of Abel:

O, my offence is rank: it smells to heaven;
It hath the primal eldest curse upon't—
A brother's murder.

(3.3.36–8)

That curse spreads to all Denmark: the Edenic orchard in which
Claudius murdered his brother becomes an unweeded garden,
possessed by things rank and gross in nature. Hamlet again recalls
this primal sin as he comes upon a skull in the graveyard: "How
the knave jowls it to the ground, as if 'twere Cain's jawbone, that
did the first murder" (5.1.72–3). These Biblical echoes enlarge
the political murder into a mythic transgression. The Gravedigger
rings a humorous change on this enlargement, defending his claim
that Adam was a gentleman because he "bore arms" (i.e. a coat
of arms): "What, art a heathen? How dost thou understand the
Scripture. The Scripture says Adam digged. Could he dig without
arms?" (F, 5.1.33–5). The punning constitutes the punch line and
wittily parodies literalistic exegesis; the references to Adam and the
digging evoke the penalty of the Fall, replayed in Denmark where
sin again brings death into the world, and all our woe.

The bleak allusions to the Old Testament and the human
condition find a kind of answer in Hamlet's extraordinary recol-
lection of the New Testament when he accepts the fateful invitation
to duel with Laertes:

There is special providence in the fall of a sparrow. If it be, 'tis
not to come. If it be not to come, it will be now. If it be not now,
yet it will come. The readiness is all.

(5.2.197–200)

Compare Matthew 10.29: "Are not two sparrows sold for a
farthing, and one of them shall not fall on the ground without your
Father?" Christ's metaphor for God's loving care of his creation
here introduces the mesmerizing cadences that betoken faith and
serenity in every eventuality. The words sound surprisingly in the
mouth of Hamlet, the revenger who admired Pyrrhus, roasted in
wrath and fire, who declared himself ready to drink hot blood;
they move him beyond his predecessors and deepen the profound
ambivalence of his action. Is the killing of Claudius finally bloody
vengeance or faithful cooperation with the divine plan?

The sophisticated and fluent juxtaposition of Old and New Testament passages constitutes a governing artistic principle in *Measure for Measure*, the only play of Shakespeare to allude directly to the Bible in its title. In the closing moments of the play, Angelo confesses his crimes and begs for "sequent death" (5.1.370). Ordering him to marry Mariana and then go to execution, the Duke utters climactically the titular phrase:

> An Angelo for Claudio; death for death.
> Haste still pays haste, and leisure answers leisure;
> Like doth quit like, and Measure still for Measure.
>
> (5.1.407–9)

Here the Duke evokes the Old Testament *lex talionis*, "an eye for an eye and a tooth for a tooth" (see Exod. 21.23-5; Lev. 24.17-21; Deut. 19.21). However theatrically satisfying, this threat does not illustrate the Old Testament justice it pretends to: the Duke and audience know that Claudio lives and there is no measure to be re-measured. But the phrasing evokes also New Testament passages that warn against judging others and predict the return of judgments upon the judges, "For with what judgment ye judge, ye shall be judged, and with what measure ye mete, it shall be measured unto you again" (Mt. 7.2; cf. Mk. 4.24, Lk. 6.38). This moment in the play enacts this return of judgment upon Angelo, now facing the same harshly retributive justice and penalty he levied upon Claudio. But in the same instant, the underlying New Testament passages raise serious questions about the Duke as judge. How can his neglect and abnegation of rule, his disguise as a cleric and hearing of confession, his lie to Isabella about her brother's death, his grand assumption of moral superiority in the end, all exempt him from judgment, from returning measures? Contemporary commentators on the New Testament passage could not agree on who should mete out the requisite measure, the earthly magistrate or God. The play raises that crucial indecision to a higher level of urgent questioning.

Francis Bacon famously commented: "Revenge is a kind of wild justice, which the more man's nature runs to, the more ought law to weed it out" ("Of Revenge"). In *Measure for Measure* the law that weeds out revenge is the law of mercy, phrased in resonantly New Testament terms as the "remedy" by Isabella the postulant:

Why, all the souls that were, were forfeit once,
And He that might the vantage best have took
Found out the remedy. How would you be
If He, which is the top of judgement, should
But judge you as you are? O, think on that,
And mercy then will breathe within your lips,
Like man new made.

(2.2.73–9)

The play turns these very words back on Isabella, measure for measure, when Mariana begs her to plead for the life of the man she thinks has executed her brother. Isabella's gracious plea for Angelo's pardon shows that mercy is a divine gift that sometimes costs humans not less than everything.

On this quadricentenary celebration, where might we go from here? One promising direction is the study of Biblical reception, the examination of how preceding ages understood, translated, glossed, inflected, and transformed the ancient languages and stories. Among our classical colleagues, reception studies now flourish and enrich the field. Biblical reception study will return early modern scholars to patristics as well as to medieval and early modern appropriations and in turn bring new gifts to the study of literature, including Shakespeare.

Shakespeare's Sources

Ania Loomba

In Shakespeare studies, as in literary studies more generally, the relationship between the text and its sources has fueled charged debates about the purpose, formal properties, and politics of art. Rather than something that distilled and transcended its sources, the literary text began to be understood as existing in a similar plane and in dialogue with other historical and cultural materials. It thereby became a source in itself—a source for understanding history and culture. For self-avowedly political critics, to think about literature thus was to expand its contours and importance, while for their opponents, this approach devalued the unique properties of literary utterance. During these debates it became clearer than ever before that source studies, like other aspects of literary critique, are far from ideologically innocent.

Nowhere was this more evident than when issues of race and colonialism began to be raised. Could early modern images of Native Americans be considered sources for *The Tempest*, and would admitting them as such ignore or devalue the play's formal properties, reducing it to a text "reeking of the discourse of colonialism," as Jonathan Bate put in his 1977 book *The Genius of Shakespeare*? Or was it the case, as postcolonial critics argued, that to attend to New World and other early colonial materials was in fact to engage with the linguistic and formal properties of the play *more* deeply, and to be *less* moralistic than those who held the former position?

These earlier debates continue to haunt contemporary critical controversies over the limits and shortcomings of historicism (especially New Historicism), the resurgence of a new formalism, and calls to practice "surface reading" and abandon the "hermeneutics of suspicion" towards the literary text. In relation to early modern sexualities, for example, it has been suggested that the literary critic can trace the play of fantasy and desire only if she unshackles herself from historicism, which necessarily works to reinforce a heteronormative view of the past. For those of us who work on questions of race and colonialism in premodern Europe, ignoring history in the name of recovering fantasy is simply impossible. We have had to battle entrenched historiographies, but also to question dominant readings of fantasy itself. It is the literary text in all its literariness (its rhetoric, its fantasies, its margins) that has alerted us to what is occluded in dominant historiography, and inspired us to expand and reinterpret the historical archive, and to reorient our gaze on literary history. This may be one reason why literary critics have been central to the study of premodern racial ideologies and geopolitics in early modern Europe.

The Shakespearean text has been a particularly fertile ground for such work, allowing a constant rethinking of both our concepts and the archives, sometimes becoming a source for thinking about race, and sometimes leading us to new sources. Thus, for example, a long critical history that ignored the blackness of Othello was propped up by a sanctioned ignorance of the historical archives which were rich with evidence of a considerable black presence in

England, as well as widespread English contact with black people abroad. Early revisionist readings drew attention to Geoffrey Whitney's *A Choice of Emblemes* (1586), which showed two white men washing a black man alongside a poem that reiterated the futility of battling against the power of Nature and trying to whiten the "blackamore." Such images contested M. R. Ridley's influential assertion that Othello, even if dark-skinned, could not possibly have been conceived by Shakespeare as a "veritable negro." As *Othello* criticism reinterpreted history and text in tandem, the "sources" for the play expanded dramatically to include early modern travel documents, such as George Best's *A True Discourse of the Late Voyages of Discovery, for the Finding of a Passage to Cathay by the Northwest* (1578), which claimed that black men's intercourse with white women would result in black offspring; Queen Elizabeth's edicts expelling "blackamoors" from England; and English slaver John Hawkins's crest showing a shackled slave.

But the next decade saw yet another major rethinking of both text and its sources. In the opening scene of *Othello*, Brabantio responds to Roderigo's hysterical images of miscegenation by confessing that even before he received the news about Othello stealing his daughter, he had anticipated some such event: "This accident is not unlike my dream, / Belief of it oppresses me already" (1.1.140–1). Even as Brabantio "loved" Othello and "oft invited" him to his house, he harbored fears that his daughter might be stolen from him by such a stranger. But did he imagine that this theft would involve a "black ram" with a "sooty bosom," or did his fantasy center around the figure of a "malignant and turbanned Turk," a "circumcised dog" who threatens not just individual Venetians but the Venetian state (5.2.351–3)? Both sets of images are used to describe Othello and establish his difference from Christian Venetians. In establishing Othello as black, critics had downplayed the other—and historically prior—meaning of the word Moor—a Muslim. Cinthio's *Gli Hecatommithi* (1545), long acknowledged as a source for the play, had pointed in this direction, depicting the disastrous marriage of a Venetian lady to a jealous and murderous Moorish captain. Similar stories circulated in English books such as William Painter's *The Palace of Pleasure* (1566) and Richard Knolles's *Historie of the Turks* (1603) and proliferated as the Ottoman Empire expanded its borders. Turkish harems were reputed to be filled with beautiful Christian girls. But

England's mercantile ambitions nevertheless compelled its subjects to "traffick" with Muslims; as many traders and pirates converted to Islam, English preachers railed against Christians who "turned Turk." *Othello* repeatedly evokes the possibilities of such conversions, even as its hero is one who appears to have turned in the other direction, towards Christian civility.

The play compels us to take a second look at contemporary writings on blackness, which, it turns out, are often about faith as well. Some twenty years earlier than Whitney, Thomas Palmer's *Two Hundred Poosees* (1565) had also depicted two white men washing a black man in vain. In this case the accompanying poem warned that the stubborn "heart of heretics" is black and impossible to wash clean. The image harked back to a medieval tradition in which Saracens and Jews were described as metaphorically and often literally black. Whereas in these earlier texts religious conversions could result in a whitening of the skin, early modern writings underlined the impossibility of whitening an "Ethiopian," a "Man of Inde," or a "blackamoor" by comparing blackness to the inflexible nature of unbelievers. Like the term "Moor" itself, which could mean Muslim and black, Shakespeare's play indicates that the intersecting histories of religious and somatic difference have together shaped ideologies of race.

But even as medieval and early modern writings depicted religious difference in somatic terms, they made much of the *differences* between North African Muslims and supposedly faithless sub-Saharan blacks. Leo Africanus, a convert to Christianity himself, detailed these in an influential history of Africa that was translated into English four years before Shakespeare wrote *Othello*. Like Othello, Africanus draws a distinction between himself and the savages he has encountered, admiringly describing the possessiveness of North Africans who need to see a bloody napkin as evidence of a bride's virginity, and contrasting them with Negroes who keep harlots in common. He suggests a necessary contradiction between dark skin and civility, which also resonates with Shakespeare's play. But *Othello* also *fuses* these two sets of differences, offering us a "Moorish" alterity that indicates the messiness of racial ideologies that draw, often contradictorily, upon popular beliefs, elite ideas, older histories of difference and newer global relations. It reminds us that the burgeoning African slave trade, the Spanish expulsion of Moors and Jews, Ottoman imperial expansion, English mercantilism, and imperial ambition were coterminous, and their histories need to be understood as interconnected.

Finally, *Othello* also alerts us to a longer literary history. The romances between Christian women and Moorish men have shaped European literature since the Crusades, including *The Song of Roland*, *Parzival*, *The King of Tars and the Soudan of Damas*, and Chaucer's *Man of Lawe's Tale*. Whether or not we include such texts as sources for the play, they are certainly crucial resources for understanding the history of race. As Joan Scott once observed in relation to feminist work, fantasy can become a critically useful tool for historical analysis.

I have suggested why the study of race demands an expansion of what we think of as the proper sources for literary study, and why, at the same time, literary writing allows us to retheorize race and rethink the histories of global contact. In this mutual cross-fertilization, the literary text emerges as valuable precisely because it is the repository of histories, ideologies, and fantasies, and because it demands that we read it with both pleasure and suspicion.

Volver, or Coming Back

Sarah Beckwith

The measure of the worth of a play is that we return to it. What Coleridge said about poems is true of plays.

I have been teaching a new Shakespeare class recently under the loose and capacious rubric "Shakespeare Now and Then." Most of the materials we study are versions of *The Winter's Tale*, beginning with one source, Robert Greene's *Pandosto*. Eric Rohmer's beautiful film, *Conte d'hiver* (1992) is an evident homage to Shakespeare's play. We watch Félicie watching the animation of the statue as a performance that confirms and helps articulate her self-understanding. George Eliot's *Daniel Deronda* (1876) features the statue scene in *The Winter's Tale*. But the other films and novels we examine, such as Jane Austen's lovely and late novel, *Persuasion* (1818), or the Dardennes Brothers' haunting film, *L'enfant* (2005), and Pedro Almodóvar's scintillating melodramas, *Talk to Her*

(2002) and *Volver* (2006), never explicitly reference Shakespeare's play. But they are Winter's Tales: that is my claim. They share the promise and the terror of those words that sound the idea of return, (coming back, *volver*), recovery, renewal, but too remembrance, repentance, resurrection, remorse, recognition, redemption. They are all books of second chances. When read together they mutually illuminate each other, interweaving the themes of childhood, forgiveness, remarriage, the role of art, and the relation between the past and the present. To our class *The Winter's Tale* seemed so deep and generative in these works that source, influence, analogue, adaptation, homage, or re-creation gave way to words such as: incarnation, resurrection, echo, haunting.

In philology source is distinguished from influence. Source was supposed to be determinate. In the compendious and welcoming pages of Geoffrey Bullough's *Narrative and Dramatic Sources of Shakespeare* we could distinguish a source from an influence by tracing direct minings, citations, copyings, and outright plunderings. The sources helped us to see the contours of writerly intention. When Shakespeare, unlike Plutarch, makes Caesar deaf; when in Shakespeare, not Plutarch, Cinna is mobbed and murdered even when it is established he is not the poet; when he adapts Plutarch to create a world love-sick for Cleopatra, Shakespeare's Rome or Egypt come into view as places where authority is vulnerable, where crowds are sometimes inchoate, and where Cleopatra creates new laws of attraction that will dislimn the world. Yet we also distinguish a source from an analogue. An analogue provides a similar story but it is not clear to whom the story belongs. The analogue is not "sourced"; it has no copyright. No one seems to own it, yet everyone is telling it. Influence is disastrously woolly from the philologist's point of view, and how much more so in a writer so porous to his surroundings, so generative of new worlds, whose nature is subdued to what it works in, like the dyer's hand.

So *The Winter's Tale* returns in the work of a filmmaker who cannot be said to be consciously quoting him and yet who sounds Shakespearean themes of *revenance* and return, remorse and forgiveness. Almodóvar and Shakespeare in *Volver* and *The Winter's Tale* tell winter's tales as old wives' tales and redeem the power of stories and the community of women who create the very conditions of the stories' inheritance, their issue.

Neither *The Winter's Tale* nor *Volver* is exactly a ghost story, though both tease us with ghostliness, and in both works the putative ghosts need to come back, for the past is not dead and buried. Hermione's ghost appears to Antigonus in a dream more like a waking (3.3.16–18). Her specter is conjured by Paulina and Hermione when they agree that Leontes should not marry again lest Hermione's "sainted spirit" again possess her corpse (5.1.57). Hermione is metaphorically dead, turned to stone by Leontes who has mortified her. But Hermione in her flesh and blood, with her history of Leontes' harm, might be more difficult to confront than a ghost. In both Shakespeare and Almodóvar, it is the medium of art (the statue, the flamenco song "Volver"), not ghosts, that allows the deep damages of Leontes's jealousy and perversion of justice, of Irene's ignorance and neglect of her daughter's abuse, to be confronted and forgiven.

The scene that grants the film its title features the luminous Penèlope Cruz as Raimunda lip-syncing the tango song *Volver* sung by Estrella Morente, a song that tells of the great difficulty of keeping open a simple hope that a love can be refound after even twenty years. Raimunda sings a song her grandmother taught her to her daughter Paula, who has never heard her sing. (That she has not done so is a measure of the harshness and difficulty of Raimunda's life. So the song is a vehicle of a returning joy.) In the car her mother, Irene, presumed dead, and who has not yet "appeared" to Raimunda, hides and cries at her daughter's song. She is estranged from her daughter, who has withdrawn from her in her adolescence. We later find out that this is because her mother, unaware of her father's abuse, failed to protect Raimunda, who has carried his child, Paula, also, then, her half-sister. Irene is herself presumed dead, having set light to the house in which she finds her husband and his lover (Agustina's mother) in a deep, postcoital sleep. The incident of the fire ties together the disappearance of Agustina's mother, Irene, and her husband's death.

The women of the village (Alcanfor de las Infantas) have "sighted her," but they presume Irene is a ghost. Their superstitions both shield her from discovery and make possible her return. Though she farts, works out on an exercise bicycle, and needs help to get out of the back of Solé's car, so she can clearly not pass through walls, Solé and young Paula simply accept her return without fussing about whether she is a ghost or not. Her unfinished business is with Raimunda. Irene has returned to ask forgiveness of her daughter, for she discovered only on the day of the fire the terrible harm suffered by Raimunda at the hands of her father. The disappearances and burials of the past that estrange the women from each other are thus excavated gradually through the care and kindness the women show to each other.

House-cleaning, keeping house, is brilliantly imaged as tidying up the men, sometimes quite literally as Raimunda cleans up the blood young Paula has spilt in defending herself from Paco, who has repeated history by trying to rape her. The film begins in a stunning tracking shot of the village women sweeping the graves of their family and their own future graves (their second homes) in the mistral wind.

In each work a woman (Hermione, Irene) who is ambiguously a ghost returns and becomes flesh and blood. The ability of the statue to assume life, for Hermione to take the risk of return, as for Irene to "appear" to Raimunda, is predicated on the full, open-hearted acknowledgment of the other, which means acknowledgments of the particular harms visited on Hermione, on Raimunda. "Whilst I remember / Her and her virtues, I cannot forget / My blemishes in them, and so still think of / The wrong I did myself" (5.1.6–9). Each return is predicated on the necessary, yet insufficient, superstition and the necessary, sufficient, hopes and faith of the women. "It is required / You do awake your faith" (5.3.94–5) says Paulina as she leads Leontes and his party to the statue of Hermione. Solé will only tell Raimunda about Irene's return when she has extracted her promise that she will credit her story. Irene's return is "covered" by the superstition of the village women who believe in ghosts and so accept her return, and by her nurturing of old Paula till she dies.

In each case the women have reasons for vanishing and reasons for coming back from a past not yet settled. Irene returns to Solé, but her appearance to Raimunda is long delayed. Irene was angry with her daughter and felt rejected and unloved. Her own pain blinded her to her daughter's pain and this made her daughter seem unreal to her. The process of assuming flesh and blood, of taking on reality, existence, is in both works a slow process of forgiveness and acceptance by which mother and daughter, husband and wife, can accept each other again.

Irene announces herself through her signature farts. The daughters smell her before they see her. This is Almodóvar's comic and visceral return of the flesh and blood mother, an insuppressible piece of wind, the past's comical mistral. Ghosts don't fart. They don't need someone to open a trunk to get out of a car. Irene moves from ghostliness to reality as she is accepted in relations of forgiveness.

Perhaps *The Winter's Tale* and some of its haunting "versions" provide us with a new vocabulary for source study: echoes, hauntings, resurrections, as it gives us a new vocabulary for imagining the return of the past in the present. In so doing the stories of women are given their due place.

9

Text and Authorship

Collaboration 2016

Gary Taylor

Only Shakespeare, that lad unparalleled, our myriad-minded one-of-a-kind, could have written *that*. Haven't we all, happily or guiltily, been struck by Shakespeare's singularity at one time or another (even when it was politically or professionally incorrect to do so)? At other times, though, we have to talk ourselves into believing that Shakespeare wrote something. For most of the twentieth century, Shakespeareans talked themselves into believing that he wrote every word of the thirty-seven plays that had been canonical since the eighteenth century. The evidence that some of those plays were cowritten by other playwrights was dismissed as "The Disintegration of Shakespeare," a heresy labeled and discredited by that great British bureaucrat of orthodoxy, E. K. Chambers, in his 1924 British Academy lecture. Half a century later, in 1974, even Chambers's doubts about *Timon of Athens, Pericles, Henry VI, Part 1*, and *Henry VIII* were ignored by the Riverside Shakespeare. But by 2016 it has become apparent that anywhere from a quarter to a third of Shakespeare's plays contain material written by other professional playwrights. And even those numbers underestimate the pervasiveness of collaboration in the Shakespeare canon.

Why this radical change in the consensus about collaboration? And what does it mean for our reading, performing, editing, and teaching of Shakespeare and his collaborators?

The radical change was powered by the convergence of three apparently unrelated developments: the increasing academic legitimacy of theatrical approaches to Shakespeare's work, the theoretical and historical challenge to Kantian ideals of authorship, and the development of digital databases, statistical linguistic analysis, and empiricist approaches to the arts generally, and to attribution scholarship particularly.

Resistance to the mono-authorship monopoly began on the critical and geographical periphery, in studies of Massinger, Beaumont and Fletcher, and Middleton. New Zealander MacDonald P. Jackson, who began investigating authorship in the unfavorable climate of the 1960s, has done more than any other scholar, over half a century, to transform the field, and he is now the world's most experienced, influential, and widely admired attribution specialist (and also the most modest). In the mid-1980s, the Oxford Shakespeare's emphasis on his plays as scripts for performance included a synthesis and endorsement of much neglected scholarship on collaboration. Those claims were, at the time, resisted by many traditional literary scholars, including Brian Vickers. But in 2002 Vickers himself produced a monumental—and fiercely polemical—summary of earlier, calmer scholarship on Shakespeare as "co-author." Meanwhile, in a French part of the critical forest, Barthes, Derrida, and Foucault pioneered another kind of disintegration, not of Shakespeare but of the Kantian aesthetic of the disinterested author producing an organically unified work of art. Two other Frenchmen, Lucien Febvre and Henri-Jean Martin, in *The Coming of the Book* (1958) inaugurated the emergence of book history as a discipline that redefined authorship in an evolving relation to machines, capitalism, and the commodity market. Assumptions about authorship have changed over time, and we have learned to historicize earlier claims about attribution. John Jowett's "Disintegration, 1924," for example, situates Chambers's influential lecture within the social, scientific, and educational policy debates of the 1920s.

Even on an island, no man is an island, and no early modern acting company satisfied Kant's criteria for disinterested artistic activity. We never experience Shakespeare in isolation from collaborators, living or dead. Lukas Erne describes editors as "Shakespeare's Modern Collaborators," and Diana Henderson characterizes modern adaptations of Shakespeare's work in fiction,

film, and performance as "Collaborations with the Past." Insofar
as Shakespeare wrote for the theatre, he wrote for shareholders,
performers, composers, patrons, censors, and for the owners,
controllers, and audiences of particular venues, all with their
own agendas. Even Shakespeare's poems survive for us only
because of the collaborative work of printers and publishers,
or the scribes and compilers of manuscript miscellanies. It is an
axiom of book history that authors do not make books. Books
are material objects created by specialist craftsmen. Shakespeare
was never a member of the Company of Stationers: the texts of his
playbooks and poetry books that we read and interpret are objects
produced by anonymous compositors, pressmen, and proofreaders.
Three pages of *Sir Thomas More*, written by what paleographers
identify as "Hand D," preserve—in the opinion of most, but not
all, specialists—Shakespeare's own handwriting: his trained hand
touched those pages and applied the ink that formed those marks
on that paper. But those pages belong to a profoundly and pervasively collaborative document, and even Hand D's three pages have
themselves been overwritten by someone else ("Hand C"). What
Hand D and Hand C wrote may also incorporate material from
the lost original version of that scene, written by Anthony Munday
or Henry Chettle.

Nevertheless, this collaborative milieu needs to be separated
from the solitary executive act of formulating strings of hundreds
or thousands of words, and putting them down on paper, for the
first time. Jeffrey Knapp's *Shakespeare Only* (2009) demonstrates
that most plays were always written by a single playwright, and that
single authorship was the norm for Shakespeare, too; Will Sharpe,
"Framing Shakespeare's Collaborative Authorship" (2014), establishes that most of Shakespeare's plays and poems were originally
written solo, and that even in the collaborative plays Shakespeare
usually wrote more than his partner poets. Gabriel Egan reminds
us of "What is Not Collaborative About Early Modern Drama in
Performance and Print?" (2014). The most important and most
common "not collaborative" activity of the early modern professional theatre was writing new scripts. Shakespeare, in particular,
seems to have escaped from his collaborative London life regularly,
for trips to Stratford, and for all we know he might have written
most of his plays there. Certainly, there must have been times
when Shakespeare was the only person in a room, alone with

his thoughts, composing a complete poem or speech or scene or entire play script that, in our legal world, would be regarded as his personal intellectual property.

But, in our legal world, much of what Shakespeare wrote "alone" would be condemned as an appropriation of someone else's intellectual labor. Even in solitude, sharpening his own penknife, Shakespeare carried in his memory song lyrics composed by other people, alongside proverbs and lines of poetry, and he recycled them all, without qualm or embarrassment, in his own writing, never acknowledging (as John Webster did in the quarto of *The Duchess of Malfi*) "the author disclaims this ditty to be his."

Shakespeare also had books by other people open in front of him, or stored in his memory. The National Theatre production of *The Curious Incident of the Dog in the Night-Time* won a record-breaking seven Olivier Awards in 2013, including "Best Play." Printed editions of that play, on both the front and back cover, identify the author as "Mark Haddon," and then add (below, in smaller and less conspicuous type) "adapted by Simon Stephens." Modern copyright law here recognizes the distinction between two kinds of writing: Haddon is responsible for the narrative, itself a best-selling and award-winning novel, and Stephens is responsible for adapting that story to the different genre and the different text technologies of theatrical performance.

If we applied modern notions of intellectual property and international copyright law to the works of Shakespeare, then we would have to recognize, on title pages and book covers, that *Othello* was "based on a story by Giovanni Battista Giraldi, or Cinzio, adapted by William Shakespeare." *Julius Caesar, Antony and Cleopatra,* and *Coriolanus* were "based on Plutarch's *Lives*, translated by Thomas North, adapted by Shakespeare"; *Henry V* and most of the other history plays were "based on Raphael Holinshed's *Chronicles,* adapted by Shakespeare." Perhaps most embarrassing of all, *The Winter's Tale* was "based on a story by Robert Greene, adapted by Shakespeare." Shakespeare also stole the feathers of other writers by incorporating passages from their work in his own texts. Both John Florio's translation of Montaigne and Arthur Golding's translation of Ovid are plagiarized in passages of *The Tempest*. In all these cases, Shakespeare adapted for the stage material in another medium by another writer. Cinzio, North, Holinshed, Greene, Golding, and Florio (or their heirs) would all be covered by modern copyright.

Shakespeare also adapted other men's plays. *Measure for Measure* adapts George Whetstone's *Promos and Cassandra,* and the subplot of *The Taming of the Shrew* adapts George Gascoigne's translation of Ludovico Ariosto's *I suppositi.* Shakespeare's *King John* demonstrably recycles the plot of *The Troublesome Reign of John, King of England,* possibly by George Peele, and certainly by someone other than Shakespeare. Even if copyright had existed in the sixteenth century, Plautus would have been in the public domain; nevertheless, *The Comedy of Errors,* like *A Funny Thing Happened on the Way to the Forum* (1962), is an English-language adaptation of Plautus, and owes most of its comedy to the Roman playwright. Shakespeare made an honest living stealing other men's work.

Shakespeare collaborated with the living and the dead. The word *collaboration* derives from the word *labor,* and co-laboring means "working with," implicitly working side by side. Our normal uses of the word presuppose an interactive social relationship. By contrast, Greene in *The Winter's Tale* was what Harold Love, in *Attributing Authorship,* called a "precursory author." Nevertheless, these many authorial precursors reveal three fundamental characteristics of Shakespeare's writing habits, which are all relevant to the texts he wrote in active collaboration with other professional playwrights.

First, much of what we label "Shakespeare," in lights on Broadway, broadcast from Hollywood, enshrined at Stratford-upon-Avon, or guarded in the underground bunkers of the Folger Shakespeare Library, is actually the creative work of other people. Second, Shakespeare co-opted other men's narratives because he recognized the value of a particular story, particular characters, particular passages, created by someone else; he had no difficulty cohabiting with another man's imagination. (And it was always the imagination of another *man,* not a woman.) Third, Shakespeare worked primarily by adapting an existing artifact.

In all these ways, Shakespeare's practice as a playwright belonged to the social world of the artisan and the workshop, a world of collaborative trial-and-error tinkering. Not the imaginary theocratic or autocratic black-and-white world of a single moment of divine creation (and the Lord said, let there be light, *Fiat Lux*) but a quieter evolutionary spectrum world: *Fiat Flux* (as Randall McLeod punningly puts it). The Romantic ideology of originality warps our perspective on early modern creativity. As I have argued at greater length in "Human Object" (originally delivered at a Shakespeare Association of America conference in 2008, not published until 2016), we need to look at the work of Shakespeare, Middleton, and other early modern playwrights as an expression of "artiginality": the creativity of artisans who tinker with inherited forms and stories.

Artisans are always collaborating with previous artisans, and this habit lends itself to other forms of interactive creativity. Tinkering can be done collaboratively, and so can thinking (as we acknowledge when we talk about "brainstorming"). Most modern collaborative writing—like *Some Like it Hot* and other screenplays by Billy Wilder and I. A. L. Diamond, or many of the songs of Lennon and McCartney—takes the form of two writers in a room together hammering out a text line by line: this is what Lennon called "eyeball-to-eyeball" collaboration. But the records of early modern scriptwriting suggest that the actual penning of speeches and scenes was done separately, in what psychologist James W. Pennebaker calls "lazy collaboration," which we might more neutrally describe as "structural" or "parceled" collaboration. These two kinds of collaborative writing produce strikingly different results, and the early modern norm makes it much easier to differentiate the work of the two (or more) authors of a cowritten play.

Easier, that is, if we use massive digital databases, reliable search software, consistently applied protocols, tests that have been proven to work with texts of known authorship, accurate statistics, objective prose, and ethical reporting. It may seem snarky to mention ethics, but deliberately falsified results have become an increasingly visible problem in the sciences, and there is no reason to believe that humanists are intrinsically more ethical than scientists. (Books on the philosophy of ethics are exceptionally likely to be stolen from academic libraries.) Even scrupulously honest scholars make mistakes, and all human brains are susceptible to cognitive error. Occasional spectacular failures, like Donald Foster's attribution of *A Funeral Elegy* to Shakespeare, should not surprise us, and Foster had the good sense and good grace to accept that his hypothesis had been disproven. Conclusions based on empirical methods should always be tested by other scholars, to see if the results can be replicated. For instance, Vickers's claim that

Peele wrote 4.1 of *Titus Andronicus* (2002) has been challenged by William Weber (2014) and Anna Pruitt (2016). In an evolving discipline, new tools can invalidate honest investigations based on old databases or old methods. And we shouldn't be surprised by disagreements between the advocates of opposing hypotheses. Empiricist disciplines evolve by a constant process of challenging and discarding weak theories (Taylor, "Empirical Middleton," 2014). We could wish that such disagreements were conducted with some civility, but there are bullies, blowhards, and lunatics in every human community.

Despite all these potential pitfalls, twenty-first-century empiricism is immeasurably more robust and objective than the fledgling attribution scholarship of the Victorians and Edwardians. Earlier studies of dramatic verse have been reconceptualized by Marina Tarlinskaja, and John Nance is discovering criteria for distinguishing Shakespeare's dramatic prose from that of his contemporaries. Pioneering digital humanists like John Burrows and Hugh Craig have confirmed many well-established hypotheses about Shakespeare's collaborations, developed a battery of new statistical techniques, and introduced traditional humanities scholars (like me) to new ways of visualizing linguistic patterns. In 2015 Douglas Bruster teamed up with an anthropologist, Genevieve Smith, to apply sophisticated statistical techniques for dating archeological objects to the chronology of the Shakespeare canon—which among other things provides new evidence for collaboration. Younger digital scholars are exploring new realms like "Nearest Shrunken Centroid" and "Random Forests" (Jack Elliott and Brett Hirsch, 2016), or demonstrating that standard data compression software can isolate idiosyncratic patterns of authorial repetition (Giuliano Pascucci, 2012 and 2016), or applying techniques developed in the social sciences to Shakespeare's unconscious stylistic habits (Boyd and Pennebaker, 2015).

As a result of this evolving coalition of theory, history, and big data, the major editions of Shakespeare's *Complete Works* in the twenty-first century have all acknowledged the importance of collaboration. The updated Oxford Shakespeare (2005) added *Edward III* to the canon. The RSC edition (2007) acknowledged George Peele's presence in *Titus Andronicus*—though its editor, Jonathan Bate, had summarily dismissed that possibility a decade before; Bate and his partner Eric Rasmussen later produced an entire volume of *Collaborative Plays* by "William Shakespeare and Others" (2013). The Arden Shakespeare included *Double Falsehood* for the first time (2010). The textual editors of the new Norton edition (2015), Suzanne Gossett and Gordon McMullan, are both well known for their exemplary editorial and critical work on collaborative plays. *The New Oxford Shakespeare* (2016) includes an entire companion volume of new research on *Shakespearian Authorship*.

We now know that any "Complete Works" of Shakespeare is also an anthology of selected work by Middleton, Fletcher, Marlowe, Peele, Nashe, Wilkins, and the "Anonymous" who was so important to the early English theatre from 1580 to 1594. This means that such editions offer teachers the opportunity to introduce students to many other instruments in the early modern orchestra. It also means that actors and directors have often, without knowing it, performed scenes by these other, less familiar playwrights—and that audiences, without knowing it, have often applauded and admired the work of those other playwrights. The interviews with theatre artists in the appendix to the Bate–Rasmussen edition of *Collaborative Plays* document this productive creative disorientation; so does Terri Bourus's essay on the differences between directing Fletcher and directing Shakespeare ("*Poner en escena*," 2013).

"Why did Shakespeare collaborate?" I asked in 2014. Shakespeare, unlike Jonson, recognized the *artistic value* of collaboration. Only Shakespeare could have written the great misanthropic tirades in the second half of *Timon of Athens*. But only Middleton, "our other Shakespeare," could have written half a dozen brilliantly satirical scenes in that play. We should not assume that soloist Shakespeare is always better than Shakespeare-in-company. Shakespeare indisputably wrote all of *Lucrece;* just as clearly, he did not write all of *Edward III*. But the collaborative play offers a less misogynistic, more interesting, modern, and imaginative retelling of the Lucrece myth: the story of a king's imperious sexual desire for the wife of one of his own subjects, and its political consequences. As William Poel recognized, Shakespeare's Countess of Salisbury scenes make a compelling one-act play. (They would make a great double bill with Middleton's equally succinct *Yorkshire Tragedy*.) If forced to choose, I would lose all 1,855 "tedious (though well-labored)" lines of *Lucrece* to gain the 834 lines of Shakespeare's two Countess of Salisbury scenes in *Edward III*. Shakespeare apparently thought so too: despite the commercial success of *Lucrece,* and the praise it earned him from contemporary academics and anthologists, immediately after its publication Shakespeare chose to abandon narrative poetry and commit himself instead to collaborative playmaking.

Did Shakespeare write the Additions to *The Spanish Tragedy*? Who were his collaborators on *Arden of Faversham, Edward III,* and some parts of the three *Henry VI* plays? How much of *Macbeth,* or *Measure for Measure,* did Middleton write? Did he (as Laurie Maguire and Emma Smith conjecture) author parts of *All's Well that Ends Well*? Did Shakespeare write the "fly scene" added to *Titus Andronicus* in 1623—and if not, who did? Can we identify, and strip away, the passages by Theobald (or Davenant) in *Double Falsehood*? Can we isolate, and authenticate, fragments of Fletcher and Shakespeare's original *History of Cardenio*?

Whatever the coming century's answers to those questions, they will alter the way that we understand Shakespeare's art, his biography, and the history of the early modern theatre. And those answers, whatever they are, will result from the collaboration of scholars with each other and with their evolving machines.

The Value of Stage Directions

Laurie Maguire

Stage directions have not been underused by textual critics in the past century but they have been valued for different reasons. For W. W. Greg in 1954, they were useful in assigning textual origin: discriminating among an author, playhouse personnel, and a reporter. E. A. J. Honigmann's interest in 1976 was editorial: how modern editors misinterpret or misplace stage directions. For Alan Dessen and Leslie Thomson, writing as theatre historians in 1999, stage directions offered a "theatrical vocabulary" (conventions shared by early modern playwrights, players, and audiences). Similarly, in the same year, Linda McJannet chronicled their "theatrical code."

Whereas Greg was interested in author versus non-author, Dessen and Thomson discriminate between different authors:

"Chapman is more likely than any other professional dramatist to use Latin terms, but it is Massinger who is particularly fond of '*exeunt praeter* ...' where another dramatist would use *manet.*" This moves the enquiry from theatrical vocabulary to authorship studies—a move possible because, as Dessen and Thomson explain, they assume that "most stage directions are authorial in origin." This logical assumption was also made by Greg because, although many stage directions are generic, many are not. Thus in 1999 McJannet could speak of a Munday "signature" in stage directions—"midscene directions for action expressed as phrases." It is R. V. Holdsworth, however, who has made the most detailed study of stage directions' usefulness in authorship studies, from his unpublished (but much consulted and cited) thesis of 1982 to recent articles. Stage directions, for instance, are one of several stylistic factors distinguishing the hand of Thomas Middleton from that of William Shakespeare in *Timon of Athens.*

"Here enters"

McJannet notes a "here" formula—"here enters"—in stage directions in *Henry VI, Part 2* [*sic*: actually *Henry VI, Part 1*] and *Henry IV, Part 1.* "Here" is not infrequent in texts of masques, where it is accompanied by past-tense description of action; this is a logical collocation when putting into print a one-off court performance. It is less logical in printed drama. Temporal-spatial markers ("then" and "here") occur throughout the Jacobethan period but are much more frequent in the texts of the early professional theatre in the 1580s and 1590s. The marker "here" occurs at the beginning of stage directions in only six Shakespeare plays: *Titus Andronicus* (once), *Richard II* (once), *Richard III* (twice), *Henry IV, Part 1* (four times), Q *Merry Wives of Windsor* (once), Q1 *Hamlet* (once). It occurs five times in *Henry VI, Part 1.* Noting this preponderance in *Henry VI, Part 1* and *Henry IV, Part 1*, McJannet calls them "exceptions" (i.e. exceptions to the Shakespearean norm). What she does not note is the concentration of examples in *Henry VI, Part 1*—all are in Act 1 (scenes 2, 3, and 4). This act is generally agreed to be non-Shakespearean, with Thomas Nashe one of the favorite candidates for authorship. In Nashe's *Summer's Last Will and Testament* we find nine stage directions beginning with "here."

Stage directions may thus add to other stylistic evidence for Nashe's contribution to *Henry VI, Part 1*. Holdsworth, who also notes this example, comments that "Little use has been made of stage directions in authorship studies of early modern plays" but reminds us that "in their form and diction, directions directing even the most standard kinds of action can differ sharply."

Point of view

Here are two entrance directions in *Tamburlaine, Part 1* (1597):

To the battaile, and Mycetes comes out alone

(B6v, 2.4.0)

Sound trumpets to the battell, and he runs in.

(B7v, 2.4.41)

Where is "out"? Where is "in"? A modern playwright (and many early modern playwrights) would code these directions as *Enter Mycetes / Exit Mycetes*—which answers the question: "out" means onstage (he comes *out* of the tiring house) and "in" means backstage (he runs *into* the tiring house). (The out/in prepositions are retained in extensions such as "a bed thrust out" or "hallowing within.") The point of view is that of the audience. This out/in phrasing occurs in only two Marlowe texts, the other being *The Massacre at Paris* (although this text has not come directly from Marlowe's pen).

McJannet notes that the *Tamburlaine* directions are unusual in that they "reverse the usual prepositions": Mycetes "exits by running in." But unusual by what measure? Only by our expectations. They are not unusual by Elizabethan practice where the formula continues throughout the Jacobethan period: although it is eclipsed, it is never extinguished by the more standardized *enter* or *exit*, continuing to coexist with the Latin verbs, often in the same sentence: "Sacrepant ... *goes out* and his man *enters*" (Robert Greene, *Orlando Furioso*, 1594); "As the young princes *go out*, *enter* Tirill" (Thomas Heywood, *Edward IV, Part 1*, 1600; my italics).

Shakespeare infrequently uses out/in. "In" appears in Q1 *Romeo and Juliet* (1597) (*Nurse offers to goe in*, G2r; *Paris offers to go in*,

G2v), in *Richard II* (1597) (*The murderers rush in*, K1r) and in Q *Henry V* (1600) (*Enter* Flewellen *and beats them in*, C2v) where the same prepositions mean opposite things: "*Nurse offers to goe in*" means the Nurse offers to exit, whereas "*The murderers rush in*" means they enter. This linguistic duality collapses in on itself in *Sir Clyomon and Sir Clamydes* (1599) where an exit cue—"now come and follow after me"—is followed by the prima facie contradictory direction *Enter out*.

An unusual example in *Comedy of Errors* can tell us about the genesis of the Folio text: *Runne all out* at TLN 1445 is followed half a line later by *Exeunt omnes, as fast as may be, frighted*. The two directions, separated by four words cueing the exit ("Away, they'l kill us"), are duplicates, choreographing the same exit. Arden 2 combines the directions: [*They*] *run all out, as fast as may be, frighted*. Charles Whitworth's World's Classics edition explains how compositor B saw *Runne all out* in his MS copy, thought it to be a complete stage direction, then noticed the continuation and invented an expanded opening *Exeunt omnes* to accommodate it. Shakespeare's manuscript was the copy for this F text. Here we have an example of early Shakespeare using "out," a formula that he later drops or which has been edited out of the extant texts.

There are other ways in which stage directions can indicate authorial copy. In *King Lear*, 3.7 (the blinding of Gloucester), Q contains a stage direction for Regan to kill the mutinous servant: *Shee takes a sword and runs at him behind* (H2r). (For the same action, F offers the prosaically blunt *Killes him* [TLN 2155].) As Peter Blayney first pointed out, the Q SD is a perfect pentameter line and is thus unlikely to originate from other than an author's pen. This stage direction can be added to other textual details to make the case for authorial copy as underlying the Q text.

It was the unusual nature of the stage directions in *All's Well that Ends Well* that first drew the attention of Emma Smith and myself to this text's possible links with Thomas Middleton. The most distinctive is that at TLN 1089–90 (*Paroles and Lafew stay behind, commenting of this wedding*) but analogous directions abound: *Enter the King with divers yong Lords, taking leave for the Florentine warre* (TLN 594–5); *Enter one of the Frenchmen, with five or sixe other souldiers in ambush* (TLN 1911–12). The conventional explanation is that these indicate an author pausing, with a cue to himself about how to resume later—but other evidence suggests that he may be pausing to hand over to a collaborator and providing a cue for the collaborator.

The feature in *All's Well* of introducing characters with a generic or status marker in the stage direction and giving them a specific name in speech prefixes is akin to Middleton's practice. *All's Well* has *Enter Count Rossillion* followed by speech prefixes *Ber.* (TLN 1730ff.). In *Michaelmas Term* the stage direction provides an entrance for *Quomodoes wife* (C3v) but her subsequent speech prefix is *Toma.* (for her name, Thomasine). At the end of *Your Five Gallants* Katherine is instructed to enter as follows: *Enter the Virgin betweene two antient gentlemen.* (I2v); her speech prefix is *Kathe.*

Middleton is also unusually fond of appositive explanations in stage directions: *Enter Lussurioso, and Infesto two Lords* (*Phoenix* I2r); *Enter Vindici and Hippolito, Vindici in disguise to attend L. Lussurioso the Dukes sonne* (*Revenger's Tragedy* B2v); *Enter Misters* [*sic*] *Katherine with Fitzgraue a Gentleman* (*Your Five Gallants* B2r). It seems likely that the unusual stage direction at *All's Well* TLN 2601—*Enter a gentle Astringer.*—is a misreading of *a gentleman, a stranger* as the subsequent speech prefixes are *Gent.*; this speech prefix is more likely to be an abbreviation of a noun (*Gentleman*) than of an adjective (*gentle*). If so, the original stage direction, with its noun in apposition, is typical of Middleton.

Collectively, stage directions and speech prefixes invite renewed attention.

The Author Being Dead

Adam G. Hooks

The death of the author was announced by Thomas Walkley in 1622. In the first edition of *Othello*, which Walkley published that year, he noted the necessity of providing a prefatory epistle: "the Author being dead, I thought good to take that piece of worke vpon mee." Since Shakespeare had never contributed preliminary material to his printed plays, Walkley capitalized on the unfortunate, if convenient, condition of the author to advertise the book to customers. For Walkley, "the Authors name is sufficient to vent his worke"—that is, the title-page ascription "*Written by* William Shakespeare" would help ensure a profit. Shakespeare's death was both a matter of fact and a matter of business. The author was a function of the marketplace.

In Shakespeare studies, the death of the author was accomplished with a combination of post-structuralist theory and historicist investigation into the materiality of texts. By recovering the agencies and investments of Walkley and his fellow stationers, this work showed how the book trade created the concept of literary authorship. The value of an author and his work was defined in commercial rather than aesthetic terms; indeed, the latter were partly determined by the former. The material turn dispersed the traditional authority of Shakespeare. But the author has now once again returned: in approaches that define collaboration as a matter of individual agencies, in empirical attribution studies, and above all in attempts to infer Shakespeare's literary intentions from his bibliographic presence. These are powerfully appealing critical narratives because they claim Shakespeare's own authorization. We should remain skeptical, however, as this familiar version of authorship required the literal death of the author.

A year after Walkley published *Othello*, a more elaborate tribute to the dead author appeared, in the form of *Mr. William Shakespeares Comedies, Histories, & Tragedies*—the volume we now call the First Folio. In their dedicatory epistle, John Heminges and Henry Condell pledge that Shakespeare's plays will outlive him, "he not having the fate, common with some, to be exequutor to his owne writings." They have thus "done an office to the dead" by conflating Shakespeare's corpse and corpus, as they "humbly consecrate" his "remaines." Shakespeare is not simply embodied but also entombed in a book that both memorializes and revivifies him, as Ben Jonson claims in his memorial tribute. John Taylor "the Water Poet" had earlier, if more prosaically, made the same point: in praising the virtues of paper, made from nothing more than "rotten rags," he includes Shakespeare in the society of dead poets immortalized "in paper" who thus "Do liue in spight of death, and cannot die."

Confronted with the fact that Shakespeare never explicitly expressed a desire to see his plays in print, critics have conjectured that he was merely prevented from doing so by his death; or they have taken Heminges and Condell—colleagues in Shakespeare's theatre company who were remembered as "ffellowes" in his will—as proxies for the playwright's intentions. Yet the Shakespeare presented in the First Folio could only be a posthumous artifact. If the book is a replacement for the body, then immortality (in paper) demands mortality. What we need now is a posthumous criticism, one that reinterprets the connection between Shakespeare's life and his afterlives in print.

The intersection of Shakespearean bibliography and biography dates back to the beginning. Nicholas Rowe is credited with being the first critical editor of Shakespeare, and also the first biographer. Rowe was hired by the Tonson publishing house to edit *The Works of Mr. William Shakespear* (1709), advertised as "Revis'd and Corrected, with an Account of the Life and Writings of the Author." However idiosyncratic or inadequate Rowe's biography was, it inaugurated the modern biographical tradition, displacing an earlier reliance on what has been characterized as a mixture of bare antiquarian reporting and literary gossip. As an editor, Rowe's task was to attend to the text—and that is where he found his Shakespeare.

The collected works of Rowe and his editorial successors were in part a result of the Tonsons' attempt to maintain control over their valuable Shakespearean property within the newly instituted system of copyright—it was a publishing venture as much as a scholarly project—and so, paradoxically, it has caused us to neglect other approaches that defined Shakespeare through his books, rather than his texts. Starting half a century earlier, booksellers like Francis Kirkman compiled catalogs of all the plays "that were ever yet printed and published." These catalogs were the first sustained attempts to assemble a comprehensive bibliography of English printed drama and they led directly to the development of a kind of dramatic and biographical criticism rooted in the material basis of commercial artifacts. (W. W. Greg complained about his inaccuracies, but Kirkman was a New Bibliographer *avant la lettre*). The brief biographical notices of Shakespeare that appeared in the collections of William Winstanley (1687) and Gerard Langbaine (1691) were accompanied by lengthy lists of all the plays attributed to Shakespeare in print. Shakespeare's life was found not in his writings, but in his books.

The very same books were later enumerated and evaluated in *A Census of Shakespeare's Plays in Quarto 1594–1709* (1916), compiled by Alfred W. Pollard and Henrietta C. Bartlett. (Note that the date range of the census ends with Rowe's edition, thereby marking the end of one historical era and the beginning of another.) Pollard's introduction begins by defining the competing ways the quartos are valued: for their "intrinsic interest," and because they are "worth their weight in banknotes." Although Pollard claims that the quartos beyond the first editions are of no importance textually, they do indicate Shakespeare's popularity in the seventeenth century—and his appeal to subsequent collectors (including eighteenth-century editors) into the twentieth. But Pollard's inattention to, and even denigration of, the quartos themselves is ironically juxtaposed with his obsession with contemporary sale prices, as the introduction devolves into a kind of auction catalog.

At the tercentenary of Shakespeare's death, R. B. McKerrow outlined the prevailing bibliographic view in *Shakespeare's England: An Account of the Life & Manners of his Age* (1916). McKerrow lamented the sorry state of the early English book trade, which consisted of an "inferior class" of "tradesmen pure and simple, regarding their business solely from the point of view of immediate returns." Stationers such as Thomas Walkley likely would have agreed with the emphasis on "immediate returns," and may even have recognized the insulting epithets. McKerrow, like some early modern observers, objected to the way in which the book trade inverted systems of value: economics rather than ethics or aesthetics determined a book's worth.

It was Pollard more than anyone else who contributed to this characterization of the book trade (the lectures that would comprise *Shakespeare's Fight with the Pirates* [1917] were delivered in 1915). He divided the quartos into "good" and "bad," blaming "pirate" stationers for the latter. The profit motive ruled; they had no concern for the textual value of their products, or for the supposedly unethical means used to acquire and sell them. The New Bibliographers analyzed the material artifacts of Shakespeare's plays with greater detail than ever before, yet they condemned the business practices that produced those artifacts, while failing to question their own investment in a narrow conception of Shakespearean authorship. Shakespeare could not be held responsible for deficiencies in his texts—but "tradesmen pure and simple" certainly could.

The narrative has undoubtedly changed. We now embrace the multiple manifestations of Shakespearean texts. Instead of challenging the integrity of printers and publishers, we consider the "book" and the "play" (and "Shakespeare") as unstable entities produced within intersecting cultural and commercial networks. The new bibliography is "cultural bibliography," which aims to recover the ways in which all the agents involved in the production and circulation of texts made meaning out of Shakespeare. It also aims to demonstrate that historicist inquiry is a fundamentally interpretive practice. Scholars continue to discover (and to reconsider what constitutes) evidence; more importantly they continue to tell new stories, with an awareness of the motives that drive critical narratives.

The infamously interventionist editor Alexander Pope once said that Shakespeare "For gain, not glory, wing'd his roving flight / And grew Immortal in his own despight." His faults—particularly the errors found in the Folio—could thus be extenuated; the author was freed from imputation, and problems of textual transmission were blamed on other agents. Editorial methods would change radically, yet this fundamental belief remained. In more recent years, some have simply reversed the old orthodoxy: if Shakespeare's plays were valued by readers and playgoers—if they are good, and not bad—then Shakespeare himself must have made it so. We should not need to resurrect Shakespeare to authorize our own critical narratives. The condition of possibility for our familiar, powerful conception of Shakespearean authorship was Shakespeare's death. As we reflect on the anniversary of that death, and on his place in our time, we should let the author rest in peace.

10

Globalization

Against Our Own Ignorance

Susanne L. Wofford
President, SAA 2002–03

So many approaches to Global Shakespeare and globalization in Shakespeare have burgeoned in the past two decades that we now have a richer and often surprising picture of how Shakespeare has been drawn on in cultures around the world, sometimes to open a space for political or personal comment, sometimes to reinforce the educational goals of the colonial or even postcolonial project. These crucial ways in which globalization has animated our scholarship—studies of how the "global" emerged from the imperial, and now encompassing new ideas about global cosmopolitanism—have led to valuable interpretations of Shakespeare against and within complex cultural imperatives, creating a textured quality of the global inter-mixed with the English in how we read Shakespeare today.

Globalization might have meant many things to Shakespeare and his London contemporaries, including: encountering Ragusan and Arab traders on the docks of London; developing global trade routes; tensions, trade, and alliance with the powerful and wealthy Ottoman Empire; Christian captives converting to Islam; New World discovery and rivalries; the founding of the great corporate trading companies; xenophobia in tension with a cosmopolitan outreach to the world and a desire not to be insular; and growing access to exotic goods (such as the "mummy" that Othello refers to as the dye for his handkerchief). The power and impact of these complex interactions with the world beyond the borders of England transformed the literary and cultural productions of the period, as many scholars have demonstrated.

This essay will look instead at the "global" and "globalization" through the lens of our own ignorance, considering how a globalizing study of Shakespeare has revealed limitations in interpretation and an inability to understand issues that might have been clearer to Elizabethan audiences and readers than to Shakespeareans in more recent times. The development brought about by post-Cold War readings of the geography in Shakespeare's Mediterranean plays, for instance, has exposed a blindness or blankness in the interpretations of my generation (at least in the United States), a generation who encountered Shakespeare during a period in which much of Eastern Europe and Yugoslavia was inaccessible, even invisible, and much of the Arab world relatively unknown. I believe that we may have brought our own ignorance to the plays we read, projecting our lack of understanding onto Shakespeare and his contemporaries. It seems important, then, to ask what globalization was for early modern writers, and to be attuned to the way Shakespeare's plays are "global" productions that entwine the English and the foreign, creating a cosmopolitan English theatrical canon through importing words, emotions, plots, and ways of understanding from other cultures.

Illyria

In his great mapping project, *Theatre of the World* (*Theatrum Orbis Terrarum*) (1570 and after), Ortelius identified the eastern coastline of the Adriatic sea and the surrounding countryside as "Ilyricum," and maps of the period commonly marked "Illyria" or its Latin name along today's Croatian coastline, going significantly south of Dubrovnik. The Illyrians, as a seafaring trading people, were tributaries of the Ottoman Turk and competed with the Venetians, having been under Venetian control through the late medieval period. Illyrian Ragusa (present day Dubrovnik), a republic, paid tribute to the Ottomans and, after aiding the Spanish to build the Armada, reestablished relations with the English and sent trading ships to London. Understanding Illyria as a border space between the Ottoman Empire and the Western Christian world provides an interpretive lens for Shakespeare's *Twelfth Night,* linking it to other Mediterranean plays like *Othello*, the last four acts of which, set on Cyprus, take place in a similar border space between Christian and Turk. Indeed, after the dismemberment of Yugoslavia as a state, we today have a vivid sense of this area as a borderland between Catholic Christian (Croatian), Russian Orthodox Christian (Serbian), and Muslim (Bosnian) populations. This space is marked by the histories of empires in a concrete, localized, and tragic way: Bosnia being the farthest west that the Ottoman Turks reached in terms of geographic incorporation.

At the university level I encountered in a Shakespeare seminar a very different picture of Illyria. As Viola says when recovering after the shipwreck: "And what should I do in Illyria? / My brother he is in Elysium" (1.2.2–3). The common sounds of these two names and the strong genre markers of what we then called "romance" combined to suggest that Illyria was a fantasy place, a magical space somewhat like Oz with dangerous pirates (like Ragozine in *Measure for Measure*, named for Illyrian Ragusa) but fundamentally a place where desire and love can find fulfillment and where the faith that the dead can be recovered can be upheld. "Prove true, imagination" (3.4.372): that could happen in Illyria! And of course, this reading is right in many ways. After all, Illyria seems to be a place at which one arrives only by shipwreck, and it is a country where there are no parents, so the traditional blocking figures of comedy don't pose a problem. In this parentless country of song and festivity, the children of a gentleman who has died and apparently left his twins a fairly modest inheritance can end up marrying a Duke and a Countess. The Illyria of the play can feel like a romance place, colored by the sea and infused with the scent of wetness—where love "is all as hungry as the sea" (2.4.100), that slippery shapeless ocean of all the forms of imagination. Illyria indeed marks out a place where the theatrical imagination does prove true and desire can be fulfilled, and as such, it is a figure for the world created by theatre and for the power of dramatic fiction itself.

But Illyria was also was a geographical place well known to early modern writers and travelers—a trading partner with most countries and city-states that participated in Mediterranean trade, and located on that crucial border between the Ottomans and the Christians, a border that was pushed to its westernmost in 1571 with the Battle of Lepanto off the Gulf of Corinth in western Greece (near Illyria!). Latin Illyria, referred to by Ovid and a somewhat larger region than early modern Illyria, would also have been within an early modern geographical imagination. So the location or geographical meaning of Illyria would not likely have been obscure for Shakespeare, and an early modern audience would not have understood Illyria primarily as a utopian no-place. Seeing this geography in a post-Cold War light allows us now to recognize that the play connects this borderland quality to the power of theatre, theatre becoming an important border place itself.

Why was the understanding of the geography of the Mediterranean and Eastern European world brought to bear so rarely in the 1970s, at least in the United States? As a college student reading *Twelfth Night* for the first time my critical blindness to this rich geographical set of meanings mirrored a broader cultural blindness created by the Cold War. Many American scholars, especially those of us who had grown up after World War II and were coming to critical consciousness in the 1970s, were, I suspect, vague about the geographical boundaries and ethnic histories of the Balkans precisely because these were areas closed off and blocked from our experience. The lack of contact between countries and their peoples on either side of the "Iron Curtain" made our Western scholarship start out ill-informed in relation to what early modern audiences might have known and assumed of this part of the world. In other words, they may have been more "globalized" than we were, and we may have projected onto Shakespeare and his contemporaries an ignorance that was in fact our own.

This "not knowing"—marked by a blindness created by ideology and lack of knowledge—is what has begun to change as a desire to understand the global has become an urgent focus in Shakespeare studies. A series of works that came out in the 1990s and early 2000s (including John Gilles' *Shakespeare and the Geography of Difference*, 1994) started to give a very different picture. I take as an example *Shakespeare's Illyrias: Heterotopias, Identities, (Counter)histories* (2002), a volume edited by Martin Procházka, which emerged from a Seminar at the 7th World Shakespeare Congress in Valencia in 2001 in which the work of scholars from this region like Goran Stanivukovic were featured. Published as

Volume 32 of *Literaria Pragensis*, it was edited by a Czech scholar, featuring Bosnian and Croatian scholars along with writers from the US and UK. Shakespeareans had begun to think seriously about the meaning of the early modern Mediterranean, and the Valencia conference drew scholars interested in the ethnicities and submerged histories of this region.

A very different sense of the role of the Illyrian location is developed in Sulayman Al-Bassam's play *The Speaker's Progress*, which imagines a reenactment of *Twelfth Night* in the context of an Arab totalitarian kingdom, in the political present tense of a space neither inside nor outside of that regime—a theatre in another country where the "deep state" has its continuing presence in a surveillance recording camera and the mandates that authorize the performance. For the "Speaker" in this play, Illyria is partly a past when theatres were still open and performance was allowed, a past outside the boundary of the modern totalitarian Arab state. But as the play is set in the present tense in the theatre itself, in the very location of its audience, and intended to be spoken mostly in the language of its audiences (with the "envoys" speaking in Arabic, and the play mainly in English), it captures the doubleness of the border space of Illyria in *Twelfth Night*. The play's theatre marks a border of Arab and Western customs, and is set in two idioms, in the space between no performance being allowed and a performance that takes over.

In this theatre the Mullah who plays Malvolio's role leaves the stage having been whipped, as Shakespeare's revelers have become "the people," represented by the booted Young Woman whose heel, as a stage direction indicates, "marks the rhythm of the chant 'Al Sha'ab Yurid Isqat Al Nidham'—'the people demand the fall of the regime'—the signature slogan of the Arab popular uprisings." This reworking of *Twelfth Night* uses Shakespeare to comment on the politics of repression while simultaneously mounting a critique of *Twelfth Night* for coming too easily to a comic conclusion. Here in the Arab Shakespeare, the people's torture/revenge on the Mullah helps to create the very ending of the play, and the "new ending" brings neither romantic fulfillment nor easy liberation through art.

Al-Bassam's play thus opens up a dual space marking the border between modern secular theatre and Islamic values and practices, present tense performance and reenactment of the past, as a way of rethinking what Illyria as a borderland between Christian and

Ottoman might mean today. His play artistically embodies and "knows" that *Twelfth Night* mobilized theatre as this border space, and it uses a parallel symbolic geography to highlight the idea that theatre can occupy the border between cultures, between two kinds of politics, between the globalized opening and the local imperative.

Egypt, Cleopatra, and Isis: Shakespearean Globalization

Notions of "globalization" for Shakespeare also came from the past, especially from the cosmopolitanism of Greek and Roman Hellenistic letters, which suggested ways of understanding other cultures that focused on symmetries and congruencies of belief. We may have partially lost the capacity to see the world through this intercultural lens, available to an Elizabethan coming up through a grammar school education that taught Latin first and reminded the English writer of his marginality. Such engagement with the broader world of humanist and philosophical speculation about the religions and intellectual traditions of the "East" and especially Egypt would have come to Shakespeare in part through the ancient writers recently edited and translated, whose work reshaped the early modern intellectual world. Roman and Greek culture—and Hellenistic globalization and Alexandrian cosmopolitanism—were also foreign countries whose understandings Shakespeare incorporated into his own representation of the East and are part of what made up the "global" in his plays.

For audiences of *Antony and Cleopatra*, then, "the East" and "Egypt" might have been understood through the syncretism of Plutarch, so influential on Shakespeare especially in Sir Thomas North's 1579 translation of the *Lives*. When Antony admits to himself that "I'th' East my pleasure lies" (2.3.39), he not only suggests he will choose love and pleasure over Rome, but he reminds us of the Mark Antony of Plutarch's *Lives*, an Antony who was deeply associated with the East, who ruled the eastern part of the Roman Empire, who spent more than a decade receiving "divine honors" from the subject towns and cities of Lebanon, Syria, and the eastern Mediterranean, and who was associated with the Asiatic or the Eastern rhetorical style. Shakespeare also could have read Plutarch's extraordinary syncretic and imaginative rethinking of the myth of Isis and Osiris in his essay of that name, which was widely available in Latin and in French by the second half of the sixteenth century even before it was translated in 1603 into English by Philemon Holland. There Shakespeare would have encountered a multicultural internationalism and a method of respecting and adapting the myths of foreign cultures. Here Hellenistic globalized thought became the model for early humanist efforts to incorporate the classical non-Christian past:

> Whensoever therefore you shall heare the Aegyptians tell tales of the gods, to wit, of their vagarant and wandring perigrinations, or of their dismembrings, and other such like fabulous fictions, you must call to minde, that which we have before said; and never thinke that they meane any such thing is or hath beene done according to that litterall sense. ...

For Shakespeare, then, but perhaps not for modern Western Shakespeareans, Egypt was a place of sophistication, the center of Hellenistic culture and society, a place being interpreted through the lens of philosophy. This Hellenistic world available to Shakespeare in classical writing was doubled by a contemporary resonance, since Egypt was also a part of the Ottoman Empire, itself a sophisticated and tolerant culture.

So when we read of Cleopatra dressing as Isis and Antony as participating in this ritual, we can also read through the deeper lens of Hellenistic philosophy:

> I'th' market-place, on a tribunal silvered,
> Cleopatra and himself in chairs of gold
> Were publicly enthroned. [...]
>   She
> In th'habiliments of the goddess Isis
> That day appeared, and oft before gave audience,
> As 'tis reported, so.
>
> (3.6.3–5, 16–19)

Plutarch, himself a priest who officiated at Delphi, read Egyptian myth into Greek religion, seeing them as pointing to the same truths, and he interpreted the stories of the gods in Greece and Egypt as ways to understand the generative forces in the universe:

> They say also, that *Isis* (which is no other thing but generation) lieth with him; and so they name the Moone, Mother of the world; saying, that she is a double nature, male and female: female, in that she doth conceive and is replenished by the Sunne: and male, in this regard, that she sendeth forth and sprinkleth in the aire, the seeds and principles of generation.
>
> For *Isis* is the feminine part of nature, apt to receive all generation [...] yea and the common sort name her *Myrionymus*, which is as much to say, as having an infinite number of names, for that she receiveth all formes and shapes, according as it pleaseth that first reason to convert and turne her.

For Shakespeare, having a global perspective meant in part learning to use these myths in ways not consonant with his own culture's expectations about love, sexuality, fertility, or death. If Isis has an infinite number of names because "she receiveth all forms and shapes," perhaps we can understand better Cleopatra's "infinite variety": if "Age cannot wither her, nor custom stale / Her infinite variety" (2.2.245–6), it is in part because Cleopatra comes to embody larger forces that exceed her individual being—she is thus "Egypt" and "Isis" herself and not just Cleopatra. If these words also seem to capture an aspect of Shakespeare's writing itself, it may be because of his capacity to incorporate and remember (after the dismemberment) the globalized learning of the past as well as of his present moment.

A recent exhibit at NYU's Institute for the Study of the Ancient World, "When the Greeks Ruled Egypt," underlined the centrality of the myth of Isis and Osiris under the Ptolemies. Alexander, when he entered Egypt, had shown respect for Egyptian religion, and the Ptolemies, the family line of Cleopatra, strategically reinterpreted and appropriated Egyptian divinities, especially the Isis–Osiris–Horus triad. The synchretism of the Ptolemies allowed them to centralize power by appropriating Egyptian religious practice and myth, so that the rituals of Isis that Cleopatra enacted and that Plutarch described reflect what we might call the early practices of a kind of globalization, in this case a result of empire.

For Shakespeare, Egypt was a source of exotic practices and symbols that provided languages for a discussion of how fertility and generativity can reshape a human and a political narrative. *Antony and Cleopatra* is both a globalizing and an orientalist play, then, with Egypt as a sign of the exotic and the excessive, as well as a place of highly sophisticated and complex mythic traditions representing a globalized understanding of culture. Plutarch's uniting of Greek, Egyptian, and Near Eastern religions could be seen as just another form of imperial imposition—like Alexander appropriating local myths for his political purpose—but it arguably provided a model of cosmopolitanism for Shakespeare. These same questions—imperial/cultural domination versus cosmopolitanism—can be asked of the global today, since the same double-edged sword cuts through our modern moment of globalization.

Circumnavigation, Shakespeare, and the Origins of Globalization

Daniel Vitkus

Until the early modern period, the *global* as a concept existed as a *geometrical* notion, not a *geopolitical* one. In the English language, early usages of the word "globe" referred to small-scale physical objects. After 1492, Europeans and non-Europeans eventually "discovered" that the lands forming the Western and Eastern hemispheres were part of one planetary globe. This new geography allowed for the mapping of imperial and commercial desires onto a circumscribable planet. Elizabeth I appears in the famous "Armada Portrait" with her right hand resting on a globe, her royal fingers tracing a desire for imperial expansion over the Americas, as if her commanding gaze could direct the same English ships that defeated the Spanish in 1588 to traverse and conquer that globe at will. During the early seventeenth century, writers began using the word "globe" to describe the objects that were spherical representations of the earth, and to designate the material form of the earth itself.

In Shakespeare's day, the English were not yet an imperial power on the scale of the Portuguese or Spanish empires, but they were ambitious to overtake and surpass their European rivals. On August 10, 1519, the Portuguese explorer Fernão de Magalhães (aka Magellan) had set sail from Spain with same goal as Columbus:

to find a new, westward route to the Indies. Magellan's voyage would not have taken place without Christopher de Haro, a Flemish financier representing the Austrian Fuggers, who loaned the money to Magellan's patron, Carlos V of Spain, at a very high interest rate. After Magellan's death in the Philippines, Juan Sebastián Elcano led the expedition home to Seville via the Cape of Good Hope. On September 6, 1522, he and his crew completed the circumnavigation. Carlos V of Spain, in recognition of this feat, bestowed on Elcano a coat of arms with the motto *Primus circumdedisti me* (You went around me first).

Of the original 237 crew members who set out from Spain, only eighteen survived, but the sole returning ship, the *Victoria*, contained twenty-six tons of cinnamon and cloves. A small profit was made for the investors, but the crew members were not paid their full wages. Then, as now, the hard labor that makes the investors' gain possible was poorly rewarded: maritime labor was almost a disposable commodity and subject to the cruel fortune of the sea. After the voyages of Columbus and Magellan came those of Sir Francis Drake, who returned from his plundering circumnavigation of the globe in 1580 and went on to serve as second-in-command of the English fleet that repulsed the Spanish invasion in 1588. The globe had become something to be *encompassed* by imperial and commercial enterprise. A colonizing capitalism produced new forms of violent commerce, new economies of scale, and new world systems. Many European Prosperos went forth with their knowledge and technology, seeking to enslave new Calibans and Ariels wherever they might be found. And many merchants like Antonio stayed home awaiting news about their investments in long-distance ventures.

But what does this history of circumnavigation and emergent globalization have to do with the London theatre and with playwrights like William Shakespeare? Let us consider the career path of Shakespeare for a moment: bored and frustrated by the dull cold rain falling on the wool-producing sheep of Warwickshire, Shakespeare followed the bales of wool to London. By the time that Shakespeare arrived in London (yet another provincial migrant seeking employment and fleeing the idiocy of rural life), the growing city already boasted a highly sophisticated multi-media time–space travel machine—the theatre. These newly constructed permanent playhouses (along with gun-bearing ships and joint-stock corporations) were among the leading cultural and technological innovations produced by the Elizabethans. The early modern theatre offered an imaginative geography of elsewhere: it was a site of cultural production that thrived on the reception and reformulation of information from and about other parts of the world. In 1599, Thomas Platter, a Swiss physician, visited London where he attended a performance at the newly built Globe theatre and reported in his journal: "With these and many more amusements the English pass their time, learning at the play what is happening abroad; indeed men and womenfolk visit such places without scruple, since the English for the most part do not travel much, but prefer to learn foreign matters and take their pleasures at home."

These theatrical representations of the world beyond England were not merely escapist fantasies: plays like *The Merchant of Venice*, *Othello*, and *The Tempest* drew upon actual experiences and the reports that were flooding back into London as a result of England's intensified participation in the global trade matrix. Commerce, diplomacy, plunder, plantation, and even travel for travel's sake brought back people, commodities, and texts bearing information about places beyond Europe. English merchants sent their vessels, goods, sailors, and factors to Livorno, Crete, Venice, Tunis, Aleppo, Constantinople, and beyond—where they met with Jewish, Italian, Greek, and Armenian merchants, bankers, and commercial officials in the employ of Catholic or Muslim authorities. English factors and diplomats encountered Moors and Turks and witnessed the struggle between the Venetian Republic and the Ottoman Empire. Londoners learned about the Mediterranean slave trade, met African servants in the streets, and heard of English sailors taken captive and enslaved in North Africa. They heard rumors about that struggling outpost called Jamestown in the Virginia colony, and listened to tales about shipwrecks off Bermuda. Some read the travel narratives printed in Richard Hakluyt's *Voyages and Discoveries*, and the numerous manuscript and pamphlet "true reports" penned by those who did "travel much" and had sailed far from London. This information was new, exciting, compelling, and frightening. The name of Shakespeare's theatre, "The Globe," suggested the capacity of that playhouse to contain a world of foreign settings and characters. When playgoers at the Globe heard about the dangers that destroyed Antonio's

argosies in *The Merchant of Venice*, the storm that wrecked the
Turkish fleet in *Othello*, or the tempest that begins the play of that
name, these staged events were reminders of very real dangers. The
spectacle of the storm invoked the vulnerability of all those who
risked the fortune of the seas.

Shakespeare certainly felt the urgency and novelty of the new
maritime mobility, with its imperial ambition, profit-taking, and
knowledge-gathering. Perhaps the newly proven ability to circum-
navigate the globe was on his mind when, twenty years after
Drake sailed around the earth, Shakespeare wrote *A Midsummer
Night's Dream*. In that play, the local English sprite, Robin
Goodfellow, could boast, "I'll put a girdle round about the
earth / In forty minutes" (2.1.175–6) and declare, "We the globe
can compass soon, / Swifter than the wandering moon" (4.1.96–7).
The imagined fairy flight around the world, to the Indies and back
in search of a rare "herb," is only one example of the way that
Shakespeare associated the magical potency of his theatre with
the new sense of global mobility that seemed to bring the world's
commodities within reach.

We have come a long way since 1616: from those empire-
builders who followed in the wake of Drake's circumnavigation,
guided by map, compass, and sextant, to those today who play
Puck on Google Earth and whose every word and movement is
traced by GPS and archived within a Big Data surveillance system.
We have all borne witness to a new generation of post-human
fairy-flyers who do the bidding of corporate King Oberon in an age
of globalized media and transnational neoliberal empire. But we
should not understand these digital and technological innovations
as the source of our salvation or as the means to reclaim a divine
or cosmic perspective. Rather, we should acknowledge the abiding
and intensifying force that rules these postmodern measurers and
their seductive wizardry—a globalizing capitalism. In spite of the
small eddies and pockets of resistance, let there be no doubt that the
power of postmodern capital, energized and globalized by digital
technology, is today a triumphant force driving permanent war
and environmental destruction. What began in 1492 has achieved
its dark telos, the catastrophe of our Anthropocene end times.
The Puck pursues us still, chanting: "Up and down, up and down,
/ I will lead them up and down; / I am fear'd in field and town"
(3.2.396–8). And though Hippolyta declares that she "love[s]

not to see wretchedness o'er-charg'd / And duty in his service perishing" (5.1.85–6), Theseus insists that the show must go on. How much longer will today's rude mechanicals dance their unsustainable jig for the pleasure and profit of a neoliberal plutocracy? As our climate changes, what will become of this planet by 2116— will we "make a sop of all this solid globe" (*Troilus and Cressida*, 1.3.113)? And will "th'affrighted globe" yawn at this alteration? The tragic problems represented by Romeo's "gold, worse poison to men's souls" (5.1.80) and Lear's "Poor naked wretches" (3.4.28) were intensified with the emergence of capitalism during the early modern period, and they afflict us still. Ironically, it is too much "degree" (in the form of our global class system) that has threatened to fulfill the prophecy of Shakespeare's Ulysses:

> Then everything includes itself in power,
> Power into will, will into appetite;
> And appetite, an universal wolf,
> So doubly seconded with will and power,
> Must make perforce an universal prey
> And last eat up himself.
>
> (*Troilus and Cressida*, 1.3.119–24)

Today, Ulysses's conservative call for a restoration of order and obedience will not save us from the universal wolf of global capital. If we fail to control neoliberal power and its appetite for profit—if we do not rein in the rapacious beast that has evolved from the commercial energies that excited and alarmed Shakespeare when the age of global empire began—then "endless jar" will follow.

The Bard in Calcutta, India, 1835–2014

Jyotsna G. Singh

I was recently in the heart of Calcutta (now Kolkata, but the earlier spelling more accurately evokes its colonial history) on College Street, where the educational establishment of the city is based in a group of handsome, somewhat fraying buildings dating from the mid-nineteenth to early twentieth centuries: these house

Calcutta University's various colleges and departments. Adjoining the university enclave is Presidency College, recently declared a university, with its elegant, colonnaded verandahs along long passageways. Its walls are covered with numerous portraits and photographs of male teachers, British and Indian, associated with the college for two hundred years. Women students were only admitted in the early 1950s, with female faculty arriving in the 1960s. This was the famed Hindu College, established in 1817 and renamed Presidency College in 1855. What is striking about this urban landscape today is an architecture that reincarnates Victorian and Edwardian England in the teeming bazaar-like atmosphere. The elegant Victorian architecture is sturdy and imposing, though somewhat marked by the grime and dust produced by the contemporary, densely populated city. Across College Street is a long snaking row of bookstalls, where one can find even today varied editions of Shakespeare in English and some in Bengali. The East India Company, and later the English government, called the Presidency, had their roots in Calcutta in the late eighteenth century. My friend, Saikat Majumdar, giving me an historical tour of Calcutta University and its environs, reminds me that "Calcutta's history, unlike Delhi's, only goes back a few hundred years, but in the nineteenth century, it was the capital of colonial British India." And, crucially, it was in these university buildings that the formation of anglicized Indian subjects took shape in the early development of English educational policy, with its related cultural practices such as the dissemination and teaching of Shakespeare in India.

The seminal moment of this English educational agenda can be traced to Thomas Babington Macaulay's famous "Minute" or memorandum of 1835. This policy called for producing elite Indian subjects to be "interpreters between us and the millions whom we govern ... a class of persons Indian in blood and color, but English in tastes, in opinions, in morals, and in intellect." Soon thereafter, the English Governor-General, Lord Bentinck, withdrew funding for education in Sanskrit and Arabic, replacing it with English literature, which placed Shakespeare as the center of aesthetic awe and moral exemplarity. While from the late eighteenth through the nineteenth centuries English playhouses in Calcutta had staged a medley of plays with Shakespeare figuring prominently, the bard's works were now being discovered as classroom texts, as the Indian bourgeoisie and intelligentsia in Calcutta embraced the English education agenda. In fact, since the Calcutta theatres were supported and patronized by the various Governors General and other colonial dignitaries, Shakespeare's plays were significant in privileging the culture of the colonizers—both among the English expatriates as well as the elite Indians who gradually became associated with these theatres. For instance, a significant recognition of Shakespeare's new role came from students of Hindu College and Sanskrit College who staged several Shakespearean plays between 1837 and 1853. And most of Shakespeare's plays were translated or adapted for the Bengali language, with a number of them being produced on the public stage from the late 1800s through the early twentieth century.

I was keenly reminded of this history of "Shakespeare in India" in colonial Calcutta (Kolkata), as I stood amidst the eighteenth- and nineteenth-century architecture in this "ground zero" of the former English presidency, which signaled the creation of colonial subjects. I was a participant at a conference at Presidency College on "Global Shakespeares," ably organized by Amrita Sen, a recent US PhD. The graduate student and faculty presenters at Presidency were the descendants of Macaulay's colonial subjects, and the range of papers revealed both an awareness of the genealogy of Shakespeare in India as well as the impact of a hyper-real modernity—both in its local and global contexts—through which contemporary Shakespeare was being refracted. Paper topics included adaptations of *Hamlet* in nineteenth-century Bengal; contemporary adaptations of *Macbeth*; early nineteenth-century translations of Shakespeare in Calcutta; Boydell's influence on Bengali illustrations of Shakespeare; Shakespeare on Facebook and on the video games circuit; Shakespeare and sovereignty in relation to theories of Agamben and Schmitt; Shakespeare as inflected by queer desire in fan fiction; and readings of Shakespearean sources in Ovid.

These topics reflected a rich, Janus-faced, double perspective: from specific, native genealogies of Shakespeare in nineteenth-century Bengal to global modernity with its digital technologies and new forms of hybridity. This conference was an excellent example of a fairly recent "coming of age" in Indian engagements with the bard. Many generations of scholars in India (as elsewhere) were caught up in the myth of a "universal" Shakespeare, without any acknowledgment of the text in history and ideology. In India this veneration often signaled an unhistoricized "love" of Shakespeare that echoed the colonial past. However, at this conference, while many papers evoked life in Calcutta, the home of colonial (and global) Shakespeare in the eighteenth and nineteenth centuries with its distinct native and local inflections, they did so with an historical self-consciousness, aware both of Macaulay's shadow on Bengali cultural history and their break from that history in contemporary global modernity. Collectively, the papers brought to life the topicality of history and the history of topicality as it related to the presence of Shakespeare in colonial, postcolonial, and global contexts in Calcutta and the world at large.

Leaving the halls of Presidency University, among the crammed bookstalls on College Street outside I found many English and American editions of Shakespeare on sale. Among these I discovered a roughly bound edition of *Julius Caesar*, edited by a Professor N. Ghosh and published by a local press, the Modern Book Agency, in several editions from 1993 to 2003. The paper was of poor quality and the price was equivalent to one dollar. The editing mode was reminiscent of popular help books, with copious notes in a somewhat pedantic, formal style. Given its several reprintings, it was obvious that it had a broad readership, including perhaps some students at Presidency and others who had limited access to libraries or books in English. What was remarkable, however, was the continuing and almost ubiquitous presence of the Shakespearean text at so many levels of cultural and economic life in contemporary Calcutta.

As an American-based South Asian academic, invited to give an opening address on Shakespeare in global modernity and on the new Indian adaptation of Hamlet, *Haidar*, I became keenly aware of my role as a *passeur* or a "go-between" faced with mediating nearness and distance: between histories and cultures, and between temporal and spatial divides: as, for instance, between the English/European Renaissance and its postcolonial, cross-cultural, and New Media appropriations and dissemina-tions—some of which were presented at this conference. In fact, the burgeoning field of "postcolonial Shakespeare"—spawning related studies on travel writing, on cross-cultural encounters, on global trade, among others—that now seems commonplace at meetings of the Shakespeare Association of America or Renaissance Society of America, got its direction and impetus from a seemingly localized, then marginal, and "exotic" scholarship on Shakespeare and the Indian Empire in the late 1980s and early 1990s. Of course, this interest in colonial and postcolonial contexts within which Shakespeare was reproduced went on to offer rich cultural transmutations, going far beyond the British Empire in nineteenth-century India. And today, anthologies on "native" Shakespeares or "world-wide" Shakespeares oscillate between charting a variety of non-Western, postcolonial, local contexts and an awareness of the global commodification of Shakespeare's plays.

Such cross-pollinations—and tensions—between the local and global, indigenous and global histories, and between colonial and postcolonial contexts continue to shape the scholarly debates of *Shakespeare in Our Time*. We have come a long way from accessing Shakespeare mainly through the mythos of Burckhardt's "Renaissance Man," though the grip of this Anglo-centric approach has not been adequately loosened in many English departments. Attending the conference on "Global Shakespeares" at Presidency University, the former bastion of the colonial educational project, brought home to me the importance of an experiential (and not purely discursive) sense of history that accretes to locations and objects—a set of buildings, photographs, portraits, and dusty books sold on pavement stalls. Such literal spatial and temporal trajectories of travel, I believe, are also analogous to the cultural transmutations of early modern travelers crossing cultures as they traversed the globe—such as the English officials and traders who arrived in Anglicized Calcutta in the late eighteenth and early nineteenth centuries. Finally, I was filled with a keen appreciation of the newer generations of Shakespearean scholars in India who are reclaiming the bard on their own terms—local and global, native and cosmopolitan. They also play an important role as *passeurs* or "go-betweens," mediating the many pathways that lead to Shakespeare in our time.

11

Bodies and Emotions

Bodies without Borders in *Lear* and *Macbeth*

Gail Kern Paster
President, SAA 2003–4

For early modern scholars, the signal achievement of literary criticism's "turn to the body" in the mid-1980s was twofold—to write the human body into the history of the subject and to situate the body and its emotions materially within the natural world. Whether knowingly or not, these historians of the body were heeding the wise words of Shigehisa Kuriyama in *The Expressiveness of the Body* (1999): "the history of the body is ultimately a history of ways of inhabiting the world."

For early modern people themselves, however, the terms of living within this basic history seem inverted. Their experience was less one of inhabiting the world than of feeling inhabited *by* it. As Timothy Reiss has suggested in *Mirages of the Selfe* (2003), the early moderns were embedded within circles that included the material world, the family, the state, animal being, and spiritual agents, both human and divine. These circles both preceded a person and constituted him; they "*were* what a person was: integral to [his] very substance." Reiss names this conception of selfhood *passibility*. In early modern English, being *passible* denoted the capacity to suffer or to receive impressions, physical and mental. As opposed to *impassibility*—a quality imputed to God—*passibility* was synonymous with being human.

As I and other body historians have long proposed, the passible body is characterized by its openness to the environment, its humoral instability, and the extreme volatility of its passions. With its faulty borders and penetrable stuff, such a body interacts differently with the world than the "static, solid" modern bodily container constructed by the followers of Descartes. At times, the humoral body took the environment into itself; at times it spilled out of its boundaries. What cultural historians now require is a more precise understanding of that environment's significant traits, including the character of its interaction with the human body. Early modern nature, James Bono has suggested in *The Word of God and the Languages of Man* (1995), was endlessly metamorphic, creative, and playful. And full of appetite: in this idea of nature (according to Lorraine Daston in "The Nature of Nature in Early Modern Europe," 1998) only things of human manufacture were incapable of appetite and the self-love justified and enabled by it. Shakespeare scholars have described this dynamic natural order in different, but overlapping discourses. Leah Marcus, in *"King Lear and the Death of the World"* (2016), argues that the play is "steeped in early modern vitalism," which she defines as "a belief in some type of invisible, immanent force or network of forces, whether material or immaterial, that operates in and between things, linking them and determining their relations with each other." According to Mary Floyd-Wilson in *Occult Knowledge, Science, and Gender on the Shakespearean Stage* (2013), people lived their lives "with the conviction that their emotions, behavior, and practices were affected by, and dependent on, secret sympathies and antipathies that coursed through the natural world." Bulls naturally loved fig trees; serpents hated the smell of garlic; elephants hated dragons, mice, and swallows. What this means is that the bodies brought to life for us on Shakespeare's stage, like the bodies that filled his theatre, inhabit a plentiful, dynamic cosmos pervaded by forces and spirits of diverse kinds and filled with natural objects moved by appetites (desire and aversion, sympathy and antipathy, attraction and repulsion) that explained their behavior. The transmission of emotion from stage to playhouse yard, from actor to spectator, about which Allison Hobgood has written so powerfully in *Passionate Playgoing* (2014), is one instantiation of this desire-filled cosmos.

It is important to be clear about what is entailed by seeing early modern embodiment in this light. It does not mean pathologizing early modern selfhood, reducing human agency, or privileging the involuntary work of an appetitive body over the voluntary work of reason, will, and purposeful cognition, as some scholars have maintained. Rather, it is to recognize within the terms of early modern embodiment a host of distributed agencies that reach beyond the human body into a world constituted by what Jane Bennett, in *Vibrant Matter* (2010), has described as "the capacity of things—edibles, commodities, storms, metals—not only to impede or block the will and designs of humans but also to act as quasi-agents or forces with trajectories, propensities, or tendencies of their own." In *Politics of Nature* (2004), Bruno Latour names these capacities "actants"— whatever has efficacy, can do things, and has sufficient coherence to make a difference, produce effects, or alter the course of events. While we moderns may need to be instructed in matter's vibrancy, the early moderns certainly did not.

Here I want to look at vibrant matter and forms of distributed agency in two iconic apostrophes in Shakespearean tragedy—King Lear's address to the storm and Lady Macbeth's invocation of the spirits. I want to use these moments in order to reconsider the reciprocal interactions of body and world, matter and spirit, force and resistance in early modern thought, interactions now being designated as the ecology of the passions. And I want to argue that to recognize the vitality of matter in Shakespearean drama and other early modern texts is not a postmodern theorization but rather a welcome return to early modern ways of conceiving the dynamic relation of the human body to its world from our side of the Cartesian mind–body split.

At these moments in the two tragedies, Shakespeare's characters invoke cosmic forces for transformative purposes, both of self and others. Lear asks the elements—"rain, wind, thunder, fire" (3.2.15)—to wage violent destruction on the land below. Lady Macbeth famously asks the spirits "That tend on mortal thoughts" to "take"—i.e. exchange, transform, or accept—her "milk for gall" (1.5.41, 48). The question I want to ask of these two moments is twofold: what kind of agency—material, purposive, affective—is embodied in the forces being invoked; and what are the cosmological implications of apostrophe, which I consider here less as a heightened form of poetic address than as a genuine example (like blessings, curses, or magical charms) of early modern cosmological thought and practice.

King Lear

King Lear rushes furiously out into an oncoming storm, preferring to contend "with the fretful elements" (3.1.4) rather than face the escalating cruelty of his daughters. His apostrophe in 3.2 is marked not only by a variety of possible relations to the storm but also by the various forms of agency Lear imagines it to have:

> I tax not you, you elements, with unkindness.
> I never gave you kingdom, called you children;
> You owe me no subscription. Why then, let fall
> Your horrible pleasure. Here I stand your slave,
> A poor, infirm, weak and despised old man.
> But yet I call you servile ministers
> That will with two pernicious daughters join
> Your high-engendered battles 'gainst a head
> So old and white as this.
>
> (3.2.16–24)

Lear begins by absolving the elements of blame for his suffering, telling "rain, wind, thunder, fire" they are not his daughters. But, by the speech's end, he has changed his mind, not equating the storm with his daughters but finding the elements actively leagued with the daughters against him—being, in his word, unkind.

The movement of this speech from portraying the weather first as entirely separate from, then subservient to, human powers serves as a reminder of sharp distinctions relevant both to the play's world and the real world outside it—distinctions between physical and mental suffering, accidental and deliberate infliction of pain, natural and human agency. Lear draws a bright line between the social sphere of reciprocal obligation and a natural world devoid of it. The weather owes Lear no gifts, having received none; it owes him no service ("subscription") since he cannot do it any benefit. His word "kingdom" adds to the differences between the social and natural spheres. The weather makes no distinctions among the world's kingdoms because it does not recognize their existence.

And so, Lear goes on to merge the social and natural spheres and to reverse the cosmological order of things by subsuming the natural within the human. He endows the elements with an appetite for destruction—they fall oxymoronically with "horrible pleasure"—but then arranges them in a hierarchy of hostile forces. He, a "slave" at the bottom, serves their will by suffering, and they, being intermediate agents, serve punitive daughters by turning their "high-engendered" battles with each other against him.

While Lear's self-destructive narcissism is evident here, it is his serious distribution of ethical agency I want to emphasize instead. Early modern English described many phenomena as "unkind"—meaning unusual, unpleasant, severe, causing hardship to man and beast. Unusual meteorological events were classed with monstrous births, sudden sinkholes, or miraculous fasts. Lear's re-signifying of the storm's elements—first as above, then as within the human sphere—has the effect of critiquing anthropocentric understanding and instead foregrounding the problematic agency and purposes of matter, as when Lear wonders what "breeds" about Regan's heart and asks: "Is there any cause in nature that makes these hard hearts?" (Q 3.6.74–5). His various reactions to the storm—absolving it, blaming it, urging it, shrinking before its violence—oscillate between the human desire to bring the storm within an ethical compass by blaming its cruelty or to absolve it from human signifying practice altogether. These ethical options in turn provide a context for Lear's confrontation with the nearly naked body of Poor Tom, whose position in the natural order is no less ambiguous than that of the king. Laurie Shannon's brilliant reading of "the thing itself. Unaccommodated man" (3.4.104–5) in *The Accommodated Animal* (2013) emphasizes the moment's critique of negative human exceptionalism in relation to animal being—what human beings lack in relation to animals. But it is also possible to read the moment as recalling the vibrancy and generosity of animate matter, since Tom is pitied for lacking access to the affordances of the natural world which, by covering him, would make him more recognizably human: "Thou ow'st the worm no silk, the beast no hide, the sheep no wool, the cat no perfume" (3.4.101–3). Even Lear's description of clothes as "lendings" suggests the mutuality of human and animal worlds. If Lear's decision to strip himself for Tom—"Off, off, you lendings" (106)—marks the onset of compassion and fellow-feeling, it is an inner transformation (however partial, however temporary) that witnesses the play's insistence upon human indebtedness, both positive and negative, to the affordances of matter and to the agency of the storm outside and inside the body of the king.

Lady Macbeth

Lady Macbeth's famous invocation to the spirits "that tend on mortal thoughts" is also an example of distributed agency and vibrant materiality in a cosmos which John Sutton (*Philosophy and Memory Traces*, 1998) has described as a theatre of pneumatological interaction filled with nested systems of spirits. In *Sylva Sylvarum* (1627), Francis Bacon defines spirit "as a natural body, rarified to a proportion, and included in the tangible parts of bodies, as in an integument." Despite being invisible, the spirits are no less material than Lear's storm: Lady Macbeth calls them "sightless *substances*" (1.5.49, emphasis added). It is not crucial to the literalism of my argument here whether these spirits are supernatural or preter-natural, or even whether Lady Macbeth's invocation is understood by us as fantasy or imagined possibility. What matters is that her world is full of accessible spirits just as Lear's is full of rain, wind, thunder, and fire. For her, the spirits are already out there filling the cosmos with their own invisible plenitude, waiting for assignment from the passible human selves whose thoughts they "tend on"—a crucial phrase whose meanings include attending, overhearing, executing, being drawn sympathetically towards:

> Come you spirits
> That tend on mortal thoughts, unsex me here,
> And fill me from the crown to the toe, top-full
> Of direst cruelty. Make thick my blood,
> Stop up th'access and passage to remorse,
> That no compunctious visitings of nature
> Shake my fell purpose, nor keep peace between
> Th'effect and it. Come to my woman's breasts,
> And take my milk for gall, you murdering ministers,
> Wherever, in your sightless substances,
> You wait on nature's mischief.
>
> (1.5.40–50)

Criticism has been most interested in the emotional, psychological, and bodily changes that Lady Macbeth requests. I would like to query, instead, the material agencies involved in effecting the transformation she so desires and fears. In her complex bodily self-image, she proposes two kinds of actants in Latour's sense— the spirits and the gall they would somehow mysteriously enable. The physiological transaction imagined here would redistribute agency twice, first to the powerful spirits who are to enter her body and then to the bitter matter—the gall—she would have them exchange (or accept, or transform) for her woman's milk in order to effect her unsexing. Such an imagined action is made possible first of all lexically: in early modern English, cruelty and gall—the bodily humor also known as choler that was produced in the gall bladder and sent thence into the bloodstream—were synonymous, the substance indivisible from the act. She is, at this moment of invocation, virtually emblematic of the passible self, presenting her embodied self to the attending spirits as their vessel to fill—or perhaps first to empty (of milk), then fill (with gall). In terms of agency, it is not only that the cruelty she desires would therefore be in significant measure externally derived but also that her blood, newly thickened by the currents of cruelty, would have the capacity to overcome the psychological and physiological forces she finds within her female self—her remorse, her compunctious visitings of natural feeling—that might resist this pneumatological importation of the spirits and shake her "fell purpose."

There is no ambiguity about the naturalness of the material forces within and without her body. Gall, though bitter, is not poison. It is as natural as milk and as requisite for the action of self-preservation and the maintenance of life. My interest lies rather in the ethical open-endedness of natural bodily capacities—the kindly compunction and the hellish mischief that she describes as natural. Milky, thin-blooded female embodiment seems to involve bodily openness within—"access and passage" to the second thoughts of remorse and compunction stored materially within her. She worries about harboring these thoughts and feelings within as she waits for the spirits to manufacture instead their aversive opposite. This is "Nature's mischief" involving the material agency of gall— the choler, the yellow bile—that she is counting on to give her masculine firmness and strength of purpose, changing her bodily texture and substance in order to transform her disposition, harden her mind, and expand the scope of her capacities. It is here in the conflict of elements—milk versus gall, sweet versus bitter, thin versus thick, soft versus hard, remorse versus fell purpose, nature's compunction versus nature's mischief—that the spirits in the cosmos surrounding Lady Macbeth come to resemble the contentious storm whose fretful elements Lear experiences with such complex variety of response. For both of these characters nature is a conflict of elements, a conflict of actants in Latour's terms, to be recognized within and without the body, a conflict that both of them wish—in different ways, for different reasons—to invoke, encourage, inhabit, and make their own within the parameters of early modern possibility.

It is the volatility and materiality of these embodied selves—of a piece with the volatility of their environments—that are on view at these two moments in Shakespearean tragedy as the two characters struggle with the destructive power of their own appetites at a moment of crucial self-reckoning. And we should also recognize the significance of the rhetorical form that addressing the environment takes as they attempt to seize control of forces outside themselves. At such moments, apostrophes become a mode of address symptomatic of early modern cosmological thought and practice, examples of the ecology of the passions when the early modern self hails the myriad forces that surround it and recognizes the similitude of appetites for nurture and destruction that self-sentient life in the body shares with nature's vibrant matter. It is at such eloquent moments that the history of the embodied self reveals itself most truly as a history of ways of inhabiting—and being inhabited by—the world.

Potions, Passion, and Fairy Knowledge in *A Midsummer Night's Dream*

Mary Floyd-Wilson

When I teach *A Midsummer Night's Dream*, students are troubled that Demetrius (unlike Lysander or Titania) remains under the spell of the love juice. His love for Helena, they insist, cannot be genuine. Surprisingly, Demetrius's charmed state causes little consternation among critics. For them the fairy influence is symbolic, reminding us that Demetrius showed a similar inconstancy before the play began. Magic, in these readings, is analogous to fickle love. But Demetrius questions whether he has actually been roused from his slumber in the woods. In his enchanted state, he asks, "Are you sure / That we are awake? It seems to me / That yet we sleep, we dream" (4.1.191–3). Altered by fairy magic, he hints that his perception feels hallucinatory.

How might it affect our reading of the play if we resist translating the love potion into a symbol? Almost everyone in Shakespeare's era believed in some form of natural magic, as well as in the existence of demons. Fairies, spirits, and magical potions were authentic spurs of human desire and knowledge. Even Reginald Scot accepted that hidden forces of antipathy and sympathy resided in minerals, plants, and animals. Do we gain a different perception of early modern emotion and embodiment if we account for preter-natural influences? (Here preternature encompasses strange but natural forces, including the demonic, in a culture that attributes supernatural phenomena only to God.) Critics have read Bottom's union with Titania as a commentary on cross-class relations, sodomy, and bestiality, but Shakespeare's audience may have been most titillated by the play's more overt question: how do these airy entities interact with mortal bodies? How, demonologists asked, did spirits copulate without flesh?

Historians of the body debate the degree to which corporeal processes were thought to determine behavior or inhibit agency. Early moderns recognized themselves to be embedded in, and constituted by, an animate world that influenced their thoughts, emotions, and health. But they also privileged their capacities to intervene in this world and redirect its forces. Interventions could encompass attention to the six Galenic non-naturals, such as diet or air quality, or they might involve the shaping effects of custom or education. More esoterically, while early moderns feared the disruptive power of invisible forces, they also pursued control of the secret workings of nature. As David Houston Wood in *Time, Narrative, and Emotion in Early Modern England* (2009) and Tanya Pollard in *Drugs and Theater in Early Modern England* (2005) have shown, potions and poisons regularly unsettled and resolved fictional accounts of emotional experiences.

Whether fairies were categorized as sprites or demons (and Reformation writers such as Niels Hemmingsen and Thomas

Jackson discounted fairies only to deem them demonic), they operated within the confines of nature. When humans performed magic, they manipulated the same properties and virtues—hidden in nature—that fairies and demons were thought to deploy. As Allison Kavey argues in *Books of Secrets: Natural Philosophy in England, 1550–1600* (2007), lay folk recognized that "sympathy and antipathy between objects determine the composition of the natural world, ... they act as levers by which readers could mold it ... to their needs and desires." "Receipt" books list countless recipes that rely on occult qualities in human fluids and flesh and on hidden properties in animals, insects, minerals, and plants.

Recipes for love magic prove more obscure, perhaps because it became a capital offense in 1542 to "provoke any person to unlawful love." The illegality of love magic suggests that authorities believed that such spells worked. Evidence indicates that when people wanted a love potion, they consulted their local cunning man or woman. In 1582, Goodwife Swan of Margate claimed she could make a drink that would make any young man love her. Some love recipes appear in books of secrets: Thomas Johnson's *Cornucopiae* recommends ingesting creatures that love most, such as the turtle or the swallow, drawing an implicit sympathy between animal and human passion. Particular herbs generated desire: vervain would procure love if rubbed on one's mouth before kissing the beloved.

If we accept Egeus's version of events, magical influences began well before the lovers entered the woods:

> This hath betwitch'd the bosom of my child.
> ...
> And stol'n the impression of her fantasy
> With bracelets of thy hair, rings, gauds, conceits,
> Knacks, trifles, nosegays, sweetmeats (messengers
> Of strong prevailment in unharden'd youth):
> With cunning hast thou filch'd my daughter's heart,
>   (1.1.27, 32–6)

The exchange of gifts—rings, gauds, and handkerchiefs—was often identified as a means of enchantment. In *Eighteen books of the secrets of art and nature* (1660), Johanus Wecker notes that love may be sustained by "procur[ing] ... a quantity of hair of the

... beloved as will make a ring or a bracelet, and then wear[ing] it either on your finger or wrist, and it shall by secret exciting the Imagination procure its certain effect."

While Lysander could gain such secrets from a cunning man or woman, the cunning folk themselves often attributed their knowledge to fairies, as Owen Davies has shown in *Cunning-Folk: Popular Magic in English History* (2003). Agnes Hancock insisted she got advice from fairies whenever she pleased. John Walsh explained in 1566 that he would speak with the fairies to learn which clients were bewitched. As Davies reports, Joan Willimott allegedly obtained healing abilities when a man "willed her to open her mouth, and hee would blow into her a Fairy which should doe her good." Early moderns attempted to conjure fairies with the secret properties in flowers and plants. A fifteenth-century spell instructs one to anoint the eyes with an unction from flowers gathered near where fairies go.

That humans and fairies might share knowledge of the natural realm is brought home in the scene when Bottom rests in Titania's bower. Bottom easily recognizes Titania's fairy attendants, Peaseblossom, Cobweb, and Mustardseed, as familiar entities. As Wendy Wall notes in "Why Does Puck Sweep?" (2001), the fairies can be viewed as incarnate simples, regularly named in household cookbooks and medical guides. As if reciting his own homey recipes, Bottom knows that mustardseed will make his eyes water and go well with ox-beef. Cobweb stanches bleeding. For Wall this scene "Shrink[s] the power of the magical sphere to homespun remedies." But perhaps the home-space and the magical sphere are not separate. The flowers, berries, and worms that comprise Titania's bower are the same ones humans use to intervene in nature.

The mingling of the magical and the mundane is epitomized in Oberon's description of the love juice he tells Puck to collect. The western flower appears to be a purple pansy or a violet. In observing that maidens call it "love-in-idleness," (2.1.168) Oberon reminds the audience of its domestic familiarity. Its purple color places it among the venereal plants—those herbs ruled by Venus—and it was also called "heartsease" for its power to comfort those grieving. Rather than representing the potion's main ingredient as exotic, Shakespeare points to a flower available in any local garden.

Although Oberon attributes the flower's origins to the virginal Queen's watery beams, he uses this magic to reestablish his masculine authority. While under his spell, Titania deploys her own knowledge of nature's secrets in a scheme to "purge [Bottom's] mortal grossness so, / That [he] shalt like an airy spirit go" (3.1.153–4). As Gail Kern Paster has shown in *The Body Embarrassed* (1993), Titania's undertaking is moral and physiological, erotic and infantilizing; in thrall to Titania, Bottom loses control of his body's boundaries. But Titania's endeavor also suggests that human grossness could be made less material and more airy by ingestion and expulsion. When the Fairie Queen purportedly came to Godwin Wharton in his sleep, he claimed she sucked out the very marrow of his bones. Perhaps the purgation of one's mortal grossness is a transformative effect of having sex with a fairy.

It was a pervasive fear among early moderns that devilish spirits could, without their knowledge, have carnal relations with them. Oberon claims that Titania has repeatedly intervened in Theseus's love life, yet Theseus's dismissal of fairy toys suggests that he is ignorant of her interference. And if Hippolyta is also Oberon's mistress, has this union occurred without her awareness? Is it possible to categorize Oberon as an incubus and Titania as a succubus?

As Regina Buccola notes in *Fairies, Fractious Women, and the Old Faith* (2006), Oberon's most blatant intervention in the human world—the potion's lingering effects on Demetrius—ultimately succeeds in accomplishing Helena's will, her wish to possess an "art" that would sway Demetrius's heart. There were many real-life Helenas, lacking fairy intervention, who sought out cunning folk to resolve unreciprocated passions. But can we find this source of knowledge in *A Midsummer Night's Dream*? In "Taken by the Fairies" (2000), Mary Ellen Lamb observes that when Puck topples the wisest aunt, he overturns the author of his own narrative: an old wife telling fairy stories. But Puck's humiliation of the wisest aunt may be an act of policing knowledge boundaries. For her wisdom could include a recipe for remedying the sadness of her tale. In the world outside the play, the wise woman may have known the very same secrets as Oberon and Puck.

Shakespeare and Variant Embodiment

David Houston Wood

To call disability an identity is to recognize that it is not a biological or natural property but an elastic social category both subject to social control and capable of effecting social change.

TOBIN SIEBERS, *DISABILITY THEORY* (2008)

For most of us, William Shakespeare's limping, hunchbacked king, Richard III, serves as the representative example of the dramatist's engagement with disability. And why shouldn't it? By far the most staged of all Shakespeare's plays (and thus in some sense the most popular), *Richard III* links Richard's various deformities with murderous evil; Shakespeare himself seems to have been sufficiently interested in exploring this metaphorical association to have pursued Richard across fully three of his early history plays: *Henry VI, Part 2*; *Henry VI, Part 3*, and *Richard III*. Within these works, Richard famously suggests he is

> not shaped for sportive tricks
> ...
>   curtailed of this fair proportion,
> Cheated of feature by dissembling Nature,
> Deformed, unfinished, sent before my time
> Into this breathing world, scarce half made up,
> And that so lamely and unfashionable
> That dogs bark at me as I halt by them—
>   (*Richard III*, 1.1.14, 18–23)

His deformities, as he itemizes them, include an arm like a "withered shrub," a back like a "mountain," and legs "shape[d]" of an "unequal size," so that he is "disproportion[ed] ... Like to a chaos." By others' accounts, Richard is an "elvish-marked, abortive, rooting hog," a "poisonous bunch-backed toad," a "bottled spider," a "hedgehog," a "cockatrice," a "cacodemon," and, repeatedly, a "dog," a "hog," and, as his own mother bitterly addresses him: "Thou toad, thou toad." These are the familiar terms that can generate uneasy laughter in any performance. But while it is tempting to rely upon this characterization of Richard as singularly representative of Shakespeare's engagement with disability, the truth is decidedly more complex. In fact, if we define disability as any frequently stigmatized sensory, somatic, or cognitive impairment which is either congenital (deriving from birth), acquired (secured during one's lifetime), or periodic (from which one phases in and out), then it becomes rather difficult to identify examples of Shakespearean drama that fail to stage disabilities of some sort.

Of course, Richard III and his deformities have recently become front page news, and not just in the Arts section but, as they say, above the fold. The 2012 discovery of Richard's remains buried in a Leicester parking lot, complete with his death wounds and a moderately severe case of adolescent-onset scoliosis, has exposed his body to newfound popular scrutiny: terms like the "Tudor Myth," titles like Josephine Tey's *The Daughter of Time* (1951), and even the rich foods and wine of his diet, for example, find themselves thrown about nowadays in the common discourse of *The New York Times*. With the discovery of Richard's body the familiar literary reliance upon disability depictions as metaphors for something else has yielded, for the time being, to the material fact of his deformity, as plain as the curvature of his actual spine. But what happens when, as literary scholars lacking recourse to other such corporeal remains, we engage the full range of Shakespeare's disability representations for what they really are— acknowledging the period-specific metaphors that accrue to depictions of variant embodiment, that is, but pushing beyond them to the medical, legal, theological, aesthetic, and ethical realities that underlie such representations? In other words: how might we pursue this thing called *early modern disability studies,* and what might such research reveal about early modern England more broadly? About Shakespeare? About ourselves?

Toward that end, my epigraph comes from disability theorist Tobin Siebers, who expresses here the stakes of the field, the central project of which is to examine the contingent and constructed nature of what a culture deems "normal." Over the past thirty years, disability studies has appealed to many professionals beyond the familiar domains of medicine, rehabilitation, special education, and social services; these domains are often criticized for pathologizing human variation, and thus individualizing, and

R3—"Reclaiming" reputation linked to "he wasn't THAT disabled" depoliticizing, personal medical experience. As pursued in the arts and humanities, disability studies seeks to establish disability as a social category on a par with class, race and ethnicity, or gender and sexuality, and thus to promote an understanding of how mental and physical variation are continually reinterpreted by various material, discursive, and aesthetic practices. Disability studies thus "reimagines disability," as Allison Hobgood observes, as "a social category more than an individual attribute, a discursive construction instead of a bodily flaw, and a representational system rather than a physiological problem to be cured by modern medical interventions" (2013). Crucially, historical studies of disability revise what we know about disability in the past, and, in doing so, help clarify disability in our own cultural moment. As Siebers observes:

> The experience of contemporary minority people, once brought to light, resound back in history, like a reverse echo effect, to comment on the experiences of past minority peoples, while at the same time these past experiences contribute, one hopes, to an accumulation of knowledge about how oppression works. (2008)

Interpreting Shakespearean drama through contemporary disability theory makes a number of important sparks fly. My two coedited collections with Allison Hobgood—*Disabled Shakespeares* (2009), and *Recovering Disability in Early Modern England* (2013)—have sought to correct a significant omission in Shakespeare studies: while scholarly interest in the politics of early modern embodiment has been pursued with alacrity over the past two decades, there has been until very recently next to no engagement with disability as such, or with the vocabularies, methodologies, and ethical considerations that have arisen to account for it in its early modern iterations. This oversight is especially puzzling because, of course, disabled bodies and minds serve as some of the signature character features in Renaissance texts.

Within Shakespearean drama alone, in fact, such impairments are legion: from Gloucester's blindness in *King Lear* to Simpcox's feigned blindness in *Henry VI, Part 2*; from the "deformed" Caliban to the "deformed" Thersites in *Troilus and Cressida*; from Julius Caesar's epilepsy to Othello's; from the "distracted" Ophelia to Leontes's derangement in *The Winter's Tale*; from

Michael Cassio's alcoholic "infirmity" in *Othello* to Antony's besottedness in *Antony and Cleopatra*; from the maimed Lavinia in *Titus Andronicus* to Katherina's ostensible limp in *The Taming of the Shrew*; from Lear's senectitude to Adam's in *As You Like It*; from Coriolanus's war wounds to Falstaff's fat; and still more broadly, perhaps, from the two queens unable to bear male children in *Henry VIII* to the inwardly deformed, disenfranchised bastard sons in *Much Ado About Nothing, King John,* and *King Lear.* Such depictions deserve examination in the context of the prehistories of stigmatization that early modern disability studies takes as its purview, and can contribute to current Renaissance scholarship involved in exploring forms of embodied difference by situating such representations between medieval discourses of marvel, wonder, and prodigiousness, on one hand, and burgeoning early modern protomedical models, on the other.

Engaging Shakespeare via disability studies thus prompts any number of salient questions: what sorts of medical, theological, legal, aesthetic, and ethical traditions informed Shakespeare's ideas about disability? In what ways did he take these received opinions and make them new on the Renaissance stage? What is the underpinning logic of ability in early modern England, and how do categories of "normal" and "nonnormal" function in pre-Cartesian contexts? How does our ability to examine the literary record with reading strategies developed from contemporary disability theory transform our understanding of Shakespeare's plays, and what are the methodological challenges and ethical responsibilities we face in doing so? What are the unique significations of congenital impairments in Shakespearean drama in contrast with those associated with acquired or periodic disabilities? How do representations of disability staged within drama—in which "character" is always a personation, always an embodied performance of some sort—contrast with depictions of disability situated within nonperformed literary texts? And in historicizing disability, what is the precise relationship between early modern impairments of the body and those of the soul?

As scholarship turns to address genuinely new questions such as these, it seems safe to say that the topics of embodiment and emotion remain alive and well in Shakespeare studies. The masterful dramatic achievement that is *Richard III* will always offer a formidable disability representation, of course, not least in its problematic depiction of Richard as a beguilingly charismatic, "elvish-marked" changeling deposited in this world as if by fairies on loan from another Shakespeare play. And yet the full range of Shakespeare's depictions of disability difference ought to spur us to expand our consideration of early modern nonnormative embodiment as a crucial means by which Shakespeare assays and delimits the human. As we move forward, that is, our attempts to answer the questions I pose here can provide us the opportunity to reveal both the historicized ways in which Shakespeare once meant, and the powerful ways in which he continues to do so.

12

Social Context

Social Contexting

Frances E. Dolan
President, SAA 2004–5

The usefulness of the word context has always been, for me, the double connotation of "con," suggesting both texts one reads with and against other texts, and the reminder that we access the social through texts that pose the same interpretive challenges as Shakespeare's plays. However wide we cast the net for those texts to be read with and against Shakespeare's texts—to include fabrics, codpiece points, ink stands, pamphlets, ballads, depositions, recipes, and legal statutes—they demand and reward the same tactics of analysis we turn on Shakespeare's plays, even as they also challenge us to be more agile and resourceful critics. Thinking about a Shakespeare play in relation to other kinds of evidence has never meant ignoring or disparaging all of the ways in which a play is different from a muster roll or a will. Quite the opposite. To examine the many different forms with which early modern people engaged is to see what sophisticated and labile readers and writers they were and the very particular resources each kind offered them. Only by placing plays in relation to others within their class as well as in relation to other kinds of evidence entirely can we interrogate the operations of form, the persistence (and sometimes repurposing) of some ideas, practices, values, fears, and things, the transformation of others, and the emergence of the new. Placing variously situated texts in debates or contestations, we can test hypotheses about processes of change, cycles of return, throbs of resonance, webs of association. Our agency in that placing and testing—in context as a verb rather than a noun—is what will ultimately concern me here.

However much disparaged, a distinction between text and context insistently reasserts itself. Yet we have also developed a more supple language for discussing the participation of plays in making the social. Critics describe texts as actors in networks, ecologies, constellations, assemblages, and affinities. All of these terms suggest a span across space and time, a patchwork rather than a line; they helpfully shift our gaze away from the author's intention (and individuation). Refusing to see the Shakespeare text as the origin or the target, network models emphasize, diffuse, and sometimes mystify the agency of various actors, including texts. In part because of the weightiness of "Shakespeare" and in part because of the privileging of what seems the indisputably literary, the Shakespearean text can throw an ecology out of whack because it remains so challenging to articulate exactly how it relates to the other actors in a given network or what its "literariness" contributes to its agency. Rita Felski points to certain works' "dexterity in generating attachments" ("Context Stinks!" 2011). Generating attachments as well as hogging the limelight and setting the agenda, the Shakespeare play can sometimes seem to be an actor-manager, an impresario, a ham.

While we can never nail down exactly how it pulls this off, puzzling over that power requires thinking the Shakespeare play in relation. But attending to the "social contexts" of Shakespeare plays does not mean assembling materials, issues, or events as much as it means raising a series of questions about the cultural embeddedness of literary invention. Why tell this story in this way at this time? What other versions of this story were in circulation? What were the materials available from which Shakespeare constructed his story? What were the functions of particular fictions? That is, how did they manage the social conflicts they engaged? What, if anything, distinguishes Shakespeare's versions of popular stories from others? In placing a Shakespeare play into dialogue with other versions of the story, other accounts of a problem, we rarely resolve anything but rather complicate understandings of a play's operations—how it achieves its effects—and of the problems and issues with which it engages.

For example, Shakespeare constantly draws our attention to anxiety about men's dependence on women to perpetuate their names and transfer their property, anxiety about the prevalence of adultery and the conjectural nature of paternity. Shakespeare revisits this anxiety not only in cuckold jokes and nervous remarks about paternity but in four plots that constitute an extended inquiry into the individual, social, and formal resources needed to give the dilemma of misplaced jealousy a comic conclusion (*Much Ado*), a tragic one (*Othello*), or a fantastical one (*Winter's Tale*, *Cymbeline*). In each of these plays, the jealous husband falsely accuses his wife. But other playwrights consider the wife who is actually unfaithful and suggest that, even in that case, it is possible for the marriage and the story to find various resolutions. Shakespeare depends on temporary deaths to buy the time and create the remorse jealous husbands need to surrender their doubts and reclaim their wives (and that accused wives need to get over their anger, although Shakespeare is much less interested in that). Wives can be forgiven on the condition that they are innocent and that they have seemed to be dead for days or years. But Thomas Heywood, whose adulterous wives have usually done the deed, has them eliminate themselves, and the problems they pose, either through suicide (*A Woman Killed with Kindness*) or through the helpful expedient of dropping dead (*The English Traveller*) rather than simply appearing to have done so, as Hero, Imogen, and Hermione all do. In a wonderful play to which Bradin Cormack has drawn our attention, the Webster and Rowley collaboration *A Cure for a Cuckold*, the cuckolded husband, Compass, whose wife Urse has had a child by another man while Compass was away at sea (and presumed dead), "cures" his own cuckoldry first by delighting in his wife's baby and claiming it as his own and second by feigning death so that he and his wife can marry again. Shakespeare's husbands invent or fall for fictions of their wives' adultery. Compass cooks up a story that restores his marriage and expands his family and serves his own comic plot by playing the Shakespearean woman's part of pretending to be dead. In another twist on the story of marital infidelity, in *The Tragedy of Mariam* Elizabeth Cary imagines that there might be betrayals more troubling than adultery. One could go on and on. My point is that one of the most valuable "contexts" for thinking about Shakespeare's choices and inclinations is the different ways other playwrights tackle similar conflicts and work through similar scenarios. If writers work with story kits containing familiar elements—here the triangle of jealous husband, suspected wife, and purported lover—what is the range of configurations and outcomes possible in early modern drama?

Attending to "social contexts" is usually assumed to require looking beyond the drama to illuminate the telling differences among writers, across time, and across genre, as well as the tantalizing overlaps between, for example, the blood-sport bearbaiting and the various suffering Shakespeare characters who describe their situation through reference to the procedures of the arena. As Gloucester says in *Lear*, "I am tied to the stake and I must stand the course" (3.7.53). Understanding this image begins with a gloss—to what kind of stake does Gloucester refer? What is the scenario he conjures up? But the more one tries to visualize and relate the suffering man's situation to that of the bear (on whose perseverance an early modern theatregoer might have placed a bet) the more one enters a knowledge-making process that, for contemporaries, required the ability to link the stage and the arena, human and animal suffering, and, for readers and viewers now, demands the imaginative leap of entering another time and place. A crucial part of this knowledge-making process, then and now, is the recognition of its limits: we can never fully know, for example, what animals—or other humans—feel. But we can begin to understand the available terms in which suffering could be described and the most well-worn paths of connection between one arena of exposure and trial and another.

What might be called social context, here the practice of bearbaiting, might work as a kind of frame or foil. Foil first referred to a thin sheet of metal placed under or behind a precious stone to enhance its luster. By extension, it came to mean, according to the *OED*, "Anything that serves by contrast of color or quality to adorn another thing or set it off to advantage." With this meaning, foil is used to describe how one character relates to another as a revealing contrast. But if we think of social context as a foil, then it threatens to elevate the Shakespearean text as a jewel, superior to its setting, and simultaneously to fix it in place, framing it but also shutting it in. This would foil the expansive possibilities of contexting.

For the jewel is not without flaw, nor is it set unshakably in its illuminating foil. As we all know, it is itself unstable, in process, and under negotiation. Shakespeare, famously, seems to have started with a crowded calendar and a crammed notebook rather than a clean slate, borrowing and upcycling. Some plays survive in multiple versions; these might include quarto and folio versions, which cannot be explained simply as earlier and later, bad and good versions. Recent work has drawn our attention to a play not as one text but as a congeries of mobile pieces, which might have included the scrolls actors used to learn their parts and their cues, the letters and proclamations read on stage, music, the actor's memory of other parts he had played or other actors who had played similar parts. Plays in performance challenged their audiences to engage in piecework and in guesswork, as William N. West has shown. Before they ever reached the printshop, then, playtexts were con-texts.

Reminding ourselves that Shakespeare's plays are as much works in progress as are "social contexts" can also remind us that a contextualizing practice might require us not just to venture out, but to dig in. What is the play's provenance and authority? A speech that seems familiar—Hamlet's "to be or not to be" soliloquy—looks different when we read it in the context of the play as a whole, attending to why it appears when and where it does. Every time I reread *Hamlet*, for instance, I find it jarring that he laments that no traveler returns from the "undiscovered country" (3.1.78) of death after he has encountered the Ghost, who so unsettlingly has. Even after we accept a given text as our object of analysis, need we necessarily look away from it to find social contexts? Might we think of the play itself as a kind of historical "evidence"? It is often a useful exercise to consider: If I had only a given play, what might I think I knew about early modern attitudes toward grief or marriage, sexuality or kingship, or anything? Now that it is so easy to find answers on the Internet, the questions we ask have become more pressing.

Furthermore, if we think of context as an open-ended and interactive process, what readers are doing or making rather than what they find, then contexting need not contain or delimit meaning, hedging Shakespeare round with a policeable perimeter of the historically accurate (as opposed to the anachronistic). We might trace paths of connection across texts and across time and find new nodes of connection that light the play up in new ways or open it out. Passages about, and images of, bearbaiting may offer both the romantically dusty whiff of the archive and the bracing appeal of newly acquired information. But contemplating where we ourselves witness images of someone tied to the stake might provoke reflection on the many, many depictions of restraint and torture we see in contemporary media and the way that Shakespeare's use of this image invites us to imagine what it is like to be the one immobilized, the one tortured. Focusing on suffering bears can make it too easy to forget our own complicity in brutality, the ways in which we have not made as much progress as shock at bearbaiting or public execution might assure us we have.

If context is a process, then it is ongoing and might include afterlives, revivals and survivals, as well as the surprising tenacity not only of a Shakespeare play as a whole but of a character, a phrase, or a plot that floats free from it and latches on to new conditions. Divorced from the play, what meanings does a famous line or speech jettison and what new meanings does it seem to pick up? Many people who have not read *The Merchant of Venice* might have seen Jon Stewart, responding on the Daily Show to Joseph Biden's reference to "shylocks," screaming "Fuck you Shakespeare ... I've been waiting four hundred years to say that." Biden's grouping of unscrupulous moneylenders under Shylock's name, and Stewart's vehement response, suggest the far-reaching social implications of Shakespearean representations. A character's name can trail clouds of association, some of them obscure, even as it also accrues new resonances. Thinking about a play's afterlife can seem to position it as a kind of origin, the stone dropped in the water from which the ripples fan out. But the Shakespeare play is not as rock solid as that.

I would like to turn, finally, to two kinds of objects documenting early modern reading practices—marginalia (or the annotations in the margins of a printed text) and compilations (by which I mean a whole range of texts produced through breaking down and reassembling texts)—in order to figure two different processes by which one might "context" Shakespeare. What we once thought it meant to attend to social contexts might best be figured in the image of the printed text with marginalia. Such texts were central evidence in crucial case studies in the history of reading. The notes in the margins might gesture in different directions and be written in different hands. But picturing the page or even interleavings—blank pages bound in to make space for a reader's notes—we might still think of one text as at the center and its contexts gathering around it. For Shakespeareans, that central text is usually Shakespeare, and everything else gains value through its association with him or supplements our understanding of Shakespeare's works. As has been much discussed, marginalia pose various evidentiary problems. Those annotated texts that survive tend to have been the work of elite male readers and notetakers, either because they were more likely to annotate their texts or because their notes were considered valuable and so preserved. Many libraries cropped or erased the very annotations scholars now treasure. Yet the model of reading they document or perform remains one that structures many new reading platforms. *Internet Shakespeare Editions*, for example, focuses on playtexts, but offers pathways outward to "supplementary and related materials," including what could be called "social contexts" (under the "Life & Times" tab). For many readers, academic and non, the center of attention remains the play, and we depend on editors to decide what goes in the margins.

The counterpoint to the printed book with its marginalia is the compilation, commonplace book, or scrapbook. Scholarship on reading practices suggests that many early modern readers broke texts down, collected fragments, and then combined texts they'd written and texts they'd collected into new texts. The compiler makes meaning by materially asserting the relations he or she sees or creates among texts, composing what we might now call collages, textual clusters, or word maps, using scissors, glue, and pins rather than data searches. Like the elite readers who entered their notes in the margins of printed texts, these compiling or relational readers posit relationships among texts, ideas, and experiences. Sometimes there was an interactive dimension to these transactions as well, as one reader added to or critiqued what another had written, using the process to forge relations among readers and their readings. The social aspect of some digital platforms is starting to open up a similar space for collaboration and interaction. Descriptions of the Folger Luminary Shakespeare, for example, promise to promote social reading, content creation, networking, and mobile learning. New technologies might, then, facilitate a venerable process. At present, such platforms downplay what conventional editions have included as contexts, in part because crowds don't always know about or have access to the sources. But if contexts are as dynamic as the Shakespeare con-text itself, as I have been arguing here, then there might be more room for the collaborative compilation of contexts.

Whereas I have taken the printed text with its marginalia as one model for a contextualizing practice, focused on one central text and, often, the commentary of one self-documenting reader, I propose the compilation as a model for an altogether messier process, which decenters (even breaks up) the texts it engages, emphasizes the compiler's agency in forging connections, and relates the contexter to the crowd of others. Shifting attention to our own practices erodes the distinction between text and context by reminding us that we are not talking about stable objects of study so much as about the dynamic interpretive processes through which we engage and constitute them. The Shakespeare text may be adept at generating attachments but it doesn't do it alone. In our creative and critical practice we assemble and relate ideas, texts, moments, images, people, and objects. In owning up to our own agency, we can also refuse the false distinction between historicism as the recognition of difference, rupture, and change and presentism as the insistence on relatedness. We might also consider surrendering the pleasure of scolding others for failing to master their contexts in favor of the abashed recognition of the limits of our own knowledge. Pieces are missing. The glue connecting one piece to another keeps coming unstuck. We misunderstand some of what we feel most sure about. Join the crowd.

"*Hic et ubique*": *Hamlet* in sync

Bradin Cormack

Set off as it is here, the *social* in *social context* can be seen to name both a particular kind of context among others and, paradigmatically, almost tautologically, a quality pertaining to context generally, as alliance or fellowship or, most basically, relation. Like background, a context is never given, but always made or in the making, just at the moment when its use brings it into relation with the other text or texts it is to help stabilize. In the past thirty years, it has become a commonplace (no less correct for that) to note that contexts are as fluid and dynamic as the partners they serve. This openness pertains to context not only as a cultural phenomenon, whereby everything is seen to participate, always partially, in an only emergent, always elusive networked whole, but also as a logical consequence of the thing context is. *Text* and *context* name aspects of a practical, social operation whose discursive product *is* the relation we name in those two parties and by those two names. Even if it doesn't usually come out so, therefore, this means also that a play might as easily be a context for grasping the force of a legal report or husbandry manual or conduct book as the reverse. (Properly speaking, of course, this implies neither relativism nor subjectivism; nor, equally, must it disrupt the hierarchies that today, as we know, *literary* critics must import when they attend to their objects.) At another level, indeed, the playtext is always going to be contextual, since, in the ongoing shuttling of position inherent in the interpretive dynamic, it is the text that makes the context *as such* visible, the text that is the context for context, in the Derridean sense Claire Colebrook identifies when she writes that "any sense or understanding of context already differs from the 'context itself,'" the difference lying in the "repeatable and distinct shape" that makes the specific event, even in its specificity, "readable" and "repeatable" ("The Context of Humanism," 2011). This repeatability is a transcendence of which the historicist in particular is aware, inseparable as it is from the specificities against which a presentist reckoning is sometimes, and too blandly, measured.

Context specifies. "What means this, my lord?" (3.2.129), Ophelia asks of the dumb action onstage, thereby repeating the terms in which Horatio has earlier asked after the mere sound, offstage, of a trumpeted flourish: "What does this mean, my lord?" (1.4.7). The context Hamlet offers in explanation of the latter—the king is following a norm in social drinking—specifies with a (customary) here and now the meaning of a sound that would otherwise not have *no* meaning, but, rather, a more general one, which, steady, persists, however, into the other. The custom, Hamlet then avers in a further application of a now personal context for the extraction of the right significance from sound, is "to my mind ... / More honoured in the breach than the observance" (1.4.14–16). Hamlet's answer to Ophelia's question is of a different order. The show, he says, "means mischief" (3.2.130–1). Similarly specifying a meaning that would otherwise be more general than it might or must be, this answer has the curious effect also of reversing for Shakespeare's audience the relation between a show and the context of performance that the audience themselves are instantiating. If the meaning of the show *is* mischief, that is because the show has become context for the other thing Hamlet is in the process of specifying, namely the act of reception that remains (and, Hamlet's art aside, would merely have been) the social context for the show-as-event. The text *becomes* the context by making what had been context speak. And what does this fit between text and context feel like, such that, in the shuttle, a meaning, a reading, might stick? Like a resonance, we sometimes say, like a satisfying harmony or shudder:

OPHELIA   The King rises. ...

HAMLET   Didst perceive?

HORATIO   Very well, my lord.

HAMLET   Upon the talk of the poisoning.

HORATIO   I did very well note him.

                                        (3.2.258; 279–82)

Context places. It promises if not to fix a meaning then to settle it in the minimal sense of placing it in a posited, usually distant, here and now. Alert to the *topos* of the rhetoricians, the place and seat of their arguments, we may even say that context promises meaning itself, since without a place—some place, however complex—the datum remains undisciplined, impertinent to the disciplinary life that is the text's knowledge. When Hamlet in his table book converts his uncle into text, pinning him there as a specimen under his proper word, the satisfaction in the nephew's slow sentence speaks just to the fit of the placement: "So, uncle, there you are." But then, as Hamlet turns to himself—"Now to my word. / It is 'Adieu, adieu, remember me'" (1.5.110–11)—Shakespeare undoes the comforting thought that placing and knowing something might aspire always to this kind of stillness, this *there*-ness. The near context for the potent word that might subsume the person, the word that might be personal, be mine, be me, is theological: "In the beginning was the Word, and the Word was with God, and the Word was God." And the gentle joke in Hamlet's textual self-poiesis is that the form of the Ghost's farewell, "a-dieu," has suggested and already activated the context his sentence reaches for. And so the joke releases Hamlet into the place of the father, the ghostly thing that has evaded knowing by refusing to stay still, to stay in place, for anyone but Hamlet, and then, paradigmatically, even for him. As Hamlet asks his companions to swear their silence about what they have seen, the thing under the stage cries, "Swear," first here, then there, then there. "*Hic et ubique*," Hamlet says (1.5.155–6), as he moves his party along the felt trajectory, placing the thing here, but just to the extent (as is also said of God) that it is also everywhere.

Not in *a* here or *a* place, but not not there, not not in that place. The challenge of the kind of reading the play stages is of letting both aspects of meaning pertain to the text the ghostly thing is and, equally, to the thing the playtext is. Rather than asking how to know something that *is doubly, is itself* by being here and not only here, we might notice just the urgency with which a play about placing things, getting them right in the way students were and are taught to do, ends up there. The stage is partly responsible, since it trades, by definition, not only in the doubling of here and now, but also in a staging of action that is necessarily in touch with the place of its own futurity. As my examples of Hamlet's words suggest—these phrases that cause the action to pause in the face of its own displacement—the effect is a consequence also of the syntax that puts meaning in and out of place. Consider one more sentence. In Act 2.2, after Polonius has, with all the satisfaction of a contextualist, laid out unrequited love—a commonplace—as the cause of Hamlet's condition, the King wonders if it can be so, which makes Polonius ask, with precise generality, if he has ever hitherto been wrong: "Hath there been such a time—I would fain know that— / That I have positively said 'tis so / When it proved otherwise?" (2.2.150–2) No, the King agrees, to which Polonius adds, as warrant, a sentence so general as to be aspiring to its own formalization:

Take this from this if this be otherwise.

(2.2.154)

We know how the line is to be played—head and torso, head and neck, tongue and mouth, whatever. But if the acting body allows the play coherently to proceed past the crux, the singular sentence nevertheless functions as a stop, a pause coincident with how the action has been said and thereby placed. Almost entirely deictic in force, the sentence insists on a hyperspecificity, even as it also unmakes itself into the opposite, a sentence so empty as to seem to be socially nowhere. Alternatively put, the sentence that means by waiting for its emptiness to be filled (the actor's dream sentence, then) manages also to be comprehensive, a kind of ur-proposition. For, enacting a tautology, Polonius's words may be said to stand under any statement whatsoever: take *this* from "this" if "this" be other than *this*. In Polonius's fumbling eloquence, the play invents the semantic equivalent of the thing under the stage: *hic et ubique*, the sentence reaching from its here to index and grasp the possibility, even in its *here*-ness, of its meaning being elsewhere and everywhere.

Then, not, not not then. Context means in alliance with the text that will still be pointing it out. There, not, not not there.

Playing in Context, Playing out Context

William N. West

For the last generation at least, scholarship on Shakespeare's poems and plays, in all its wild variety, has largely shared an imperative to set these works in the contexts of the social worlds in which they appeared and intervened. Contexts need not be social, of course, or even historical—they may be generic, philological, ideological, among other possibilities—but recently we have looked above all to social circumstance to enliven these powerful works. At its liveliest, context is no static frame within which objects of analysis are fixed, but a dynamic, reciprocally shaping interplay of interpenetrating elements. Text and context, foreground and background, readily switch places, so that one moment's focus blurs into a background that highlights something different. The claims of context are bifurcated. In *Taming of the Shrew*, Petruccio makes a show of refusing to dine on the burnt meat he and Katherina are served,

For it engenders choler, planteth anger,
And better 'twere that both of us did fast,
Since, of ourselves, ourselves are choleric ...

(4.1.161–3)

Context for this passage may claim to declare either what would have been obvious to everyone (that is, everyone *in that context*) but which in another context has become obscured, for instance a humoral physiology that linked diet to temperament, or what can now be articulated (that is, because of our distance *from that context*) but that from another perspective would have been invisible or unsayable, like patriarchy as a systematic subjugation of women.

"Context" is not a word that Shakespeare used, nor is it frequent among the writings about early modern playing. More often in Shakespeare's time it appears when different religious factions accuse others of ignoring context in order to advance their heretical interpretations of the Bible. We sometimes talk about putting something in context as if contexts were like the cozy cases in which, according to Walter Benjamin, nineteenth-century bourgeois lapped their possessions and their selfhoods. But early modern contexts weave more continuities than distinctions. When John Foxe, or John Milton, talks about the "context" of the gospels, neither means a setting that determines meaning, but a composite knitted together from differing accounts, discontinuities patched and smoothed to produce a narrative with no designs on originality. *Context* is not what cradles a text that is already given, but the articulation of scattered pieces into a text.

But although they did not use the word, early modern producers of playing—I mean not only playwrights, players, and playgoers, but interested onlookers, bystanders, even opponents—attended insistently to playing's social contexts. We have few accounts of the performances of plays that people actually saw. We know much more about how the world was carried into the playhouse: paying or being pickpocketed, standing in the crush of the yard or sitting in the galleries, gaping, groping, eating and drinking, hissing, shouting. We hear of how playing reached in turn out into the world, applying morals and allegories to echo or interpret it. But it is hard to see plays in early records; mostly they must speak for themselves.

They often do. When Hamlet hears the player recite the death of Priam, he thinks not of the King of Troy but of a player's skill in a fictional Denmark; he thinks as well of the actual, present London of Marlowe's *Dido and Aeneas*, and the boy playing companies whose competition threatens adult companies like the one in which Burbage rehearses this scene. He thinks above all of other playhouses, set apart from the rest of the world and pressing back against it. Early modern playing is not, or not only, a medium, it is a self-resembled content: it is about itself, its novelty, its capacity, its fantasy of failing to fit into any position defined for it by society. Playing sets itself into a determinate relation of likeness with contexts outside it, not the same and not the opposite, but contiguous and registering the contact. This is how playing requires a context: it claims a place both within and apart from the culture it sketches and inhabits. Playing flashes up emergently from an undifferentiated environment, throwing other features into shadow, making them its contexts. Its contexts are as much its product as anything else it figures. The claim of self-resemblance continues to shape our own aesthetic, epistemic, and hermeneutic assumptions about theatre today.

Playing in Shakespeare's time reflects insistently on its own situation as something within the world yet apart from it. Its action is "the abstract and brief chronicles of the time" (*Hamlet*, 2.2.462–3), showing "the very age and body of the time his form and pressure" (3.2.23–4), at once informing and informed. The discourses around playing reify it as an inset mirror or a world within the world, as a still *theatre* that turned simultaneously outward and inward to show playgoers to themselves. To understand playing, as Hamlet does, as beside its out-of-joint time is to insist on the imperfect framing of a synchronous context, in which what pleased once will not please the same way again, like changeable fashions, "richly suited, but unsuitable" (*All's Well*, 1.1.156–7), to which playing was often compared. To the extent that Hamlet's Mousetrap works, it is because of the context in which it is played, from which it differs and in which it is sheltered. The compelling fantasies playing expresses of overreaching its boundaries, exposing guilty creatures sitting at a play or taking murderous revenge upon them, only underscore its difference from the real world within which it is contained.

The playing Shakespeare knew was a gallimaufry of practices, materials, institutions, and agencies, some familiar and some innovative, that insistently represent themselves as novel, local, and clearly circumscribed events: as plays. This was not entirely true, certainly not so radically as was claimed. But playing localizes distributed practices and phenomena to focus on a particular moment, space, or action, capturing and managing its audiences' attentions through its props, structures, institutions, gestures, voices. In Shakespeare's London playing was multiply set off from other fields of activity, through physical boundaries, with legal injunctions and recognitions, and above all by ways of speaking that developed around it. Perhaps foremost among the imaginative tactics of Shakespeare's contemporaries for placing playing was the magic circle of the playhouse, which cut out a space privileged as uniquely unserious. As they set aside their contents from the social world, these boundaries rendered the rest of the culture as their context, the great shared world that playing took up and commented upon in its representations, and within which its activities made sense. Playing's reflection of the world is its power, its circumscription is its constraint, but circumscription is what enabled it to claim its potent reflection.

By localizing action in the play, the playhouse, and the player, the discourses of early modern playing made their contexts rise around them. Not all other discourses did this. Take two writers who, for us, are part of the social context of playing, Philip Stubbes and Stephen Gosson. Stubbes and Gosson alike vehemently condemned playing, but while the vicious effects they ascribe to it are similar, in their accounts playing works very differently. In *Anatomie of Abuses* (1582), although he writes it "dialogue-wise," Stubbes is not especially interested in playing, which is only one vice among many, including dancing, gambling, gluttony, careless Sabbath-keeping, football, and usury. Stubbes is not in fact particularly interested in anything, because for him everything shows equally the depravity of the land whose name he transposes as Ailgna: "All wickedness, mischief, and sin ... springeth of our ancient enemy the Devil, the inveterate corruption of our nature, and the intestine malice of our own hearts" (B3r). Fallenness is a condition of playing, as it is of living, but it is not a context. In the "Theatre of Heaven" (L3v) that Stubbes pictures in place of worldly playhouses, the details of earthly existence are all equally insignificant in God's eyes.

Gosson, unlike Stubbes but like many other antitheatrical writers, had been a playwright (Stubbes' dystopian Ailgna was invented by another, Thomas Lupton), and wrote against playing as playing thought about itself. In *Schoole of Abuse* (1579) and *Playes confuted in five actions* (1582), playing is not just one problem among others, it is a center of vice that organizes other kinds of vice around it. Playing is set into a world which it ornaments, or mars, and which in turn explains and generates it. Gosson localizes playing, distinguishing it from the fabric of culture that it nestles within. From playing, vice radiates outward into that culture, as its emblem, symptom, index. This is not to say that playing was a master discourse of early modern social formation; far from it. It is to point out that our attempts to comprehend playing's social contexts are anticipated by some of the ways Shakespeare's playing presented itself as that world's mirror. Have we learned our habits of seeking context in part by reoccupying the practices of Elizabethan playing, finding among them new questions for old answers?

13

Historicism

Historicizing Historicism

William C. Carroll
President, SAA 2005–6

Always historicize! This slogan—the one absolute and we may even say "transhistorical" imperative of all dialectical thought—will unsurprisingly turn out to be the moral of "The Political Unconscious" as well.

FREDRIC JAMESON, THE POLITICAL UNCONSCIOUS (1981)

I began with the desire to speak with the dead.

STEPHEN GREENBLATT, SHAKESPEAREAN NEGOTIATIONS (1988)

History lies to us if it seems to offer us any completely realized "past" which we are able to see independently of what happens in the present.

TERENCE HAWKES, "MACBETH IN THE PRESENT" (2013)

Shakespeare scholars have, since 1980, taken Jameson's slogan to heart, though often not in the ways he intended. Greenblatt's *Renaissance Self-Fashioning* (1980)—the launching pad for the historicizing impulse in Shakespearean scholarship—impelled a generation of scholars to converse with the dead. Yet "historicism"—New, not Old—apparently vanquished formalism only to turn into a type of formalism itself. Recent developments in presentist theory, as Hawkes suggests, qualify the historicizing impulse while harnessing it to new concerns. My three epigraphs thus represent key moments in historicist approaches to literature across the past several decades. Perhaps a fourth should be added, encompassing all of the above: Faulkner's "The past is never dead. It's not even past."

The brief narrative outlined above is far too simple, of course. "Historicism" is a mode of thinking, not just an approach to literary-critical interpretation; historicist thinking posits social context as central to understanding culture, with the corollary notion that supposedly immutable, universal laws of nature and of human nature are necessarily contingent. The history of the idea goes back at least to Vico and Montaigne, to Marx and Hegel; its modern philosophical and sociological critics include Karl Popper and Leo Strauss. Historicism has always had to steer carefully (if it is even possible) away from the twin shoals of determinism and relativism. Still, in the study of "early modern" literature—the category itself finding currency from the theoretical developments of the 1980s—"historicism" has come to refer not so much to the philosophical tradition as to the literary mode of analysis announced by and embodied in the work of Stephen Greenblatt, followed by multitudes of others offering support or critique. The "New" Historicism marked itself off from the "Old" Historicism by embodying the latter in the work of Tillyard and others, and by invoking the writings of Foucault and other postmodern theorists to argue for "the historicity of texts and the textuality of history," as Louis Montrose put it. Culture was a text—Greenblatt's often-cited phrase was "cultural poetics"—which could be read if one were skilled enough, and alert to historical difference. Historicists found authority and inspiration for these concepts in Clifford Geertz's method of "thick description," which aimed at understanding the actions and symbols in any given culture as the people living in that culture would understand them. To speak with the dead one first had to hear their own discourse.

If New Historicism was undertheorized, as some asserted, writers like Jean Howard and Montrose began to articulate its underlying assumptions. Critics of the approach, from Edward Pechter and Alan Liu to Stanley Fish, offered often fierce analyses of the method. Further critiques from feminist, psychoanalytic, textual, and religious approaches soon followed, as well as socio-logical analyses of how American and British English departments had been "taken over" by this now hegemonic discourse; in 1987 Don Wayne prophesied, with considerable accuracy, that New Historicism would become the "new orthodoxy in Renaissance studies." Moreover, the New Historical "anecdote"—the Geertzian synecdoche of culture so tantalizing and useful in the beginning—was eventually seen by many as a late twentieth-century fatal Cleopatra, leading the New Historicist (as Dr. Johnson said of Shakespeare's quibbles) "out of his way, and sure to engulf him in the mire. It has some malignant power over his mind, and its fascinations are irresistible." The more politically-oriented "cultural materialism," brought to its sharp point by mainly British academics, offered a different path to historicist analysis, one that openly engaged in contemporary social struggles and tended to see New Historicism as a formalism itself. As one side looked to Geertz and Foucault for inspiration, the other looked to Raymond Williams.

The most powerful challenge to historicist premises has come from "presentist" studies, which, as Hugh Grady (2003) puts it, "underline the salient point that all our knowledge of works from the past is conditioned by and dependent upon the culture, language, and ideologies of the present, and this means that historicism itself necessarily produces an implicit allegory of the present in its config-uration of the past." And New Historicism especially has, from its beginnings, seemed too easily to dismiss or ignore form—that is, aesthetic questions; "context" has seemed to some to displace "text." Indeed, among the recent counter-strategies to historicism are the "new formalism" and "thin reading," the latter a method for reading texts "that employs techniques developed originally to analyze behavior" (Heather Love).

This too brief history of historicism omits much influential and profound thinking on the subject; moreover, "1980" as a starting point for New Historicism is merely conventional shorthand, ignoring the multiple discourses and pressures that led up to the work of Greenblatt and others. This essay turns, then, from a more thorough genealogy of historicism to a single question: what difference has the historicist turn made to the study of Shakespeare in the past decades? The answer is simple: it has made an enormous difference. The texts we now read, teach, and edit (and how we edit them), the myriad approaches we deploy in our scholarship and our classrooms, the expansion of the canon, the questions we now take up: it is difficult to imagine most of these developments issuing from the continuation of the New Criticism alone. The historicist turn produced editions of the plays quite specifically designed to provide "context," while the *Norton Shakespeare*'s introductions to the plays modeled deeply engaged historicist approaches. The eventual fusion of feminist theory with historicist approaches vastly expanded the literary canon, and provided new foundations for the exploration of Shakespeare's work—even leading some into rejecting it. To investigate how Shakespeare's works were imbricated in race, class, and gender can no longer be dismissed as a marginal activity.

It is difficult to think of any of Shakespeare's plays that have not been profoundly, even radically, rethought through the pressure of historicist approaches. Some plays achieved a new prominence in criticism because they were so susceptible to these approaches—such as *Measure for Measure*, which for a time seemed written to a Foucauldian prescription in which surveillance and state power figured as central, and the Duke's formerly godlike power of punishment and forgiveness came to be seen as, at least in part, sinister and coercive. More canonically central plays, such as *The Tempest*, were no longer the bard's farewell to the stage but an exploration of colonialism (including Ireland), of Old and New World encounters with the Other, and of patriarchal power in collision with its own contradictions. *King Lear*, too, was seen to interrogate contemporary political and social issues: debates in early Jacobean London about possession and exorcism, vagrancy and state power, the proposed unification of England and Scotland and the creation of "Great Britain," the disintegration of feudalism and the impact of a new transactional economy on social relations, among others. Many of these topics had been considered prior to 1980, but each took on a new urgency and was pursued in new directions. And while the history plays and the tragedies seemed most responsive to historicist analysis, Shakespeare's comedies also benefited from historicist lines of inquiry: geography and empire in *The Comedy of Errors*; inheritance and deforestation in *As You Like It*; the early modern history of Jews in England and the rise of a neocapitalist economy in relation to *The Merchant of Venice*.

I will briefly consider *Macbeth* to illustrate how historicist approaches have transformed critical interpretation. The Romantics and Victorians especially admired Macbeth's heroic criminality and Lady Macbeth's "unnatural" ambition as superb, even "sublime" constructions of character. The apotheosis of this interpretation was Bradley's comment that Macbeth was Shakespeare's "most remarkable exhibition of the *development* of a character." Cleanth Brooks's famous 1947 essay, "The Naked Babe and the Cloak of Manliness," took formalist analysis of the play's language about as far as one could imagine. Just three years later, however, Henry N. Paul's *The Royal Play of Macbeth* firmly marked a historicist turn in the play's interpretation, although not in a New Historicist direction, as the book's subtitle reveals: *When, Why, and How it was Written by Shakespeare.* Paul's book raises (or begs) the distinction between topicality and historicism—a distinction still too-often elided in historicist writing. Paul deployed a deep knowledge of local and national history surrounding the play, appealing to known facts (King Christian of Denmark's Hampton Court visit in 1606) with some license (asserting that *Macbeth* was written for and first performed at this visit, though no play titles for these performances exist). Paul was not above inventing history, as when he imagined that George Buc, acting Master of the Revels, "must have been at Oxford" with King James in 1605 and that "it would have been quite in order for Buc to tell" Shakespeare to "write a better play for his king" than those on offer in Oxford, "with suggestions as to subject matter." Buoyed by this advice, the pliable playwright "was conscious of the face of the king looking straight at him" as he "sat at his desk and wrote." Here is almost a parody of the New Historicist anecdote *avant la lettre*. The result of Paul's exhaustive treatment was an (old) historicist account of the play as, ultimately, a text designed to "flatter" James.

Historicist approaches post-1980 began to call into doubt, or even reverse, much of what Paul and those who followed him had claimed for the play. Essays by Harry Berger Jr., Jonathan Goldberg, Stephen Orgel, and David Norbrook, among others, dismantled the "flattery" reading of the play, noting contradictions and fissures in the play's structure, language, and sources. Feminist approaches analyzed the play's demonization of the maternal, and linked these projections to the anxieties of patriarchal power. Coupled with deconstructionist-tinged close readings, these approaches turned the play's historical position from one of a "reflection"—one of the key metaphors of the Old Historicism—of contemporary order, to one of intervention in, and skepticism of, that order. Jan Kott had offered an explosive rethinking of the play (1964), rejecting restorative readings; Kott saw "the image of history itself" as a "Grand Mechanism," in which "Every successive chapter, every great Shakespearean act is merely a repetition," one totalitarian regime succeeding another. Kott's vision of history offered little in the way of Geertzian "thick-reading" detail, but his provocative recasting of the play found positive correlation in some of the historicist approaches after 1980, while Paul's vision of the play continues to find adherents. Perhaps the best way to illustrate the difference between the two approaches to *Macbeth*, and to indicate the virtues and limitations of New Historicist analysis, is to look at three elements of the play as they figure in each kind of interpretation.

Consider the witches. A few years after the first performance of *Macbeth*, Middleton (most likely) seems to have adapted the play, adding two songs that also appeared in his play *The Witch*. Davenant added more singing and dancing, Thomas Duffet parodied it, more and more singing and dancing witches were added (up to fifty or sixty in Kemble's production), until eventually the Shakespearean/Middletonian text was restored to the stage, and in much criticism of the twentieth century they became pure agents of evil, "instruments of darkness," external to Macbeth but speaking his own dark desires. Then, in 1986, Terry Eagleton made his notorious comment: "To any unprejudiced reader—which would seem to exclude Shakespeare himself, his contemporary audiences and almost all literary critics—it is surely clear that positive value in *Macbeth* lies with the three witches. The witches are the heroines of the piece, however little the play itself recognizes the fact." Eagleton's was one of many recent attempts to recast the witches in a more positive light—usually as demonized projections of patriarchal anxieties; they were read as the inevitable by-product of state power, the necessary Other against which power reasserts its supposed legitimacy. Such efforts have had considerable success. The work of Diane Purkiss, Dympna Callaghan, and Peter Stallybrass, among many others, has gone far to place the witches in patriarchal, religious, social, and political discourses. Not only external agents of evil, not only psychological projections, the witches are seen as *systemic* elements of a diseased, masculinized hierarchy. For Greenblatt, "Witchcraft provided Shakespeare with a rich source of imaginative energy upon which he could draw to achieve powerful theatrical effects."

A comparable transformation occurred with Lady Macbeth. Along with Macbeth, she became in the nineteenth century a greatly admired *character*, even as her image bifurcated into "barbaric and passionate or domesticated and caring," as Georgianna Ziegler has shown. Mrs. Siddons's tremendous portrayal long dominated the critical conversation. Some writers, like Anna Jameson and Mary Cowden Clarke, worked to understand Lady Macbeth by providing an imagined childhood, filling in perceived lacunae in the play's narrative, and delving into her supposed psyche. From the time of Gordon Bottomley's *Gruach* (1918) forward, however, an unusual historicizing process has been at work. The "actual" history of the historical Lady Macbeth has been unearthed and/or invented: her very name, Gruach (never mentioned in either Shakespeare or his chief source, Holinshed), now appears in contemporary plays and novels; her royal blood (descended from King Kenneth III) is now cited as the chief means by which Macbeth's rule is (tenuously) legitimated; her first marriage and child by that marriage, Lulach, are revived. None of these elements is present in Shakespeare's play, and none present (except Lulach's brief reign) in Holinshed. Yet some scholars now critique not only male scholars but Shakespeare himself for "suppressing" this historical information—to which he in fact had no access. Playing a historical trump card, one scholar notes that historicist scholars who have investigated the often contradictory succession issues in the play "have not addressed the historical Lady Macbeth's dynastic claims and revenge motive lurking at the margins of historical and dramatic master texts or the public transcript." This conflation of a literary character with elements of a historical figure blurs the line—how self-consciously is unclear—between literature and history in a way that gives one pause. This feminist/historicist impulse has, ironically, provided a scholarly platform for contemporary adapters to invent other aspects of Gruach's personal history to somehow explain the literary character's actions: more precisely, that a miscarriage (or whole series of them) must have occurred—hence the "babe that milks me" passage is explained (and L. C. Knights answered) as is Lady Macbeth's ambition, which seeks to fill the hollowness of her womb. We have, in some quarters, thus returned to Clarke and Jameson via a "historicist" detour.

Consider, finally, how historicist inquiry has altered critical conceptions of Malcolm. The prominent Stuart triumphalism of earlier criticism, in which Malcolm is seen not only as the "rightful" successor to Duncan but also as a righteous man, like the sainted Edward who shelters him, was central to Davenant's version and to virtually all accounts of the play into the twentieth century; many contemporary readers of the play, even those who adopt historicist methods, continue to see him as "Scotland's rightful heir," though he does seem "ineffectual" and the play's ending "like one more needlessly crude disappointment," as one critic lamented. Yet historicist approaches have cast considerable doubt on just what a "rightful heir" is, what the principles of Scottish succession are (both in the play and in Holinshed, Boece, Major, and other chroniclers), and how Malcolm's conduct in 4.3, the difficult scene set in England, might be justified. On the latter, John Drakakis (2013) has observed, fusing an informed historicism with Agamben's analysis of sovereignty, that "Malcolm incorporates into himself all that sovereign power necessarily *excludes* or 'abandons' as ethically unacceptable, but that is symbolically central to its operation." Certain recent playwrights— Ionesco (*Macbett*), Heiner Müller (*Macbeth: After Shakespeare*), David Greig (*Dunsinane*)—now give audiences a depraved and murderous Malcolm. Müller has Malcolm's followers kill Macduff; when Malcolm is then crowned, the Witches speak the final line: "Hail Malcolm Hail King of Scotland Hail." (In German it is the even more ominous "*heil.*") Not to be outdone, Greig, whose sequel begins after Macbeth's death during Siward's ongoing invasion of Scotland, gives us a Malcolm without human feelings at all—ordering the murder of innocent families, the burning of villages, and worse. In one speech, Malcolm, promising "total honesty," tells his nation that

> I will periodically and arbitrarily commit acts of violence against some or other of you—in order that I can maintain a more general order in the country. I will not dispose my mind to the improvement of the country or to the conditions of its ordinary people. I will not improve trade. I will maintain an army only in order to submit you to my will.

These playwrights understood Malcolm's duplicitous language as, well, duplicitous, and if their versions are not precisely historically informed, they are certainly informed by their own histories. Construing Malcolm as "rightful heir" or duplicitous machiavel figures the kind of old/new difference revealed in historicist approaches.

The history of Historicism in Shakespeare studies is not simply one of rise and fall—generically, a tragedy—but something far more complex and interesting. The turn to presentism, the turn to religion, the turn to a new formalism: Historicism continues to evolve. Paraphrasing Ovid, I want to speak, not with the dead, but about bodies changed into new forms: "That which has been, is not; that which was not, / Begins to be; motion and moment always / In process of renewal."

Minding Anachronism

Margreta de Grazia

Shakespeare's works, especially those set in antiquity, abound in anachronisms. Trojans, Greeks, and Romans refer to persons, things, events, customs, and beliefs belonging to much later periods. But Shakespeare could not have identified them as anachronisms for the simple reason that the word did not exist in England until a couple of decades after his death, and even then in its Greek form and primarily in recondite treatises on universal chronology. That the term anachronism postdates Shakespeare, however, does not mean that we should drop the category from historical inquiry. Rather it should prompt us to ask what these temporal anomalies might have indicated before they were judged anachronisms: errors in how time is computed, by chronology and in periods.

The first anachronism in Shakespeare to receive critical attention appears in *Troilus and Cressida*. In council, the Trojans debate whether to return the abducted Helen or fight to keep her. Paris and Troilus argue for her keeping, but their older brother Hector dismisses them as too young to reason responsibly. They have argued, he maintains, "not much / Unlike young men, whom Aristotle thought / Unfit to hear moral philosophy"

(2.2.165–7). Eighteenth-century commentators were appalled by this chronological error of almost a millennium. Did Shakespeare think the fourth-century BC Greek philosopher existed prior to the twelfth-century BC Trojan warrior? "Small Latin and less Greek" indeed.

The first eighteenth-century editor of Shakespeare, Nicholas Rowe, tacitly corrected the gaffe, replacing "Aristotle" with the indeterminate but metrically equivalent "graver sages": the two princes are "not much / Unlike young Men, whom *graver Sages* think / Unfit to hear moral Philosophy" [italics added]. Rowe's successor, Alexander Pope, followed suit, blaming the error on Shakespeare's publishers: "Any man with a tincture of education (or in conversation with anyone who had it)" would have known better. Subsequent editors retained "Aristotle" in the text, but flagged the anachronism in their notes, along with others they detected throughout the plays. Lewis Theobald made a policy of highlighting Shakespeare's anachronisms, believing it the critic's "duty" to "expose" the playwright's "Transgressions in Time." For Samuel Johnson, Hector's blunder becomes typical of Shakespeare's disregard for historical and cultural difference: "He had no regard to distinction of time or place, but gives to one age or nation, without scruple, the customs, institutions, and opinions of another." What began as a single slip becomes a characteristic failing. Toward the end of the century, Edmund Malone, dedicated to devising a chronology for both Shakespeare's life and his works, is particularly exasperated by Hector's anachronism, "Our author here as usual, pays no regard to chronology."

Throughout the twentieth century and even into the twenty-first, from the 1953 Variorum to the 2008 Norton, editors continue to signal Hector's anachronism, sometimes, because the error is so obvious, apologetically. But would it have been so obvious when the play was performed or imagined in 1600?

The Prologue tells us that the play's action takes place in the middle of the Trojan War. But what indication would there have been onstage that the action happens at a vast distance from the present? Before the Restoration, we have no sure evidence that the ancients onstage were visually differentiated from the moderns. Whether set in ancient or modern times, plays were performed in contemporary attire. Characters from antiquity, whatever their rank, sex, or profession, wore the same garb as their English counterparts, just as they read codices, wrote in tablebooks, and told time with clocks.

In *Troilus and Cressida*, Trojans and Greeks appear alternately armed and unarmed. Armed, they would have been clad in the same war gear that would have been worn in any of the other staged historical battles, at Philippi (42 BCE), for example, or Dunsinane (1054) or Agincourt (1415). And their trappings would have resembled items still in use, on ceremonial occasions if not on the battlefield. Unarmed, the Trojans and Greeks would also have appeared in sixteenth-century attire. Perhaps in council they would have worn dignified ruffed robes not unlike those worn by the delegates in the group portrait now at the National Portrait Gallery in London of *The Somerset House Conference, 1604*, where another war was at issue. (The Anatolian carpet on the conference table would have added a nice Trojan touch.) In such a contemporary setting, would a reference to Aristotle have seemed out of place? In assuming so, are we, like the eighteenth-century editors, being ourselves anachronistic?

When Hector's reference to Aristotle registers as an anachronism, the play is being imagined "in period"—as if the setting were in sync with the historical span being represented. But as Stephen Orgel has boldly stated, not until the late eighteenth century was Shakespeare staged to look like history: "All at once, in 1786, Shakespeare stopped being our contemporary and became history." Shakespeare ceased to be performed as if occurring in the *now* of the audience and was instead set back to the *then* of its historical moment. In 1790, John Philip Kemble considered staging an historically accurate *Troilus and Cressida*, but the first in-period production was in Germany, at the end of the nineteenth century, in a setting and costumes that purported to be archaeologically authentic, probably inspired by Heinrich Schliemann's Mycenaean excavations. One assumes the Aristotle reference was omitted.

But when a production is not in period, when it is instead sutured to the present of its audience, there is nothing untimely about what later generations would identify as anachronisms. There would have been nothing dissonant about *Troilus*'s numerous references to the particulars of its own early seventeenth-century day: to Winchester geese, mince pies, plackets, leather jerkins, pressing to death, the Neapolitan bone-ache, playing at bowls, dancing the "high lavolt," wall hangings, tablebooks with clasps, shoe horns, fee-farm, primogeniture, potatoes and tithes. Nor would the play's invocations of Christianity have jarred: of chapmen, the conjuring of devils, the seven deadly sins, the state of Grace, as well as expletives like God-a-mercy, Amen, praise be the Lord, 'sfoot, Friday fast-days and Sunday feast-days, and the world's end.

These references are better classified as updatings than misdatings, modernisms not anachronisms. They conform to what since Plato and Aristotle has been seen as the basic generic distinction between drama and epic. Drama is mimetic, it reenacts in the present. Epic is diegetic, it narrates the past. Modernisms give immediacy to a drama set in the past. But modernisms also occur in the process of translation from ancient tongues to modern. Vernacular equivalents to ancient Greek and Latin vocabulary often require modernization. Consider Golding's *Ovid*, in which Balearic slings are modernized as guns, catapults as cannons, rocks as bullets, tablets as books, and urns as coffins. Chapman's *Iliad* features buttons, coachmen, longbows, and man-of-war frigates.

Hector's "Aristotle" would also qualify as a modernism. Circa 1600, there would have been nothing anachronic about citing Aristotle. Indeed fathers and schoolmasters in the audience might well have quoted to headstrong sons and pupils the very passage that Hector cites: the maxim from *Nicomachean Ethics* that young men were unfit for philosophy was commonplace, quoted by Erasmus, Richard Mulcaster, Nicholas Grimald, Francis Bacon, as well as in popular handbooks of paraphrases. And if, as scholars have speculated, the play was written for the Inns of Court during what has been termed the Aristotelian revival, Aristotle's name might have had something of the topicality critics attribute to the insubordinate Achilles in the wake of the Earl of Essex's rebellion. Modernisms and topicalities all work to meld the time of the play into the audience's *here* and *now*.

This is not to say that the play effaces its Trojan past. No event, certainly none outside of Scripture, was as momentous as the Trojan War, in the epics of Homer and Vergil, to be sure, but also in the Matter of Britain. (Holinshed's *Chronicles* follows Geoffrey of Monmouth in opening with the Fall of Troy and the diaspora that sends Aeneas to Rome and later his grandson Brute to Britain.) It is also the event that in both Hesiod and Ovid divides the myths of the gods from the history of men. Thomas Heywood dramatizes the ancient metallic ages into four plays, the first three (Gold, Silver,

Brazen) on the escapades of the gods and the last (Iron) on the Trojan War. *Troilus and Cressida* is situated at a time more ancient than the ancients, since it precedes both the Greco-Roman and the Judaeo-Christian traditions. Not only was there no Aristotle to cite, there were no authors or authorities of any kind. It is with this play that precedents are first set, most markedly by Pandarus: "Let all constant men be Troiluses, all false women Cressids, and all brokers-between panders! Say 'Amen'" (3.2.197–9).

To an age enjoined to "Always historicize," anachronism is an embarrassment. It is an offense to historical thought that depends on maintaining a clear distance between the present of historians and the past of their historical subject. But anachronisms are not necessarily antithetical to historical criticism—only to one that sticks fast to chronology and periods.

The Historicist as Gamer

Gina Bloom

The Tempest's climactic revelation scene begins, oddly, with occlusion: the curtain to the stage's discovery space opens to reveal Miranda and Ferdinand playing chess, the former accusing the latter of cheating, but the audience—unable to see the chessboard—cannot decipher with certainty whether foul play has transpired. Instead of revealing all plots and identities, Shakespeare uses the architectural affordances of the early modern stage to hide information. The move is all the more interesting insofar as chess is, as scholars of gaming have argued, a game of "perfect information," where players and the spectators who make a game of betting on them see the board equally and thus share knowledge of the game's status. As it does on and offstage spectators, the scene leaves critics to inhabit a state of imperfect information and has consequently provoked debate. Does Ferdinand cheat? The happy conclusion of the play may be compromised if he does, so the answer, which the play refuses to provide, matters. I want to suggest that the irresolvability of this question presents us with a model for historicist reading wherein the historian is less an archaeologist who digs up evidence from the past than s/he is a gamer who navigates imperfect information in the course of playing with history.

The Tempest is an ideal play through which to deploy such a model of historicist reading because the information we have about its performance history poses intriguing links with the play's plot. Evidence that the play was performed to celebrate the dynastic union of King James I's daughter has, not surprisingly, invited speculation about how members of the English court might have responded to, or even shaped, the play's representation of good governance and dynastic marriage. Instead of taking sides in the debate about whether evidence of the play's court performance is useful or pertinent, I want to consider how information about historical performance of Shakespeare's plays puts literary scholars in a position much like that of audiences of *The Tempest*'s chess game. The revelation of evidence occludes even as it shows, reminding us that historicist reading, like *The Tempest*'s staged chess match, is a game of imperfect information. No matter how many pieces of data we can find, we can't really know the past; we, like theatre spectators adjudicating Ferdinand's honesty, can only speculate.

What might be gained by recognizing that historicist readings of Shakespeare are necessarily speculative? That the historian is not so different from the theatre spectator? And what would speculation of this sort look like as a historicist methodology? A good place to start is by recalling the gaming resonances of the term "speculation." In the context of gaming, the risks of speculation are central to the pleasures of play and crucial to reaping rewards from it. The more one has invested in a game and the less that is known about its outcome, the greater the financial, and often emotional, gains. What would happen if Shakespeareans bracketed their anxieties about speculation as a failure to maintain rigorous evidentiary standards and instead took seriously (or, perhaps, less seriously) our roles as speculators about, and players of, the past? What are the advantages of approaching historicist readings of Shakespeare as a kind of gaming?

The model of historian as gamer is already being enacted by Shakespeareans who apply historical research on what are sometimes called "original practices" (OP) to contemporary productions of the plays. For instance, a company may provide their actors only with "sides" (just the character's lines and cue words) instead of the entire script during rehearsal. Performances may be done with no artificial lighting in theatre spaces that mimic those of early modern London. And the troupe performing the play might be comprised of no more than fifteen actors, replicating the size of early modern professional theatre companies. Reenactment of this sort sometimes raises eyebrows among historically minded Shakespeareans, often for good reasons. Archival evidence of early modern rehearsal and production practices is incomplete and contested, so if the aim of OP is to relive the way Shakespeare's theatre "really was," the method rests on shaky foundations. Even in the best of circumstances, OP productions can seem a bit too much like nostalgic Shakespeare tourism.

However, OP performance techniques have been productively integrated with scholarly projects where these practices function not as instantiations of, but testing grounds for, theatre history research and literary analysis. Staging plays in one of the reconstructed historical theatres, such as Shakespeare's Globe or the Blackfriars Playhouse in Staunton, Virginia, yields insights into, for instance, how actors communicate to audiences whose sight lines are blocked by pillars or to audiences standing close to or sitting on the stage. Such insights impact our analysis of the plays. Consider again the climactic chess game scene in *The Tempest*. Would having audience members closer to the chess board put more or different pressure on Prospero to control what happens when he reveals the lovers at play? What happens to the dynamics of information in the scene when it is performed without a recessed, curtained space, as might have been the situation at court performances in halls with only two entrance/exit doors? Performed with what we believe are the original staging conditions in mind, theatrical productions become sites for experimental research, offering a way to assess what theatre historians believe they know as well as to consider what is at stake in that knowledge. Most notably, OP work sets up historians, and especially historians' bodies, as partners in the process of historicizing Shakespeare's plays and theatres. Performance provides a way to test and recontextualize speculations about theatre history and drama criticism, such that what we know about the past emerges through playful embodied engagement with it. For at the center of OP is a desire to play with the play.

OP can help us think more broadly about gaming as a model for historicism and particularly how the framework of gaming alters the focus of historicism to emphasize less what we find than how we find it. In his essay "A Theory of Play and Fantasy" in *Steps to an Ecology of the Mind* (1972), anthropologist Gregory Bateson observes that games are intrinsically about, indeed are forms of, metacommunication, for they not only prompt but are constituted by debate about their boundaries. Such debate is often enormously productive. Bateson argues that recognition of the "frame" of a game makes transformation possible: when players debate the rules, they enter into a different "logical type" and can return to play with modified, nuanced rules. In effect, discussion of rules and methods of play creates more critically astute players and often a better game. In a process that has come to be called "modding" in the digital gaming community, players alter even the material fabric of a game (its software or hardware). Modding is central to the history of analog games, too, including the game of chess staged in *The Tempest*, which was a modification of an early medieval version of chess where, among other things, the Queen piece had much less freedom of movement. Changing a piece's affordances could be seen as a violation of the game's rules from one perspective but, from another, this modification made a better game: faster paced, more interesting, and more conducive to wagering—arguably one reason for the changes. The point is that games change over time because debate about their rules and boundaries is an inevitable part of play. The history of a game is a history of debate about what the game is.

A metadiscourse about historicism has functioned in similarly productive ways in Shakespeare studies, which has been at the center of transformations in literary historiography. Shakespeare scholars have often been at the front lines if not the founding thinkers in new critical movements around historicism—New Historicism, unhistoricism, queer temporality, presentism, historical phenomenology, to name a few. Perhaps this is because the canonicity of Shakespeare's writings and their consequently familiar content frees us up to think more about method. Or maybe Shakespeare's unique position as both an icon of his early modern English moment and an author whose work has been pervasively read and performed in just about every moment since makes Shakespeare a particularly useful case for the study of historicism. Whatever the reason, Shakespeare studies has been a site of ongoing and often cantankerous debate about historicism. In figuring such debate as gamelike, I do not mean to minimize the serious stakes of disagreements about historiographical method. Rather, I want to invoke Bateson's view of play as inevitably metadiscursive and of discourse as constitutive of gameplay in order to observe that our histories of Shakespeare's time are bound up in, facilitated by, and indeed produced through critical disagreement about historicism and through continuous, scholarly modding. The historian who is a gamer is not only able to shift ground with changes in historiographical methods, but also to position herself as one of history's agents, one of the players, who brings change about.

14

Appropriations

American Appropriation through the Centuries

Georgianna Ziegler
President, SAA 2006–7

July 2014—two American cities, two *Romeos*. In New York, actors from the Classical Theatre of Harlem, in hoodies and bare midriffs, face off in *Romeo N Juliet* at Marcus Garvey Park, where the production's Soca music blends with hip-hop from a nearby ballgame. In a Washington DC bar, patrons, divided into teams Montague and Capulet, get the play started with a game of flip cup and continue to interject cheers and songs into LiveArtDC's production of *R+J: Star Cross'd Death Match* (*New York Times*, July 8, 2014; *Washington Post*, July 19, 2014). These are just two recent examples from a long history of Americanizing Shakespeare that began in the eighteenth century and shows no signs of slowing down. From the very beginning, Americans have appropriated Shakespeare into a variety of formats to serve their own cultural needs. Before going any further, I'd like to look more closely at what we mean by appropriation and its companion, adaptation— two terms that are often used interchangeably, as they will be here, but which literary theorists have tried to disentangle.

Linda Hutcheon in *A Theory of Adaptation* (2013), refers to appropriation as "taking possession of another's story," while

Julie Sanders in *Adaptation and Appropriation* (2006), attempts to distinguish the difference between the two. While both an adaptation and an appropriation assume a source text, what distinguishes the latter, according to Sanders, is that it often moves farther away "from the informing source into a wholly new cultural product." Thus LiveArtDC's *R+J*, though it used many of Shakespeare's lines, morphed into a type of performance art, involving the audience in a drinking game as well as direct participation in the telling of the story. Here the *process* is as important as the *product*, and indeed, the product or, in this case, performance, will always change depending on the venue and audience. Its style thus reflects our culture's comfort with online participatory media where anyone can virtually add to, act out, mash up, transpose, or translate anyone else's story, in full view of thousands of others with similar interests.

Indeed, much of American—and global—popular culture can be seen as appropriation, pushing against the old restraints of copyright and property law. In some respects we have circled back to Shakespeare's England, where stories from a variety of sources including folk and fairy tales, new translations of old works, classical literature, and even other people's plays circulated freely and were available to any playwright or poet who needed inspiration. If you'd read Plutarch in school, for example, part of the fun was seeing how Shakespeare had revamped his characters in *Antony and Cleopatra* (1606–7). Or if you had seen *The Taming of A Shrew* (c. 1594), you might have enjoyed seeing Shakespeare's almost simultaneous recasting of the story in *The Shrew*, and the subsequent adaptation, John Fletcher's play *The Woman's Prize, or, The Tamer Tamed* (c. 1611), a sort of "Shrew III."

Appropriations are more fun if you are "in" on the game by knowing the source text(s); as Sanders writes, this knowledge is what provides "this inherent sense of play, produced in part by the activation of our informed sense of similarity and difference between the texts being invoked," and there can be more than one text involved. But even if you don't know the novel or play or film upon which the appropriation is based, if it is itself an engaging work, it can be enjoyed on its own. Furthermore, the enriched enjoyment can occur afterward. Many people liked the film *Clueless* or the musical and movie *The Lion King* without having read *Emma* or *Hamlet*, but if they came to Austen's novel or Shakespeare's play later, the films and show would have taken on extra resonances.

Sanders points out that "adaptation and appropriation are dependent on the literary canon for the provision of a shared body of storylines, themes, characters, and ideas upon which their creative variations can be made." In English culture, and increasingly worldwide, Shakespeare's works have the highest literary recognition and are the most often adapted and appropriated. Sometimes the appropriation is more obvious, as in Jane Smiley's novel *A Thousand Acres*, which rewrites the King Lear story. Sometimes it is more subtle and wide ranging, as in Melville's use of Shakespeare in *Moby Dick*. But as John Bryant has written in *Adaptation Studies* (2013), "The delight that a culture takes in revising works by Shakespeare or Melville ... speaks directly to that culture's own evolving identity. Readers show their love of a work by changing it, remaking it, retelling it, adapting it."

Americans have been particularly fond of appropriating Shakespeare throughout our relatively short history. Indeed, next to the Bible, Shakespeare became the most influential writer in America, providing a common language through which Americans grappled with important issues such as independence, slavery, war, immigration, gender, civil rights, and multiculturalism. I'd like to focus here on a moment in American culture where Shakespeare was appropriated as a highly recognizable medium through which to process important events and ideas—the era of the American Civil War.

Though references to Shakespeare were used in letters and poems on both sides during the colonies' break with Britain in the eighteenth century, it was during the nineteenth century that real appropriations began. By this time the country had expanded westward, newspapers and magazines had proliferated, many people owned copies of Shakespeare along with the Bible, and they had memorized speeches in school from their McGuffey readers. Thousands flocked to theatres or makeshift stages, large and small, from New York to New Orleans, St. Louis, and San Francisco, and on barges along the Mississippi, to watch performances by traveling actors. Writers and the popular press could thus assume that their audiences knew enough Shakespeare to recognize references in their books, essays, and political cartoons.

When the abolitionist movement took hold in the 1830s, feelings ran high, along with the fear of miscegenation or intermarriage between whites and blacks. Edward Williams Clay was an illustrator and printmaker who capitalized on this fear in his series titled *Life in Philadelphia*, which ridiculed what might happen if blacks were freed and got "above themselves" in society. One of these prints from the 1830s is titled "The Fruits of Amalgamation." It features a black father reading *The Emancipator*, official paper of the American Anti-Slavery Society, while his dainty white wife holds their mulatto baby at her breast. Between them stands an older boy holding a black-and-white cat, while a portrait of abolitionist William Lloyd Garrison hangs on the wall. But over the couch where the family sits is a print titled "Othello & Desdemona," showing her pleading for her life in the bedroom scene. Clay appropriates Shakespeare's play as a warning of what might happen when the races mix. Buying into the culture of fear which is generated by the unknown, Clay suggests that beneath the veneer of domestic tranquility violence lurks, articulated by Desdemona's impending murder.

Events surrounding the Civil War in particular gave rise to expression through appropriations from Shakespeare. In spite of (or perhaps because of) the fact that William Holmes McGuffey's *New High School Reader* (1857) quoted from Hazlitt: "The striking peculiarity of Shakespeare's mind was its generic quality; its power of communication with all other minds; so that it contained a universe of thought and feeling within itself, and no one peculiar bias or exclusive excellence, more than another," Shakespeare's works continued to be used to support one political philosophy or another when discussing issues of the day, such as slavery. For example, an 1864 political cartoon from the Southern point of view shows "Lincoln and his cabinet ... in a disorderly backstage set, preparing for a production of Shakespeare's 'Othello.' Lincoln (center) in blackface plays the title role. He recites, 'O, that the slave had forty thousand lives! I am not valiant neither:—But why should honour outlive honesty? Let it all go.' Behind Lincoln, two men ... comment on Lincoln's reading." The first says, "Not quite appropriately costumed, is he?" and the second replies, "Costumed, my dear Sir? Never was such enthusiasm for art ... Blacked himself all over to play the part, Sir!" (Library of Congress website http://www.loc.gov/pictures/item/2008661674/). The implication is that

Lincoln has blackened more than his face to take the side of the slaves he would free.

The derogatory reference plays off white actors who donned blackface in the rowdy minstrel-hall adaptations of *Othello*, with titles like *Dar's de Money* and *Desdemonum*. In "Playing with (a) Difference: Early Black Shakespearean Actors, Blackface and Whiteface," Francesca Royster has suggested that since most of the actors of these burlesques were white immigrants—Italians, Jews, Germans—"performing the minstrel show's artificial codes of blackness was a way of both becoming American and becoming white" (in A. Vaughan and V. Vaughan, eds., *Shakespeare in American Life*, 2007). In other words, making fun of blacks in color and speech was a way of adapting a stance taken by the broader white American public, and thus becoming part of that public, even if you were a European immigrant. But Lincoln was not making fun of blacks, and the cartoon criticizes him for seriously "becoming" black as a way of supporting their cause.

The antislavery side also appropriated Shakespeare. The design for a political cartoon from the 1860s shows Columbia as Lady Macbeth, washing her hands of slavery while Lincoln and Grant look on. Lincoln had appointed Ulysses S. Grant as Chief General of the Army in 1864. Columbia was the female precursor to Uncle Sam, an allegorical figure used especially during the war to represent the preservation of the Union. The cartoon's caption reads: "Yet here's a spot / Out, damned spot, out, I Say!" making an emphatic statement about the stain of slavery on the Union. Years later in 1878 when Grant visited Otto von Bismarck, the powerful Prussian ruler, the German asked Grant about the American Civil War, supposing it was fought to save the Union. It was, Grant admitted, but "we all felt, even those who did not object to slaves, that slavery must be destroyed." Then echoing the sentiment of the Lady Macbeth political cartoon, Grant said, "We felt that it was a stain to the Union that men should be bought and sold like cattle" (John Russell Young, *Around the World with General Grant*, 1879).

Even during the war, Shakespeare continued to be performed. In November 1864 the three famous American acting brothers—Edwin, Junius Brutus, and John Wilkes Booth—playing together for the first time, starred in a production of *Julius Caesar* to raise money for a Shakespeare statue in Central Park, New York, commemorating the 300th anniversary of Shakespeare's birth. During the performance, fires raged outside the theatre, set by Confederate sympathizers trying to burn down New York. Five months later, John Wilkes, passionate for the Southern side, assassinated President Abraham Lincoln at Ford's Theatre in Washington. The popular press appropriated Shakespeare as a means of disseminating this terrible tragedy. A print titled "The Martyr of Liberty" shows Booth firing a shot at Lincoln's head in the theatre box. Beneath is the quotation: "Hath borne his faculties so meek; has been / So clear in his great office; that his virtues / Shall plead, trumpet-tongued, against / The deep damnation of his taking off." No attribution references the description of Duncan from *Macbeth*, and none was needed. Those who knew the play would recognize its source; those who did not would no doubt recognize that the language was Shakespeare's, but the attribution hardly mattered. The effect came from the "rightness" of the words to express the deepest tragedy.

Similarly, a handbill announcing the death places the name Abraham Lincoln at the top, followed by three quotations compiled from passages in *Macbeth*, again not identified. The quotations are constructed to make points: first, about "our Honored President" who "Hath borne his faculties so meek" and second, the "Duty of the Hour." The populace is advised, "Let's briefly put on manly readiness," for "Dread horrors still abound—Our Country, it weeps, it bleeds; and each new day / A gash is added to her wounds."

It is not clear that the compilers of these two pieces of popular ephemera would have known that Lincoln himself was drawn to *Macbeth*, among all of Shakespeare's plays. In 1864 Lincoln had written a letter to American actor James Hackett saying, "I think nothing equals *Macbeth*," and five days before his assassination, he read aloud to some colleagues Macbeth's speech about "the torture of the mind." Burdened by the thousands killed in the war and by dreams of his own death, Lincoln turned to Shakespeare's words to express his own torment. Ironically, his assassin, John Wilkes Booth, also drew on Shakespeare. In the closing words of his diary after shooting Lincoln, whom he hated, and while he himself was on the run and soon to be captured, Booth compares himself to Brutus and quotes from *Macbeth*, "I must fight the course. 'Tis all that's left me."

But Brutus echoed on the abolitionist side as well. Some time after he had escaped from slavery, Frederick Douglass quoted from *Julius Caesar* in a letter he wrote to his former owner, Thomas Auld, in Maryland, which was published in *The Liberator* on September 22, 1848. Recasting Brutus's speech in Act 4 of the play which reads:

> There is a tide in the affairs of men
> Which, taken at the flood, leads on to fortune:
> Omitted, all the voyage of their life
> Is bound in shallows and in miseries.
>
> (4.3.216–19)

Douglass wrote, "I embraced the golden opportunity, took the morning tide at the flood, and a free man, young, active, and strong, is the result." Reaching back into the play again, he continued, "It is not that I love Maryland less, but freedom more," thus appropriating Brutus's words about Caesar and Rome.

It was precisely because, in Hazlitt's words, Shakespeare "contained a world of thoughts and feelings within himself," that northerners and southerners, abolitionists and slave holders, liberals and conservatives could all appropriate his words as a means of expressing their views in a troubled time. What was true in the nineteenth century is still valid internationally in the twenty-first century as well; the 2012 London Shakespeare Festival performances included the Iraqi Theatre Company in a *Romeo and Juliet* infused with the poetry and music of that country; a version of *Troilus and Cressida* performed by New Zealand Maoris, and a new piece by African American author Toni Morrison dramatizing a conversation between Desdemona and her African maid, Barbary. The appropriation of Shakespeare's works continues to provide our virtually connected age with a common medium through which to express our similar anxieties, fears, triumphs, and loves, and to share them with each other.

Appropriation 2.0

Christy Desmet

Within Shakespeare studies since the 1990s, we have examined the ways in which individual writers, from Aimé Césaire to Jane Smiley, have appropriated Shakespearean plots and characters to explore such crucial topics as race, gender, and national identity. For critics, the guiding questions have been: what did the artist do to Shakespeare and why did she or he do it? Studies of Shakespeare in mass media, consumer culture, and popular films may shift the focus from single artists to cultural systems and institutions; but even considering the complications introduced by the relationship between local and global Shakespeares, the overriding concern remains with analyzing *what* was done and *why*.

As an unintentional consequence, "the Shakespearean text" tends to be reified as a concept. This claim is counterintuitive, as the New Bibliography and post-structuralist approaches have long since debunked the notion of a single text or an ur-text. Nevertheless, many recent adaptations, from novels to new media, remain focused on Shakespearean plots and language, and the pieties of scholarship have done little to stem the tide by which adapters have rewritten Shakespearean plots and transferred Shakespeare's words into the mouths of revived Ophelias and redeemed Lady Macbeths. Under the banner of Web 2.0, however, "the Shakespearean text" is palpably revealed to be not a literary entity, but an artifact of appropriation as a creative and critical process.

The dismantling of the Shakespearean text, as Lev Manovich (*The Language of New Media*, 2001) has argued of Web 2.0 applications generally, results from a tension between the logics of database and narrative. While narrative sutures together units of meaning on a horizontal continuum, database logic disperses units of meaning, or "memes," into different classifying containers, from whence they may be extracted and remixed in new narrative combinations. We can see the interplay between narrative and database most clearly in the phenomenon of YouTube Shakespeare, where remix is the dominant principal of composition. One particularly appealing genre of YouTube Shakespeare combines clips ripped from DVDs of commercial *Hamlet* films with a popular music soundtrack to rewrite Shakespeare's play from an Ophelia-centric perspective. The young, often female videographers borrow readily from one another, creating a storehouse of *Hamlet* clips that can be recombined to make new narratives that transform Shakespeare's doomed maiden into a protagonist of her own version of *Hamlet*.

Even more radical changes to "the" Shakespearean text take place, however, in computer applications that turn Shakespeare's plays and related texts into "big data" archives. Sampling, as John Unsworth argues, is the basic trope of database construction, chopping up narrative into categorical bytes that then become available for new narrative permutations ("Scholarly Primitives"). One of the simplest demonstrations of database logic at work on Shakespearean text is the kind of diagram produced by running the plays through an application such as Wordle (http://www.wordle. net/) to produce a scatter graph of names, nouns, verbs, adjectives, and adverbs, whose relative size and placement is algorithmically determined. We can see the dialectic between database and narrative play out more explicitly in a simple word search with the *Folger Digital Texts* (http://www.folgerdigitaltexts.org/), in which database and search engine do the hard work of sampling the Shakespearean playtexts, extracting a given word from its narrative contexts and arranging the examples in a list. Readers can then click back through the hyperlinked words to resituate them in their specific narrative context. Search engines of this kind are by no means new, but two features of Web 2.0 applications worked particularly to bring text, as the bedrock unit of Shakespearean study, into the realm of appropriation. The first is the increased power and scope of textual mining made possible by computers, the second the dissemination of these tools to a wider audience by Web 2.0.

The larger the database, the more vigorous the oscillation between distant reading and fine-grained data maps, the more dispersed—and less readable—the text becomes. Just compare a Shakespearean Wordle, where the size of certain names and proximity to one another in the graph might function as a visual analogy of actions and character relations, with one of the diagrams in Hugh Craig and Arthur Kinney's *Shakespeare, Computers, and the Mystery of Authorship* (2012). Craig and Kinney have been able to distinguish Shakespearean tragedy from history based on small function words, such as "a" and "the." These findings, although significant, are so far removed from everyday concerns of action and character as to forestall any easy application of them to critical or even classroom discussion. Big data findings, to enter the critical discussion as textual mashups, must produce and engage with one or more framing narratives. One current set of such narratives is centered around the question of authorship for "Shakespeare's" plays, with arguments being made for different kinds of collaboration between Shakespeare and other playwrights, rival poets, and—even more appropriate to the dispersed realm of text 2.0—loose collectives of notetakers who reconstitute texts such as the Q1 *Hamlet*.

The Web's ability to make tools available to a wider range of users also changes the afterlife of Shakespearean texts. In a provocative article, Peter Stallybrass argues that the advent of digital texts of all kinds can move literary study from a pedagogy of consuming ideas to one of *doing* things with texts ("Against Thinking," 2007). Stallybrass's point is that having access to primary materials such as EEBO (Early English Books Online) allows students to create meaning through a process that is more a remix of textual, visual, and other materials than an exercise in generating Romantic "ideas." Doing things with primary texts using Web 2.0 applications often involves not only sampling the texts but comparing targeted samples of text. In the *Enfolded Hamlet*, for instance, the Q2 and F1 *Hamlet* texts can be viewed either separately or superimposed over one another to create a *Hamlet* palimpsest (*Hamlet Works*, http://triggs.djvu.org/global-language.com/ENFOLDED/index. php). For an even more sophisticated example with facsimile texts, we might turn to the Shakespeare Quartos Archive (http:// www.quartos.org/). Building toward a comprehensive database of digitized Shakespearean quartos, the site now offers only *Hamlet* as a functional prototype. The British Library's Shakespeare in Quarto site, part of the core of the proposed archive, allows users to place different quarto versions of many plays side-by-side for comparison. In the *Hamlet* prototype for the Shakespeare Quartos Archive, viewers can also create a facsimile palimpsest by overlaying a snippet from one copy of Q1, perhaps from the Folger Shakespeare Library, with another from New Zealand. Anyone now can perform an action that once was the province of a small, specialized guild of scholars—but what can most of us make of a tiny difference in font impressions or even of marginalia from one quarto to another?

This final exercise in close versus distant reading points out new tensions in scholarly manipulations of Shakespearean texts. When access is expanded, expert narratives falter. Increasingly, I think, there is a divide between what we can do with Shakespeare texts and what conclusions we can draw from those textual manipulations. Database threatens to overshadow completely the explanatory narratives that bring together into consensus the scholars of Shakespeare studies. Most of us know our Shakespeare, but few can identify with any degree of confidence the contributions of Shakespeare and Wilkins in any given swatch of text. This ascendency of database and the concomitant deconstruction of narratives that make sense of big data might seem daunting, but it offers also an opportunity to recognize Shakespearean scholarship as a species of appropriation. There has been some effort to recognize that Shakespeare himself was an entrepreneurial appropriator of others' texts, whether the source was Ovid or Robert Greene. But Shakespeareans have been slow to see our own scholarship as appropriations. If appropriation 2.0 is a species of remix, as demonstrated graphically by Shakespeare 2.0 artifacts, archives, and applications, then all interactions with Shakespearean text(s) that engage in a dialectic between database and narrative are acts of appropriation.

The revelation that "all is appropriation" in Shakespeare studies may be part of what some academics see as "The New Modesty in Literary Criticism" (*Chronicle of Higher Education*, January 7, 2015), a rising generation of scholarship engaged less with theoretical speculation than with the empirical study of data. Recognition of the constructed and contingent nature of scholarly argument, however, is salutary for Shakespeare studies, rather than a symptom of our increasing social irrelevance. To recognize that all is appropriation is not to concede the equal status of all arguments—that "all is true," in *Henry VIII*'s phrase—but to demand of ourselves a greater level of self-scrutiny and methodical care, and most important—to accept from the outset the possibility that we will, at some point in the future, be proven wrong. The art of remix, whether in Shakespeare's Globe or on YouTube, is guided by a spirit of play, but it is, in the terminology of Clifford Geertz, a species of "deep play"—entrenched in, informed by, and responsive to core cultural imperatives.

Appropriation in Contemporary Fiction

Andrew Hartley

Though the adaptation of Shakespeare's work into contemporary fiction enacts a shift in genre, the artistic processes involved are often akin to those undertaken by theatre companies. While some novels are more radically adaptive, many are driven by something resembling a directorial impulse to stage a "take" on a play, to tell a version of Shakespeare's story which is consciously single, shedding the infinite possibilities of the unstaged text in embodying a single set of production choices. These productions—and the novels which resemble them—do not seek ways of presenting the plays "correctly" but ways of making them new.

Theatre is an immediate art form defined by its ephemerality, so it is unsurprising that companies seek relevance and urgency in their productions. The question many stage directors ask when they are choosing texts for their upcoming season is "why this play and why now?" Novelists adapting Shakespeare invariably start from similar points, seeking in the plays that which seems pressing in the present, even if that means filling absences or solving problems raised by the original. For a novelist working solely with words on the page, the directorial "take" on the play cannot be rendered simply with costume or set, and must necessarily push a book's brand of newness into difference from the original.

My own reimaginings of *Macbeth* and *Hamlet* (cowritten with David Hewson) fall at the less adaptive end of the spectrum, refashioning the core stories as historical thrillers in the style popularized by George R. R. Martin's *Game of Thrones* (itself inspired in part by Shakespeare's history plays). Even our fairly unadaptive retellings of the stories began with the choice of a directorial angle of approach, an attitude to core ideas and characters very much on a par with the principles which might emerge from the first week of production rehearsals. With *Macbeth*, we set out to render the core couple likeable, even admirable, at the beginning of the story, drawing on historical sources Shakespeare did not incorporate in order to push back against the perceived demonization of Macbeth and (in particular) Lady Macbeth. With *Hamlet*, we decided to draw on the first quarto's emphasis on action while also creating a new character, a young Yorik, son to the dead jester, who would be Hamlet's (possibly imaginary) confidant. In so doing we did what novelists always do in this kind of work, taking elements from inside and outside the primary text in pursuit of something familiar but surprising, a hybrid form which is both the thing itself and the shadow cast by something prior.

At the opposite end of the spectrum are adaptations so radical that the original is barely apparent in the shape of the story but makes its presence felt in other ways. In *The Black Prince*, for instance, Iris Murdoch builds a *Hamlet* novel which bears little resemblance to Shakespeare's play in plot, setting, or character but which is nevertheless saturated by some of that play's central preoccupations and concerns, drawing self-consciously on *Hamlet* as a literary and philosophical source text without retelling the play's core story. *The Black Prince* is a character-driven murder mystery, but it is also replete with the psychosexual and existential angst of *Hamlet* as imagined by mid-twentieth-century scholarship, complicated by a specifically novelistic take on the epistemological issues which characterize the play. Hamlet's persistent but problematic attempt to deduce the truth of his predicament from the behavior of others is, in Murdoch's novel, extended through the device of an unreliable narrator (the protagonist, Bradley Pearson) whose version of the events leading to his conviction for murder are called into question by postscripts penned by the secondary characters.

Matt Haig's *The Dead Fathers Club*, by contrast, relies upon the familiarity of the *Hamlet* narrative and invites the reader to make direct connections between what is happening to Phillip, the bereaved eleven-year-old who tells the story in strangled and ungrammatical first person prose, and the story line of the Shakespeare play the book so closely resembles. As in Murdoch's novel, the play's study of epistemological crisis takes center stage as the book begins to call into question the reality of the paternal ghost with which Phillip converses, so that the novel's study of fractured families, disconnected children, and communicative collapse is made all the more unsettling by the child's pursuit of a vengeance against his uncle that is surely unjustified. Though Haig and Murdoch are telling quite different stories, both use *Hamlet* as a reflecting glass to deepen and complicate not only their own projects, but the reader's sense of the original play as well.

This is a frequent goal of Shakespearean adaptation, and while many rewritings are made in pursuit of the topical or, more generally, the "relevant," others seek to revisit or even invert the original, bending it to meet the prevailing concerns of the present. This is particularly the case in youth-oriented fiction aimed at school-aged students who may be wrestling with Shakespeare in English classes and exploring the problematics or absences of, for instance, gender in the plays. So Lisa Klein's *Ophelia* and Michele Ray's *Falling for Hamlet* rethink Ophelia as the emancipated and defiant hero of her own story. In Paul Griffiths's *let me tell you*, by contrast, she is the complex, psychologically scarred victim whose story can be expressed only by rearranging (but not by adding to) the words assigned to her by Shakespeare, an approach which gives her voice while acknowledging the constraints placed on her by the original text.

This last is representative of a whole swathe of fiction which wrestles with Shakespeare as author and cultural force, reimagining his characters as straining against their familiar bardic confines (as in Stoppard's *Rosencrantz and Guildenstern are Dead*) or trying to imagine them as emerging from a different time and a different author. These books enact the kind of imaginative leap made by Virginia Woolf, who wondered what Shakespeare's sister might have produced had she been able to escape the misogynistic confines of the age, but they go beyond regendering the author through rescripting his stories, and many of them tackle other shaping political contexts and those elements of the early modern which seem most out of joint in the present. In short, and to maintain my guiding theatrical metaphor, such books enact a version of Stanislavski's "magic if," in which the behavior of characters (and, in this case, authors) can be imagined in a set of given circumstances by the actors (or authors) who must inhabit them. What if *King Lear* were an Ohio landowner (Jane Smiley's *A Thousand Acres*)? What if *Romeo and Juliet*'s Benvolio were a cat-burglar who falls in love with Rosalind (Rachel Caine's *Prince of Shadows*)? What if *The Tempest*'s Miranda were the head of Prospero Inc., a benevolent corporation which uses magic to further a program of global improvement but which is under assault by demonic forces (L. Jagi Lamplighter's *Prospero's Daughter* series) ...?

As those last examples suggest, many contemporary adaptations are whimsical and self-conscious about their refashionings of Shakespeare, though this does not necessarily render them frivolous or flippant. Many authors take seriously what generations of critics did not—Shakespeare's fascination with magic and the supernatural—finding in those sensational elements the stuff of moral and philosophical tension as well as a drama of the imagination which, in some respects, trumps the physical limits of theatre. Neil Gaiman drew heavily on the fairy elements of *A Midsummer Night's Dream* to create his groundbreaking *Sandman* series of graphic novels, while several incarnations of *Macbeth* revel in witchcraft and magic as much as they do in military and domestic politics.

The twenty-first century has embraced postmodern notions of authorship and originality and moved steadily in technological and cultural terms towards the adaptive amalgamation popularly known as "mash-up." In 2009, Seth Grahame-Smith hit the bestseller list with *Pride and Prejudice and Zombies*, spawning a slew of tongue-in-cheek revisionings of classics, including Ian Doescher's 2013 *William Shakespeare's Star Wars: Verily a New Hope*, which recounts the Luke Skywalker space opera in iambic pentameter. Websites house millions of instances of fan fiction in which contributors play in other authors' sandboxes, reconfiguring character relationships, reimagining plot points or settings, mixing together the worlds and characters of different books, series, and authors. This does not mean that people no longer care for the original work of individual authors, but it does mean that they are more comfortable with some of the conditions that defined Shakespeare's own cultural moment than were intervening generations. The artistic realm of the early modern was one in which collaboration, combination, and the adaptive retelling of familiar stories was common and valued. That contemporary authors should use similar strategies in response to Shakespeare's plays seems to me natural and healthy as marks of engagement and ownership. In the process, they enact a complex—if occasionally unselfconscious—negotiation of the value of the past and those literary and dramatic works which continue to be seen as its cultural summit.

15

Biography

Shakespeare and Biography

Peter Holland
President, SAA 2007–08

Raised upon a little eminence which his independence has made for
him, he sees his subject spread about him. He chooses; he synthe-
sizes; in short, he has ceased to be a chronicler; he has become an
artist.

"The New Biography" (1927)
VIRGINIA WOOLF

Shakespeare never met a biographer. Nor did he ever read a
biography. Or perhaps that ought to read that he "never met a
'biographer'" or "read a 'biography,'" for the point is simply that
the words themselves were not available to him. It is somehow
pleasing—at least to Shakespeare scholars—that the *Oxford
English Dictionary*'s current first citation for each word (which is
not, in the case of the latter, its first occurrence in print) is from a
work with intriguing connections to Shakespeare.

For the first, it is John Bulwer's *Chirologia* (1644), a study
of gestural language often linked to early modern acting styles
and to its construction of the meaning of somatic behavior, a
treatise that had this to say about the function of the hand: "The
hand, according to the primitive intention of Nature, having by a
necessary consent of nations been ever chosen chronologer of all

remarkable actions, hath consequently proved its own biographer."
The hand becomes autobiographer precisely because it is the
chronologer of itself, the recorder of events in temporal sequence,
the author of what Roger North (1651–1734) would delightfully
describe in his own autobiography as "Notes of Me."

For the second, it was John Dryden, in his life of Plutarch prefaced
to the new translation of Plutarch's *Lives* (1683), who praised his
subject, for "[i]n all parts of biography ... Plutarch equally excelled."
The *Lives*, that volume doubly translated (by Amyot into French and
then by Sir Thomas North into English) that, more than any other,
was the place where Shakespeare read biographies, may construct
its thematics as a comparison of individuals, one Greek, one
Roman, each pair separately biographied and then compared and
contrasted, but it constitutes, for Dryden, not the supreme example
of a discipline in its own right but, instead, one that acts as a branch
of history. "History is principally divided into these three species.
Commentaries or annals; history properly so called; and biographia,
or the lives of particular men." And Dryden has no doubt that, of the
three, biography is the lowest, lacking in the quality and generality
of the other forms but making up for it in readers' delight and in
its ability, as a result, to have a beneficial effect on its readers: "in
dignity [it] is inferior to the other two; as being more confined in
action, and treating of wars and counsels, and all other public affairs
of nations, only as they relate to him, whose life is written," yet "in
pleasure and instruction it equals, or even excels both of them."

There was nothing new in Dryden's tripartite division: Bacon,
in *The Advancement of Learning*, wrote of chronicles, lives and
"relations," the last being narrative histories. Shakespeare—or
whoever titled or glossed the titles of his plays in print—could
conceive of a form of history that combined and in some ways
transgressed such a division in *The Life and Death of King Richard
the Second* or the *True Chronicle History of the Life and Death of
King Lear* or *Pericles ... with the true relation of the whole history,
adventures and fortunes of the said prince*. In drama, history as
biography is also chronicle and a relation. The terms overlap, as in
Warwick's definition of the analysis of the individual life:

There is a history in all men's lives
Figuring the nature of the times deceas'd

(Henry IV, Part 2, 3.1.80–1)

History, here, is seen as the narrative of the lived past that may, Warwick will go on to say, prefigure the future. Or Orsino's asking about the "history" of Cesario's father's daughter ("A blank, my lord," 2.4.110) which is her lost biography. Or the Duke in *Measure for Measure* seeing in Angelo "a kind of character in thy life / That to th'observer doth thy history / Fully unfold" (1.1.27–9), that character that reveals the history to the other (an assumption that, in this play, may well not be true). Shakespeare ties character to history and each to the individual, his own network for the make-up of the plays which become, in effect, a clustering of individual biographies. Shakespeare imagines biographies, dramatizes them, makes them histories and chronicles and narratives. Shakespeare's plays—and, indeed, the *Sonnets*—create characters who character their histories as a performance of their biographies.

Biography—etymologically, life-writing—is multiply an investigation of character, of the charactering of a life in writing it (that handwriting that is a gathering of characters and which disguises or reveals its author, so that Maria can make her writing "much like the character" of Olivia, 5.1.340) and of the writing of a character in finding the person in that life, just as the comparison of the pairs in Plutarch acts as an exploration of character. It was precisely in Sir Sidney Lee's definition of "the aim of biography" as "the truthful transmission of personality" that Virginia Woolf found "the whole problem of biography" in the turn it had newly taken, as she perceived it: "On the one hand there is truth; on the other, there is personality." The former was of "granite-like solidity," the latter of "rainbow-like intangibility," the aim being "to weld these two into a seamless whole."

But the seams always show. Nicholas Rowe's edition of Shakespeare's plays (1709) announced its bonus features on its title page: that it is illustrated ("Adorn'd with Cuts") and that it includes "an Account of the Life and Writings of the Author," Shakespeare's first substantial biography. Perhaps Rowe was asked to include it by his publisher, Jacob Tonson, who had published such an account in that 1683 Plutarch where Dryden wrote of "biography." The function of the account is, for Rowe, both "a kind of respect due to the memory of excellent men, especially of those whom their wit and learning have made famous" and a way of appeasing the eagerness people have for "discovering any little personal story of the great men of antiquity" so that "we are hardly satisfied … till we have heard him described even to the very clothes he wears." The hunger for biography of the "man of letters" creates a particular desire because "the knowledge of an author may sometimes conduce to the better understanding his book." Yet Rowe does little to connect the life and the writings. The two projects sit, for the most part, side by side, an account of each, not an account of the writings formed and informed by the account of the life.

There are exceptions, even for Rowe: it is "probable" that Shakespeare "acquired that little Latin he was master of" at Stratford's "free-school" but, withdrawn from school by his father to help out in the family business, "unhappily prevented his further proficiency in that language." But the proof that Shakespeare "had no knowledge of the ancient poets" lies in "his works themselves," not in external anecdote, let alone evidence. Rowe wishes he knew more, especially about the chronology of the plays (something that would have to wait for Shakespeare's next biographer, Edmond Malone), for "it would be without doubt a pleasure to any man, curious in things of this kind, to see and know what was the first essay of a fancy like Shakespeare's." But it is precisely the strangeness of Shakespeare's imagination that means that normal rules may well not apply: "for aught I know, the performances of his youth … were the best."

For the most part, though, the two accounts, biographical and critical, sit in a kind of random adjacency with Rowe reluctant, unable, or unconcerned about how to move from one to the other. Significantly, the *Sonnets*, the collection that, more than any other, has been read as Shakespeare writing autobiographically, is never mentioned. Tacked on at the very end of the account is a sudden reference to "a book of poems, published in 1640, under the name of Mr. William Shakespeare" that Rowe claims to "have but very lately seen" and which therefore "I won't pretend to determine whether it be his or no." And of course it is Malone, working long after the expiry of the Tonson copyright, who is the first editor to unite poems and plays.

The biography of an author, any author, recognizes a yearning, a desire to bridge between works and life. But the chasm remains and what Shakespeare's apparently endless line of biographers can do about it is, most often, little more than a variation on Rowe's adjacency. None of this is in any way to doubt

Shakespeare's authorship, only to record his conformity to the mystery of creativity itself. As Shakespeare read Plutarch, so biographers read Shakespeare, as a spur to their own imaginations, as both the material out of which and because of which they write at all and as a search for a compatibility, not only because of those necessary gaps that all biographers are aware of—the fact unknown, the connection unknowable—but also because engaging with Shakespeare's writings is, despairingly, to yearn to be able to imagine as he is uniquely able to imagine. So, for instance, Stephen Greenblatt ends the preface to *Will in the World* (2004) with a recognition that, "to understand how Shakespeare used his imagination to transform his life into his art, it is important to use our own imagination." Then he begins the biography with "Let us imagine," a phrase that reappears when, for instance, he exhilaratingly imagines Shakespeare meeting Edmund Campion: "Let us imagine the two of them sitting together then, the sixteen-year-old fledgling poet and actor and the forty-year-old Jesuit."

Shakespeare biographies have always been a space of "perhaps" and "what if" and "might have." It takes rare confidence to begin one with "There is no need to doubt," as Katherine Duncan-Jones did in *Ungentle Shakespeare* (2001), even when the rest of the sentence turns out to be "whether a grammar-school boy from Stratford-upon-Avon could grow up to write great, and enduring, plays and poems." Duncan-Jones's point, that the West Midlands was "much the likeliest region of England to produce a major secular poet and playwright," is a device to argue for the significance of the cultural geography that becomes the basis for the first of her "scenes from his life," something that suggests fragmentation and discontinuity, choices of significance, "important topics or issues associated with particular periods," as a way of avoiding the need to cover everything, the complete biographing that, intriguingly, she describes as "chronicling." Selectivity within a form of cradle-to-grave account produces a method that is "more thematic than narrative."

The overall theme of her approach is that of the title, a refusal "to idealize my subject," something that not only works against the assumption that bardolatry depends on approving of everything about Shakespeare but also is embedded in a form of historicism, a recognition of the otherness of early modern culture in which no "Elizabethans, even Shakespeare, were what might now be called

'nice'—liberal, unprejudiced, unselfish." Is there an ironic turn
to her phrase here, "even Shakespeare," or is he still distinctively
exceptional? Shakespeare's abnormality, his removal from the
normal ranges of social behavior whether historically differentiated
or not, is a mark of his being not simply a subject for a biography
but perhaps *the* subject, the perfect exception who demands that
bridging from life to work because of the remarkable nature of
the achievement and the unremarkable nature of the life, as if the
former demands something different of the latter.

And from that interconnection comes the inevitability of
Shakespeare biography constituting a space of fiction, precisely
as it seeks to find the mind, to find the art, to find that which
lies behind and beyond and within and in spite of the facts. As
Hermione Lee showed, in the incisive last pages of her *Biography:
A Very Short Introduction* (2009), biographers seem unable to
help themselves inventing fictions—for what else can they be?—to
describe Shakespeare's response to the death of his son Hamnet
in 1596: a Shakespeare of whom one cannot say that he did not
feel his loss deeply (James Shapiro), or who seems never to have
recovered from the loss (Park Honan) or who suffered "a crisis of
mourning and memory ... a psychic disturbance that may help to
explain the explosive power and inwardness of *Hamlet*" (Stephen
Greenblatt) or who "may, or may not, have become inconsolable"
(Peter Ackroyd). As Lee sums up the list, "All biographers have at
times to suppose and infer." Yet the body at work, that shifting,
expanding, contracting construction of a Shakespeare who created,
as we create and recreate it, a matchingly shifting body of work, a
corpus (with, now, say, parts of *Arden of Faversham* and without
most of *Henry VI, Part 1*), has to be inferred from the plays and
the plays inferred from the life that created them.

If there is to be a moment at which, for me, Hamnet Shakespeare
must be recalled, at which the absence, whatever it may have meant
to Shakespeare as father, must be present, privately but with consequences for the creation of a play, it is less in *Hamlet* and more
in *Twelfth Night*, Shakespeare's exploration of a sister's response
to the apparent death and miraculous return of a twin brother. I
simply cannot see how Shakespeare could have avoided thinking
of Hamnet and Judith in turning to this narrative. I do not for a
moment mean—for that is precisely the temptingly dangerous next
step of inference—to suggest that Viola either represents Judith's

grief or is at the opposite extreme from, say, Judith's absence of grief. But rather I mean that here, without any question, is *some* form of interconnection, of biography turned to drama and/or drama as a response to biography, of fact becoming fiction or fiction remaking fact, of a convergence that brings work and life unknowably together. I can—others have—fictionalize the event, describe a Judith who is, by turns, pleased or furious when she sees, reads, discovers *Twelfth Night* or who never knows of its existence. It might make for a good Shakespeare fiction (the subject of Lois Potter's piece in this volume) but we can sensibly assume that, whatever may yet appear from the archives about Shakespeare's contacts (the subject of David Kathman's piece), it will not change our knowledge of the event, just as nothing will show quite how autobiographical the *Sonnets* are, precisely how far they are a self-dramatization by the man whose "name is Will" (Sonnet 136). As Barbara Everett has argued, "If his biography is to be found it has to be here, in the plays and poems, but never literally and never provably."

In confronting that impossibility of certainty and proof biographers continue to take different routes. The traditional plan was not only to narrate the cradle-to-grave "relation" that biography for so long appeared to prescribe but to do so in terms of the provable, of the factual basis from which all hypotheses ought, along this track at least, to emerge, even as they also manifest their construction of their fictions. What constitutes that provable fact outside the works could of course be arguable: take, for instance, the still powerful attack by C. J. Sisson, in his 1934 lecture on "The Mythical Sorrows of Shakespeare," on those who thought they knew what was happening inside Shakespeare's head and heart. The documents and records, the materials Samuel Schoenbaum so superbly assembled in *William Shakespeare: A Documentary Life* (1975) and its sequel, *William Shakespeare: Records and Images* (1981), offer a materiality that ostends solidity but which tempt towards those wished-for certainties beyond the material object.

We can narrow the scope of the investigation: Shakespeare in Warwickshire (Mark Eccles) or Shakespeare in 1599 (Shapiro) or Shakespeare lodging with the Mountjoys in Silver Street (Charles Nicholl) or Shakespeare's wife (Germaine Greer). We can construct an angle to define a context: the theatre for Lois Potter or Shakespeare as the "soul of the age" which, by tracing the "cultural DNA" enables us to read "a biography of the mind of William Shakespeare" for Jonathan Bate. We can lean more towards afterlife than life (my own emphasis in my entry for Shakespeare in the *Oxford Dictionary of National Biography*). But we all know that the result will not be *Shakespeare Revealed*, the probably ironic title of René Weis's biography.

We can, instead, accept the inevitability of failure and rearticulate the biography as ours not his, flipping the topic from him to ourselves, as Dominic Dromgoole did in *Will & Me: How Shakespeare Took Over My Life* or in the collection of articles by Shakespeare scholars in *Shakespeare and I* (edited by McKenzie and Papadopoulou). Or, as Graham Holderness exhilaratingly explored in *Nine Lives of William Shakespeare* (2011), we can fragment the life into nine aspects (the writer, the player, the businessman, and so on), give for each the facts, the traditional myths and some speculations, and then move unequivocally beyond the limits of the documentary by accompanying each chapter with a brief fiction, riffing off the tense stresses of the biographical into the pleasures of the imaginative. As Virginia Woolf noted, "it would seem that the life which is increasingly real to us is the fictitious life; it dwells in the personality rather than in the act," for "each of us is more Hamlet, Prince of Denmark, than he is John Smith, of the Corn Exchange."

What we cannot do is stop ourselves writing and rewriting some version of the Shakespeare biography, addressing the impossible, enjoying the desire, never despairing, always hoping. And yet always knowing that it is bound to fail, for—Woolf again—"Nor can we name the biographer whose art is subtle and bold enough to present that queer amalgamation of dream and reality, that perpetual marriage of granite and rainbow."

Shakespeare's Friends and Family in the Archives

David Kathman

It's sometimes said that all the documented facts known about William Shakespeare could fit on a single sheet of paper. That's probably an exaggeration, depending on what one counts as a "documented fact," but it's certainly true that we know less about Shakespeare as a person than most people would like. Nearly all of the documents mentioning William Shakespeare by name, the ones that still form the backbone of all Shakespeare biographies, were uncovered in the eighteenth and nineteenth centuries. A few more, such as the Bellott-Mountjoy suit (including the sixth Shakespeare signature) came to light in the early twentieth century, but by the time of the Shakespeare tercentenary in 1916, the list was essentially the same as it is today. A handful of new references have been discovered in the century since then, such as a 1596 writ tying Shakespeare to theatrical entrepreneur Francis Langley (announced by Leslie Hotson in *Shakespeare Versus Shallow* in 1931), but these have not changed the essential story of what we know, or think we know, about Shakespeare's life.

However, documents that directly refer to William Shakespeare are only one part of the tapestry that makes up Shakespeare's biography. Any biography needs to put such bare-bones facts into context, and that's especially true for someone like Shakespeare who lived 400 years ago. One particularly important source of context for any Shakespeare biographer is the lives of his friends, relatives, and coworkers, and this is an area that has seen a wealth of important archival discoveries over the past century. These discoveries have not attracted nearly as much attention as the latest speculation about Shakespeare's love life, but they have provided invaluable insights into the people closest to Shakespeare, in some cases forcing scholars to revise the views of previous generations.

One example is the poet's father, John Shakespeare. Biographers have long known that John Shakespeare was a glovemaker, a fairly high-status artisanal trade, and that he was a prominent citizen of Stratford-upon-Avon, serving many years as an alderman and one term as bailiff, the equivalent of mayor. Traditions depicting John Shakespeare as a butcher or a wool dealer were supposedly debunked by Edmond Malone and other early biographers, but twentieth-century researchers uncovered documentary evidence of John's extensive activities as a "brogger" (illegal wool dealer) and moneylender in the poet's youth. In 1949, Leslie Hotson announced his discovery of a lawsuit in which John Shakespeare sued another man over payment for 588 pounds of wool that Shakespeare had supplied in 1569, and in 1984 D. L. Thomas and N. E. Evans found that John was accused in 1572 of illegally selling more than four tons of wool. Thomas and Evans also found that a few years earlier, John Shakespeare was accused of lending a total of £180 (an enormous sum) at usurious interest rates.

These revelations have complicated our view of John Shakespeare, and shed potential light on the unspecified financial problems that caused him to withdraw from public life in the late 1570s, as William entered adolescence. Many scholars have suspected that religion also played a part in John Shakespeare's troubles, and here, too, discoveries from the past century have influenced conventional thinking. A Catholic "Spiritual Testament" signed by John Shakespeare was found in the rafters of the Shakespeare Birthplace in 1757 and printed by Edmond Malone in 1790, but the original subsequently disappeared, and by the early twentieth century it was widely assumed that the document Malone examined was a forgery. However, printed editions of the testament found in 1923 (in Spanish) and 1966 (in English) proved that the text transcribed by Malone was largely genuine, written by Archbishop of Milan Carlo Borromeo and probably brought to England in 1580 by Jesuit missionaries. These discoveries have provided support for those who argue that John Shakespeare was a secret Catholic, though sons did not necessarily follow the religion of their fathers, and the question of William Shakespeare's religion remains a hotly contested one.

Research into Shakespeare's theatrical colleagues has been a particularly fruitful area over the past century. Perhaps the best-known such colleagues are John Heminges and Henry Condell, Shakespeare's longtime fellow actors in the King's Men and editors of the First Folio edition of his plays. Although both men's wills were printed by Malone, and their theatrical activities were well documented by the early twentieth century, virtually nothing was known about their personal lives, including when or where they were born. Research over the past several decades has revealed much new information about Heminges and Condell, including the fact that both were younger than Shakespeare and also from the countryside; their paths to the London stage thus provide valuable context for Shakespeare's similar path.

Heminges was baptized in 1566 in Droitwich, Worcestershire (about twenty miles west of Stratford-upon-Avon), and was sent to London at age eleven to be apprenticed as a grocer. He became a freeman of the Grocers' Company of London in 1587, and remained a member of the Grocers after becoming an actor; between 1595 and 1628 he bound at least ten apprentices in that company, nearly all of whom can be traced on stage with the Chamberlain's / King's Men. From 1608 to 1626 Heminges also served as a sea-coal meter of London, a lucrative position available only to freemen, and in 1621 he joined the livery of the Grocers, the top echelon of the company's members. Condell was born in Norwich in 1576, the son of a fishmonger, and may have gone to London at age fifteen after his father's death in 1591. There he could have stayed with his uncle Humphrey Yeomans, who lived on Fleet Street a short walk from the Bell Savage inn-playhouse and the Inns of Court. At age twenty, Condell married Elizabeth Smart, who had recently inherited London real estate from her father that instantly made the couple financially comfortable, and in 1603 he inherited £100 from his uncle's estate that he may have used to buy a share in the King's Men soon afterwards. Despite their relatively humble origins, Heminges and Condell both became financially comfortable and respectably middle class in London, quite apart from their status as sharers in the King's Men and the Globe and Blackfriars playhouses.

Finally, over the past century such scholars as Edgar Fripp, Mark Eccles, and Leslie Hotson have uncovered a wealth of new information about William Shakespeare's known associates in and around Stratford-upon-Avon. This information has proved that these associates were a cultured lot, and has refuted the frequent Victorian depiction of Stratford as a cesspool of dirt and ignorance. For example, in *Master Richard Quyny* (1924), Fripp demonstrated that Quiney, longtime Shakespeare friend and writer of the only surviving letter to the poet, was proficient in Latin, friendly with such Warwickshire notables as Sir Fulke Greville, and able to correspond easily with courtiers and other power brokers on his many trips to London. Similarly, Hotson's *I, William Shakespeare* (1937) provided valuable information about Thomas Russell, one of two overseers of Shakespeare's will. Russell was the stepfather of Leonard Digges, author of a famous eulogy to Shakespeare in the First Folio, and of Sir Dudley Digges, mathematician and member of Parliament; he was also close friends with writer Sir Tobie Matthew and courtier Endymion Porter, among others.

More recently, Robert Bearman has provided an admirably thorough account of the life of Shakespeare's friend Thomas

Greene, building on the work of earlier scholars. Greene was living in Shakespeare's house, New Place, in 1609, and referred affectionately to "my cosen Shakespeare" in his diary. A Warwickshire native, Greene studied law for seven years in London at the Middle Temple, where John Marston was his sponsor and diarist John Manningham (recorder of a famous bawdy joke about Shakespeare) was a friend. After finishing his legal studies, Greene briefly tried his hand at poetry in 1603, when he published a poem honoring King James (*A Poet's Vision and a Prince's Glory*) and wrote a commendatory sonnet for Michael Drayton, another friend. The same year he moved to Stratford to become town steward, a post he held until 1617, the year after Shakespeare's death, when he sold his Stratford properties and moved to Bristol while remaining an active member of the Middle Temple in London.

Many more of William Shakespeare's friends and relatives have been the subject of biographical investigation over the past hundred years, but these are among the most important. Each of them had a significant impact on a major area of Shakespeare's life: John Shakespeare as he was growing up, Heminges and Condell in his theatrical career as an actor and shareholder, and Quiney, Russell, and Greene in his life as a Stratford gentleman and property owner. The documentary information that scholars have uncovered about these men has deepened our knowledge of William Shakespeare's network of social relationships, thus giving us a clearer picture of the world inhabited by one of the greatest writers in the English language.

Biography vs. Novel

Lois Potter

As Shakespeare says, most Shakespeare biographies are "simply novels by non-novelists." It is, of course, a fictitious Shakespeare who says this, as he chats with Cervantes during the interval of a rewritten *Cardenio*. I shall return to Robin Chapman's *Shakespeare's Don Quixote* (2011), but first I want to look at this comment. What, in fact, is the difference between "Shakespeare novels" and Shakespeare biographies? For Paul Franssen and Ton

Hoenselaars, "The most reliable criterion would seem to be to what extent the work is openly presented to the world as fictional and to what extent as documentary" (*The Author as Character*, 1999). But, as they admit, the distinction is not always obvious. For example, it is on the biography shelves that you will find *Who Killed William Shakespeare?: The Murderer, the Motive, The Means* (2013), by Simon Andrew Stirling, who argues that Ben Jonson murdered Shakespeare after their drunken meeting; his evidence includes Henry Wallis's 1857 painting, which shows the sculptor of Shakespeare's bust pointing to its forehead, the spot where Jonson stabbed him. This, surely, is novel as biography.

At the other extreme are the scholars who write "Shakespeare novels." The first and perhaps most interesting, Clara Longworth, Comtesse de Chambrun, wrote a French PhD on Giordano Bruno in 1921 and published extensively in both French and English. *Two Loves I Have: The Romance of William Shakespeare* appeared in 1934 with a preface by the Shakespeare scholar G. B. Harrison and was later expanded (with appendices supplying the scholarly background) into *My Shakespeare, Rise!* (1935). The novel looks sentimental and dated now, but many of its theories have come back into fashion. Chambrun believes that scholars should pay attention to the traditional stories about the poet, and she is convinced of his Catholic background and sympathies ("The Phoenix and the Turtle" is interpreted here, not for the last time, as an allegory of Catholic martyrdom). Her idea that Shakespeare arrived in London by the Oxford Road and saw the corpses at Tyburn anticipates (and is geographically more probable than) Stephen Greenblatt's suggestion (in *Will in the World*) that he was struck by the sight of the heads on London Bridge. She had read the latest scholarship, such as Leslie Hotson's discovery (published in *Shakespeare Versus Shallow*, 1931) that one William Wayte had included Shakespeare in the list of people who supposedly made him fear for his life. In her novel this becomes a comic episode: Shakespeare deliberately terrifies the dimwitted Wayte in order to aid the escape of a Catholic priest. Chambrun went on to write another biographical work, published posthumously, which continues to argue the "Shakespeare was Catholic" case and prints the John Shakespeare Spiritual Testament in full.

The choice between "period" and "modern" style is crucial for a "Shakespeare novel." Few biographers can resist quoting from Shakespeare. Novelists are likely to fill their pages with famous words, spoken either by the author himself or by people who (we realize with hindsight) inspired all his best lines. The dialogue that surrounds these quotations is likely to be based on the assumption that normal Elizabethan speech was a riot of simile, metaphor, oaths, and proverbs. But the alternative is worse: modern English, stripped of everything that makes it too recognizably modern, and turned into a flat and colorless instrument. The comic potential of Elizabethans speaking modern English, as exploited in Bernard Shaw's *The Dark Lady of the Sonnets* (1921), the Caryl Brahms–S. J. Simon *No Bed for Bacon* (1941), and the Marc Norman–Tom Stoppard *Shakespeare in Love* (1998), usually depends on our knowledge that the apparently ordinary man, with bad memory, writer's block, etc., is really (as no one else seems to know) *William Shakespeare*.

Shaw's Shakespeare in fact introduces himself in capital letters, but the question, "Did Shakespeare know he was Shakespeare?" haunts all attempts to portray the character, and explains why so many authors choose someone else as their narrator. Chambrun anticipates many later Shakespeare novels in her solution: *My Shakespeare, Rise!* pretends that John Aubrey's search for biographical data led to a letter from a Restoration actor-playwright who had played boys' roles for Shakespeare. Two later Shakespeare novelists, John Mortimer and Robert Nye (in, respectively, *Will Shakespeare*, 1977, and *The Late Mr. Shakespeare,* 1998), also used a former boy actor as narrator. Nye's narrator, the eccentric clown Pickleherring, takes the book on Rabelaisian detours such as a discussion of the various possible Dark Ladies and a description of the wonderful brothel run by his favorite candidate, the prostitute Lucy Negro. Other narrators have included Anne Shakespeare (*Mrs. Shakespeare: the Complete Works*, 1993, also by Robert Nye, who does not believe that Anne was illiterate); Shakespeare's daughter (e.g. *My Father Had a Daughter* by Grace Tiffany); his siblings. The most ingenious (and surprisingly convincing) narrator is *Shakespeare's Dog* (1981, 1983), by Leon Rooke, which depicts Shakespeare's life in stifling Stratford up to the point where frustrated poet and equally frustrated dog finally set off for London. The two novels called *Will*, by Grace Tiffany (2004) and Christopher Rush (2009), are told through the poet's eyes and, in Rush's case, in his voice as well, since the poet's conversation with his lawyer about his will is juxtaposed with his own interior monologue in lyrical prose. Indeed, he also speaks from beyond the grave, giving his views on drama and many other topics, especially sex. Anthony Burgess remains the most successful of those who have presumed to impersonate a creative genius. The multilayered narrative in *Nothing Like the Sun* (1964) leaves it unclear who inhabits what at times seems to be meant as Shakespeare's voice, but the characters speak in an idiom that is recognizably different without being embarrassingly pseudo-Elizabethan.

The difficulty is that fiction can easily become fact when it sounds poetically and imaginatively right. Some of Burgess's statements in *Nothing Like the Sun*—that Thomas Kyd was tortured by having his fingers broken (particularly horrible for a writer who may also have been a professional scrivener), that Shakespeare had a poor memory even for his own lines, and that he got Will Kemp fired for too much ad-libbing—sometimes turn up as fact in other writers, and in Burgess's own biography (*Shakespeare*, 1970). Rodney Bolt's *History Play: the Lives and Afterlife of Christopher Marlowe* (2004) is an alternative history based on Calvin Hoffman's thesis that Christopher Marlowe survived his apparent murder and went on to have an interesting life abroad, letting the greedy and unscrupulous William Shakespeare take the credit for his plays. For this negative view of the Stratford man, Bolt's playful work, posing as a scholarly biography, cites Katherine Duncan-Jones (*Ungentle Shakespeare,* 2001). But he also refers to such figures as "Dr. Samuel Clemens" and the actor "Henry Brodribb" (better known as Mark Twain and Henry Irving, respectively). Fact is carefully distinguished from invention in the notes, though readers can skip them if they prefer fiction.

Both Shakespeare biographies and Shakespeare novels, after all, must entertain as well as inform, and appeal both to the uninformed reader and to the critic who has already seen far too many similar works. Graham Holderness's *Nine Lives of William Shakespeare* (2011) combines facts, traditions, speculations, and frankly fictitious responses, all clearly distinguished, but also argues for the recognition of the "compelling" truth value of fiction (something that Shakespeare novelists have insisted on for some time). It is a tour de force. Similarly, reprinting his short story, "Will and Testament" (1984) in *Enderby's Dark Lady* (1986), Burgess followed it with an account of Enderby's attempt to write songs for an American musical comedy about the life of Shakespeare, thus displaying his ability to write pastiche Elizabethan, complex modern song lyrics, and American theatre-speak. Robin Chapman's novel, mentioned earlier, is its nearest rival. Also combining drama and novel, Chapman goes one better than Burgess, printing the complete text of his recreation of *Cardenio*, probably the most successful of several recent attempts to imagine the lost Shakespeare–Fletcher collaboration, and surrounds it with description and comment that would have been impossible in a play. His Shakespeare, Fletcher, Cervantes, and (in a brief cameo) Lewis Theobald are credible modern equivalents of themselves. One might compare Greenblatt's imagined encounter between Shakespeare and the Jesuit Edmund Campion, mentioned by Holland, with the scene, invented by Chambrun, in which the disguised Jesuit Robert Southwell recites "The Burning Babe" and Shakespeare replies with "Poor soul, the center of my sinful earth," adding that it was written under Southwell's influence. The difference is that Greenblatt, having proved himself as a novelist, goes on, as a scholar, to admit that his meeting could never have taken place. So why invent it? It is as if, in order to write about Shakespeare, one needs to prove that one belongs to the same imaginative world as Shakespeare. Mere academic biographers, trapped in their self-constructed prison of "might have" and "perhaps," need not apply.

16

Classicism

The Classics as Popular Discourse

Coppélia Kahn
President, SAA 2008–9

For months, half-consciously meditating on this essay, I assumed that Shakespeare's classical sources meant the Latin and Greek sources of his "classical" works, from *Lucrece* to *Cymbeline, Titus Andronicus* to *Timon of Athens*. Then I happened to be reading *Love's Labour's Lost* one day, and a light went on: Shakespeare drew on the classics all the time, 24/7 as we say, not just in plays based on Roman or Greek history, but in all his works. The *Aeneid* is constantly present in *The Tempest* as well as in *Antony and Cleopatra*. Ovid's *Metamorphoses* suffuse *A Midsummer Night's Dream* as much as they do *Titus Andronicus*. As I began to realize, though, sometimes his "classical sources" weren't "classical" at all. Sometimes they were English, contemporary, unlettered, and oral.

Generations of scholars have traced the poet's indebtedness not only to giants such as Vergil and Ovid, but also to an array of major and minor Greek and Roman writers. As Robert Miola has noted, like other writers and educated people of his era, Shakespeare got his classics not only from the actual Latin texts he read, and read closely, but from a proliferation of commentaries, anthologies, colloquia, handbooks, florilegia, translations, abridgements, epitomes, excerpts, reference books, digests, encyclopedias in English. There were many roads to Rome, or to Athens.

In this essay I'd like to take a road less traveled: Shakespeare's use of popular discourse *about* the classics: jokes, hearsay, loosely theatrical entertainments, mocking allusions, deliberate misquotations, and mistakes. Furthermore, to discuss examples of how Shakespeare drew on popular sources for his use of the classics, I will move outside the plays he sets in Roman or Greek locales, to plays whose settings are contemporary with the poet and not "classical," specifically, *Love's Labour's Lost* and *Measure for Measure*.

C. L. Barber's early, groundbreaking *Shakespeare's Festive Comedy* (1959) introduced a new and mostly nonverbal kind of source material to Shakespeare studies: holiday celebrations with roots deep in folk custom. His book had no immediate descendants, however. Janet Adelman's *The Common Liar: An Essay on "Antony and Cleopatra"* (1973) greatly expanded the idea of sources, treating "any tradition which shapes our attitudes toward the protagonists, or love, or politics, or any other concept in the play" as a source. She read certain images—the baited hook, the knot, the crocodile—"in the light of the appropriate traditions," to illuminate moral judgments, political issues, and conflicts of feeling that run through the famous story that Plutarch, plainly Shakespeare's major source, tells. Then, from the eighties on, under the influence of the New Historicism, the relatively straightforward notion of "source" as a text that Shakespeare had demonstrably read, then consciously adapted or echoed verbally, became ambiguous, broader, looser, and, I think, truer to the mystery of the poet's creative process. We began to look at social contexts, analogues, and, more seriously than before, at folklore and popular culture. We also began to treat sources as influences over which the poet might not always have had conscious control.

The traditions whose operations Adelman so astutely discerned, however, were mainly written ones, and in this her work was typical of source study in general. As Catherine Belsey remarks in *Why Shakespeare?*, her book on the poet's use of fairy tales, "When it comes to sources, scholars have generally preferred to see Shakespeare in their own image, sitting in a library diligently studying books in quest of material he could reassemble to make his case." No wonder—as literary scholars we are, after all, trained to work with what's written down rather than what's heard on the street. So in what follows I'm going out on a limb. I have no training as a folklorist to imbue with authority my readings of sources that are oral, unlettered, undocumented, and casual: street talk about the Latin heritage that Shakespeare's sharp ear picks up and puts into plays that have nothing to do with Rome. Well, in for a penny, in for a pound (to invoke a folk saying).

I focus on how Pompey, Pompeius Magnus as he was called in his day, figures in the two comedies mentioned above. Named "Magnus" in recognition of his victories in Africa on behalf of Sulla, he was entrusted by the Roman Senate with ridding the Mediterranean of pirates, which he did, and with waging war against Mithridates, king of Pontus on the Black Sea, whom he defeated. He subdued a swathe of kingdoms in the Middle East, but the Senate refused to ratify those victories, whereupon he entered into the first triumvirate with Julius Caesar and Crassus, and married Caesar's daughter Julia. As Caesar gained power in Gaul, though, Pompey lost it in Rome, and they became enemies. Defeated by Caesar in 48 BC, Pompey was then murdered, by Caesar's direction. Along with Caesar and Augustus, he went down in history and legend as a heroic conqueror, one of Rome's greatest military heroes. In *Parallel Lives*, Plutarch pairs him with Agesilaus; Lucan's heroic poem *Pharsalia* narrates the struggle between Pompey and his rival.

Most readers will recall Pompey in the first scene of *Julius Caesar*, where he is a strong presence without even being a character. "O you hard hearts, you cruel men of Rome, / Knew you not Pompey?" (1.1.37–8), says the tribune Murellus, bitterly reminding the people of how they once celebrated "great Pompey" (1.1.43), and rebuking them for making a holiday of Caesar's triumph— Caesar, the murderer of his former ally, "That comes in triumph over Pompey's blood" (1.1.52). Murellus mentions Pompey's name three times in fifteen lines, translating the title awarded him by the Senate into a common—perhaps too common—epithet, in "great Pompey." Shakespeare has a fondness for that name, mentioning it almost ninety times in his works, not merely because Pompey's son is a character in *Antony and Cleopatra*. I suspect that the poet appreciated the sound of the name. The anglicized version of the Latin Pompeius takes the name out of the honorific realm of "the classics," domain of the gentry and aristocracy, to familiarize it and make it common property. That "Pompey" chimes so readily with the words "pomp" and "pompous" may be the reason that

Shakespeare uses the name so often. Its very sound makes it an emblem of the transience of military glory, of Fortune's fickleness, of the treachery of Roman politics in the last century of the republic—as it is in the first scene of *Julius Caesar*. "Great" Pompey wasn't great for very long. I hazard the speculation that this idea, attractive to the powerless who felt the sting of low status, joined with a certain resentment toward those whose knowledge of Latin signified their entitlement to lord it over others, and so charged "Pompey" with meanings that were heard rather than read.

In *Love's Labour's Lost*, Shakespeare goes out of his way to situate Pompey midway between humanist letters and popular culture, by making him one of the Nine Worthies. It is Holofernes the pedant who determines that the "delightful ostentation, or show, or pageant, or antic, or firework" (5.1.104–5) commanded by the King for the entertainment of the Princess shall be that of the Nine Worthies. A conventional entertainment presented throughout Europe in the late Middle Ages and the Renaissance, the Nine Worthies consisted of three trios of exemplary heroes— biblical, Greco-Roman, and medieval—who stepped forward in costume to describe their careers, edifying and entertaining in equal measure. In this device, humanist knowledge was reduced to sound bites, giving the many casual access to what was reserved for the few. Traditionally, Hector, Alexander, and Julius Caesar made up the classical trio, but Shakespeare changes that in this play by putting Pompey in Caesar's place and adding Hercules. He also eliminates the medieval heroes and includes only one biblical hero, Judas Maccabeus, reducing nine to five, which suggests that Navarre, despite the pretensions of its aristocrats, is thin on the ground as far as learning goes. This shake-up of the nine heroes calls attention to Pompey and Hercules as interlopers.

Performed or perhaps deformed by Costard the clown, Pompey gets the most stage time and comes in for the most jokes. Costard announces the coming attraction as "the three Worthies" (5.2.486), declaring "I am, as they say, but to parfect one man in one poor man—Pompion the Great, sir" (5.2.500–1). His approximation of the name marks him as a country clown, a "poor man," who assimi- lates the foreign word to an English one, and to what he knows best, apples and pumpkins. More tellingly, when he declares "*I Pompey am, Pompey surnamed the Big*" (5.2.546), he initiates a series of jokes on "the Great," Costard mistaking the epithet to mean "large in size" like a pumpkin rather than famed for noble achievements. After the Princess compliments his performance by saying, "Great thanks, great Pompey," he acknowledges his mistake with a malapropism: "I hope I was perfect. I made a little fault in 'Great'" (554–5).

Like the mechanicals' play in *A Midsummer Night's Dream*, which it anticipates, the Nine Worthies serves as a class marker, setting off the noble audience onstage, who pounce on the commoners' mistakes with clever wordplay, from the performers, who are, as Costard says, "a little o'erparted," overwhelmed by the grandeur of their parts, lacking as they do any context for them that might come from humanistic learning. On balance, the comedy works against the lowly, who can only pretend to the sophistication of their betters. When Costard and Armado nearly come to blows over Jacquenetta's pregnancy, and Costard takes off his shirt in preparation for the fight, Bakhtin's "lower bodily stratum" rudely undercuts the Nine Worthies' ceremonious nod to classical heroics.

That balance shifts a little when Shakespeare names one of the bawds in *Measure for Measure* Pompey. He appears in five scenes (1.2, 2.1, 3.2, 4.2, and 4.3), and in each he raises the play's unregenerate countervoice that speaks for tolerance of and mercy toward sinners, against Angelo's harsh, hypocritical regime. He is a wit rather than a clown. In his exchange with Mistress Overdone, his terseness downplays the crime of which Claudio is accused:

POMPEY	Yonder man is carried to prison.
MISTRESS OVERDONE	Well! What has he done?
POMPEY	A woman.

(1.2.79–81)

In the course of Escalus's vain attempt to discover "what was done to Elbow's wife" (2.1.115–16), Pompey disarms Elbow with double entendres ("There was nothing done to her once," 2.1.140). He cleverly thwarts the constable's attempts to get Frost arrested by introducing a mass of irrelevant circumstantial detail into the conversation: the stewed prunes, only two of them, in a fruit dish that cost three pence, the rest having been eaten by Master Froth, "a man of fourscore pound a year; whose father died at Hallowmas" or rather, "All-hallond Eve" (2.1.122–3, 125).

It is when Escalus turns to examine Pompey himself that Shakespeare repeats the joke he made in *Love's Labour's Lost*, the joke that turns on the historical Pompey's title, Pompeius Magnus. This Pompey's surname being "Bum," Escalus exclaims,

> Troth, and your bum is the greatest thing about you; so that, in the beastliest sense, you are Pompey the Great.
>
> (2.1.214–16)

Again, the dignity pertaining to a legendary hero of the humanistic tradition is trumped by the lower bodily stratum, the realm to which that tradition relegates common people such as Pompey, the same realm from which the common people hit back. Furthermore, Arden 2's note cites Tilley to the effect that "Your bum is the greatest thing about you" is "a common expression." Escalus, an educated man, can speak the language of the streets when he pleases. Pompey's retort to Escalus's defense of the law prohibiting fornication is one of the most resonant lines in the play, because it rephrases Angelo's agenda in the most explicitly physical terms possible: "Does your worship mean to geld and splay all the youth of the city?" (2.1.227–8). Pompey voices a counterargument to the idea that sexuality is "beastly," representing it rather as innate to the body, to be identified with life itself, ineradicable.

Escalus concludes his examination of the unrepentant Pompey with a threat: if the bawd comes before him again on any charge, he declares, "Pompey, I shall beat you to your tent, and prove a shrewd Caesar to you: in plain dealing, Pompey, I shall have you whipped. So for this time, Pompey, fare you well" (2.1.245–8). That he repeats the name three times in four lines suggests, again, the ironic demotion of the namesake's glory to this Pompey, bawd and criminal. In the same lines, by alluding to the rivalry between Caesar and Pompey, Caesar's deviousness in gaining the upper hand, and the circumstances of Pompey's defeat, Shakespeare reminds us of the name's classical provenance. In his life of Caesar, Plutarch portrays Pompey at the final battle as forgetting "that he was any more Pompey the great which he had been before, but rather ... like a man ... affrayde and amazed ... and so retired into his tent speaking never a word." Thus Shakespeare moves back and forth between the Pompey of common talk and the Pompey of the classics.

He keeps Pompey's story going, as the rascal is arrested for being a bawd, and this time rebuked by the disguised Duke for making his living from "their abominable and beastly touches," on which the bawd is "So stinkingly depending" (3.2.23, 26). Ever the relativist, Pompey replies, "Indeed it does stink in some sort, sir" (3.2.27). Lucio taunts him by recalling his namesake: "How now, noble Pompey! What, at the wheels of Caesar? Art thou led in triumph?" (3.2.42–3). The allusion is, strictly speaking, inaccurate: Caesar never led Pompey in triumph but rather defeated him on the battlefield. Shakespeare may be alluding obliquely, though, to the opening scene of his own *Julius Caesar*, when Murellus refers to Caesar's triumph as coming on the heels of Pompey's. Or he may simply be drawing on a widely recognizable Roman image of the nadir of humiliation, the leader being led, chained to the wheels of the victor's chariot. For some forty lines, Lucio jeers at the prison-bound bawd, calling him by name twelve times, so that our ears ring with the sound. Since Pompey would probably be under some kind of restraint on the stage—his wrists bound, perhaps—the idea of a great Roman hero's reversal of fortune is strongly present, superimposed as it were on what must also have been a frequent sight, a commoner arrested in the street. Akin to Lucio's ironic denigration of Pompey is the custom, in British North America and in the antebellum United States, of giving Roman names to slaves. The frequency of such names meant that by the mid-nineteenth century, in print satire or onstage, a character named Caesar or Pompey was assumed to be a slave.

Once in prison, Pompey agrees to assist the hangman Abhorson; long an "unlawful bawd," he becomes "a lawful hangman" (4.2.14–16). The difference, the Provost says to Abhorson, is arbitrary: "Go to, sir, you weigh equally: a feather will turn the scale" (4.2.28–9). The Provost echoes Pompey's earlier remarks on prostitution being "the worser of two usuries," alluding to a traditional association between issue and interest as the profit to be made, respectively, from prostitution and usury. By his last scene (4.3), Pompey is quite at home in prison, with a soliloquy cataloguing the kinds of gallants now resident there, whom he knew before as Mistress Overdone's "old customers" (4.3.3–4). He concludes by lumping them all together as "great doers in our trade … now 'for the Lord's sake'" (4.3.19–20). Appropriately, the last phrase is language heard on the street: according to

Arden 2, "the cry of poor prisoners begging from the grating or window of their prison." After a few lines taunting Barnardine about his upcoming execution, Pompey simply drops out of the play. Shakespeare has made his point: a bawd named for a Roman hero may have something to tell us about the fickleness of fortune and the questionable morality of the law. The irony of his name resonates with the moral inversions dramatized in the play, and as I have been arguing, attests to the currency of "the classics" in popular discourse, as does Pompey of the Nine Worthies in *Love's Labour's Lost*.

There's a powerful tendency to think of the classics as immutable, remaining the same forever, as permanent as marble, but of course, however hard and heavy it is, marble isn't permanent. Columns fall, are shattered, and repurposed. Like Shakespeare studies, the field of classics itself has undergone great changes since the eighties, and Shakespeareans who study Shakespeare's relations to the classics can benefit from knowing that field. Classicists today are interested in the afterlife of classical texts, not just Vergil and Ovid but compilations, collections of anecdotes, biographies. In such texts, one can sometimes hear the voice of the street. It's that voice that I've tried to hear in this essay.

Shakespeare's Classicism, *Redux*

Lynn Enterline

The academic study of "classical sources" brings with it assumptions deriving from twentieth-century scholarly practice that do not align well with Tudor classicism. For an ever-increasing number of male writers in the sixteenth century, humanist grammar schools ensured that classical texts were understood in distinctly rhetorical terms—and were woven into the fabric of everyday life, informing vertical as well as proximate, horizontal relationships. While we may trace Latin "sources," Shakespeare and his contemporaries translated, memorized, and imitated ancient authors *to and for one another*. These scenes of address, and their authors, were judged according to the rhetorical desiderata of "wit" (*ingenium*), "energy" (*enargeia*), and "force" (*vis*). As one schoolboy put it in his commonplace book, masters aimed to cultivate *actio*, "eloquence of the body," as much as of the tongue. Whether in public recitation "without book," examination day declamations, school theatricals, or disciplinary meetings in which boys brought "complaints and accusations" against one another, and the "favour shewed to Boyes of extraordinarie merite" was the "honour ... to begge and prevaile" on behalf of classmates for "remission" from punishment, school exercises lent the classical past a performative as well as judicial dimension (*Annals of the Westminster School*). *Imitatio* required more than collecting, memorizing, and writing: it required public performances that determined a schoolboy's place in his social world. Given this institutional context, the texts of antiquity took on a far more vivid—and personally complex—presence than we can gauge through literary history alone, whether that history be construed as a question of allusion or intertextuality. Roland Barthes observed that Augustan Rome saw a wholesale conversion of rhetoric into poetic technique. As a consequence of humanist pedagogy, the same is true of sixteenth-century Britain—and the institutional practices that encouraged this conversion left their mark on early modern conceptions of the body, masculinity, and the passions.

The school's *habitus* meant that certain Roman texts exercised a palpable force on lived experience. Tudor masters tend to personify classical authors as if they were speaking with familiar, living beings: Roger Ascham remarks in *The Scholemaster*, "right choice of wordes, saith Caesar, is the foundation of eloquence," or "Tullie would have placed this worde here, not there." In *Timber*, Ben Jonson construes *imitatio* as impersonation: poets should "make choise of one excellent man above the rest, and so to follow him, till he grow very he: or, so like him as the copy may be mistaken for the principal." Shakespeare vivifies ancient characters with equal force. But in contrast to Ascham and Jonson, he often imagines these interlocutors to be female. As I argued in *Shakespeare's Schoolroom*, he has a marked tendency to explore the school's curriculum and practices through the voices of those it would have excluded. When Shakespeare translates rhetorical practice into poetic technique, we frequently encounter cross-voiced impersonations—a habit that is hardly consistent with the masculinist endgame of Tudor pedagogy. Indeed, his forms of classicism cast a skeptical eye on the claims schoolmasters made for a Latin education, revealing a former schoolboy keen to exploit the school's contradictions and unintended consequences.

In the past fifteen years, scholars generally have read early modern ideas of embodiment and the passions alongside medical discourse and humoral theory. But given the grammar school's disciplinary regime, there is good reason to read these representations in light of early modern classicism. This is especially true because a schoolboy's experience of Latin occurred during the transitions of puberty: just as a student was beginning to decipher what counted as "male" and what "female," there were two languages and cultures to contend with, not one. In addition, while humanist theories about training in oratory aimed to produce embodied, gendered identity in its Latin-speaking "gentleman," their methods may well have kept such identity at a distance. In one sentence set for translation, for example, a Tudor *vulgaria* cites a "master" telling his student to learn to "play the mans part and not the boyes." Though dedicated to the social reproduction of eloquent masculinity, school exercises sent signals indicating that the social identities masters encouraged were not essential, but rather "parts" one "played" in an elaborate social script.

Early rhetorical training was shot through with impersonation—whether under the rubric of imitation (as in *Timber*) or that of *prosopopoeia*, the Roman rhetorical practice of inventing voices for literary, historical, and mythological characters. An implicit demand for impersonation informs preliminary as well as advanced exercises. *Vulgaria* required boys to translate sentences into Latin by adopting a series of familiar voices; Corderius's *Dialogues* trained them to imitate imaginary conversations about daily life; Erasmus's exercises in letter writing proposed a series of hypothetical circumstances and *personae*. In the case of the most widely used rhetorical manual in England, Aphthonius's *Progymnasmata*, a lesson in *ethopoeia* ("character making") required students to invent speeches according to such propositions as "the words Hecuba would say at the fall of Troy," or "what Niobe would say over the scattered bodies of her children." And, of course, boys performed both male and female parts in school theatricals and interludes. Such training laid the groundwork not only for cross-dressing, but also for what Elizabeth Harvey aptly called "cross-voicing" (*Ventriloquized Voices*, 1992).

Grammar school training promulgated a culturally significant distinction between English and Latin, the "mother" and the "father" tongue. But Shakespeare's cross-voiced impersonations—Lucrece, Philomela, Hecuba, Venus, Ariadne, Beatrice (among others)—give Latin training an epicene twist. As Lily's *Grammar* puts it, the epicene is an "indiscriminate" case (*promiscuum*) because "both sexes are embraced" (*complectimur*) under "the sign of one gender." This "common" case has particular purchase on Tudor literature for well-known reasons: transvestite theatrical performance and Galen's influential "one sex" model of anatomy. More important here: from the point of view of humanist Latinity, English was not an inflected language—which posed a problem for those who acquired the cultural capital of a Latin education and so struggled under Rome's shadow to define vernacular eloquence. "English nouns," as Jenny Mann observes in *Outlaw Rhetoric*, "are nearly all *de facto* epicene terms." Ancient theorists used physical metaphors to capture oratory's aim and function, terms that tended to produce decidedly gendered figures for verbal power: a speaker's goal is to "move" an audience (*movere*)—hence the appeal of moving statues—and words acquired the ability to move by exercising *vis*, a noun that covers a wide terrain in English: "force," "power," "might," "violence." Clearly such metaphors inform the humanist habit of equating weapons with pens—an analogy captured succinctly, for instance, in Gascoigne's self-portrait on the frontispiece of *The Steel Glass*. And Shakespeare's humanist tendency to think about persuasion as a "force" can lead to phallic figures for words-as-weapons—for instance, Titus's arrow wrapped in "a verse in Horace" read "in the grammar long ago" (4.2.22–3). But his female characters are quite capable of doing battle with verbal "poniards" and "stings" (Beatrice, Katharina) and of winning competitions in persuasion (Hermione). And many of them—Lavinia, Bianca, Lucrece, Venus—display considerable classical learning; in Bianca's case, she's a better Latinist than her would-be tutor.

Shakespeare's habit of revisiting ancient texts and grammar school habits *as if* in the voices of women tends to unleash powerful epicene fantasies. For example, when his satire on schoolmasters turns Venus into an obtuse, Ovidian *praeceptor amoris* conducting a failed lesson in classical desire—"O, learn to love; the lesson is but plain" (407)—Shakespeare indulges in famously promiscuous gender trouble: Venus would imitate the boar's tusk by penetrating Adonis with her kiss; and Adonis, "the field's chief flower" (8), is destined to be castrated, then cropped. *Venus and Adonis* also engages a series of schoolroom exercises (*in utramque partem* arguments; "themes"; ekphrases; *prosopopoeiae*; Ovidian *imitatio*), but the poem shifts from mocking Venus to adopting her perspective, her sorrow—a shift that occurs when the narrator imagines her "as one on shore" like Ariadne, calling after her vanishing lover (817–18). In *The Rape of Lucrece*, similarly, a lesson in Tarquin's "school for lust" leads Lucrece to compare herself to Philomela. Lending Ovid's character a voice becomes a virtuoso performance and a "burden." The duet allows Lucrece a glimpse of Orphic power; but that power "strains" the speaker, wounds like a thorn at the singer's breast. The plot of rape relies on a violent instantiation of gender difference; but Lucrece's imaginary duet with Philomela repeats the narrator's inaugural act. And it is in their shared attempt to lend a tongue to ancient female suffering that the narrator and Lucrece most resemble one another.

The intimate, disconcerting link between rhetoric and violence in his Ovidian epyllia may be an index not only of ancient metaphors for verbal energy and force, but also of the schoolroom, where the Latin master's rod loomed. But that rod may not have worked as efficiently as expected: the epicene energy of Shakespeare's impersonations indicates that Latin training could unleash emotions and voices that hardly corresponded with the kind of "masculine" identity that masters claimed their Latin training would produce.

Time, Verisimilitude, and the Counter-Classical Ovid

Heather James

I begin with an admission: when writing on classicism in Shakespeare's age, I find myself juggling terms. Some are matters of conviction: I spell Vergil's name roughly as he did rather than use the symmetrical, postclassical, and ideological "Virgil." I waffle on others. Do I go with the forward-looking "early modern"— which has the added benefit of hedging the question of the "medieval" period—or do I stick with "Renaissance"? For many Shakespeareans, the question seems moot in relation to classical transmission, which aims to recover the past for present but not obviously "modern" uses. In matters classical, it is counterintuitive to buck the older trend. But how are we to characterize an object or text unearthed from antiquity and adapted to new forms that is already a classical antibody? I refer to Ovid, the "classically unclassical" poet, who inaugurated a "counter-classical sensibility" and wrote the "counter-epic" (W. R. Johnson) *Metamorphoses*. These oxymoronic terms refer to a powerful strand of dissidence that Ovid introduced to Augustan poetry: in his hands, poetry defied the decorum and mores that were shaped by Horace and Vergil and defined by an ultimate reader, Augustus Caesar.

In Shakespeare's England, Ovid inspired the cultivation of letters from the rise of lyric eroticism in the sixteenth century to the rise of libertinism in the seventeenth century. The delicious boldness of his verse persisted, I suggest, because it was tied to a fundamentally *political* concern for the liberty of bold and open speech: Ovid's poetic iconoclasm recalls *parrhesia* in Greek and, in Latin, *licentia*, which may refer to licentious abuse or the liberty of speech, the hallmark virtue of republicanism. Ovid fascinated bold thinkers, writers, and readers of Shakespeare's day and inspired them to test the scope and limits of imaginative expression that seemed both "classical" and "counter-classical" even to them. One feature of this kind of verse is a perplexing relationship to time and ethics that makes the term "early modern" seem as hidebound as "Renaissance."

Why did English poets and readers go for Ovid? Any number of answers is imaginable, from the moral alchemy of allegorical reading (the *Ovide moralisé*) to the sensual compulsion of Petrarch and a Marlovian penchant for fusing formal invention with ideological rule-breaking. I take up the latter response to Ovid, who shook things up and broke them down, disordered proprieties and orthodoxies, and unleashed novel forms of expression in abundance. He had an enviable supply of wit, especially in response to political times that restricted poetic expression.

Two techniques belonging to the counter-classical sensibility seem opposed, not conjoined: the fantastic and the verisimilar. In Ovid's verse, they are phenomenally aesthetic, animated by *enargeia*, and broadly political. Shakespeare's contemporaries recognized that Ovid borrowed and repurposed a poetic technique central to Horace's *Ars Poetica*. Memorably, Horace's speaker implores poets to give up the fantastic for the verisimilitude associated with Augustan Rome. Horace also presents a dissenter, who asserts that "poets have always had the *right* to *dare* whatever representations they please." Elizabeth I translated "right" as a "lien," or right to retain possession of property. But Horace is usually conflated with his main speaker and so Ovid sides with his dissenting interlocutor. In the *Metamorphoses*, Ovid devotes himself to the fantastic transformation of bodies and a reworking of the concept of verisimilitude, which he re-creates in his own—not the prince's—inalienable image. In his hands, verisimilitude fails to naturalize ideals of Augustan decorum: it instead depicts scenes of violence in light of the readers who are caught up—intensely—in the moment of perception and judgment.

Shakespeare understood Ovidian verisimilitude as an assault on decorum that pitted aesthetic allure against ethical functions. An example appears in the scenarios presented to Christopher Sly by the Lord and his servants in the Induction to *Taming of the Shrew*:

> 2 SERVANT Dost thou love pictures? We will fetch thee straight
>   Adonis painted by a running brook
>   And Cytherea all in sedges hid,
>   Which seem to move and wanton with her breath
>   Even as the waving sedges play with wind.
> LORD   We'll show thee Io as she was a maid,
>   And how she was beguiled and surprised,
>   As lively painted as the deed was done.
> 3 SERVANT Or Daphne roaming through a thorny wood,
>   Scratching her legs that one shall swear she bleeds,
>   And at that sight shall sad Apollo weep,
>   So workmanly the blood and tears are drawn.
>   (Induction, 2.47–58)

These scenarios have at first glance an uncomfortably transparent agenda. The audience seems meant to be caught up in the here and now of erotic solicitation: there is no easy escape from the message that desire is as predatory as it is intensely visual. Verbal suggestions that our sympathies might lie with the objects of rapacious desire are present, but they seem dragged into play to suggest that even sympathy is a predator's passion: the god Apollo is sad that Daphne heedlessly mars her own beauty as she flees from him. Yet Shakespeare's readers are not fully Apollo: his Ovidian scenarios solicit both assent to erotic invitations and ethical resistance to scenes in which there is no consent. Are readers to position themselves as desiring subjects, vulnerable objects of desire, or bystanders, blindsided by the passions of voyeurism (the side of the gods) and solicitude for the victims? Readers may well respond in this order: yes, no, probably.

Shakespeare follows Ovid, who formally makes his case for an ethics of verisimilitude in his story of the inventive and insolent weaver, Arachne, who refuses to cede credit for her talent to a goddess, Pallas, and instead weaves a powerful complaint about the gods' abuse of mortal women in a vivid, engaging, and sensuous tapestry that epitomizes Ovid's own stories of divine passion, deceit, and rape. In contrast to the goddess's classical tapestry— ordered, hierarchical, iconographic, and triumphal—Arachne weaves a phantasmagorical image of the rapes of nineteen women by five gods who often assume the shape of beasts to accomplish their ends. To back up Arachne's theme of rape as crime (*caelestia crimina*), Ovid furnishes a specific artistic quality: verisimilitude. Each story of rape is set out with accurate representations of "the face" of all persons, beasts, elements, and places of the story (*Met.*, 6.121), and each story speaks to the reader as if from the violent moment of experience. In Golding's 1567 translation:

> The Lydian maiden [Arachne] in hir web did portray *to the full*
> How *Europe* was by royall *Jove* beguiled in shape of Bull.
> That Bull and Sea in very deed ye might them well have thought... .
> The Ladie seemed looking back to landwarde and to crie
> Upon hir women, and to feare the water sprinkling hie,
> And shrinking up hir fearfull feete.
> ... Of all these things she missed not their proper shapes, nor yit
> The *full* and *just resemblance* of their places for to hit.
>
> (6.126–32, 150–1)

This passage redirects the art of verisimilitude from an ethic of decorum to one of witnessing and truth telling.

In this scene, verisimilitude, *ekphrasis*, and *enargeia* create a speaking picture that engrosses readers in the here and now and does nothing to speed up the process of reading. The picture tells us to *do* something, since both gods and men have failed to address the abuses perpetrated by the powerful on the comparatively powerless. In Ovid's verse, verisimilitude generates strong and immediate feeling in readers and directs it, as if in slow motion, towards ethical action in the world. For the poetic justice anticipated is just that: anticipated and imminent in the reader's experience but not in historical time. Justice comes in the future perfect tense—"it will have happened"—and this is a problem of art that Ovid and Arachne acknowledge. Art is a counter and parallel to the punishment of Tantalus: the here and now of desire is enlarged in the act of reading while justice is just out of reach. In this context, Ovidian allusions link imaginative fables from the classical past (Theseus's antique / antic fables) to the here and now of readerly acts absorbed in the present while leaning into a future tense of action. As Golding suggests, the Ovidian form of verisimilitude inaugurates a literary tradition of historical witness.

For Shakespeare, Ovid's poetry created a productive tradition of poets thinking furiously about the future of justice and the form of writing that may help it come about. Shakespeare's Ovid cultivated a boldness, force, and audacity in poetic invention and expression that addressed and ameliorated a void in public discourse: poetry allows for bold thought even as it leaves open the question of how and when readers will be moved to action. Ovid inspired a boldness of imagination and form that tested the capacity of poets to engage and enlarge the liberty of speech through poetic rather than topical allusion. Holofernes got it right: "Ovidius Naso was the man," so named for his skills in "smelling out the odoriferous flowers of fancy, the jerks of invention. *Imitari* is nothing" (*Love's Labour's Lost*, 4.2.123–5).

17

Public Shakespeare

The Publicity of the Look

Paul Yachnin
President, SAA 2009–10

Shakespeare's *Cymbeline* develops a remarkable representation of vision, relationship, and identity as well as a forward-looking consideration of the possibilities of egalitarian public association within an oppressive visual field. The play is interested in optical magic, enchantment, and the evil eye. It connects ideas about an infectious visual field with monarchical hierarchy and with monarchy's close cousin, tyranny; and it suggests how the visual field might be altered so as to allow all people, regardless of gender, nationality, or social standing, to recognize and be recognized by each other and to be able to look each other in the eye.

Julia Lupton and Henry Turner, collaborators in this section, raise urgent questions about the kind of public space I am describing. My twofold claim is (1) that *Cymbeline* imagined such a space and (2) that Shakespeare's playhouse made it real for his playgoers—that they were able to see and be seen on an equal basis and that they thereby anticipated the democratic political culture of modernity. But, it must be asked, what kind of public space was the playhouse? Perhaps becoming public at the Globe was no more politically creative for early moderns than going out to the local shopping mall is for us.

I focus on seeing and being seen; Lupton's focus is speaking and being heard. It is one thing to be seen in public, it is another to speak out and to act in the world, especially for women such as Juliet or Imogen. Lupton's argument about "courage, action, and publicity" challenges my view, and it also suggests a way forward: Juliet's or Imogen's courageous speaking from the heart has the power to transform private into public space. On this account, the playhouse made itself public in a strong sense—more like a parliament than a shopping center—by dint of its playful but heartfelt representations of family, society, and polity.

Turner moves the question closer to home by reminding us how the humanities and the university have lost social influence. What kind of hold on the world can Hamlet's father's ghost or a scholar of Shakespeare's drama have? All they seem to do is raise questions that neither they nor anyone else can answer. Turner follows a hint from Derrida to suggest how Hamlet's father's ghost and people like us can achieve public life. We Shakespeareans might feel "*trapped* by theatricality ... estranged from *other* forms of public associational life that might have situated [us] more securely." But Derrida tells us that acts of interpretation presume a politics, not in the usual sense, but as an act of gathering many individuals into a public, political body. Feeling deeply, questioning, appearing to others, and speaking out made Shakespeare's predominately commoner audience into a public, a form of association able to speak back to the larger world of Church and State. Could *Hamlet* teach us about the courage needed to become public? Could *Cymbeline* provide us with a model of public life?

At the start of *Cymbeline*, the play is obsessed with what to us moderns are strange beliefs in the evil eye. The wicked queen, the stepmother of the king's daughter Imogen, attempts to deceive her stepdaughter into trusting her by assuring her that she will not practice ocular enchantment against her:

> No, be assur'd you shall not find me, daughter,
> After the slander of most stepmothers,
> Evil-ey'd unto you.
>
> (1.2.1–3)

Most editions do not gloss the phrase, "evil-ey'd unto you," perhaps assuming that it is being used metaphorically and that its meaning is transparent—something like "looking harshly at you" or simply "wishing you harm." In fact the phrase is the first indication of a large and complex interest in ocular enchantment. An active belief in evil eye magic was a normal feature of early modern culture. When Phoebe in *As You Like It* protests that "there is no force in eyes / That can do hurt" (3.5.26–7), early moderns would not have heard merely metaphorical language. For them, eyes could indeed hurt. "What gives eyeing such power?" Bruce Smith asks in a recent essay on the play. "The eyes' force is not just metaphorical, but physical" ("Eyeing and Wording in *Cymbeline*," 2010).

The early modern archive is full of evidence that supports Smith's claim. In a 1612 trial, one Elizabeth Sowthernes was accused of possessing an "ill Eye, ill Tonge" and was recognized by the court as a witch because of an ocular deformity (*The Wonderfull Discoverie of Witches in the Countie of Lancaster*, 1613). Even highly educated people such as Reginald Scot (who wrote a book debunking belief in witches) and the pioneering scholar and jurist Francis Bacon believed in the effects of ocular enchantment. In his 1625 essay, "Of Envy," Bacon wrote, with a leavening of skepticism, about the dangers of "fascination," by which he meant "evil eye." He speaks about fascination as "an ejaculation or irradiation of the eye." The early moderns, Bacon too it seems, believed that bad blood could actually transform into eyebeams, which could then infect or poison the person at whom the evil looker was gazing.

Against this background, the play's interest in evil eye magic becomes more readily apparent. In their parting scene, Imogen tells her beloved Posthumus that his banishment from England will leave her vulnerable to a hail of ocular attacks:

You must be gone,
And I shall here abide the hourly shot
Of angry eyes: not comforted to live,
But that there is this jewel in the world
That I may see again.

(1.2.19–23)

She will be able to go on living, even under the ocular barrage she anticipates, because she will know that her husband, "this jewel," lives also somewhere in the world and that she might one day be reunited with him. The last half-line refers primarily to "this jewel," which is the direct object of "may see": "you are a jewel that I might one day see again." There is, however, a secondary sense of the half-line that connects to the wounding looks that are the subject of the second and third lines. The "jewel" is in this sense an amulet that will protect Imogen against the evil eye and that will allow her to look freely at others, unafraid that their looks might be able to enter her eyes, the most penetrable entry points for visual harm, and thereby injure, poison, or infect her. Looked at this way, Posthumus is an apotropaic charm. "Jewel" is not the direct object of "may see"—not the thing the heroine sees, but rather the thing that makes it possible for her *to see*. In time, Imogen might be reunited with her husband; she will then be able to "see again," will then be able to use her eyes to see everything and everyone without hesitation or fear.

This idea of the difficulty of seeing in a dangerous visual field, a space where Imogen's stepmother (among others, including her own father) is looking daggers at her, is repeated a few lines later, when she expands those who are visually afflicted to include her husband as well as herself:

> O the gods!
> When shall we see again?
>
> (1.2.54–5)

Again, the primary meaning makes the verb "see" effectively transitive, with "each other" being understood: "when shall we see each other again?" But a secondary meaning makes "see" effectively intransitive: "when shall we be able to see again at all?"

The king enters just after these lines, interrupting the young couple's parting and ordering Posthumus's departure in terms that confirm the normality of ideas about ocular infection in the world of the play. Posthumus is like the basilisk mentioned later (2.4.107), an animal thought to be able to kill people by looking at them or sometimes just by being seen. Note also how the king's description of Posthumus reverses Imogen's, transforming Posthumus from a charm against the evil eye into a powerful source of ocular infection:

> Thou basest thing, avoid hence, from my sight!
> ... Away!
> Thou'rt poison to my blood.
>
> > (1.2.56–9)

In light of Imogen's need for her husband's presence to protect her from ocular injury, to clear her field of vision, and inoculate her against a kind of blindness, it is not surprising that she should seek desperately to keep him in view. That is exactly what she imagines when she describes how (if she had been at the port) she would have gazed after him as his ship carried him away from the English shore and eventually out of sight. His disappearance has the effect of turning her eyes from seeing to weeping and so losing the function of vision altogether:

> I would have broke mine eye-strings, crack'd them, but
> To look upon him, till the diminution
> Of space had pointed him sharp as my needle:
> Nay, followed him, till he had melted from
> The smallness of a gnat, to air: and then
> Have turn'd mine eye, and wept.
>
> > (1.4.17–22)

During the period of their forced separation, Posthumus does not lose his sight, but he suffers a disastrous and culpable collapse of judgment. Not only does he bet on his wife's ability to resist the seductive charms of the villain Iachimo but, in ways familiar from other Shakespearean plays about male jealousy and the pursuit of sexual certainty, Posthumus puts absolute trust in what he takes to be "ocular proof," to use Othello's phrase (3.3.363), the bracelet that Iachimo has filched from the sleeping Imogen, and he discounts entirely what he knows from experience about his wife's virtue.

On her side, while Imogen retains her faith in her husband, she undergoes actual visual impairment, becoming unable to see the world or people distinctly and accurately. We hear about this affliction when she says (on the night of Iachimo's visual rape of her), "mine eyes are weak" (2.2.3); or when she claims that she can see only the way to Milford Haven (where she thinks her husband awaits her), and that all else within her range of sight is utterly obscured: "I see before me, man: nor here, nor here, / Nor what ensues, but have a fog in them, / That I cannot look through. ... / Accessible is none but Milford way" (3.2.79–83).

In the event, her diminishing sight prevents her from finding Milford Haven. Lost in the hills of Cambria, she recalls how close Milford seemed when seen from a mountaintop. It was "within a ken" (3.6.6), the distance from which a sailor can sight land, but now it has fled from her and cannot be seen. More striking is her inability to tell the headless corpse of Cloten from the body of her husband. Even her part-by-part visual inspection of the body misinforms her about what she has right before her eyes.

The scene is extraordinary. It recapitulates her inability to reach Milford Haven, the nightmare helplessness to move toward a goal one dearly wants to reach, then shifts to a reflection on the unreliability of vision, and then to her horror-filled inspection of the body of the man she takes to be her husband. As she begins to speak here, she is just waking from a drug-induced sleep, still half in a dream state:

> Yes sir, to Milford-Haven, which is the way?
> I thank you: by yond bush? pray, how far thither?
> 'Ods pittikins: can it be six mile yet?
> I have gone all night: faith, I'll lie down and sleep.
> ...

> [*Seeing the body of Cloten.*]

>   ... Our very eyes
> Are sometimes like our judgements, blind.
> ...
> A headless man? The garments of Posthumus?
> I know the shape of's leg: this is his hand:
> His foot Mercurial: his Martial thigh
>   (4.2.291–4, 301–2, 308–10)

Toward the end of the play, Imogen regains her full powers of sight and presides over a restored visual field, free from ocular enchantment. This conclusion is achieved in part by way of a remarkably complicated unfolding action. The total effect is to transform the visual field from a space of affliction and socially induced blindness, where no one can look at anyone else, to a place where people can see and be seen and where each person recognizes and is recognized by his or her fellows. The new social healthfulness of the visual field results from the radiant looks of Imogen, both how she is seen and how she sees, here enabled by the loving and protective gaze fixed on her by her husband and the newly loving gaze of her father, who describes the scene:

> See,
> Posthumus anchors upon Imogen;
> And she (like harmless lightning) throws her eye
> On him: her brothers, me: her master hitting
> Each object with a joy: the counterchange
> Is severally in all.

(5.5.393–8)

The "counterchange" is the highly mobile network of looks among the characters onstage, an ocular network that knits them together into a restored and open society, a notional space that recent theory would call a public sphere. The fact that the king's description directs the spectators in the playhouse to join the network of restorative looking, itself anchored on the boy actor playing Imogen, even suggests something about the power of theatrical performance itself to reform the visual field.

As a matter of fact, before we even meet the lovers or hear mention of the evil eye, the play tells us that the British nation is beset by toxic looking relations, caused not by the queen but rather king Cymbeline himself, whose fury against the marriage of his daughter with the relatively lowborn gentleman Posthumus compels his subjects to hide their true happiness for what seems to everyone to be a worthy union. The source of the general state of ocular affliction is therefore not some otherworldly evil-eye magic but the this-worldly power of the monarch. In a scene where the courtiers find a moment of private respite, the First Gentleman says,

> not a courtier,
> Although they wear their faces to the bent
> Of the king's looks, hath a heart that is not
> Glad at the thing they scowl at.

(1.1.12–15)

Since they are hiding their true faces from the king and usually from each other, the courtiers cannot be recognized or recognize others. Each is like the distracted Imogen when she fails to acknowledge the men who saved her from perishing in the forest (note how her failure to recognize them persuades them that she is not who they at first take her to be—the boy Fidele):

BELARIUS   Is not this boy reviv'd from death?
ARVIRAGUS   One sand another
  Not more resembles that sweet rosy lad,
  Who died, and was Fidele! What think you?
GUIDERIUS   The same dead thing alive.
BELARIUS   Peace, peace, see further: he eyes us not, forbear;
  Creatures may be alike: were't he, I am sure
  He would have spoke to us.
                                    (5.5.120–6)

How, finally, does the reformation of ocular relations and the proto-democratization of the visual field in the world of the play come about? A clue is in the fact that it is the king in the final scene who directs our attention to the radiant Imogen, and from her to all the other characters on the stage. At the start of the play, the political world has a single focal point—the king himself. Everyone looks at the king, and everyone feels himself or herself under the royal gaze. The courtiers "wear their faces to the bent / Of the king's looks" (1.1.13–14). Their faces are not theirs; they are like masks fashioned after the scowling look of the monarch. The unfolding plot, with the eclipse of the king by way of his political impotence, the victory over the Romans in which he has no part, the revelation that the queen did not love him, the discovery of a living male heir to the throne—all these elements devalue the king and remove him from the center of the visual field, allowing the other characters to look around themselves far more freely and even to see each other truthfully. So it is no surprise that the king directs attention away from himself and toward his daughter, and from his daughter toward his son-in-law and the other characters on the stage. It is as if the king were teaching the spectators in the playhouse how to make their looks more mobile, quick, and inclusive.

But of course, the playgoers have been looking freely all along. The playgoers in Shakespeare's theatre were not subject to the visual habits of the deference culture in which they lived, where commoners were expected not to look directly into the faces of their social betters. The playgoers did not have to avert their eyes from a mere player-king, and they were certainly not required to wear their faces to his bent. On this account, the Globe was already the kind of proto-democratic visual field that the play seems bent on creating in the play world. One of the pleasures of playgoing must have been the freedom of looking openly, critically, and with great mobility at the characters on the stage—kings, queens, gentlemen, or peasants. And it must have been a pleasure too, and one that had long-term political effects, for playgoers of all social, vocational, and confessional sorts to see and to be seen by other playgoers and to be recognized by others in moments of self-disclosing responsiveness to the play, where their responses were not keyed to what some aristocrat or even the monarch might think; rather, audience responses were remarkably public, interpersonal expressions of each playgoer's thoughts and feelings. On this account, the play *Cymbeline* bends all its energies, its thematic interest in evil eye magic, its staging of characters alone or in groups, and its considerable narrative complexity toward the realization onstage of the kind of reformed visual field that Shakespeare, the players, and the playgoers were creating in the Globe playhouse itself.

Public Women / Women of Valor

Julia Reinhard Lupton

November, 2014, UC Irvine: My colleague Robert Cohen leads a cohort of MFA acting students through a unit on the Shakespearean monologue. In each segment, an actor portraying, say, Richard III or Henry V or Mark Antony is surrounded by the other students, who assume roles as courtiers, soldiers, or citizens. When Juliet delivers her stirring speech in Act 4, scene 3, in which she contemplates and then finally downs the sleeping potion, the actress kneels on a "bed" built out of stacked exercise mats while the other students stand around her, assuming the poses of family portraits hanging on her bedroom wall. This technique of engaging the whole class in the dramatic fabric of the scene, Cohen explained to me, heightens and clarifies the stakes of the speech. Cohen's method reminded me how attention—the embodied and directed eyes and ears of those present—helps sustain the public sphere as the place where "people can see and be seen and where each person recognizes and is recognized by his fellows" (Yachnin).

Much of the pathos of Juliet's speech, however, resides in the terrible aloneness that she voices:

> I'll call them back again to comfort me.
> Nurse! What should she do here?
> My dismal scene I needs must act alone.
> Come, vial.
>
> (4.3.17–20)

Juliet uses dramatic language to describe her predicament: hers is a "dismal scene" that she must "act alone," and the speech's deliberative movement culminates in her decision to act: "Stay, Tybalt, stay! / Romeo, Romeo, Romeo, here's drink. I drink to thee" (4.3.57–8). Cohen's pedagogy alerted me to an undercurrent in Juliet's own thought processes: finding herself forsaken, she proceeds to repopulate the room, conjuring first the absent women, then the Friar, then Tybalt and her ancestors, and finally Romeo himself. Even the drug she is about to take assumes the character of an interlocutor: "Come, vial," she says, addressing the object in her hand as if in hope of an answer. In filling the stage with ghosts, she is trying to stage this private and indeed privative moment as a semipublic one, since what she wants to risk is not only her life and her sanity, but also the disclosure of who she is to others.

The scene poses for me the relation between courage, action, and publicity, especially for the women in Shakespeare's plays. What if, instead of the ancient Capulets, we ringed Helen, Cordelia, Imogen, Marina, and Miranda around Juliet's bed? What will they have learned from her, and what might they urge her to do?

In *The Human Condition*, Hannah Arendt defines courage:

> To leave the household, originally in order to embark upon some adventure and glorious enterprise and later simply to devote oneself to the affairs of the city, demanded courage because only in the household was one primarily concerned with one's own life and survival. Whoever entered the political realm had first to

be ready to risk his life, and too great a love for life obstructed freedom, was a sure sign of slavishness. Courage therefore became the political virtue par excellence, and only those men who possessed it could be admitted to a fellowship that was political in content and purpose and thereby transcended the mere togetherness imposed on all—slaves, barbarians, and Greeks alike—by the urgencies of life.

As so often in Arendt, there is something unabashedly masculine, elitist, and Greek about her definition of courage. The Homeric warrior and the Athenian citizen, exercising overlapping forms of *arête*, are freed to exercise courage by the labor of women and slaves, as Arendt reiterates throughout *The Human Condition*. Yet the use of "one" and "oneself" in the lead sentence leaves open the possibility of female courage, manifested by Arendt herself in the fierceness of her commitment to public life. Arendt's closing reference to the "mere togetherness" shared by "slaves, barbarians, and Greeks alike" implicitly democratizes the potential circle of civic actors by zoning the *oikos* (roughly, the household) as a space that can become political when the noncitizens within it choose to speak. If courage begins with the act of leaving home, for some subjects exodus from *oikos* can occur without actually leaving its precincts, by simply raising one's voice. "Courage," from *cœur*, originally designated "the heart as the seat of feeling, thought, etc." (*OED* 1a); at stake in courage is the will to put forward one's person and reveal one's personality in situations where such manifestation involves a real risk to the speaker's life or livelihood, her standing or estate. Courage is the self- and world-constituting movement out of the *oikos* of the soul and creaturely life into a widening polis of shared concerns that remains anchored in anima.

There are no Arendts in Shakespeare's canon, but he does give us a series of compelling dramatic analyses of how women might exercise courage. Cordelia is courageous when she decides not to play the love test before the fully assembled court. Helen is courageous in professing medicine and then publicly choosing Bertram as her spouse. Hermia and Imogen are courageous when they defend their marriage choices to their fathers in semi-judicial settings. Juliet helps initiate this line of verbally adventurous, authority-testing heroines, but she practices a more secretive form of courage whose immediate consequence is not to expand her capacities for action but rather to sink her into a sleep like death. Juliet's isolation is not of her making: the play details Juliet's progressive desertion by her mother and her nurse in the face of Capulet's blustering paternity, while also equipping these flawed adults with enough life story to render their actions comprehensible. In the course of attending over twenty rehearsals and performances of *Romeo and Juliet* at UC Irvine in the summer of 2014, I increasingly felt the weight of the play falling in the series of missed encounters for full disclosure in Act 3, scene 5, culminating in Lady Capulet's chilling, cowardly, but totally real declaration to her daughter: "Do as thou wilt, for I have done with thee" (3.5.204).

Let's fast-forward to Imogen. Capulet becomes Cymbeline, Lady Capulet becomes the stepmother, and Paris is replaced by Cloten. (Posthumus merges lyric Romeoanticism with emulative Tybullying.) The play begins with Imogen defending her election of Posthumus before the assembled court. Later, on the road to Milford Haven, she recounts her actions to the steward Pisanio, and to her husband in absentia:

And thou, Posthumus, thou that didst set up
My disobedience 'gainst the king my father,
And make me put into contempt the suits
Of princely fellows, shalt hereafter find
It is no act of common passage, but
A strain of rareness: and I grieve myself
To think, when thou shalt be disedg'd by her
That now thou tirest on, how thy memory
Will then be pang'd by me.

(3.4.89–97)

Imogen recognizes, perhaps for the first time, that her choice of Posthumus as her husband separated her from the household and established her ethical freedom by exercising her capacities for "disobedience" and "contempt," close relatives of courage in virtue's playbook of dynamic ambivalences. Imogen's decision may have been "no act of common passage," but it was most certainly *an act*, a life-changing deed exercised in concert with another and witnessed by the world. The consensual, contractual, and egalitarian character of Imogen's election of Posthumus lifts her deed above the merely personal without draining it of its singularity. The couple's courtship and elopement, the central interest of *Romeo and Juliet*, has occurred before *Cymbeline* begins; it is the recognitive effort of coming into a hard-won relationship to that action in the presence of new audiences and unexpected challenges that interests the author of *Cymbeline*. At the end of the scene, having risked death but choosing life, Imogen will adopt a "waggish courage" (3.4.159) and a "prince's courage" (3.4.186) along with boy's clothing. Courage for Imogen consists in matters of the *cœur* or heart, the roiling, restless seat of love and anger, fidelity and disobedience, a courage that requires her to avow her commitments in public, but whose link to marriage also feminizes that classical definition as she passes through the creaturely landscapes of romance. Her courage in its social dimensionality leads to the "counterchange ... severally in all" (5.5.397–8) that Yachnin associates with the play's "restored and open society."

Like Robert Cohen with his students, and like Arendt in her life and work, Shakespeare affirms the public nature and social conditions of courage as a resource for drama. Courage directs the affective and existential manifestation of personhood in search of public acknowledgment and in response to real dangers and intractable constraints. The very word *courage* enacts the virtuous realization of the ardent, willful, deliberative self through its action with, against, and before others. Shakespeare's women of valor are also *public* women, and Juliet is struggling towards this truth as she conjures an infernal host of companions to witness her secret deed.

The Ghost of the Public University

Henry S. Turner

Shakespeare in *our* time? For those of us who teach at public universities, that time has never been more out of joint. Hamlet's phrase is probably inevitable in the context of a volume commemorating not the 400th anniversary of Shakespeare's birth but of his *death*. We find enrollments in English departments across the country in precipitous decline and departments of literature in other languages disappearing before our eyes, victims of administrative decisions that have become unhinged from the systems of value that have long defined the public university as a teaching body that remains, in principle if not in fact, open to all. "Remember me": all of us know the terrifying injunction of the Ghost who stands before Hamlet (1.5.91). There seems to be no danger of forgetting Shakespeare, who has never been more public and whose power— imaginative, pedagogical, institutional—remains undiminished. And yet like Hamlet, we, too, should remember the angry, worried Ghost. For it has something to tell us.

It has often been observed that the Ghost is an epistemological and ontological ambiguity, a thing whose reality—whose identity, properties, and purposes—appears under the sign of a question. Horatio calls it an "illusion" (1.1.126). The Ghost is a "thing" (1.1.20) returned from elsewhere, a *revenant* from the world of fiction, which has begun to fill the space of the offstage, as Peter Womack has shown ("Off-Stage"). When Hamlet returns from speaking with the Ghost to declare that "There are more things in heaven and earth, Horatio, / Than are dreamt of in your philosophy" (1.5.165–6), he is not only referring to Reformation theological problems but to figures of a "mythic" type, in the sense that Jean-Pierre Vernant has given the term (*Myth and Society in Ancient Greece*): he is referring to theatre, which can begin only when philosophy has withdrawn and left a space to fill. Spectacular, the Ghost stands before Hamlet as the empty form of a person, a character peeled away from the actor, as it were, a figure defined through repetition—"has this thing appeared again tonight?" (1.1.20)—and likeness to another. It is "like the King that's dead" (1.1.40), a visual echo, an after-image, a memory come to assume an uncanny physical presence. Onstage, death and life alike have become indeterminate, replaced by a state of suspended animation: in a word, *mimesis*. In this way the Ghost is the counterpart to the virtuoso demonstration by the First Player later in the play, as he transforms himself into the "fiction ... a dream of passion" (2.2.487) in the manner that Hamlet finds so powerful but also so absurd, since it is "all for nothing" (2.2.492).

As a mimetic creature, the Ghost thus also voices a demand for interpretation, both about itself—*who* is it? *what* is it? *why* is it here?—but also about the nature of fiction as a condition of being. The ghost disturbs Hamlet and Horatio, both "scholars," because it provokes them to consider what existential qualities fictional beings, and especially fictional *persons*, might have. For are they themselves not persons of a similar type? This realization need not be tragic: Rosalind or Puck shows us how generative it can be. But after his encounter with the Ghost, Hamlet (and *Hamlet*) takes a tragic turn, undertaking a meditation on what it could mean to "live" or "die" in the artificial world of the stage by means of every possible theatrical register: the Mousetrap, role-playing and acting, hiding and dissimulating; soliloquies on suicide and Stoic philosophizing; the report of Ophelia's offstage drowning, figured as a mode of poetic song, as Scott Trudell has argued ("Mediation of Poesie"); graves, skulls, and cosmic visions of atomic degeneration; duels and poisons, and more. Even the Ghost, always ambiguous, already perhaps a "fantasy" (1.1.22), somehow manages to become *less* substantial as the play progresses. In her chamber, Gertrude professes not to see it, referring only to a "vacancy" and to "th'incorporal air" (3.4.113–14); it appears now to be a figment of Hamlet's projection; after Act 3, it ceases to appear in the play at all.

But the Ghost has become unnecessary: Hamlet has taken its place. He has become a pale imitation, an artificial person awoken to the knowledge that he lives a borrowed life, occupied by the body of another—the actor—without a body of his own. He has become *trapped* by theatricality, and this is because he has been estranged from *other* forms of public associational life that might have situated him more securely but that are dying all around him. As both a public and private person, Hamlet is a "Prince" and heir, as Julia Reinhard Lupton has shown (*Thinking with Shakespeare*, 2011), but he is unable to take possession of the King's body politic that now stalks the ground outside the castle, reduced to the Ghost it always was. He is also a university student, despite his age, as Elizabeth Hanson has discussed ("Fellow Students," 2011), but he has returned from Wittenberg to find a world in which a crisis in sovereignty has become a crisis in knowledge—as Horatio puts it, the Ghost may "assume some other horrible form / Which might deprive your sovereignty of reason" (1.4.72–3). In this world of sudden political transformation, of secrecy and opacity, of acting and violence, Hamlet drifts untethered from the university and its "philosophy," which has become irrelevant.

To understand how Hamlet's predicament might be a "mirror" for us—"the very age and body" for *our* "time his form and pressure" (3.2.22–4)—we must look harder and listen more closely, in order to apprehend another person who has been hovering over these scenes, a person for which the Ghost, and the King, and the university, and Hamlet are all figures. This person may be glimpsed in the original meaning of the word "university," which meant, simply but surprisingly enough, "corporation." That's right: the term of art in civil and canon law for the broadest class of fictional group persons was *universitas*.

In *our* time, what has the *universitas* become, and what is its future? In a typically thought-provoking discussion of the university, Jacques Derrida suggests that every act of interpretation, every act of defining our shared objects of knowledge, presumes a politics: not in the way with which we are familiar, as an ideology or an intellectual position, more or less avowed, more or less correct, but as an act of collective gathering that is sponsored by the ensituation of the text or object or event under scrutiny ("Mochlos," *Eyes of the University*; cf. "Teaching Body," *Who's Afraid of Philosophy?*). By appearing before us and demanding that its knowledge be *made public*—be heard, looked upon, interpreted—the Ghost demands two things. It demands, first, to know what will become of these fictional persons that hover before us, seeming now to address us, now to look past us, now to look through our eyes to the place where our souls might be. These creatures, after all, have consented to our looks and voices, and have even perhaps returned them; they give *us* life by allowing us to watch them, hear them, read them, write them, discuss them, teach them, dream them.

But as an event that demands an act of remembering and of interpretation, the Ghost has a second purpose: it seeks not only an individual body to bear its face and voice but a *collective* body that can carry forward the knowledge that it discloses, to Hamlet and to us, about the value of fictional persons and the tragedy that awaits our political life if the *universitas* withdraws from the scene. Who will this collective body be? Perhaps an audience, although Hamlet's own turn to theatre as a model for interpretation and action is not encouraging. His play's real tragedy may be that it invents the modern subject but forgets the *group,* along with the notion that political action always concerns not the action of the individual but rather the actions of that peculiar being, the *group person*. We may, like Claudius, call this group person the "distracted multitude" (4.3.4): we hear its echoes offstage "within" when Laertes re-enters in Act 4. After the pioneering work of Paul Yachnin, we may call this group person a "public." We may call it an ensemble, or a company. We may call it an "association," even the Shakespeare Association of America. But its original word was *universitas*, and we may well wonder whether here, too, something has become rotten. As an institution for producing and protecting public knowledge, will the *universitas* become a shell, a virtual avatar or automaton, a mere "machine"? Or will the *universitas* come to its senses and embrace its identity as a group person endowed with purpose, will, and life? The time is out of joint, and Fortinbras approaches: the Ghost is watching us to see how we respond.

18

Style

William Shakespeare, Elizabethan Stylist

Russ McDonald
President, SAA 2010–11

Shakespeare is our most underrated poet.

STEPHEN BOOTH (1997)

Although literary critics in the mid-twentieth century wrote extensively about Shakespeare's verse, and while new analysts have begun to address his works' formal properties, the subject is hardly exhausted. Stylistic criticism has not yet succeeded in accounting for the unparalleled attraction of Shakespeare's dramatic poetry, its power to move and delight us as his fellow dramatists' verse rarely does. The more we listen to the language, the more Stephen Booth's claim seems warranted, and what follows constitutes a modest effort to revise that rating upward. I shall examine microscopically some features of Act 2, scene 5 of *Henry VI, Part 3*, probably the most familiar scene from an unfamiliar play (both adjectives being relative). The feckless King Henry, banished from the battlefield by Queen Margaret and Clifford, sits upon a molehill and, after deploring the life of a prince compared with that of a shepherd, ruefully overhears the keening of a son who has killed his father and then of a father who has killed his son. The first half of the scene presents the king's soliloquy, the second a trio of lamentation

among king, father, and son, while a brief coda returns the
battle to the stage. The episode is extravagantly, unapologetically,
self-consciously artificial, perhaps the most ostentatiously patterned
scene in any Shakespeare play.

The recent scholarly and theatrical activity that has rescued
the early histories from almost four hundred years of neglect has
not entirely dispelled skepticism about them, especially about
their poetic extravagance. Certain critics, exhibiting the modern
preference for the "natural," remain offended at their rhetor-
icity and histrionic formality: "The long, flat, fatuous speech of
Henry on the battlefield is indefensible in many respects, and the
crude parallelisms of this speech are matched by the symmetri-
cally conceived situations (a son who has killed his father, and a
father who has killed his son) presented immediately afterwards.
Richard is almost justified in getting rid of such a bore" (Hugh
Richmond, 1977). More sympathetic writers—Robert Y. Turner,
Mark Rose, Wolfgang Clemen—have taught us to recognize the
exorbitant rhetoric as constituting a phase in Shakespeare's artistic
growth, specifically his playful experimenting with verbal forms
and learning to link them to larger themes. Attention to the
dense poetic reticulum of 2.5 confirms the young Shakespeare's
commitment to the delights of pattern and the play's status as
a product of the Elizabethan taste for the wrought, the curious,
the composed. Rather than see the flagrant formality of the first
tetralogy as simply a naïve style which Shakespeare will put
behind him as soon as he can, we should regard the extravagantly
patterned poetic surface as a response to the marketplace and the
artistic norms of the culture.

The scene's poetic forms exhibit in little the narrative and theatrical patterns taken from Hall and Holinshed, especially those
falling into two categories: antithesis and repetition. The historical
scenario is replete with opposition and parallel in that both the
houses of Lancaster and York are fundamentally opposed and yet
fundamentally similar, made up of people who are at once savage
and vulnerable. The dynastic antithesis that governs the action of
the tetralogy, typified in the divisions of the Temple Garden scene
(*Part 1*, 1.5), also determines the structure of *Part 3*, based as
it is on the military oppugnancy of Lancaster and York. Janette
Dillon (*Shakespeare and the Staging of English History,* 2012) has
shown how the theatrical demands of this text expose the starkness

of the historical antithesis, especially with Warwick's tergiver-sation beginning in Act 3. His movements embody both kinds of figuration: reiteration, and reversal. Revenge, which motivates much of the action, necessitates both oppositional agents and parallel motives: thus the murders of young Rutland and of Prince Edward present a kind of situational rhyme, marking the success of the Lancastrians near the start of the drama and the triumph of the York brothers near the end, and thus providing another narrative case of likeness in difference. And the king's molehill scene is itself part of a repetitive scheme, a narrative rhyme: where Margaret had tormented York in 1.4, Henry flagellates himself in the same spot.

Dramatizing the Wars of the Roses prompted Shakespeare to organize his poetic materials into identical and antithetical groups, and the interplay of the identical and the antithetical fosters the poetic electricity of this play and scene. The complementary operation of antithesis and repetition can be perceived in units as familiar as the iambic pentameter line or as minute as the syllable and the letter. The two schemes also affect us differently: mostly the repetitive effects are auditory, whereas the antithetical figures are semantic.

Verbal antithesis dominates the opening lines of Henry's lamen-tation and assumes fresh forms as the long speech proceeds, especially combined with poetic parallels, echoes, and other rhetorical schemes. Such contrariety then functions visually and narratively in the entrance of the two soldiers guilty of parricide and filicide. The antiphonal voicing of father and son is augmented by the king's unheard intervention into their laments, and then by the three interweaving voices as the passage becomes a fugally-structured trio. The poetic reiterations are examined in some detail below, but here it is worth noting the quickening tempo: the poet contrives an urgency by reducing the distribution from longer speeches to two lines per speaker and then to one (103–11).

Anaphora is perhaps the most obvious of the scene's parallel schemes, and not only does the poet not stint on that figure but dilates it almost to the point of parody. The first is a simple triplet followed by two more infinitives: "To be no better than a homely swain, / To sit upon a hill, as I do now, / To carve out dials quaintly, point by point" (22–4). A slightly more ample instance follows as the king imagines the passage of time in the shepherd's life: "How many [minutes] ..." (26) is succeeded by "How many

hours," "How many days," and "How many years." This example
introduces a characteristic device of the passage: the use of a basic
phrase with an extension varying slightly at each repetition so that
both parallelism and variation are at work. The enumeration of
minutes, hours, days, and years is complicated by *anadiplosis,* or
the stairstep figure, in which the same temporal noun that ends
the line begins the next: "How many hours brings about the day, /
How many days will finish up the year" (27–8).

An augmented version of this device follows immediately, as
a logical follow-up to the temporal speculations just uttered. "So
many hours must I tend my flock" (31) initiates a series of four
lines in which these five words ("So many hours must I") introduce
the clause making up the line, and these four lines are succeeded
by four more "So" phrases (31–8). The last of these lines repeats
the temporal units just reviewed: "So minutes, hours, days, weeks,
months and years" (38). One sly turn demands remark: the
sequence of four lines that open with "So many hours must I" is
followed immediately by a line that includes, in the same metrical
position as "I," the unexploited antithetical pun on "ewes." A
thorough analysis would proceed to account for the anaphoric
choral lines with which the king and the father and son echo one
another at the end of the scene.

Verbal repetition of a less strict sort operates throughout.
Fifteen of the first 112 lines contain an identically repeated word.
This duplication occurs sometimes in a familiar phrase ("hand to
hand"), sometimes emphatically ("see, see what showers arise"),
sometimes rhapsodically ("how sweet, how lovely"), sometimes
rhythmically ("Give me thy gold, if thou hast any gold"), sometimes
more than once ("O pity, pity, gentle heaven, pity"), and in one
case with a doubled repetition ("Woe above woe! Grief more than
common grief!").

No less notable, partly because it again employs both repetition
and opposition, is lexical reiteration in consecutive lines, as in the
climax of the son's lament:

And I, who at his hands received my life,
Have by my hands of life bereaved him.
Pardon me, God, I knew not what I did;
And pardon, father, for I knew not thee.

                                                    (67–70)

The reiterated phrases ("I knew not") and major words ("pardon," "hands," "life") are supplemented by less obviously significant verbal units ("and," "I," "my"), the restatement of which also contributes musical harmony. And the antithesis of the first two lines is enriched by the semantically opposed but aurally matched "received" and "bereaved." The king begs for an end to the slaughter with a sentence that amounts to an *epanalepsis:* "Wither one rose ... / ... a thousand lives must wither" (101–2). Sometimes the repetition is ideational rather than lexical. Henry ends his first compassionate lament for the parricide with a showy chiasmus, repetition with the terms reversed in the second line: "And let our hearts and eyes, like civil war, / Be blind with tears and break o'ercharged with grief" (77–8). Less insistent cases of aural identity echo throughout Henry's speech and the succeeding laments: "neither ... nor" (4 and 12); "Here" and "there" (14 and 15); "molehill will" (14); "when" and "then" (30); "deadly ... daily" (91).

The poetic oppositions and parallels are not merely aural, however, but often interact with semantic oppositions and identities. The first sentence of the soliloquy illustrates the echoing of similarly structured and functioning words and phrases in its four "ing" terms in the first three lines: "morning's war," "dying clouds," growing light," and "blowing of his nails." Especially pleasing is the matching in the second line of "dying clouds" and "growing light," offering aural echo and semantic antithesis. Just after that opening, the simile about the ebb and flow of the battle confirms this pattern of repetition and opposition.

> Now sways it this way, like a mighty sea
> Forced by the tide to combat with the wind.
> Now sways it that way, like the selfsame sea
> Forced to retire by fury of the wind.
>
> (5–8)

Here poetic identities are even more abundant than they look. In lines five and seven, for example, six of the nine words in each line are identical and placed in identical positions; moreover, the single polysyllable in each line occupies the same metrical position, syllables eight and nine. And while the vocabularies of lines six and eight are not as close as in five and seven, the parallels are still perceptible. The middle of each line consists of a prepositional phrase and an infinitive, but the positions of the two units are reversed in each line. And where there is not identity there is near identity: the prepositional phrase of line six ("by the tide") and the infinitive of line eight ("to retire") are united by the long *i* sound in the same metrical slot: "tide" and "-tire."

The essential schemes of assonance and consonance are so abundant that they might consume an entire article. Some end rhyme chimes in the opening lines but more prevalent are the extravagant alliteration and extended cases of internal rhyme. In some lines one or two consonants dominate: "Would I *w*ere dead, if **G**od's good *w*ill *w*ere s<u>o</u>. / For *w*hat is in this *w*orld but grief and *w*<u>oe</u>?" (19–20); "How will my wife for *s*laughter of my *s*on / *S*hed *s*eas of tears, and ne'er be *s*atisfied!" (105–6). Sometimes the mixture of vowels, consonants, and similar words is so thoroughly interlaced that the music is elusive but palpable: "So many weeks ere the poor fools will ean, / So many years ere I shall shear the fleece" (36–7); "While lions war and battle for their dens, / Poor harmless lambs abide their enmity" (74–5).

Less ostentatious stylistic features include the limitation of vocabulary. The poet articulates the monarch's pastoral fantasy by means of a radically simplified lexis. In the first forty lines, except for the trisyllables "another," "conqueror," "conquered," "Margaret," "contemplate," and "created," every word is either disyllabic or—most of them—monosyllabic. As the king's mind turns from the projected "happy life" of the rustic to the pains of monarchy (42–54), his diction increases in complexity: the "sweeter shade" of "the hawthorn bush" is preferred to the "rich embroidered canopy" covering those "kings that fear their subjects' treachery," and "the shepherd's homely curds" are superior to "a prince's delicates."

This fraction of the poetic and rhetorical possibilities in this single scene may serve as a prompt for thinking more generally about Shakespeare and style. These aural and visual patterns grab the theatregoer or reader by the throat and insist on being noticed, but the scene is not atypical of its author and his normal poetic practice. As Shakespeare gains experience, such youthful exulting in poetic density will give way to less flamboyant ways of achieving similar effects, but he will employ all the same units—anaphora, *ploce*, internal rhyme, alliteration, etc. The novice emphasizes the poetic sound of his language, doing what all poets do: "the nature and primary function of the most important poetic devices ... is to release words from their bondage to meaning, their purely referential role, and to give or restore to them the corporeality which a true medium needs" (Sigurd Burckhardt, 1966). In short, the sounds are valid as sounds, textured materials created for the audience's pleasure.

Many of the devices I have illustrated here can be given names from the Tudor rhetoric manuals, some of which I have mentioned, but it is more profitable to consult those works about function. The consensus among humanist pedagogues, of whom George Puttenham is the most helpful on this point, is that the work of formal properties is twofold. The first is musical, i.e. pleasing in itself: "our speech is made melodious or harmonical not only by strained tunes, as those of music, but also by choice of smooth words." The second function is directive, i.e. serving as a vehicle for the delivery of ideas: "the mind is not assailable unless it be by sensible approaches, whereof the audible is of greatest force for instruction or discipline .... Therefore the well-tuning of your words and clauses to the delight of the ear maketh your information no less plausible to the mind than to the ear" (*The Arte of English Poesie,* 1589). What is vital, especially given our tendency to cling to practical explanations for literary phenomena, is that here and elsewhere most of Shakespeare's poetic devices do not contribute mimetically to meaning. In short, a clutch of "z" sounds grouped together in a poetic line almost never has anything to do with buzzing bees. The sounds are audible, demanding that we register their effect, but their musical contribution is generalized. They stamp the passage poetically, enhancing semantic animation with aural activity, but rarely are they dedicated to the "reinforcement" of meaning.

The reciprocal interaction of echo and opposition contributes materially to the excitement of the poetry. These devices enliven the mind, engaging listeners in the activity of the spoken text, creating an auditory alertness that less obviously designed language does not supply. Simply put, they create verbal texture. The poetic density that results from internal rhyme, rhythmic parallels, repeated syllables, isochronic syntactical phrases, the anaphoric reiteration of infinitives, and various kinds of logical opposi-tions attests to Shakespeare's distinctive command of expressive materials. William Scott, the sixteenth-century commentator whose poetic treatise entitled *The Model of Poesy* was composed in 1599 but published only in 2013, describes this cognitive effect: "Of great, especial great, sweetness is that kind of invention which is grounded on likenesses ... And this pleaseth because it adds to our knowledge and doth store our understanding with the apprehension of divers things at once, as saith Aristotle." Although Scott is here speaking specifically of metaphor, his analysis pertains to poetic figures generally: "the apprehension of divers things at once" aptly describes the operation of rhyme, alliteration and assonance, anaphora, and wordplay.

The formal properties of Shakespearean texts still have much to tell us about the unrivaled gifts of their creator and about the culture that created him. The stylistic patterning of this scene calls attention to the affiliation of Shakespearean poetry with other forms of Elizabethan art. In particular, such disciplines as architecture, gardening, limning, and domestic decoration employ some of the same principles of design that seem to govern the poetic style here displayed. As the sixteenth century proceeded, wealthy landowners began to renovate or replace their defensive, feudal residences with graceful houses designed not so much for function as for appearance. The house became a "composition," a pleasing object calculated to emphasize parallel structure, organized complexity, visual correspondence. What mattered was the design.

Patricia Fumerton has developed a helpful analogy between the limning practices of Nicholas Hilliard in his courtly miniatures—the artist boasted of his fidelity to "the truth of the line"—and the decorative poetic effects perceptible in Sidney's sonnets from *Astrophil and Stella* (*Cultural Aesthetics,* 1991). And in a different kind of analysis, Catherine Richardson has shown that Elizabethan jewelry was "connected visually to the design of other high-status, often non-essential possessions" and that highly embellished, expensively wrought objects of bodily decoration were especially valuable because they were unnecessary, because their inessential status set the wearer on a high plane, elevated above "the middling sort" ("Jewelry and the Quality of Early Modern Relationships," 2011). Something similar might be said of Shakespeare's poetic richness in the early histories.

The Elizabethan aesthetic favored ornament, artifice, material objects that had been "wrought," verbal and visual contrivances that were "curious." Their houses, their knot gardens, their jewelry, their clothing, their dances, their miniatures established a visual context in which the artifice of *Henry VI, Part 3* would have been immediately recognized, appreciated, and applauded.

Nondramatic Style

Stephen Guy-Bray

In some ways, the biggest difference between a narrative meant to be staged and one meant to be read is the latter's reliance on description. The visual is not the backdrop against which events take place, as it is in a play, but something to be created in words by the poet. A playwright such as Shakespeare has a number of solutions at his disposal. In the *Sonnets*, Shakespeare makes many of the individual poems into what are effectively soliloquies or speeches (although without a response). In the two long narrative poems, however, his approach is different. "The Rape of Lucrece" is a much more dramatic poem than *Venus and Adonis*; in many respects its style is not especially different from that of his plays: much of the poem is dramatic in a way that recalls his plays. In contrast, while *Venus and Adonis* also has a great deal of dialogue and even a certain amount of action—although never the action Venus wants—the poem is distinguished by what I see as its obsessive focus on the visual. To some extent, we can see this poem as Shakespeare's exploration of the nature of descriptive style. How does a writer tell what he cannot show?

Venus and Adonis operates on a strong, if implicit, parallel between the sexual and the visual. Each is a goal—Venus seeks a sexual experience with Adonis; Shakespeare seeks to present a vivid picture of the setting and events he describes; the readers seek to have a visual connection with the narrative of the poem—but each goal is consistently and, I think, inevitably frustrated. Just as Venus can never have sex with Adonis, so too the readers can never really know what Adonis looks like and Shakespeare can never literally show us what he depicts in words. However skillfully deployed it may be, Shakespeare's style cannot succeed either in conveying Adonis to Venus or in conveying an accurate picture of the world of the poem to the readers. Rather than see this as a defect, however, I argue that Shakespeare makes the frustration of the desire for the visual an important part—and, in fact, perhaps the most important part—of his style in this poem. That is, the style is not an instrument to convey the reality (or "reality") of the narrative but rather the thing itself: the language of the poem is the only fulfilment either Venus or we get.

One obvious illustration of my point is that rather than attempt to depict the characters of the poem and the forest landscape in which we find them through straightforward descriptions, Shakespeare uses an extraordinarily high number of metaphors and similes. A few examples from the beginning of the poem will make this clear. At the very beginning the sun is said to have a "purple-coloured face" (1), while the male protagonist is introduced as "Rose-cheeked Adonis" (3). When Venus first speaks to Adonis, she says that he is "The field's chief flower" (8) and "More white and red than doves or rose are" (10). A little later, Shakespeare describes Venus in her attempts to kiss Adonis as resembling "an empty eagle, sharp by fast" (55); a few lines later, Adonis, caught in her arms, is compared to "a bird ... tangled in a net" (67). Rather than having the narrator act as a mere recorder or copier, Shakespeare forces us to experience both the characters and the settings through elaborate and distracting rhetorical devices that are frequently in conflict with each other. The style forbids us to pass through the poem to an apprehensible reality; instead, it acts as an obstacle to any clear or sustainable visual perception.

Style, then, functions as a distraction in the poem, just as Venus's story of Wat the hare, which she begins in order to make a point to Adonis, ultimately leads her so far astray that she forgets what she meant to say. To adapt a famous formulation from another of Shakespeare's works, this is art that does not hold a mirror up to nature, but rather a painting. In fact, the mirror / painting opposition is pertinent here, as while a mirror is a flat surface in which one sees oneself and one's surroundings, a painting is a flat surface in which one only sees art. This, it seems to me, is precisely the function of style in *Venus and Adonis*: to present a beautiful but impenetrable surface to the spectators—and I think we should think of Shakespeare's thinking of the readers of his poem as being like the spectators of his plays. There are two important references to paintings in the poem: the first is the very odd comparison of

Adonis's horse to a painting of a horse; the second is the reference to painted grapes—significantly, in both cases Shakespeare makes the same association between art and sexual frustration that I mentioned above. It is to the latter of these that I wish to turn in what remains of this paper.

Exactly halfway through the poem, Venus falls on her back and Adonis falls on top of her. As Shakespeare remarks, "Now is she in the very lists of love, / Her champion mounted for the hot encounter" (595–6)—another metaphor that is ultimately a distraction, as it proves impossible to match the metaphorical and the narrative situations. In any case, Venus is doomed to sexual frustration even here, and Shakespeare expresses this frustration with a further metaphor: "Even so poor birds, deceived with painted grapes, / Do surfeit by the eye and pine the maw" (601–2). The reference is to the contest between the ancient Greek painters Zeuxis and Parrhasius that Pliny narrates in his *Natural History*. Zeuxis painted grapes that were so lifelike that birds attempted to eat them, but this was only the first part of the contest. Presumably flushed with pride, Zeuxis asked Parrhasius to draw the curtain from his own painting, only to discover that the curtain was a painting of a curtain. Zeuxis was forced to admit his defeat, and the story shows that while counterfeiting nature is a great achievement, counterfeiting artifice is an even greater one.

It is more complicated than it might appear to map this famous anecdote onto the situation in Shakespeare's poem. If Venus is like the hungry birds, then Adonis is like the piece of wood. But within the poem, Adonis is not a mere simulacrum, but a character as real as anything else. In this context, then, Shakespeare's implicit equation of his protagonist with a two-dimensional painting is the poetic equivalent of breaking the fourth wall. Here and throughout the poem, Shakespeare insists on the artificiality of verbal devices in order to resist the naturalization of metaphor, the way in which a metaphor seeks to present art as nature. We are trained to think that it is natural to see love as a flame, for instance, or a beautiful woman as a rose, when it is utterly unnatural. Thus, the comparison here cautions us against making the same error as the birds, but it also cautions us against making the same error as Zeuxis, who makes the interpretive error typical of the depth model. What Shakespeare suggests in the many metaphors and similes like this throughout *Venus and Adonis* is that if there is anything under the poem's very showy and distracting style it is only more artifice.

The proliferation of similes and metaphors in *Venus and Adonis* can be seen as a stylistic equivalent of the figurative thinking on which the theatre depends. After all, theatre depends on our ability to think that things are other things—that the prepubescent boy is Cleopatra or Ophelia or Rosalind or that the bare wooden boards are a palace or a beach or a blasted heath. But while this kind of thinking makes a successful dramatic presentation possible, in *Venus and Adonis* Shakespeare's style ultimately prevents us from having any clear sense of the settings and events of the poem. From this point of view, the ending of the poem is especially interesting. After the death of Adonis the heartbroken Venus goes to Paphos where she "Means to immure herself and not be seen" (1194). Her desire to withdraw and mourn in private makes excellent narrative sense, but it stands out in a poem that has so relentlessly focused on the visual. As the poem ends, Shakespeare refuses to show us anything at all. Perhaps it is the case that *Venus and Adonis*, rather than being a visual representation of a story—a text in which the elaborate style compensates for the lack of a visual element—is like the curtain painted by Parrhasius: instead of being merely a temporary obstacle to our apprehension of the story, the highly varnished style of the poem is all there is.

Shakespeare's Lexical Style

Alysia Kolentsis

Why is it still out of fashion to talk about style? Recently, scholarship of early modern literature has tended to move beyond the stark pendulum swings of critical taste to find points of affinity among disparate approaches. Promising methods that mediate between old and new—such as historical formalism, which unites the small-focus tools of close reading and the big-picture lens of historicism—augur well for renewed perspectives on Shakespeare's style. The digitization of early modern texts is also helping to reinvigorate the study of style; some recent work has shown how digital analysis and data mining can shine a light on patterns of genre and collaboration in early modern drama, while other studies have challenged enduring assumptions about Shakespeare's unparalleled vocabulary.

Given these developments, why must critics still argue for the consequence of language and style in Shakespeare's plays and poems? Perhaps we fear regressing to a time of myopic formalism, when scholars labored in ignorance of historicist and materialist concerns; perhaps emphasis on the "big"—big picture, big data—has instilled a lingering wariness of the "small," particularly in terms of seemingly transparent stylistic choices. There also remains a discomfiting association between assessments of style and aesthetic judgments: fuzzy verdicts on an author's skill and a work's quality often seem bound up in discussions of style. Additionally, definitions of style are notoriously vague. George Puttenham defined "stile" as the "constant & continuall phrase or tenour of speaking and writing ... many times naturall to the writer, many times his peculiar by election and arte, and such as either he keepeth by skill, or holdeth on by ignorance, and will not or peraduenture cannot easily alter into any other." In other words, the distinctive patterns of expression that define an author's style are difficult to pin down, yet they must somehow be capable of abstraction.

In this essay, I want to bring small stylistic details back into focus, and to consider the insights that they might offer without accompanying preconceptions of inconsequentiality. Here, I train my view on one dimension of Shakespeare's style: understanding "style" in the relatively narrow sense of "effects of language"—structural, syntactical, and grammatical features—I focus on the narrower-still category of seemingly unremarkable words. Shakespeare's preoccupation with the effects of individual words, his capacity to synthesize various types of words (old and new, spare and ornate), and his celebration of the constellations of meanings and associations that attend even the most ordinary words comprises one of the most enduring elements of his style. Indeed, a characteristic aspect of Shakespeare's lexical style is his eagerness to embrace the apparently unremarkable; no mere neologizer, despite his popular reputation, Shakespeare consistently demonstrates his extraordinary attunement to the linguistic potential of all of the rich and varied resources of the English lexicon.

Shakespeare had the good fortune to come of age in a culture that celebrated and took seriously literary style. His grammar-school education, with its humanist emphasis on rhetoric, would have encouraged a keen appreciation for the tools of artful expression. Moreover, the English language itself was poised at an auspicious moment in its development; during the late sixteenth century, its status was on the rise, and it featured an unusually wide range of options for its users, thanks to a transitional nature that retained antiquated forms while simultaneously introducing and embracing new ones. This unusually vibrant linguistic climate created a milieu in which speakers and writers of English were taught to pay close attention to words: their meanings, their etymology and history, and their expressive possibilities. For a poet and dramatist like Shakespeare, trading in the currency of words, such an environment fostered an appreciation of the expressive potential of even the smallest units of language.

Shakespeare's interest in the power of words is evident at both the macro-level of narrative and the micro-level of diction. As Inga-Stina Ewbank has remarked ("Close Reading"), "the texts of individual plays hammer away at certain words as if to crack them open: 'honest' in *Othello*, for example, or 'value' in *Troilus and Cressida*." Embedded narrative commentary on the nature of words, and the rules governing their use, recurs throughout the plays. Hamlet famously resists Gertrude's exhortation that he temper his grief by correcting her terminology: "'Seems', madam—nay, it is, I know not 'seems'" (1.2.76). Coriolanus calls out the tribune Sicinius for his brazen and indecorous use of the formidable directive "shall": "'Shall remain!' / Hear you this Triton of the minnows? Mark you / His absolute 'shall'?" (3.1.87–8), while in *Henry IV, Part 1* Hotspur and Falstaff offer competing disquisitions on the nature of the word "honor." In *Antony and Cleopatra*, Cleopatra admonishes a messenger about to deliver unwelcome news by parsing his words: "I do not like 'But yet'. It does allay / The good precedence. Fie upon 'But yet'!" (2.5.50–1). Here, Cleopatra's attention to the implications of "but yet" exposes the seams of language use; even simple conjunctions, the nuts and bolts of syntax, can carry portentous weight. At the same time, this phrase resonates in *Antony and Cleopatra* in a manner reminiscent of "honest" in *Othello* and "value" in *Troilus and Cressida*; "but yet," with its inherent redundancy and associations of the stubborn intrusion of reality, deftly captures the conflict between the private space that Antony and Cleopatra wish to create for themselves and the ceaseless countering pull of the public world. In making his characters perceptive critics of language, Shakespeare encourages his audience to be close readers and to appreciate the nuances of common language. In *King John*, Constance expresses her resistance by asserting, "Thou mayst, thou shalt; I will not go with thee" (2.2.67). The auxiliary verbs in her terse refusal— mayst, shalt, and will—belong to the category of modals, which encode information about permission, possibility, obligation, and desire. The parallel structure of the line highlights these words, urging listeners to recognize the distinctions between them, and to recognize the surprising force of the simple word "will" as an insistent declaration of intention and desire. In instances such as this, Shakespeare shows how words that seem shopworn can be defamiliarized and thus revived; like the speaker in Sonnet 76, Shakespeare's best stylistic gift may be in "dressing old words new, / Spending again what is already spent" (11–12).

As Sylvia Adamson has noted in *The Cambridge History of the English Language* (Volume 3), a less-recognized aspect of the saturation of rhetorical culture in the sixteenth century was a subtle appreciation of etymological contrast; prominent reformers such as John Cheke ensured that legions of schoolboys like Shakespeare would be well aware of the creative possibilities in juxtaposing Latinate and Saxon words. Accordingly, Shakespeare consistently dresses "old words new" by juxtaposing native and Latinate words to highlight the expressive force of simple English monosyllables. When Richard II declares his willingness to "give my jewels for a set of beads … My figured goblets for a dish of wood, / My sceptre for a palmer's walking staff" (3.3.147–51), there is an apt interchange between form and content. King Richard's words shed both heft and cachet alongside the projected loss of his kingly privilege; the Latinate "goblet," "jewel," and "sceptre" transform both materially and linguistically, converting to the staccato Saxon monosyllables "dish of wood," "beads," and "staff." This attention to native words is also evident in *King Lear*, where the Latin-inflected speech of the villainous Edmund is starkly contrasted with the simple speech of Edgar. When Edmund justifies his imprisonment of Lear and Cordelia, he retreats behind vague and palatable Latinate phrases: "Sir, I thought it fit / To send the old and miserable King / To some retention and appointed guard" (5.3.46–8). Here, the Latin-based words act as double-speak: Lear is not outraged and wronged, but "miserable"; he is not captured and imprisoned, but held in "retention." Latinate language, in this charged final scene of the play, is aligned with duplicity and concealment, especially when placed in context with the stirring Saxon phrases that contrast it. Significantly, the scene's most resonant lines are comprised of simple Germanic words; the monosyllables "O, you are men of stones!" (5.3.255) have the opposite effect of Edmund's speech, embracing painful truth rather than retreating to obfuscating platitudes. As the lexical contrasts of *King Lear* demonstrate, mundane words need not act as mere foils for their more ornate counterparts; rather, these juxtapositions can expose the deficiency of Latinate terms, while native words are held up as singularly expressive and true.

Shakespeare scholars will continue to find new ways to integrate the often polarized critical approaches of the past century and beyond. As part of our return to style, let's jettison lingering unease. Let's continue to renew and reinvent formalist study and to challenge notions of linguistic transparency or insignificance. And let's celebrate even Shakespeare's simple words, for they are powerful markers of his sharp attunement to all facets of language, and his recognition of the potential inherent in the slightest of utterances.

19

Performance

Pluralizing Performance

Diana E. Henderson
President, SAA 2013–14

Over the decades since the SAA was founded, the field and variety of events studied as "performance" has expanded exponentially. In the excellent Shakespeare courses I took as an undergraduate English major, we neither attended nor attended to actual productions, though we gestured at the farce of *The Comedy of Errors* and the Grand Guignol of *Titus Andronicus* as indicative of Shakespeare's less "mature" writing. Learning Shakespeare through performance had begun and ended in seventh grade, when I borrowed my sister's ballet skirt to play Titania; by eighth grade, it was all about reading (granted, the play was *The Taming of the Shrew* and my most vivid memory involves our collective obsession with the line "with my tongue in your tail?" 2.1.219). Conversely, my theatre classes did not include Shakespeare scene work, understandably focusing on texts and techniques closer to home. In college, it was only through extracurricular involvement in theatre that I became immersed in *The Spanish Tragedy*, *The Changeling*, and *Rosencrantz and Guildenstern Are Dead*—and what Stoppard's Player deems the essentials of the early modern theatrical repertoire: "love, blood, and rhetoric .... But I can't do you love and rhetoric without the blood. Blood is compulsory—they're all blood, you see." *There's* a fact which Michael Boyd's 2014–15 production of *Tamburlaine* at New York's Theatre for a New Audience nicely recalled for its viewers.

Even during my graduate studies with Bernard Beckerman, one of the founding generation of academicians who took stage practices in Shakespeare seriously, our theatre history seminar focused more on the blocking than the blood, and always in the service of better understanding the dramatist's scripted artistry—a narrow lens, as W. B. Worthen elaborates. Outside that class and its interdisciplinary artistic community, I would frequently be frustrated by articles positing "text vs. performance"—often written by English professors whose experiences and credentials indicated that they must have known how simplistic a binary that was. As if there were one phenomenological experience for all readers and reading, all types of theatrical contexts and productions. Thirty years on, I still hear such debates, albeit inflected by more sophisticated attention to media, book history, and the legacies of postmodern theory. More hearteningly, the variety of approaches to performance now makes its study richer and more diverse than when our organization began. The phenomenology of objects, the gasps from auditors, and the vast possibilities of cross-cultural theatre and adaptation: all play their parts in Shakespeare performance, even as text-based traditions and interpretations fruitfully continue.

Of course, as Worthen also points out, this may bring a certain diffuseness to performance studies and in some cases mask traditionally limiting assumptions, such as the dogged primacy of an originary text—despite there being no such definitive beast, and Shakespeare's primary art form always having been multimedial. Furthermore, even as theatre history sheds some of its empirical positivism and as digitization enlarges our experience of and access to archives, Tiffany Stern correctly notes that methodological challenges persist. The larger trends nevertheless seem exciting as well as long overdue. No longer do most scholars of Shakespeare performance narrow their attention to only a few canonical Anglo-American repertory companies; at the same time, those companies incorporate a much wider array of acting traditions and approaches. The results can illuminate both past and present—a goal worthy of scripted drama, which perforce always negotiates that same paradoxical temporality, that same double vision.

We have arrived at a moment that acknowledges the diversity of Shakespeare performances both past and present, rather than trying (primarily) to police "his" boundaries: work in many languages and media as well as variant texts and selections of text all have something to teach us. Recognizing this reality allows movement beyond critique alone, to contemplate a brighter future for performance as a key term for enhancing Shakespeare studies. I focus in what follows on an illustrative contemporary production that likely would not have counted as "Shakespeare performance" when the SAA began, but which epitomizes the possibilities and priorities now visible through the field's redefinition. My choice and analysis of this example gestures at practices we might pursue more extensively, to the benefit of both artistic and scholarly endeavors. At the same time, irreducible challenges remain—including the variety of audiences, perceptions, and cultural values, and the evanescence of the event itself. These are not roadblocks but realities, ones that actually provide the impetus for scholarship's continued vitality.

Robert Lepage is known for innovative multimedia work that includes, but is not delimited by, his Shakespeare productions. Based in Quebec City, his production company Ex Machina serves as both construction site and archive for the dazzling array of performance events that he has spearheaded, ranging from Cirque du Soleil's *Kà* (installed at the MGM Grand in Las Vegas, and seen live by more than a million people) and film (such as his 2003 remediated theatre piece *La face cachée de la lune / The Far Side of the Moon*) to the profound theatrical epic *The Seven Streams of the River Ota* (1994) and Wagner's Ring Cycle produced at the Metropolitan Opera (2010–12). As the company's name implies, it is "from the machine" or technical possibilities of theatre that "the god" arises: not—despite the sly possibility conjured by its name and marketing—Lepage himself. Nevertheless, while his productions are often noted for their spectacular visual and technical effects, story, text, and politics remain fundamental parts of the theatrical whole. Thus it is not surprising that Lepage has repeatedly returned to both magical and political Shakespeare: to *Hamlet, The Tempest, Coriolanus, A Midsummer Night's Dream,* and *Macbeth.*

His production of the 2004 opera *The Tempest* captures the narrative and history of Shakespeare's play while immersing its audience in this theatrical moment and the new. Conducted by its composer, Englishman Thomas Adès, Lepage's production debuted at Quebec City's Festival d'Opéra (July 2012) and was subsequently performed at the two cosponsors' theatres: the Metropolitan Opera (October 2012), and the Wiener Staatsoper (June 2015). Dramaturgically, however, Lepage chose to set the action within the mythically resonant eighteenth-century Teatro alla Scala. La Scala, founded "under the auspices of the Empress Maria Theresa of Austria," opened in 1778 with Antonio Salieri's *Europa riconosciuta* and in 1842 premiered Verdi's *Nabucco*, whose "strong patriotic feelings ... founded the 'popularity' of opera seria and identified its image with the Scala" (http://www.teatroallascala.org). That Milanese theatre provided a congenial background for this *Tempest*'s cast of aristocratic Italian characters—notably enlarged by the opera's requisite chorus, an elegant, shipwrecked "audience" of finely dressed Neapolitan courtiers. Indeed, one could hardly conjure a more politically and culturally rich European frame than this in which to retell the Shakespearean story of a displaced Duke of Milan—a story which has, at the same time, become a foundational text for postcolonial studies. That latter heritage was also very much part of the Lepage production, shaping its costuming of Prospero and its final tableau.

It was not (only) the high art and political associations of La Scala, however, that captured Lepage's imagination. As he recounted during the rehearsal process in Quebec, he was fascinated by one specific of its theatrical materiality: the nautical origins of the knotting that sustained its elaborate rope-and-pulley systems. Former mariners, who became La Scala's original stagehands, had carried their technical knowledge from ship to shore, from the seas back to Milan. What could be more serendipitously appropriate for *The Tempest* than this history? Those once-innovative rope systems enabled La Scala's elaborate stage sets to be revealed as curtains opened and closed, trapdoors rose and fell. Surrounding and interwoven into Shakespeare's fiction, then, Lepage's staging added the machinery and cultural resonance of a particularized performance space.

Reinforcing this attention to the (materially) performative, each of the production's three acts placed the actual theatre audience in a different perspectival relationship to the interior of the reproduced opera house. In the first act, we looked outward from an imagined perspective point at the rear of the stage space to gaze at those performing on it, sometimes seeing—past the prompter's box and occasionally blinding footlights—the shadowy rows of balcony boxes beyond. In the second act, we looked full on in a more conventional relationship to the proscenium stage. And in the final act the audience saw a bisected view of the orchestra and performance spaces, including the offstage ropes and trap machinery as well as the acting stage with prompter's box at stage right; the raked orchestra with moveable chairs stage left; and across the upstage area, first bare multilevel scaffolding and then the elaborate ornamentation of tiered audience boxes overlaid on that frame. Surprisingly, most accounts of the production barely remarked upon the set's metatheatricality, few mentioning the scene shifts and some mischaracterizing them. None that I found explored their specific function, or cited Ex Machina's website description of the *mise en abyme* nature of the play's structure (with the shipwrecked characters "acting" within Prospero's plot, which in turn …). Nor did they consider the thematic or characterological resonances—for example, in allowing Miranda's independent view of a "brave new world" its full import as the unabashedly romantic culmination of Act 2, before the opera's reinterpretation of the Shakespearean narrative returned to a more complex clash of perspectives in Act 3. Here, then, is one role for Shakespeare performance scholarship: using our interpretive skills and research (including interviews with artistic practitioners and involvement with theatrical processes as well as archival and scholarly reading) to delve into the potential meanings and effects of specific choices in modern adaptations, moving beyond descriptive summaries or sweeping evaluations alone. Of course, implicit in detailing any performance lie questions of value, putting pressure on our selection to demonstrate why it should warrant others' attention—a parallel process to that experienced by artistic producers.

By the last scene of this performance all the European characters had exited, leaving only the stunningly high-pitched tones of Ariel (who had climbed the ropes upward out of sight) and a delicately swaying Caliban, perched on the low dividing wall between La Scala's auditorium and orchestra spaces as he relished the music of the spirit. This final image may serve as an emblem for much about contemporary performances of *The Tempest* more generally, despite the departure of Meredith Oakes's libretto from its Shakespearean source. While remaining true to the characterization and retaining many textual lines of the two "natives" of the island, the last scene's displacement of an irascible, emotionally limited Prospero by the aesthetically appreciative albeit bestial Caliban allowed a harmonious concluding counter-image. The operatic ending could be deemed a nostalgic reestablishment of an ecosystem freed of European intrusion and domination—although the triumph of such a peaceable kingdom was implicitly ephemeral. Lepage's placement of it within that particular theatrical space overtly reinforced that this pastoral vision was already "framed" by the culture that the fiction would expel; moreover, as the period costumes of the Italian court had earlier made explicit, the fictional story was also located in an historically distanced moment when La Scala itself was "new" theatre, before the possibility of that New World dream was irrevocably foreclosed. The poignancy of Ariel's heavenly song and Caliban's dreamy delight thus became enmeshed with the haunting sense of a doubled European inheritance not so easily cast off as was Prospero's temporary reign: of colonial subjugation and racial exterminations, and simultaneously of exquisite art forms enclosed within places of cultural privilege.

Within this Benjaminian historical frame, Prospero's costuming as half European, half "gone native" (with feathers in his hair and a cape only half-covering his tattooed arms and trunk) resonated beyond the now-standard references to colonialism (standard among scholars and artists, at least; some reviewers were baffled by the body art). For Lepage as a French-Canadian with strong political consciousness, issues of cultural identification are always multiple and specific. His interest in Quebec's First Nations was even more pronounced in a production of Shakespeare's play he mounted in collaboration with the Huron-Wendat Nation, prior to directing Adès and Oakes's opera. But as an internationally praised impresario both cosmopolitan and Quebecois, whose works are as "at home" in Paris—or, in this case, Vienna—as in New York or Quebec City, Lepage's rendering of the European/native dichotomy is elusive, perhaps even illusive, as well as allusive. Here is an apt occasion if ever there were one for a deconstructive Derridean reading of that slash mark. As also the *mise-en-scène*—for not only does La Scala frame Lepage's (modified version of) *The Tempest*, but the Scala set itself is an incongruously obsolete fiction within a modern "New World" theatre with cutting-edge digital as well as mechanical systems now creating its magic. Additionally, because the original production for Lepage as director was not Adès's 2004 premiere at Covent Garden but rather the summer 2012 run at the Grand Théâtre de Québec, surtitled for a predominantly French-speaking audience and chorus, it doubly displaced—along with the shortened lines and interlocking rhymes of Oakes's libretto—any definitive primacy of Shakespeare's verse or native tongue. Yet its imminent transfer to the Met also constrained some of Lepage's choices from the start, he acknowledged. Most simply put, there never was, and in the twenty-first century never is, one "pure" geographic origin or site of performance, one authentic location that can trump all others—even in an art form that vaunts its "liveness," and even when the name "Shakespeare" is attached.

In Lepage's *Tempest*, as in his self-authored compositions, one is made conscious of the ongoing multiple layers of a European imperial legacy as well as of performativity, within a wider world of global exchange. This seems an apt model for a twenty-first-century paradigm of Shakespeare performance, in that it indicates the problematic nature of prioritizing the historical origins of work that has in many ways become liberatory precisely by speaking back to and against those origins, critical of a narrowly conceived myth of Europe as the origin of cross-cultural enlightenment and superior cosmopolitan discernment.

But to end here would not fully capture the production's aesthetics, nor the ways performance studies includes but is not limited to a multimedial version of cultural studies. As his use of La Scala's rope-and-pulley system may indicate, what characterizes Lepage's peripatetic productions is a delight in the magic of the media, the interactions of technology and the senses to produce thought, emotion, and wonder. Often Lepage's technological innovations produce radically split audience responses: the furor over his set of huge mobile wooden planks for Wagner's Ring is one such instance. Most responses to his first widely reviewed Shakespeare production, the 1992 *A Midsummer Night's Dream* at London's National Theatre, focused on the immersive use of water and mud. In the *Tempest,* the effects called for by the script (the storm, Ariel's transformation into a harpy) provided only the most obvious occasions for Lepage to exercise this dimension of sensory creativity: specifically, his mixture of high-tech and "low-tech" medium-conscious effects, which simultaneously enchanted the viewer and revealed their constructedness. From the opening sequence in which she hung from a rotating chandelier above billowing sheets, the vertical acrobatics of this production put the aerial back in Ariel. At the same time, the tempest-toss'd bodies of the Italians bobbed up and down through slits in the cloth, and later Ariel labored to turn the creaky mechanical wheel that lowered the trap door to dispose of Stephano and Trinculo. Although the spectacular nature of the high tech garners more journalistic attention, its interweaving with specifically theatrical magic-making—with the strings (and ropes) showing—is what has helped gain Lepage a mythic reputation in theatre circles. The final sequence, when Ariel climbed up the ropes at the side of the set frame into the fly space, displayed both the performer's daring and an appropriateness to a libretto that stresses Ariel's need to "be active / In higher spheres / Spirits must rise / Or atrophy" (Act 1, scene 5): "Oh let me rise ... Oh let me go!" (Act 3, scene 2). And even as Caliban swayed as if in dreams, it was the actor/singer's precarious balancing act on a thin beam as much as his concord with the music and sound of the sea that created an indelible, dynamic final tableau. The human body's risk and vulnerability within a theatrical space as dangerous as Prospero's "rough magic" melds the layers of performance and fiction, asking us to conjure our own visceral empathy across the boundary between stage and audience. To cite both scripts: "mine would, sir, were I human" (5.1.20).

This *Tempest*—and I hope, too, this analysis of it—thus pushes the boundaries of what cultural institutions and audiences traditionally seek or value in (Shakespearean) performance, just as it blurs territorial boundaries. Lepage's aesthetic and cultural perspectives engage mythmaking and theatrical magic, the conscious creation of an aura that need not constrain creativity or imply a dominant or dominating model of cultural production. Considering Shakespeare's place within such a project provides a corrective to the tendency among Shakespeareans to judge and mythologize performances only within the bardic subgenre, or in relation to other versions of the source play. At the same time, contemporary remixes recall the future-oriented potential within Shakespeare's plays. What better text than *The Tempest* to challenge the myth of European unity, given its unresolved fraternal discord? Viewing and discussing such performances—with bloggers, students, scholars, and Saturday night entertainment-seekers; online, in journals, and in person—makes the need for sensitivity and openness to audience diversity (of priorities, perceptions, and goals) self-evident. It also makes clear that the variability of performances—indeed, of each performance, given unique perspective lines as well as what one brings to the event perceptually, emotionally, and intellectually—will benefit from the same collaborative exchanges and sharing of ideas that the process of artistic creation itself requires ... before it and we all vanish "into thin air" (4.1.150). While we give each production a local habitation and a name, performance, like Shakespeare, is now most assuredly a plural collective subject.

The Study of Historical Performance

Tiffany Stern

When the SAA came up with its system of seminars, two subjects were thought so fundamental to the study of Shakespeare that they were guaranteed a yearly slot: bibliography and the study of historical performance, "theatre history." Over time the bibliography seminar lost its privileged position, though seminars on that crucial theme are proposed and run most years. The theatre history seminar, however, has remained a fixture ever since. What makes the history of performance of such permanent interest in the changing field of Shakespeare studies?

One reason for theatre history's durability is that it isn't exactly a subject. A collection of varied factual matter, "theatre history" can refer to any aspect of past performance—including the structure and nature of the physical playhouses, the governments and economics that brought them about, the companies that ran them, the actors that performed in them, and the props, lighting, costume, and music used by those actors. Given its reach and range, theatre history, or some aspect of theatre history, will always be modish.

For the same reason, theatre history has retained its powerful position over time. Facts have a permanent usefulness in the way that interpretations do not; they can be reassessed period by period as fashions of thought change. So E. K. Chambers's seminal work of theatre history, *The Elizabethan Stage*, published in four volumes in 1923, remains foundational, and most critics use it at some point; few people, however, read Chambers's outdated literary criticism—Chambers's least known book must be *Shakespeare: A Survey* (a collection of essays published together in 1925), the interpretation of Shakespeare towards which his other writing was directed.

Those of us who actually work on historical performance, then, have the privilege and burden of working in a fact-based discipline. The discoveries we make are likely to be of continual use to the field; the approaches we take to them, however, will speedily become dated. The ultimate value of our work is that it has an independence from the conclusions we put upon it—an independence from us as scholars.

It is presumably for this reason that many theatre historians have eschewed interpretation altogether. Worried about threatening the objectivity for which history has long been prized, and anxious not to muddy elegant new facts with "wrong" readings of them, theatre historians have often been content simply to organize and explain the discoveries they have made in archives. The result has been that theatre history has become the supplier of information for other, more adventurous approaches to Shakespeare.

That is, until recently. The theoretical questions that have shaped other aspects of the discipline have started to be taken up by theatre historians. Why? Perhaps the recognition that factual research is actually subjective, and that the questions we ask and the way we ask them are contingent on the time in which we live, has been freeing, allowing theatre historians to risk interpretation for themselves—what is there to lose? Or perhaps the varied theories that shaped the discipline in the 80s and 90s changed the attitude with which we approached the discipline in the first place. Whatever the reason, it is noticeable that theatre history has, like the rest of Shakespeare studies, moved away from the concept of the single author; it has instead championed gathering and grouping historical information around "collective" topics such as companies, playing spaces, or plays put on in certain crucial years. Likewise it has embraced ideas about fragmentation, deconstruction, and "unediting" plays, leading to books on the way plays were written, revised, and performed as a series of bits—prologues, actors' parts, songs, and so forth. A contemporary interest in moving beyond the canon, meanwhile, has pointed in new directions, and led to startling and exciting discoveries about collaboration and coauthorship—including not only collaboration with other authors but with actors, theatrical personnel, and audiences.

Theatre history has thus anchored and given shape to theoretical approaches as much as vice versa; a lot of current work makes productive use of the two. Yet the subject has not changed its quintessential nature. It is still also devoted to historical detective work, and the study of particular details—props like "curtains" or concepts like "revivals"—still has its place, not least because theatre history now has more practical outlets than ever before.

A growing interest in "OP" (original performance) has led to the formation of theatrical companies dedicated to putting on plays in "early modern" ways, whether in terms of clothing, accents, music, performance style, or rehearsal practice. To house such companies, a number of reproduction early modern playhouses have been built—Shakespeare's Globe in London, the Sam Wanamaker Playhouse in London, and the Blackfriars Playhouse in Staunton, Virginia, to name three. They depend upon, and also are laboratories for, theatre historians. As contemporary actors and directors engage with applied theatre history, there is ever more call for information about past practices—from the gestures, to the decoration of the theatres, to the storage of actors' wigs. Theatre historians, then, continue to supply information about past performance—but have discovered that in doing so they are simultaneously supplying possibilities for future performance too.

Another boost to theatre history's popularity is that it recently ceased to be a coterie subject and has become available to numbers of new scholars. For this, we must thank the Internet. With EEBO (Early English Books Online) and ECCO (Eighteenth Century Collections Online) available in most Anglophone universities, with LEME (Lexicons of Early Modern English) and DEEP (the Database of Early English Playbooks) a click away, and new manuscript sites like the Henslowe-Alleyn Digitization Project posted online by the month, theatre history is no longer the exclusive preserve of "rare book" academics with the time, money, and libraries to hand. For the first time ever, theatre history is open to scholars irrespective of location: a subject that was once archive-dependent can now also be studied from home—not least because visual aspects of the field, like pictorial images or archeological findings, are sometimes better represented online than in books, where picture reproduction continues to be awkwardly expensive.

The Internet, too, has added to the kind of research we are able to do. The archives to which we are devoted once shaped the questions we asked. They limited the number of books we could call up or look at simultaneously—with the result that we have traditionally focused on specific documents or small ranges of materials. The Internet has changed that. With EEBO, for instance, one can look at images of a huge number of rare books in a single day. Now projects that would have taken several libraries and many years—like examining the title page of every early modern play—can be undertaken in weeks or even days. Likewise it is now possible, using EEBO's searchable data, to scan a wide range of rare books for a single word or concept. Though it should be remembered that EEBO is by no means fully transcribed and scannable, it can nevertheless supply in minutes what once would have taken a lifetime to find.

There are dangers, of course, that come from Internet research. It is easy not to understand the nature of the book one is looking at: whether it is bound with others or stands alone; whether it is large or small; whether its paper and binding are grand or humble. As a result, one may not comprehend—or may misread—its context. Analyzing Internet research also requires certain sensitivities. Sometimes looking at huge quantities of data for patterns reveals telling habits yet hides the fact that these habits are not true of all theatres or all times. Nevertheless, these problems are the exciting consequence of learning how to use an incredible new research tool. The Internet has wonderfully expanded our field; we now need to learn how to analyze our "new" old material as shrewdly as we analyzed our "old" old material.

The aspect of theatre history that most needs addressing now, however, is neither method nor approach. It is use. Most of us originally chose to study Shakespeare's theatrical context in order to understand his writing better. Yet these days we do not always tie our discoveries back to Shakespeare's works; sometimes we neglect plays altogether. So over time, the close reader and the theatre historian have come to be seen as opposites, as though the "literature" of Shakespeare and the "performance" of Shakespeare are two different issues. Yet, of course, historical performance sheds crucial light on textual issues, textual referents, textual analogies.

Theatre history shows how Shakespeare's words affect, echo, and use not merely other words, but also space, people, place, objects, sounds, smells.

Now that theatre history is losing its safe, old-fashioned air, and engaging more fully in other aspects of the Shakespeare discipline, is the time to show why and how theatre history truly matters. Theatre history is a crucial aspect not simply of context—secondary, background information—but of text itself, with all the excitements, and all the interpretative possibilities, that that entails.

Shakespeare / Performance

W. B. Worthen

Although Shakespeare's plays are wildly popular on world stages, in a more scholarly or theoretical sense I think "we" have come to a kind of standoff, crossroads, or impasse when it comes to understanding or modeling "Shakespeare performance." I'm obliged to "scare quote" that "we," but this is hardly a gesture of political correctness: the field—if there is a field, a conventionally demarcated space of shared (and therefore contested) values, practices, objects—is populated by a range of agents who gesture in one another's direction (let's bridge that theory/practice divide, find the dialogic space between scholars and performers, literature and theatre) and yet barely share a common language. Not signaling through the flames. Barely signaling at all.

How have a couple of generations of "performance-oriented criticism" framed that special genre, *Shakespeare performance*? In his widely and deservedly influential book *Shakespeare as Literary Dramatist*, Lukas Erne echoes a now-ritual complaint in some corners of Shakespeare studies, that the predominance of "Shakespeare, man of the theatre" is so powerful as to have obliterated that old-fashioned figure, Shakespeare the writer, the poet, the author. Yet despite this presumed *over*emphasis on the "performance" dimension (as though there were only one) of Shakespearean drama and pedagogy, the notion of performance animating much Shakespeare criticism and pedagogy (and much Shakespeare performance, too) is often a fully literary one: the theatre exists to express the innate will of the text. And when students complain about all that reading (Shakespeare wrote for the stage, and so the plays only have their meaning in performance), this apparently opposed position reciprocally proves the rule: here, too, "performance" is merely an embodied means to express the innate Will in the text.

Much contemporary "performance criticism"—arising from the work of J. L. Styan and John Russell Brown in the 1970s—models performance as a form of textual interpretation. In this widely shared view, the stage works to realize an organic reading of Shakespeare's language—the "words" that John Barton celebrated in his BBC television series *Playing Shakespeare*—in a spatial and embodied rhetoric, offering something like a three-dimensional, processual essay on *the* play. This paradigm claims a more or less essential vision of theatre, seeing the evident changes in venue, architecture, technology, the entire socio-cultural-aesthetic-economic work of theatre separating early modern from late modern performance practice as mere window dressing to the presiding foundations of theatre practice. In so doing, a narrow conception of theatrical adequacy provides a doughty principle of interpretive regulation: no ideas that can't be staged (which often becomes, naturally, no ideas at all).

Of course, much as there is no single critical practice, no single mode of reading, so too there is no essential theatre practice. The making of theatre has always been multiple and divergent. Dramatic performance clearly served a range of purposes in Shakespeare's time: in London or on tour; at the Globe or at Blackfriars; for a theatrical audience or for the court; by adults or by adolescents. Given the multiplicity of performance in Shakespeare's theatrical milieu, and the range of ways the documents of dramatic writing were generated, intercalated, adapted, emended, copied, used, and reused, there's little warrant for seeing our own bookishly-inflected theatre as providing a privileged, performance-oriented insight into Shakespearean origins.

Shakespeare performance often instantiates a paradigm of performance that no historicist, old or new, materialist or otherwise, could readily accept. It proposes that unlike writing, which constantly changes in its practices, technologies, forms and instruments of materialization, its uses and social consequences, constantly performing its difference from a unified conception of "the work," theatrical performance is, for all its historical and practical variety (boy actors, footlights, the star trap, a picture-frame proscenium, digital projection), fundamentally unchanged and unchanging in its essentially ministerial relation to writing. Given the richness, the variety, the massive cultural authority and nearly universal distribution of Shakespearean writing, it may be challenging to understand Shakespeare performance in any other way, even knowing, as we do, that in Shakespeare's era the theatre was not, and could hardly have been, ministerial in this manner: performance can only be understood to minister to, to evoke, to replicate or interpret the literary value of texts that already have a literary presence, a culturally-acknowledged status and identity outside the theatre.

Historically, writing has functioned in a variety of ways within the scope of Western theatre and across the horizon of global performance. Like *literature, performance* or *theatre* hardly describes a single activity, nor can it be adequately conceived as having a proper or essential relation to writing, even, I think, in that familiar modern stage genre, Shakespeare performance (a theatrical genre unknown to Shakespeare and his audiences). Theatre is at once variably intermedial—using writing, bodies, space, and a range of technologies (manuscript, acting, costume, architecture, lighting) in a variety of ways—and is arguably conceived as an ongoing process of *remediation*: "the representation of one medium in another" as Jay Bolter and Richard Grusin put it in their influential study, *Remediation*. But theatre doesn't merely represent *other* media (manuscript, print, social behavior); given the extraordinary variety of theatre as a medium, theatre often appears to remediate theatre, representing earlier or alternate modes of performance in the discourse of *this* theatre, here and now. The contemporary Original Practices movement, materialized in the beams and plaster of reconstructed or restored theatres like Shakespeare's Globe and the Sam Wanamaker Playhouse in London and the American Shakespeare Center Blackfriars Playhouse in Virginia, points precisely in this direction, suggesting the modern theatre's capacity to *remediate* an earlier theatrical medium in the contemporary technologies—lighting, plumbing, seat numbers—of the stage.

To see theatre in this way, as a succession of related but distinctive technologies, a succession of related but distinctive media, draws our attention to the different kinds of work the human and nonhuman agents of theatre—bodies, texts, stages, costumes, props, instruments, architecture—do over time, the different kinds of performance they produce. We don't really need Bruno Latour to tell us about the extent to which objects have agency in the human world; our pockets and handbags, to say nothing of our eyes and organs, are home to prostheses whose humming and pulsing extends, enables, and so perhaps defines, contemporary human agency. But dramatic action—whether learned from the mouth of the playwright, read from a papyrus scroll, from a paper cue-script, from a book, or while it scrolls across the device screening a Screen Partner side—takes place at the intersection of performance technologies. It's precisely for this reason that contemporary performance is, finally, drawing so much attention to "alternative" ways of doing Shakespeare (as though there were a theatrical norm), or of "appropriating" Shakespeare (as though performance were a form of theft), and more generally to the implication of the drama in its technologies—original and otherwise—of performance. The incorporation of the "literary drama" into the structure of print tended to delegitimate the evanescent, actorly structure of performance as "the work"; "performance criticism," for its part, confirmed this undoing, praising only performances for their provisionally appropriate evocation of the text, Shakespeare's words. Today, the global commodity, Shakespeare, is no longer confined to English, no longer confined to realism, no longer confined to the modern proscenium (or the reconstructed oaken thrust, either), no longer confined to live performance, and no longer confined to that banal dichotomy, however much it may (or may not) have informed early modern theatre: Shakespeare/performance.

20

Ecocriticism

Shakespeare and Nature

Rebecca Bushnell
President, SAA 2014–15

The subject of "Shakespeare and Nature" is surely as old as Shakespeare himself. In their preface to the First Folio, John Heminges and Henry Condell celebrated their colleague as one "who, as he was a happie imitator of Nature, was a most gentle expresser of it," and Ben Jonson, in turn, concurred that "Nature her selfe was proud of his designes, / And joy'd to wear the dressing of his lines." As Margreta de Grazia (*Shakespeare Verbatim*, 1991) and Gabriel Egan (*Green Shakespeare*, 2006) have both observed, the Folio thus inscribes the idea of Shakespeare as a "natural writer," whose primary subject was nature writ large. That is, not only did Shakespeare scarcely blot a line, but also, in John Dryden's words, "he needed not the spectacles of books to read nature."

The "natural" Shakespeare in fact surfaced much earlier than these posthumous tributes. In *Greene's Groats-Worth of Wit* (1592), Robert Greene famously complained of Shakespeare as "an upstart Crow, beautified with our feathers, that with his Tygers hart wrapt in a Players hyde, supposes he is as well able to bombast out a blanke verse as the best of you." This insult tellingly portrays Shakespeare as both beast and artist: a "crow" is "beautified" and a beast's heart covered with an actor's skin (while "hide" does reek a bit of the animal). Greene's two images thus collapse together the human and nonhuman, and at the site of the collision we find art—beauty and acting. Greene's Shakespeare is thus a thing of nature "wrapped" in culture, or as Jonson put it, "dressed" in human art. But does this image suggest a fusion, the kind of grafting that Polixenes proposes in *The Winter's Tale*, where "The art itself is Nature" (4.4.97), or do art and nature, human and nonhuman, remain uneasily distinct, even if conjoined?

This vexed image of Shakespeare as the tiger-player / bird-artist evokes the extraordinarily multifaceted construction of nature in Shakespeare's time, no less complex than in our own. While nature has never left the conversation about Shakespeare, it was only in the last century that Shakespeareans began to talk seriously about what nature meant then, as opposed to now. For a long time scholars talked about the "Great Chain of Being," famously distilled for popular consumption in E. M. W. Tillyard's *The Elizabethan World Picture* (1959). In this world-image derived from medieval philosophy, all of creation was ordered in harmony and in a hierarchy where man answered only to the angels and to God. In his history of *Man and the Natural World* (1983), Keith Thomas graphically details the economic and ecological consequences of such thinking, which justified the human exploitation of all natural resources, animal and vegetable, earth and sea, as a God-given right.

However, while describing how early modern divines, philosophers, and writers celebrated human dominance over all other creatures and policed the boundaries between the human and everything else, Thomas also reveals the weaknesses in the chain, opened up when people also saw themselves reflected in the world around them. At the end of his little book, Tillyard himself blurts out that "it must be confessed that to us the Elizabethan is a very queer age," uncannily anticipating later uses of the word (leading Timothy Morton, for example, to speak of "queer ecology"). While Tillyard does not say exactly what he means, he suggests that what feels "queer" to him is the Elizabethan writers' easy ability to move "from abstract to concrete, from ideal to real, from sacred to profane," that is, to think materially and to dissolve boundaries between differences of kind. In particular, this sort of queerness saturates the old doctrine of correspondences and sympathies, and microcosm and macrocosm, that stretched across the "chain of being," in which every part of creation was seen to echo and influence other beings or things, high and low, cosmic and insignificant.

Tillyard sees this doctrine as the means to "to tame a bursting and pullulating world," but one wonders, however, if the idea of correspondences and sympathies was more a *symptom* of its "pullulating," or its overwhelming fertility and dynamism, than a way to discipline it. In *The Order of Things* (1970), Michael Foucault argues that this period was indeed less an age of order and more one of "resemblance": "The universe was folded in on itself: the earth echoing the sky, faces seeing themselves reflected in the stars, and plants holding within their stems the secrets that were of use to man." While man was imagined at the center of creation, everything in creation touched and reflected other things: in Foucault's words, "in the vast syntax of the world, the different beings adjust themselves to one another, the plant communicates with the animal, the earth with the sea, man with everything around him, as man is a microcosm of the universe, containing all within him." In her *Breaking of the Circle* (1960), Marjorie Hope Nicolson turns the image of the microcosm inside out, to suggest that it is premised on the *lack of distinction* between human and nonhuman, where "Man was so involved in Nature that no separation was possible—nor would an Elizabethan have understood such separation." This involvement could be understood as both symbolic and radically real, for example, in the function of the bodily humors, or in Paracelsus's belief (in Nicolson's words) that "Man *was* the elements; he was minerals and metals; he was fruit and trees, vegetables and flowers. He was also wind and storms and tempest."

The microcosm/macrocosm model thus both centers and dissolves the human, and is fundamentally dynamic and unstable, leading Egan to partially vindicate Tillyard's "Elizabethan World Picture" itself from an ecocritical perspective, in its emphasizing the interdependence of life on earth (*Green Shakespeare*). The doctrine of correspondences and sympathies also appears to anticipate the more radical conclusions of actor-network theory as articulated by Bruno Latour and others, whereby both human and nonhuman, subject and object, are understood to have agency and to interact in a network of exchange and mutual influence. It also possibly grounds the assertions of object-oriented ontology and theorists like Timothy Morton who urge us to abandon the construction of "nature" itself and to think instead of an "ecology without nature."

What are the implications, for human and nonhumans alike, of our mutual existence in such a network: is it a utopian vision of ecological interdependence or is it a "bursting" world terrifying to humans because it cannot ultimately be tamed? And what perspective does Shakespeare give us on such a world? How could one answer that question in a few thousand words? My cowriters of this section on "Ecocriticism," Karen Raber and Steven Mentz, and I have chosen to focus on just one Shakespeare play, *Troilus and Cressida*, as a way to approach the question from multiple points of view. Drawing on *Troilus*, of course, means probing the darker side of creation, figured in a fictional world driven by deception and predation. It depicts the vulnerability of the humans so interconnected in this saturated and teeming world, but also the overall chaos ensuing when connections fail.

Troilus and Cressida offers Shakespeare's most explicit statement of the doctrine of a "chain of being," in the debate about what has gone wrong with the war. Ulysses affirms there that "The heavens themselves, the planets and this centre / Observe degree, priority and place, / Insisture, course, proportion, season, form, / Office and custom, in all line of order" (1.3.85–8). That order can go wrong, when "degree is shaked" (1.3.101), untuning the harmony of creation and disrupting the earth and sea, and all living things. In Tillyard's view, it is "a picture of immense and varied activity, constantly threatened with dissolution, yet preserved from it by a superior unifying power." Later Shakespeare scholars are divided in their readings of this speech, while they are all quick to criticize Tillyard for not noting that the speech says more about "dissolution" and strife, ambition and appetite, than it affirms order. In his essay accompanying this one, Steven Mentz draws out the "blue" thread that runs through the speech, in its images of "oceanic dynamism," neither cosmic fixity nor human chaos. Karen Raber, in turn, explores how in *Troilus* overall, animals "confuse the story" of the order of being, eating away at all our easy assumptions about distinctions of kind.

My reading of *Trolius* looks more broadly at how its figurative language both evokes natural correspondences and empties them out. Many scholars have remarked on the copiousness of *Troilus*'s language, or its "pullulation" (see for example David Bevington's description of its "Bakhtinian 'heteroglossia'" in the introduction to the Arden edition). While as Tillyard notes, Ulysses himself says "nothing about animals, vegetables, and minerals," in fact the play is rife with natural images in its proliferating similes and rich panoply of insults. Beginning with the work of Keith Thomas, many scholars such as Erica Fudge and Andreas Höfele have linked people's living with their animals and producing their own food and medicine to the omnipresence of natural analogies in early modern literature. That living interconnectedness and inter-dependence surely overflowed into language, as it does so often in this play. In *Troilus*, however, those relationships are often not harmonious: its universe of words, things, and humans is fissured.

The habit of comparing people to other beings on this earth is signaled from the start when, for Cressida's benefit, Alexander expands on Ajax's character:

> This man, lady, hath robbed many beasts of their particular additions. He is as valiant as the lion, churlish as the bear, slow as the elephant; a man into whom nature hath so crowded humours that his valour is crushed into folly, his folly sauced with discretion. There is no man hath a virtue that he hath not a glimpse of, nor any man an attaint but he carries some stain of it. He is melancholy without cause, and merry against the hair; he hath the joints of everything, but everything so out of joint that he is a gouty Briareus, many hands and no use, or purblind Argus, all eyes and no sight.
>
> (1.2.19–30)

This passage uses the structure of consecutive similes to cobble together a man both connected to the nonhuman world and profoundly "out of joint," composed of the "additions" of many different beasts. Bevington sees that such "hybrid metaphors of man-as-animal introduce us to the terrifying collapse of boundaries between species and look forward to the apocalypticism of *King Lear*." But this passage does more than evoke a breakdown of species boundaries; the point of the list of similes is that, rather than fusing animal(s) and man, the structure of comparison and correspondences itself fails, where Ajax "has the joints of everything but everything is out of joint." Foucault's mirror of resemblances thus shatters.

In her introduction to *Troilus* in *The Riverside Shakespeare* (1974), Anne Barton observes that, in this play overall, similes do not serve to bind together or tame the world. Rather, they are "employed falsely to describe a world whose values are not stable, a world of chaos and relativity." The most notorious example of such a failure occurs when the lovers imagine that they themselves will become embedded in similes, when every true lover will be called "as true as Troilus" (3.2.177), and all those traitors known "as false as Cressid" (3.2.191) (should she ever be false). So Troilus declares, in the future, "tired with iteration," natural similes about true love like "'As true as steel, as plantage to the moon, / As sun to day, as turtle to her mate, / As iron to adamant, as earth to th' centre'" (3.2.172–7) will fade away. Then only "'As true as Troilus' shall crown up the verse" (3.2.177). Cressida responds with a vision of a world worn down to almost nothing, and with it, too, the decline of similes, like "'As false / As air, as water, wind, or sandy earth, / As fox to lamb, or wolf to heifer's calf, / Pard to the hind, or stepdame to her son'" (3.2.186–9); only "'As false as Cressid'" shall remain (3.2.171–91). In his essay Steve Mentz sees Cressida here representing "nature as dynamic change"; for Karen Raber, the moment foregrounds predation in nature. But as for me, I see that when all of the similes grounded in an enmeshed nature thus become "tired" or undone, we seem to be left only with a void, a desert with two people standing, alone, the ironic end of a blind anthropocentrism.

In the play's last act, we find Thersites also contemplating a failure of figures of the nonhuman. Thersites is, of course, both a magnet for animal images and a wielder of them himself. Ajax calls him a dog and a cur, or a "bitch-wolf's son" (2.1.10), and Thersites frequently repays the compliments. But in Act 5, scene 1, Thersites finds himself wondering how he should describe Agamemnon and Menelaus, and in particular to what "form" his wit should turn in so doing:

Here's Agamemnon, an honest fellow enough, and one that loves quails, but he has not so much brain as earwax. And the goodly transformation of Jupiter there, his brother, the bull—the primitive statue and oblique memorial of cuckolds, a thrifty shoeing-horn in a chain, hanging at his brother's leg—to what form but that he is should wit larded with malice and malice farced with wit turn him to? To an ass were nothing; he is both ass and ox. To an ox were nothing; he is both ox and ass. To be a dog, a mule, a cat, a fitchew, a toad, a lizard, an owl, a puttock, or a herring without a roe, I would not care; but to be Menelaus! I would conspire against destiny. Ask me not what I would be, if I were not Thersites, for I care not to be the louse of a lazar so I were not Menelaus.

(5.1.50–64).

This passage begins like Alexander's speech comparing Ajax to different beasts, but then Thersites retreats to consider the difficulty of comparison itself, where one animal analogy is just not enough, and the list of animals outruns the man. But Thersites's conclusion goes further than the failure of this *rhetoric*, when he declares he would rather be any kind of lowest animal, even the "louse of a lazar," than Menelaus himself. He thus moves beyond the breakdown of the animal simile to imply a literal exchange of species identity. Thus, the traditional order that values man over animal or louse is upended. In this case, the next step beyond the exhaustion of sympathies and correspondences is the collapse of the chain itself.

All three of our essays on "Ecocriticism" summon up differently, through the rage of the sea, the addling of the egg, and the unraveling of the chain of being, the dynamism and danger of the natural world evoked Shakespeare's plays. As Richard II's gardeners know, it takes a lot of work to maintain that world on land, because otherwise it will soon be overrun by weeds, "choked up," disordered, and "Swarming with caterpillars" (*Richard II*, 3.4.44–7); the human hand and its pruning knife are no match, in the end, for its inherent power. And, as Steve Mentz has amply illustrated in *At the Bottom of Shakespeare's Ocean* (2009), the sea will swallow us up unless we learn to navigate wisely. Greene's labeling of Shakespeare as "the tiger's heart wrapped in a player's hide" alludes to York's vilification of the "inhuman" Margaret of *Henry VI, Part 3*, that "She-wolf," and "tiger's heart wrapped in a woman's hide" (1.4.111, 137). It is implied that Margaret is dangerous not only because of her "unfeminine" cruelty but also because she ruptures the border between animal and human in her savagery. So, too, Greene suggests, our ambitious poet with his "tiger's heart" challenges our confidence in all forms of distinction and order. He is less "sweet swan," indeed, and more "upstart crow" beautified, the artist whose capacious imagination allows for the never-ending joining and disjoining of art and nature, human and nonhuman, in a pullulating world.

Shakespeare without Nature

Steve Mentz

When John Milton in "L'Allegro" celebrates Shakespeare as "fancy's child, / [who] Warble[s] his native wood-notes wild," he locates the dramatist beyond the human world. Shakespeare is a natural poet, and his unwillingness to follow accepted norms also makes him something of a natural fool. His words surge with wild undisciplined fancy. Milton's lines reflect a long tradition of imagining Shakespeare through Nature. Dr. Johnson called him "the poet of nature," Dryden referred to him as "naturally learned," and even his seventeenth-century rival Ben Jonson's famous coinage, "Sweet Swan of Avon," carries a whiff of nonhuman nature about it. These comments undergird the long-lasting myth in which Shakespeare represents, or somehow contains, Nature. A basic problem with these descriptions is their naïve attitude toward a nature that is assumed to be beneficent, harmonious, and green. We need to sound Milton's wild wood-notes and reject this stable nature. The poet whose plays embrace everything natural was also the poet for whom all natural things become pliable, artificial, and changeable. Shakespeare's poetic variety represents a dynamic and unsustainable vision of nature that appears neither very green nor exclusively human. Making nature less natural can help correct overly pastoral ideas about environmental harmony and imaginatively engage the changing nonhuman world of the twenty-first century. It seems time for a Shakespeare *without* nature.

Finding Shakespearean examples of what ecocritic Timothy Morton calls an "ecology without nature" is not difficult. Lear in the storm, Macbeth on the heath, Caliban among the scamels from the rock: many of Shakespeare's distinctive scenes figure a painful mismatch between humans and environments. In keeping with our group decision to read Shakespeare's Nature through *Troilus and Cressida*, this essay explores one of the critical tradition's favorite speeches about natural hierarchy, Ulysses on degree (1.3.75–137). As Rebecca Bushnell shows in her essay, the speech on degree occupies a central place in Shakespeare's discourse of nature. Famously treated by E. M. W. Tillyard as a "partial statement" of the "Elizabethan World Picture," the speech has been reformulated by ecocritic Gabriel Egan as a portrait of ecological interconnection. I somewhat agree with Egan, but in a much less "green" way than the author of *Green Shakespeare*. In my reading, the disorder and lack of harmony of Ulysses's speech, which for traditional criticism represent deviations from natural order, instead pinpoint the speech's beyond-natural portrayal of the nonhuman environment.

As Shakespeare criticism has grown less enamored of Tillyard's hierarchical unities, fault lines have been uncovered in Ulysses's speech. The Arden 3 edition of the play, edited by David Bevington, suggests that modern criticism splits over whether Ulysses provides reliable commentary on his post-heroic world or whether his speech performs the loss of order against which it protests. For my purposes, the task of finding in the Ithacan king's rhetoric evidence of lack of control, intentional or not, is both too easy and too hard. Finding evidence of radical skepticism in this thoroughly disillusioned play is easy, but precisely locating the attitude of wily Ulysses may be impossible. Instead, I propose following a blue counter-thread through the speech. Invocations of the sea, that least harmonious and hospitable element, punctuate Ulysses's speech to pluralize its vision of nature. These images open up Shakespeare's nonhuman and unsustainable vision of nature. Supplementing natural harmony with oceanic dynamism transforms a speech about stable hierarchy into a complex vision of multiply entangled systems. Recognizing the speech's invocations of ocean-flavored nature unsettles the green pastoralism that has long dominated ideas about natural order.

Ulysses's speech begins with a plea for human political hierarchy in an alien cosmos. Since, as Tillyard emphasizes, the basic principle of the speech is "as above, so below," Ulysses's reference to "specialty of rule" (1.3.78), which Dr. Johnson glosses as "the particular rights of supreme authority," implies the interdependence of nonhuman and human disorder. All Ulysses's images of stability, however, remain nonhuman. Principles of eternal order peer down upon disorderly humanity: "The heavens themselves,

the planets and this centre / Observe degree, priority and place"
(85–6). The physical geography of this image describes a vertical
ascent toward the heavens as entering an inhuman order, leaving
behind human environments. Order encloses the human experience
of nature, but does not permeate it.

Without closely engaging the speech's familiar descriptions of
what follows "when degree is shaked" (1.3.101), I advance two
oceanic moments in which the language reflects neither human
chaos nor Providential orderliness. In these two cases, the ocean
insinuates its salty fingers into Ulysses's rhetoric, providing a visual
language of disorder not directly linked to human errancy. The
"raging of the seas" (97) appears among a list of natural disrup-
tions that includes planets that "wander" (95), earthquakes, and
winds that create "Commotion" (98). Of these images, the sea's
rage appears the least out of true: earthquakes and planetary "evil
mixture" (95) are rare events, but rage is typical for the ocean.
Violent, dynamic motion comprises the "natural" state of the
ocean – which suggests that blue waters represent a very different
nature from pastoral green fields.

The culmination of Ulysses's vision of disorder appears in the
"universal wolf" (121) whose carnage stains the fields outside
Troy. Immediately preceding this passage, however, the great
waters reinforce their claim as the most disorderly of the elements:

> The bounded waters
> Should lift their bosoms higher than the shores
> And make a sop of all this solid globe;
>
> (111–13)

This depiction of flood humanizes and eroticizes the ocean, giving
the sea "bosoms" that exceed bounds. Ulysses voices his own,
and perhaps his play's, misogynistic view of female sexuality as
fundamentally disorderly, but the erroneous nature of his order-
seeking perspective shows itself in the phrase, "all this solid
globe." As early modern sailors were learning by experience,
the surface of the globe is largely not-solid. Ulysses's description
makes land the norm and encases water within bounds, as had
his previous reference to the "dividable shores" (105) of human
communities. Believing in a "solid globe" and an ocean that stays
within its bounds makes Ulysses a poor observer of his natural

environment. Land, not sea, is the exception on the surface of the globe, and coming to terms with landlessness was a central project of early modern European cultures. Blue seas posed a fundamental challenge, because the sea always represents disorder, even if that chaos can be navigated.

These visible gestures toward a blue and disorderly nature demonstrate that Shakespeare's nature was seldom one uniform green vista. Eruptions of blue oceanic chaos punctuate his works, from Clarence's dream of drowning in *Richard III* to shipwrecks from *Comedy of Errors* to *The Tempest*. Oceanic nature challenges stability and orderliness in comparable ways to the addled eggs and multiply-signifying animals of Karen Raber's contribution to this cluster. Three other references to the sea in *Troilus* support the play's commitment to the ocean as unnatural and disorderly nature. Immediately before Ulysses's speech, Nestor's stentorian voice intones an orderly oceanic ecology, divided between easy harmony, "[t]he sea being smooth" (1.3.34), and stormy chaos should "the ruffian Boreas once enrage / The gentle Thetis" (38–9). Nestor recognizes the split nature of the ocean but fantasizes that humans can recognize and understand it. Similarly Troilus, in his faux-mercantilist argument in favor of keeping Helen because of her great "price" (2.2.82), describes only the calm half of Nestor's blue vision: "The seas and winds, old wranglers, took a truce, / And did [Paris] service" (2.2.75–6). Troilus's language transforms concerns about natural order into a fantasy in which the ocean accommodates human desire. Controlling blue disorder becomes a winning erotic as well as political strategy.

Troilus's plans founder on the dynamism of Cressida's desire, and in conclusion I emphasize a moment—interestingly cited by all three essays in this cluster—in which the heroine analogizes herself to three of the four classical elements. She describes the falsehood she intends to avoid "'As false / As air, as water, wind, or sandy earth'" (3.2.186–7). In this key moment, as Troilus, Cressida, and Pandarus make their iconic vows, Cressida represents nature as dynamic change. She embodies what I, adapting Morton, call "without-nature": a post-natural, post-sustainable environment that is not reducible to human desires or conceptions. This environment is hard to love or live inside, but it speaks to our catastrophic present. The elements of Cressida's symbolic form are either mobile—air, water, wind—or imagined in mobile terms, "sandy earth." Her rehearsal of elemental motion reactivates the oceanic flood in Ulysses's speech to generate an antipastoral vision of the natural world as site of constant disruption. In this moment, as she, Troilus, and Pandarus rhapsodize about their cultural legacies as false lover, true lover, and go-between, Cressida's language recalls Ulysses's oceanic dynamism to reimagine Nature as inconstancy. In this fluid environment, human order seems fragile. Shakespeare's without-nature embraces the blue and flowing as well as the green and sustaining. Like Morton's post-human ecology, this nature sees itself in stormy seas as well as exquisite flowers.

The Chicken and the Egg

Karen Raber

There are plenty of animals populating *Troilus and Cressida*. I begin with one that might normally go overlooked: teasing Cressida, Pandarus claims that Troilus loves Helen no more than he loves an addled egg. Cressida replies, wittily, that indeed Pandarus loves an addled egg so much that she suspects he "would eat chickens i'th' shell" (1.2.9). Cressida's use of the term seems a bit off—an addled egg is either rotten or shaken and so no chick can form. Mercutio invokes this latter sense when he observes that Benvolio's egg-like head has been "beaten as addle as an egg" (*Romeo and Juliet*, 3.1.23). And since early moderns ate both eggs and chickens, what would be so bad about eating one in the shell anyway? Cressida's response makes this into a sticky egg that resists an easy reading and deserves attention for what it can tell us about the play's engagement with nonhuman and human nature.

Laurie Shannon calls Shakespeare's plays "zoographic" for their dense cross-species connections and distinctions, their animal metaphors, and their bestial characters, all arising from early modern appreciation of the remarkable diversity of creation; because Shakespeare's culture is pre-Cartesian, it is, Shannon observes, "less provincially human than ours" (*The Accommodated Animal*). Critics and scholars of the period have historically described its model of nature as relatively static and hierarchical— a Great Chain of Being in which all things, chickens included, have their place. But here, as elsewhere in Shakespeare's plays, an animal arrives to confuse the story. Shakespeare's works anticipate the principle Levi-Strauss would later articulate, that animals are good to think with, but in doing so they challenge this pleasingly organized organic model.

As David Bevington notes in his introduction to the Arden edition, *Troilus and Cressida* is muddled even in its genre—Swinburne calls it a hybrid, L. C. Knights a morality play, and T. S. Eliot can't decide what to call it at all. Endless war, miscommunication, lovers who are not so much star-crossed as victims of all-too-mundane politics all make the world of this play seem especially chaotic, and animals play an important role in mobilizing its thematics of confusion. Eggs provide a particularly appropriate image for the play's many degrees of entanglement: they are, after all, undifferentiated pluripotent matter—literally "con-fused," containing the promise of generation and productivity. An addled egg is thus one whose destiny as either future chicken or future gastronomical treat has been hijacked by a random twist of fate. It might therefore stand in for nature's occasional, arbitrary refusal to make good on her assurance that there will be a future for certain individuals or species. Like so many of Shakespeare's animal images, references to eggs don't really say much about actual chickens, but rather about humans. Bevington glosses the line: "Cressida's joke hinges on the fact that an addled egg is sometimes one that is partly hatched, and hence no longer fit for food." Such a reading suggests that what Cressida accuses Pandarus of involves a kind of cannibalism, a taste for inappropriate food that collapses together life and death. The embryo's partial birth removes the addled egg from both categories, making it a monstrous, and therefore inedible, meat.

In fact, eggs only appear in other plays to describe humans: the first murderer in *Macbeth* calls Macduff's son an "egg," and Macduff later laments the loss of his "pretty chickens" (4.2.85; 4.3.221); likewise, Leontes considers his son and himself "like as eggs" (*Winter's Tale*, 1.2.130). Lear's fool uses the two crowns of a broken egg to stand in for Lear's two daughters, newly invested with Lear's power—and he links Lear's foolish choices with a kind of addling: "Thou hadst little wit in thy bald crown when thou gav'st thy golden one away" (*King Lear*, 1.4.155–6). Eggs and chicks thus figure a pure (human, childlike) nature, while addled eggs instead signify human intellectual degradation. But Cressida's joke scrambles the threads of this referential web, to anticipate the play's eventual array of self-consuming acts and representations. Pandarus is not alone in his addled cannibalism—nearly everyone in the play suffers from the same affliction, as we might expect of a world in which war is interminable, dissension extends from the conflicts between enemies to division within camps and between friends, and a young woman can be sold off to redeem a future traitor. Greeks and Trojans are no heroes, but all too human. Thersites, from whose mouth so many of the play's animal images emerge, observes of Troilus and Diomedes, "I think they have swallowed one another. I would laugh at that miracle—yet in a sort, lechery eats itself" (5.4.32–4). Agamemnon eggs on that convenient tool Ajax with the criticism that "He that is proud eats up himself" (2.3.152), and in Ulysses's magisterial account of cosmic order, "appetite, an universal wolf, / So doubly seconded with will and power, / Must make perforce an universal prey, / And last eat up himself" (1.3.121–4). Nature is a Great Carnivorous Chain in which all creatures feed on one another without regard to species, familial, or tribal connection.

Instead of loving marital sex followed by gestation and repro-duction, the play serves up "hot" love followed by betrayal, signaling the play's broader resistance to structures of natural order. If, as Thomas Browne put it in *Religio Medici*, man is a "Microcosm, or little world," the world of *Troilus and Cressida* turns that image inside-out. Instead of in-forming—literally, shaping—a clear sense of the self in its relationship to nature, human analogical connec-tions to the animal world turn monstrous, and bleed across individuals to confound and conflate them. Of Ajax, Alexander says "This man, lady, hath robbed many beasts of their particular additions. He is as valiant as the lion, churlish as the bear, slow as the elephant," yet such a heap of animal attributes ends up gener-ating "a man into whom nature hath so crowded humours that his valour is crushed into folly, his folly sauced with discretion" (1.2.19–23). As Rebecca Bushnell points out, rather than fuse human with animal qualities, the description ends in a human who is "out of joint." Achilles, in theory Ajax's opposite, turns out to be best expressed through precisely the same set of animal comparisons. Against Ajax's lion, bear, elephant, dog, sparrow, ox, raven, horse, and "land-fish," we can list on Achilles' side cur, ox, lion, elephant, horse, and beehive. Nor is that the end of it: Cressida herself counts as a sparrow, keeping creaturely company with the two warriors, while Troilus is a tercel or hawk. "One touch of nature makes the whole world kin" (3.3.176) indeed, but not in quite the way Ulysses means it. Greeks and Trojans, men and women, men and other men, humans and animals, all fail to occupy clear or stable positions that would render supposedly God-given hierarchies or categories of nature intelligible. Cressida more than most seems hoodwinked by the promise of nature's constancy, foolishly certain of her ability to remain herself: "When they've said 'As false / As air, as water, wind, or sandy earth, / As fox to lamb, or wolf to heifer's calf, / Pard to the hind, or stepdame to her son', / Yea, let them say, to stick the heart of falsehood, / 'As false as Cressid'" (3.2.186–91). Like nature's elements, like its most reliable creaturely behaviors, Cressida promises to remain true to her mate, but it is that aspiration to constancy that destroys her. Cressida's similes depict an impoverished version of the natural world. The predatory creatures Cressida chooses for self-comparison seem to prove that the play endorses a regime of "falsehood" rather than the clarity of some fabulated account of natural design. Disrupted "natural" processes of procreation raise the specter of nature as a trickster, an infanticidal cannibalizing player in a cosmos that won't reliably reproduce either sameness or difference. If man is a little world, the world, it seems, is as muddled and corrupt as man.

Troilus and Cressida might initially seem to enact what Giorgio Agamben calls the anthropological machine (*The Open: Man and Animal*, 2003), the endless process of anthropogenesis that draws boundaries between human and animal in order to distinguish types of humans, some (male leaders like Ulysses) more, and some (women like Cressida) less worthy of participation in the *polis*, some entirely "bestial" like Achilles and Ajax. Animal metaphors provide the scaffold for human ideas about nature and the (human) self in the play, but this play confirms that they do so equivocally, and at a price. As Shakespeare would have known, once you start inviting animals into your house, you can't be sure what they'll do. They'll come in at the windows, at the doors, from the basement and the attic, and they'll make a mess. They'll nibble your cheese, or your clothes, steal your eggs, or attack the very walls, until the structure comes tumbling down. Confirmed addlers all, *Troilus and Cressida*'s animals introduce organic grit into Agamben's tidy machine, scattering chickens and eggs and nature's dilemmas all around the place.

AFTERWORD: SHAKESPEARE IN TEHRAN

Stephen Greenblatt

In April, 2014, I received out of the blue an email inviting me to give a talk at a Shakespeare event. There are always quite a few Shakespeare events, all the more so in the 450th anniversary of his birth, so the subject line of the email did not significantly elevate my pulse rate. But when I opened it, my attention spiked: the invitation was from the University of Tehran, which was planning to host the first Iranian Shakespeare Congress and wanted me to deliver the keynote address.

I had dreamed of visiting Iran for a very long time. Many years ago, when I was a student at Cambridge, I happened quite by accident across a book of pictures of Achaemenid art, the art of the age of Cyrus and Darius and Xerxes. Struck by the elegance, sophistication, and strangeness of what I saw, I took the train to London and in the British Museum stood staring in wonder at fluted, horn-shaped drinking vessels, griffin-headed bracelets, a tiny gold chariot drawn by four exquisite gold horses, and other implausible survivals from the vanished Persian world.

It was an ancient world about which I knew almost nothing. On display in a neighboring room at the British Museum, the great sculptures from the Parthenon conjured up a far more familiar antiquity, the Greek civilization that defined itself by its difference from the Persians. I had read Herodotus's great

Histories with its account of Athenian democracy heroically resisting the threat of enslavement by the vast Persian army. But that account was obviously penned from the Greek perspective. My only other shred of knowledge was that Cyrus the Great, the Achaemenid king, had freed the Jews from their Babylonian captivity and permitted them to rebuild the Temple in Jerusalem. Far from being an emblem of enslavement, the Persian ruler was celebrated in the Hebrew bible as a visionary liberator and hailed by many Jews as a messiah.

The culture that produced the beautiful Achaemenid objects on display in the British Museum at once eluded and tantalized me. A Cambridge friend recommended that I read an old travelogue about Persia. (I had completely forgotten the name and author of this marvelous book, forgotten even that I had read it, until the great travel writer Colin Thubron recently commended it to me: Robert Byron's *The Road to Oxiana,* published in 1937.) Byron's sharp-eyed descriptions of Islamic as well as ancient sites in Iran filled me with a longing to see with my own eyes the land where such a complex civilization had flourished.

In the mid-1960s, this desire of mine could have been easily and almost immediately satisfied. Some fellow students invited me to do what many others like us had been doing on summer vacations: pooling funds to buy a used VW bus and driving across Persia and Afghanistan and then, skirting the tribal territories, descending through the Khyber Pass into Pakistan and on to India. But for one reason or another, I decided to put it off—after all, I told myself, there would always be another year. I could go anywhere I wished, anytime I liked.

Years went by, and then decades, and with each passing year, each turn in our tangled, tormented history, the possibility that I might actually fulfill the desire that had once been awakened in me seemed further and further away. The naïve optimism that fueled my confidence that the world was open, and could only become more so, waned. Afghanistan descended into violence, and Herat—whose 600-year-old minarets I had dreamed of seeing— was virtually destroyed in the struggle against the Soviet invasion. Pakistan, particularly the tribal areas, became increasingly unsettled and dangerous. And after the seizure of the American embassy in Tehran in 1979 and the taking of hostages, the idea of casual visits by Americans to the newly declared Islamic Republic seemed entirely zany. Our former embassy was turned into a museum renamed "The Nest of Spies."

By the time the letter arrived inviting me to Iran, it was difficult to conjure up the old dream. I still very much wanted to go, but I would not be able to do so with the same cheerful insouciance with which I would once have ventured off. It was not only global politics— that is, the content of the daily news—that gave me pause. For the past ten years I have served as co-chair of Harvard's Scholars at Risk program, part of a network providing refuge and support for academics from around the world whose careers have been derailed and whose lives have been threatened by repressive regimes. A significant number of applicants to the program are Iranian. From them I heard dismaying, well-documented accounts of intimidation, arbitrary interference, and, on occasion, imprisonment for alleged violations of the canons of orthodox opinion. At universities, there were, I was repeatedly told, spies in the lecture halls watching for what the regime regarded as subversive views. Support for basic civil liberties, advocating women's rights or the rights of gays and lesbians, an interest in free expression, and even moderate religious skepticism have been enough to trigger denunciations.

Iran is a large and complicated country, and these stories, I understood, were only one part of a bigger picture. But if I went to the Iranian Shakespeare Congress, it could not be with the pretense that our academic situations were comparable. Sharing an interest in Shakespeare counts for something, but it does not magically erase all differences. Yet all the same, it seemed, Shakespeare had somehow bridged the chasm between us.

There was still the question of a visa which—because the US and Iran do not have diplomatic relations—I would have to get, after Iranian approval, at the Pakistan Embassy in Washington. Though I was invited in April and duly submitted my application, I heard nothing from the authorities in Iran. Months passed. I bought a plane ticket from Boston to Tehran, via Berlin, but there was still no word from Iran. More months passed. On the eve of my departure in late November, I told my hosts that there was no longer time for me to go to Washington, but that I would fly to Berlin and hope for the best. There, some twenty-four hours before my scheduled flight to Tehran, I was informed that I could go to the Iranian embassy on Podbielskiallee. The visa was issued. There was no explanation for the delay.

Thus I found myself on a Lufthansa plane listening to an announcement, just before we touched down at Imam Khomeini Airport, reminding all female passengers that in the Islamic Republic wearing the *hijab*—the headscarf—was not a custom: it was the law. "Women on board," the flight attendant put it, "must understand that it is in their interest to put on a scarf before they leave the plane." There, waiting for me when I deplaned at 1:00 a.m., was one of my Iranian hosts.

We drove into town, past the omnipresent billboards of Ayatollah Khomeini and of the current Supreme Leader Ali Khamenei and past the still more innumerable pictures of the "martyrs" of the Iran–Iraq war. It was well after 2:00 a.m. when we reached the hotel, a former Sheraton rechristened (if that is the right word) the Homa. Though I knew that the conference would begin first thing in the morning, I found myself too wound up to sleep. I lay in bed staring up at an aluminum arrow embedded in the ceiling to show the direction of Mecca. I was anxious about the keynote I was scheduled to deliver. I did not want to stage a provocation: I was less concerned for myself than I was for the organizing committee and the students, since I presumed it would be they who would bear the consequences. But at the same time I did not want to let the occasion simply slip away without somehow grappling with what it meant.

I entered a hall filled with eager faces—everyone arose as I walked down the aisle and applauded. Many held up their phones and took pictures. All the women, of course, wore *hijabs*; some of them wore *chadors*. The young men were casually dressed; the faculty wore jackets without ties. I also noticed among the men a few who stood apart and did not seem to be either students or faculty. There was a long prayer, accompanied by a video with flowers and dramatic landscapes, and then the national anthem, and then an implausibly long succession of introductions. I felt weirdly nervous as I got up to give my talk.

What did it mean that Shakespeare was the magic carpet that had carried me to Iran? I knew at least that it was highly appropriate that he played this role. For Shakespeare has served for more than four centuries now as a crucial link across the boundaries that divide cultures, ideologies, religions, nations, and all the other ways in which humans define and demarcate their identities. The differences, of course, remain—Shakespeare cannot simply erase them—and yet he offers the opportunity for what he called "atonement." He used the word in the special sense, no longer current, of "at-one-ment," a bringing together in shared dialogue of those who have been for too long opposed and apart.

It was the project of my generation of Shakespeare scholars to treat this dialogue with relentless skepticism, to disclose the ideological interests it at once served and concealed, to situate his works in their original historical context and to explore the very different historical contexts in which they are now received. We wanted to identify, as it were, the secret police lurking in their theatre or in the printing house. All well and good: it has been exciting work and has sustained me and my contemporaries for many decades. But we have almost completely neglected to inquire how Shakespeare managed to make his work a place in which we can all meet.

This was the question with which I began. The simple answer, I said, is encapsulated in the word "genius," the quality he shares with the poets—Hafez, for example, or Rumi—who are venerated in Iran. But the word "genius" does not convey much beyond extravagant admiration. I proposed to my audience that we get slightly closer perhaps with Ben Jonson's observation that Shakespeare was "honest, and of an open and free nature; had an excellent fancy, brave notions, and gentle expressions."

Jonson's praise of Shakespeare's astonishing imaginative and verbal powers—his fancy, his notions, and his expressions—is familiar enough and, of course, perfectly just. But I proposed to focus for a moment on terms that seem at first more like a personality assessment: "honest, and of an open and free nature." That assessment, I suggested, was also and inescapably a political one. Here is how I continued:

> Late sixteenth and early seventeenth-century England was a closed and decidedly unfree society, one in which it was extremely dangerous to be honest in the expression of one's innermost thoughts. Government spies carefully watched public spaces, such as taverns and inns, and took note of what they heard. Views that ran counter to the official line of the Tudor and Stuart state or that violated the orthodoxy of the Christian church authorities were frequently denounced and could lead to terrible consequences. An agent of the police

recorded the playwright Christopher Marlowe's scandalously anti-Christian opinions and filed a report, for the queen of England was also head of the church. Marlowe was eventually murdered by members of the Elizabethan security service, though they disguised the murder as a tavern brawl. Along the way, Marlowe's roommate, the playwright Thomas Kyd, was questioned under torture so severe that he died shortly after.

To be honest, open, and free in such a world was a rare achievement. We could say it would have been possible, even easy, for someone whose views of state and church happened to correspond perfectly to the official views, and it has certainly been persuasively argued that Shakespeare's plays often reflected what has been called the Elizabethan world-picture. They depict a hierarchical society in which noble blood counts for a great deal, the many-headed multitude is easily swayed in irrational directions, and respect for order and degree seems paramount.

But it is difficult, then, to explain quite a few moments in his work. Take, for example, the scene in which Claudius, who has secretly murdered the legitimate king of Denmark and seized his throne, declares, in the face of a popular uprising, that "There's such divinity doth hedge a king / That treason can but peep to what it would" (4.5.120–1). It would have been wildly imprudent, in Elizabethan England, to propose that the invocation of divine protection, so pervasive from the pulpit and in the councils of state, was merely a piece of official rhetoric, designed to shore up whatever regime was in power. But how else could the audience of *Hamlet* understand this moment? Claudius the poisoner knows that no divinity protected the old king, sleeping in his garden, and that his treason could do more than peep. His pious words are merely a way to mystify his power and pacify the naïve Laertes.

Or—I suggested to my Iranian auditors—take the scene in which King Lear, who has fallen into a desperate and hunted state, encounters the blinded Earl of Gloucester. "A man may see how this world goes with no eyes," Lear says; "Look with thine ears." And what, if you listen attentively, will you then "see"?

See how yon justice rails upon yon simple thief. Hark in thine ear: change places and handy-dandy, which is the justice which is the thief?

(4.6.147–50)

Nothing in the dominant culture of the time encouraged anyone—let alone several thousand random people crowded into the theatre—to play the thought experiment of exchanging the places of judge and criminal. No one in his right mind got up in public and declared that the agents of the moral order lusted with the same desires for which they whipped offenders. No one interested in a tranquil, unmolested life said that the robes and furred gowns of the rich hid the vices that showed through the tattered clothes of the poor. Nor did anyone who wanted to remain in safety come forward and declare, as Lear does a moment later, that "a dog's obeyed in office" (4.6.154–5).

That Shakespeare was able to articulate such thoughts in public depended in part on the fact that they are the views of a character, and not of the author himself; in part on the fact that the character is represented as having gone mad; in part on the fact that the play *King Lear* is situated in the ancient past and not in the present. Shakespeare never directly represented living authorities or explicitly expressed his own views on contemporary arguments in state or church. He knew that, though play scripts were read and censored and though the theatre was watched, the police were infrequently called to intervene in what appeared on stage.

Still such interventions were not unheard of. It is astonishing that in *King Lear* Shakespeare goes so far as to show a nameless servant intervening to stop his master, the powerful Earl of Cornwall who is the legitimate co-ruler of the kingdom, from torturing someone whom he suspects—correctly, as it happens—of treason. "Hold your hand, my lord," the servant shouts,

> I have served you ever since I was a child;
> But better service have I never done you
> Than now to bid you hold.

> (3.7.73–6)

The shock expressed by Cornwall and his reptilian wife Regan—"How now, you dog!"—must have been shared by the original audience. Though the servant is killed by a sword thrust from behind, it is not before he has fatally wounded his master. And what is most shocking is that the audience is clearly meant to sympathize with the attempt to stop the highest authority in the land from doing what everyone knew the state did to traitors. Here there is no cover of presumed madness, and though the setting is still ancient Britain, the circumstances must have seemed unnervingly close to contemporary practice.

How could Shakespeare get away with it? The answer must in part be that Elizabethan and Jacobean society, though oppressive, was not as monolithic in its surveillance or as efficient in its punitive responses as the surviving evidence sometimes makes us think. Shakespeare's world probably had more diversity of views, more room to breathe, than the official documents imply. There is, I think, another reason as well, that leads us back to why after four hundred years and across vast social, cultural, and religious differences Shakespeare's works continue to reach us. He seems to have folded his most subversive perceptions about his particular time and place into a much larger vision of what his characters repeatedly and urgently term their life stories.

What for Shakespeare constitutes the shape of a life? There is no single answer; his vision is far too various and restless. The multiple answers Shakespeare provides over the span of his works lie not only in particular details of individual plots—this or that pattern of carnal, bloody, and unnatural acts—and not only in the psychological or moral features of the individual characters who inhabit these plots, but also in overarching anthropological and, more broadly, biological considerations that governed Shakespeare's representation of what he called stories and what his great contemporary Montaigne called "the human condition."

Such considerations must, to a large extent, be our own: that is, I proposed, we can legitimately bring to our experience of Shakespeare our current understanding of the crucial traits or pressure points in the shape and trajectory of human lives. To do so will not be to turn away from Shakespeare but rather to fulfill his own design, which envisaged the ongoing vitality of his work, its survival, as dependent on the investment he could induce both his contemporaries and succeeding generations to make in the life histories he fashioned. Many of the plays end with a gesture toward recounting the story of the characters' lives. Hence, for example, the Abbess in *Comedy of Errors*:

> Renownèd Duke, vouchsafe to take the pains
> To go with us into the abbey here,
> And hear at large discoursed all our fortunes.

(5.1.393–5)

Or Hippolyta in *A Midsummer Night's Dream*:

> But all the story of the night told over,
> And all their minds transfigured so together,
> More witnesseth than fancy's images
> And grows to something of great constancy,
> But howsoever strange and admirable.

(5.1.23–7)

Or the Prince in *Romeo and Juliet*:

> Go hence, to have more talk of these sad things.
> Some shall be pardoned, and some punished;
> For never was a story of more woe
> Than this of Juliet and her Romeo.

(5.3.306–9)

"Go hence, to have more talk of these sad things" serves as an injunction to the audience, which is being indirectly addressed in all such moments. We are assigned the task of keeping these stories alive, and in doing so we might find a way, even in difficult circumstances, to be free, honest, and open in talking about our own lives.

* * * *

My talk took more than an hour, and, when I brought it to a close, I expected there to be a rush for the exit. But, to my surprise, everyone stayed in their seats, and there began a question period, a flood of inquiries and challenges stretching out for the better part of another hour. Most of the questions were from students, the majority of them women, whose boldness, critical intelligence, and articulateness startled me. Very few of the faculty and students had traveled outside of Iran, but the questions were, for the most part, in flawless English and extremely well-informed. Even while

I tried frantically to think of plausible answers, I jotted a few of them down:

> "In postmodern times, universality has repeatedly been questioned. How should we reconcile Shakespeare's universality with contemporary theory?"
>
> "You said that Shakespeare spent his life turning pieces of his consciousness into stories. Don't we all do this? What distinguishes him?"
>
> "Considering your works, is it possible to say that you are refining your New Historicist theory when we compare it with Cultural Materialism?"
>
> "In your *Cultural Mobility* you write about cultural change, pluralism, and tolerance of differences while in your *Renaissance Self-Fashioning* you talk about an unfree subject who is the ideological product of the relations of power: *Renaissance Self-Fashioning* is filled with entrapment theory. How can an individual be an unfree ideological product of the relations of power and also at the same time an agent in the dialectic of cultural change and persistence?"

I did not record my answers and will not try to reproduce them here. But what the questions demonstrated with remarkable eloquence was the way in which Shakespeare functions as a place to think intensely and with freedom. "Do you believe," one of the students asked, "that Bolingbroke's revolution in *Richard II* was actually meant to establish a better, more just society or was it finally only a cynical seizure of wealth and power?" "I don't know," I answered; "What do you think?" "I think," the student replied, "that it was merely one group of thugs replacing another."